# SRI AUROBINDO AND KARL MARX

# SRI AUROBINDO AND KARL MARX

## Integral Sociology and Dialectical Sociology

D. P. CHATTOPADHYAYA

MOTILAL BANARSIDASS
*Delhi Varanasi Patna*
*Bangalore Madras*

*First Published 1976*
*New Edition (enlarged) : Delhi 1988*



MOTILAL BANARSIDASS
Bungalow Road, Jawahar Nagar, Delhi 110 007
*Branches*
Chowk, Varanasi 221 001
Ashok Rajpath, Patna 800 004
24 Race Course Road, Bangalore 560 001
120 Royapettah High Road, Mylapore, Madras 600 004

ISBN: 81-208-0388-4

PRINTED IN INDIA
BY JAINENDRA PRAKASH JAIN AT SHRI JAINENDRA PRESS, A-45 NARAINA INDUSTRIAL AREA, PHASE I, NEW DELHI 110 028 AND PUBLISHED BY NARENDRA PRAKASH JAIN FOR MOTILAL BANARSIDASS, DELHI 110 007

TO THE MEMORY OF MY PARENTS

*Kiron Chattopadhyaya*

AND

*Parshwanath Chattopadhyaya*

# Acknowledgements

Parts of this book have already been published elsewhere: Chapter 3, 'The Concept of Man' as a monograph, *Sri Aurobindo on Man*, by Sri Aurobindo Pathamandir, Calcutta, 1972; Chapter 5, 'The Subjective and the Objective in History', in *Srinvantu*, Vol. XXI, No. 1, February 1973; Chapter 6, 'Smaller Human Aggregates: Family, Clan, Commune and Tribe', in *Sri Aurobindo Mandir Annual*, 1973.

I acknowledge my gratitude to the concerned editors and publishers for giving me permission to incorporate these materials in this book. I am thankful to Shri Tejeshwar Singh and Shri Buddhadev Bhattacharya for helping me in very many ways. I would also like to thank the members of my personal staff who have worked so hard to type the manuscript of the book.

D. P. CHATTOPADHYAYA

# Preface to the New Edition

The present work, first published under the title *History, Society and Polity*, was conceived and written to settle my accounts with the sociological and historiographical ideas of Sri Aurobindo and Karl Marx. I did not feel quite satisfied with the way I settled my accounts with the said two thinkers. The ideological elements underlying their thoughts have not been adequately dealt with in my earlier work.

The problems of ideology and utopia have been engaging my attention for the last one decade or so, i.e., since the publication of *History, Society and Polity*. The book has gone out of print. I utilised the occasion of republication of it by adding a Postscript to it consisting of three chapters, viz., 'Possibility of Ideology: A Marxian De-construction', 'Possibility of Utopia: Aurobindite Reconstruction' and 'Ideology and Utopia: A Critique'. This Postscript reflects my current thinking on the subject with special reference to Karl Marx and Sri Aurobindo. Since the original book was a comparative study of *their* ideas, I have decided to give a new name, *Sri Aurobindo and Karl Marx*, to the book without any substantial change of the original text. However, the Postscript will show a slight shift in my thought on Marx. It seems to me that some positive aspects of Marx's thought did not receive my due attention in *History, Society and Polity*.

I have utilised some material of the Postscript in my Sri Aurobindo Memorial Lectures sponsored by the University Grants Commission and delivered at Bombay University on March 18-20, 1987. I am grateful to all those who commented upon and criticised those lectures.

The index has been updated in the light of the contents of the Postscript. I am grateful to all those who helped me in various ways in the preparation and publication of the book.

*New Delhi*
*April, 1987*

D.P. CHATTOPADHYAYA

# Contents

# Introduction

## I

I have never seen Sri Aurobindo. A look at his portrait might lead one to believe that he had been an austere Yogi rather than one of the most creative thinkers that this country has ever produced. His face is calm and has an air of serenity about it. His features are sharp and reflect the thoughtful and powerful cast of his mind. Yet it is very difficult to gather from all these, the extraordinary creativity and imagination of the inner man.

Sri Aurobindo's life was quite unlike his placid outward appearance. He came from an aristocratic family of Calcutta and his father had been among the first to go to England for his medical education and return a complete Anglophile. The anglicized habits, ideas and ideals of his father had so much to do with the early life and education of Sri Aurobindo that he could not speak his mother-tongue even when he was a student at Cambridge. He was born on 15 August 1872 in Calcutta. He graduated from King's College, Cambridge, with a First Class in Classical Tripos. He mastered Greek and Latin, English and French and also picked up continental languages like German and Italian. At the instance of his family he had to sit for the Indian Civil Service, but after formally qualifying for the service, he managed to get himself disqualified, and thus escaped the bondage.

He returned to India in 1893 and took up an administrative job in the secretariat of the then Maharaja of Baroda. Later on he was appointed as the Vice-Principal of the local college and was for some time its acting Principal. During his stay in Baroda, 1893–1906, he was combining his teaching responsibility with secretarial work for the Maharaja, who had great respect for his competence and qualities. It was during this period that he started learning Bengali and reading the works of Bankim Chandra and Madhusudan.

Right from his student days he had two distinct creative dispositions, political and literary. He started writing poems, *Songs to Myrtilla*, for example, and taking some interest in Indian politics along with other Indian students in England. On his return to India, Sri Aurobindo's interest in politics deepened. Around the years 1902–3 he associated himself with some secret revolutionary societies in Bombay and Bengal. From his very early childhood Sri Aurobindo had developed a strong hatred and disgust for all kinds of cruelty and oppression. His foreign education had not diminished in the least his concern for the poor and the oppressed of India. Despite the occasional chill of poverty due to his father's financial mismanagement, Aurobindo had made very good use of his stay in England. But he had felt no regret in leaving England, for he had had no particular attachment to the past or misgiving regarding the future. He had developed definitely an attachment to English and European literature and culture, but not to England as a country. Perhaps emotionally, he had been more attached to France than to England.

Gradually Sri Aurobindo got more and more involved in the deeper issues of life and the larger issues of the nation and this could not be effectively followed up within the confines of the office he was holding in Baroda. So he decided to go to Calcutta and take up some assignments which were definitely closer to his heart. He joined Bepin Pal in the editing of the *Bande Mataram* and attended the Congress session in Calcutta at which the radicals, though still a minority, succeeded under the leadership of Tilak in getting a part of their political programmes incorporated in the resolutions of the Congress. He also accepted the position of Principal of the newly founded Bengal National College. Journalism and teaching were quite to his liking, providing him adequate opportunities to expound his political ideas which he had been silently and vigorously nurturing right from the days of his youth and which had been especially strengthened after his having read the *mantra* of *Vande Mataram* in Bankim Chandra's *Ananda Math.* The *mantra* had left a deep spiritual-cum-political impact on his mind, drawing him closer to the circle of revolutionary action in Bengal. He continued his political work behind the scenes and in silence. The hour to join in a public movement had not yet come for him. Even while he was in the Baroda State Service, he used to visit his relations in Bengal from time to time. He came in contact with the Yugantar Revolutionary Centres which had already been formed and also met those who were taking a leading part in the State's politics to perceive for himself the general mood of the people and the possibilities of the revolutionary movement. Having now permanently settled down in Bengal he started a Journal, the *Yugantar*, which was to preach open revolt against British rule and the necessity of guerilla warfare. Sri Aurobindo's historical studies in the revolutions and the rebellions which led to the national liberation of America and Italy in the Modern Age and that of France against the English in the Middle Age had left him in no doubt about the necessity of violent revolution in the Indian context. He derived much of his inspiration from these movements and their leaders, especially Joan of Arc and Mazzini. Therefore, when he finally decided to join public politics around 1905, he was influenced more by the radicals like Tilak rather than by the moderates like Gokhale. He had an idea to capture the Congress and to transform it into an instrument for revolutionary action. In the pages of the *Bande Mataram*, Sri Aurobindo openly wrote for complete and absolute independence as the aim of political action in India, and rejected altogether the timid constitutional approach and agitation which would only talk and pass resolutions and recommendations to the British Government. Sri Aurobindo soon became the recognised leader of radical nationalism in Bengal. Naturally, his ideas and actions drew the angry attention of the Government and he was arrested on 5 May 1907. He was in jail for a year during the Magistrate's investigation and the trial in the Sessions Court. He was released the next year on 6 May. He spent most of the time in jail reading the *Gita* and the *Upanishads* and in intensive meditation and the practice of Yoga. C. R. Das successfully defended his case and he was honourably acquitted. His stay in the jail and the experiences that he had there left a deep impression on his mind. A profound and ineffable change took place in him. And then he decided to enter deeper into the spiritual life which he had experienced before. However, the police were constantly after him though that does not appear to be the main reason for his ultimate decision to leave Calcutta. From Calcutta he first went to Chandernagore and from there he finally sailed to Pondicherry arriving there on 4 April 1910.

From now on, Sri Aurobindo began getting more and more absorbed in Yoga. He retired from all public political activities. Certainly this does not mean that he ceased to take interest in the political affairs of the country and in the destiny of the world as a whole. His inward involvement increased, although his outward contacts diminished. He came to the conclusion that his Yoga would keep him in living touch with the forces of history. According to him, the complete spiritual consciousness *not only* seeks the Divine but also *takes* all life and all world activities into its integral scope. After his retirement from open political life, only on two occasions did he think it necessary to express himself on specific public issues. The first was in relation to the Second World War. He opposed Hitler and Nazism and supported the Allies. The second time he spoke to support publicly the offer of Sir Stafford Cripps to the Congress leaders requesting them to accept it in the larger interest of national freedom. His advice was not heeded. He felt that, had it been accepted at that time, the partition of India could have been avoided. The date of India's Independence, 15 August, happens to be his birthday.

Between 1910 and the mid-twenties Sri Aurobindo, in spite of his deep pre-occupation with Yoga and other spiritual and literary activities, was accessible to a very close circle of friends and admirers. On 24 November 1926, Sri Aurobindo is said to have achieved his *siddhi* (realisation). Thereafter his withdrawal from the public life was almost complete. Only on four specific days in a year (21 February, 24 April, 15 August and 24 November) would he appear before the intending seers. Although he used to spend almost all his time in his spiritual solitude, meditating, contemplating and writing, he strongly disapproved of the suggestion that he was living an other worldly life. 'My own life and my Yoga have always been... both this worldly and other worldly without any exclusiveness on either side.' To be in this world, according to him, one need not be in physical or empirical touch with it. If Sri Aurobindo is right, the true form and significance of life are to be sought in 'the depth of the spirit' and not in the 'superficial' levels of thought and experience. What Sri Aurobindo has said in the context of his own biography has been consistently maintained by him in his works on psychology, sociology, aesthetics and various other subjects.

After his *siddhi* Sri Aurobindo lived nearly a quarter of a century more, keeping himself always active and creatively busy in spiritual and other works. He passed away on 5 December 1950.

## II

Sri Aurobindo was very much against the idea of writing his biography

For he thought that the true biography of a person does not consist of what he does, learns or knows, but of what he really is and inwardly becomes. An exactly similar expression is found in Collingwood's *Autobiography*, where he says that the true biography of a thinker is to be found only in the history of his thought. Perhaps Sri Aurobindo could go a step further and say that the true life-story of a man is to be found only in the spiritual depth of his being and not in the rather ' superficial ' thought-level. He advised his possible biographers not to try their hand in narrating his life-story. One can see only the surface of another's life and not its ingoings. He said, ' it would be only myself who could speak of things in my past giving them their true form and significance'.

Sri Aurobindo was essentially a creative author and not a typical scholar or academician as is evident from the 29 (Birth Centenary Library) volumes of his works. He himself confessed his intellectual reluctance and the resulting inability to go through the philosophical classics of Berkeley, Kant and Hegel, for instance. It is not that Sri Aurobindo's range of reading was not wide. His wide interests, originality and creative powers made more than good the deficiency due to his relative lack of acquaintance with the up-to-date literature on philosophy and sociology. In fact, broadly speaking, there are two types of creative authors, those who are mainly interested in expressing their own views without adequate information about what other authors have said on those subjects and those who take enough of trouble to criticise *specifically* others before trying to establish their own views. Sri Aurobindo and Wittgenstein belong to the first category, and Russell and Popper to the second one. Of course I must mention here that Sri Aurobindo's acquaintance with others' works was considerably wider than that of Wittgenstein's. Perhaps it should also be mentioned here that powerful and creative authors like Sri Aurobindo can almost always *independently*—independently of their actual study—conceive the relevant and alternative views and arguments on and also possible objections against a particular point; and for this they do not need to rely on a particular set of books. It is perhaps for this reason that one finds very few references and footnotes in the volumes by Sri Aurobindo.

In his exposition Sri Aurobindo is certainly argumentative but hardly analytical in the strict sense of the term. He himself has stated in several places that he is more interested in expressing himself in his own *spontaneous* way rather than in a laborious manner and conforming to the different expectations of the different readers. He is quite aware of the common complaint against him, that it is difficult to understand his writings. His answer, though simple, may not sound convincing to an ordinary rational man. ' People do not understand what I write because the mind by itself cannot understand things that are beyond it'. The implication is that one needs ' super-mental ' ability, or at least a deeply sympathetic disposition to understand the deeper meanings of his writings. Truth is many-sided, but as the ordinary mind is usually rigid in its cast and impresses its own ideas on whatever it comes across, it gets easily puzzled by non-existent inconsistencies. Sri Aurobindo attributes these inconsistencies to ' narrow minded inability to see more than one side of the Truth or more than their own narrow personal view or experience of things'.

To get rid of the inherent defect of mental knowledge he speaks of the necessity of 'the real or the integral knowledge'.

In his quest for integral knowledge he has carefully examined the main arguments of the opponents like Sankara and Marx and their well-known world-views. I have a persistent fear that orthodox Vedantins and Marxists would go on questioning as to whether Sri Aurobindo has *really* understood their masters or has merely attacked the men of straw. However, to come across this sort of criticism is not a misfortune peculiar to Sri Aurobindo. While it is true that Sri Aurobindo did not do enough to meet the criticisms of his 'committed' opponents, it must be admitted that he did oblige sceptical readers by refraining himself from expressing some of his compelling spiritual and yogic experiences. 'I have avoided as much as possible writing about these subjects because I would have to propound things that cannot be understood except by reference to other data than those of the physical senses or of reason founded on these alone.'

Notwithstanding all these self-imposed restraints, one cannot fail to note that while developing a serious point or a subtle argument Sri Aurobindo occasionally, 'strays' into an apparently unrelated matter, stating an object of vision or a mystic experience, which in itself might be of course very interesting, especially in his mellifluous English, but hardly adds clarity to his contention. His main objective is perhaps to communicate with the sympathetic soul rather than to clarify and satisfy the critic. Perhaps the most satisfying answer to a question is to be found or discovered by oneself and cannot be had from another as a gift.

Sri Aurobindo's is a multi-faceted personality. To the common people he is known as a mystic Yogi. In the philosophical circle he is mainly known as the author of a new system of metaphysics (*Purnadvaitavad*) as worked out in the *Life Divine*, which is very ambitious in its scope and excellent in orderly execution. His reputation as a sociologist and a philosopher of history and culture is also well founded and widespread. Some literary critics have greatly admired his poetry and aesthetic ideas. Some people have characterised him as the prophet of Indian nationalism. To his disciples and followers Sri Aurobindo is a Superman and an *Avataar*. One need not agree with all these views on Sri Aurobindo. But one who cares to follow his life and works rather closely is bound to perceive that he is an extraordinary personality and a creative genius. Referring to the pre-Pondicherry phase of his own life he said, 'I was a poet and a politician, not a philosopher'. He attributed his creative achievements, including his philosophical and socio-political ideas, mainly to the practice of Yoga and not to study and research. Sri Aurobindo was aware that logical reasoning and analysis were not the strong points of his thought. His major works represent a rare combination and integration of some of the best elements of philosophy and social sciences. But it is difficult to classify his works. Undoubtedly all of them contain strong ingredient derived from philosophy. Many of his themes spill over into the areas of history, sociology or cultural anthropology, psychology, politics, arts and religion. But these various subjects are blended into a single composition in which all lose their separate identities and form the integral parts of a harmonious whole. And this is achieved, according to him, ' not by force of logical argument... but by a clear vision of the relations and sequences of the Knowledge '. But one is advised to bear in mind that the vision Sri Aurobindo refers to is not an effortless achievement, it needs a lot of perspiration and, of course, deep inspiration.

## III

It was the late Professor Haridas Choudhuri, a follower of Sri Aurobindo and a distinguished exponent of his thought, who got me interested and initiated me in the latter's philosophy. Professor Choudhuri was my teacher and friend in my early undergraduate days. I had already started studying Karl Marx with the characteristic enthusiasm and optimism of a grown-up boy. As I was at that time a devout believer in God, the materialist background of Marxism pricked my theistic conscience and left me rather disturbed and unhappy. But Marx's concern for the exploited and the poor, and his rational analysis of the causes and cures of the exploitation and the poverty appealed to my head and heart. On retrospect it appears the appeal was mainly moral. However, the Godlessness of the Marxist world-view could not as yet shake my philosophical idealism and theism. My intellectual restlessness and unhappiness persisted. It was at that time, perhaps in 1949, that Professor Choudhuri suggested that I should read Sri Aurobindo's main works, *The Life Divine*, *The Human Cycle* and *The Ideal of Human Unity*, and assured me that I would get in them an alternative social philosophy supported by an integral world-view and which would be able to completely satisfy me, both intellectually and emotionally. Accordingly I started reading those books with great interest and expectation, but I must confess, without the required competence. Naturally the output was not proportionate to the input. In so far as *The Life Divine* is concerned, I am sure, I could hardly fathom even half its significance. But the book deeply impressed and intrigued me. The less abstract socio-political ideas of *The Human Cycle* and *The Ideal of Human Unity* convinced me that Sri Aurobindo was not merely a transcendental metaphysician and Yogi, but also a man of practical affairs and with a vision of his own.

My acquaintance with Sri Aurobindo did not, however, diminish my love for Marx; but it did persuade me that one could be a revolutionary defender of the poor without being an eclectician and without giving up one's belief in God. To a young undergraduate student of a highly emotional cast of mind, this was a matter of no mean significance.

Fortunately for me, during the years of my graduate studies, I had in Professor A.C. Das another loving teacher who sustained my interest in Sri Aurobindo and made me conscious of the necessity of being a little more critical in my approach to Sri Aurobindo and Marx. He was one of those few professional philosophers who, without being himself a follower of Sri Aurobindo, could recognise at quite an early stage the uncommon quality and comprehension of his works. Having obtained the Master's Degree, when I decided to devote my spare time to write a dissertation on Sri Aurobindo critically comparing his main social, political and historiographical ideas with those of Marx, Professor Das, I gratefully recall, encouraged and helped me in various ways. My objective was to show that the socio-political content of Marxism, at any rate its fundamental elements, could very well be integrated within the broad framework of Sri Aurobindo's philosophical system. At that time, even this modest objective seemed to me intellectually very stimulating. A first draft of the dissertation was completed by the year 1958 and by that time, as a result of further studies and reflections, my attitude towards God, Sri Aurobindo, Marx and the related matters had undergone a very serious change. *My* God proved elusive. The more knowledgeable Marxists told me that *my* Marx did not historically exist and was a product of imagination. Those who had the competence and the privilege to study Sri Aurobindo more closely than myself nearly convinced me of my failure to understand the 'real' Sri Aurobindo. The more kind and sympathetic of my friends said that my personal predisposition and somewhat arrogant rationalism and obstinate individualism stood in the way of a correct understanding of Sri Aurobindo and Karl Marx. Again, fortunately for me, Professor Das was very unlike the typical orthodox exponents of the great thinkers. He assured me that the standard of my research was 'far higher than the standard of research required by D. Phil'. But later on, when I had the occasion to read it carefully once again, I did not feel satisfied at all and abandoned the idea of publishing it. The matter was left there for a long time. The wiser people persuaded me that my queer theme of synthesising spiritualism and materialism did not deserve serious attention and certainly not resurrection in print.

After a lapse of 15 years, some time in 1972, the birth centenary year of Sri Aurobindo, I decided to re-read the major works of the thinker, forgetting for the time being Husserl, Russell, Wittgenstein, Popper, Max Weber, Levi-Strauss and the rest. That year I had been to Pondicherry for the first time on an official visit. I went to the Ashram to pay my respects to Sri Aurobindo, met the Mother and visited the room in which Sri Aurobindo had lived for a long time and had done his *sadhana*, and wherefrom I could see the boundless sea. I recalled his poem, *The Sea at Night*:

I see beyond a rough
Glimmering infinity, I feel the wash
And hear the sibilation of the waves
That whisper to each other as they push
To shoreward side by side, — long lines and dim
Of movement flecked with quivering spots of foam,
The quiet welter of a shifting world.

I do not think either my visit to Pondicherry or the year 1972 had anything in particular to do with my revival of interest in Sri Aurobindo's ideas. Towards the end of the year an idea seized me: I must settle my intellectual account with Sri Aurobindo as objectively as I can, for it does have its relevance today. I started rewriting the book. It is not old wine in a new bottle. Both the bottle and the wine, whatever they are worth, are new. I cannot say that this book does not have any structural similarity with my earlier work. But I must claim that the arguments and the conclusions of the book are altogether different and new, especially those of the longish last chapter.

I have tried to give here a critico-analytical exposition of Sri Aurobindo's sociological thought, taking *sociology* in an extended sense and setting it first in its historical context. Since most of his ideas are not ' secular ' or self-contained and require the interested reader to be aware of their philosophical presuppositions, I have briefly delineated a few of them, e.g., *Nature* and *Man*, at the very outset. Sri Aurobindo's own analysis is essentially diachronic and the relevant dynamics are invariably spiritual and hidden from the public eye and therefore to be inversely inferred from their outer manifestations. Marx's analysis is also diachronic, but his social dynamics are open to factual tests and there is nothing esoteric about them. My comparative studies in the fundamental concepts of Marx and Sri Aurobindo mainly centre round the famous controversy between ' the autonomy of psychology ' and ' the autonomy of sociology '. While Marx is often referred to as the main author of the latter concept, Sri Aurobindo's name is rightly associated with the former. But none of these thinkers is so simplistic as to be oblivious of and to disregard the force of the opponent's argument on the point. In his *dialectical* sociology Marx made an earnest effort to explain the seemingly autonomous psychological phenomena in terms of a complex causal relation between the infrastructural and the superstructural elements and processes of society. Sri Aurobindo's *integral* sociology is a serious and systematic attempt to put the matter ' upside down ', to use that famous expression of Marx, to show how the whole of our socio-political structure depends for their existence and significance on some deeper psychological forces which, in turn evolve out of a unique and dynamic Spiritual Being. Here the student of the history of sociology can hardly fail to note that the Marx-Aurobindo controversy is a *creative* extension of a very old and interesting intellectual battle which has been going on for centuries and drawing into its arena distinguished thinkers like Hobbes, Rousseau, Vico, Hegel, Comte, Mill and Morgan. Not only the battle line-up and the weapons, but also the attitude between the combatants have been undergoing encouraging change. Hopefully, this change for the better will persist.

# I

# Integral Sociology of Sri Aurobindo: The Concept and the Method

## Prefatory

Here I propose to delineate the main conceptual characteristics of Sri Aurobindo's Integral Sociology and to stress particularly its methodological aspect. The chapter is mainly expository and only incidentally critical. To make Sri Aurobindo's position clear it will be compared and contrasted with some concepts of sociology which had been very influential during the second half of the nineteenth century and the first quarter of this century.[1] It is against the background of this age that his thought has to be understood. I deliberately refrain here from referring in detail to the contemporary theories of sociology. But the discerning reader will see how they constitute the background of my exposition and criticism of Sri Aurobindo's thought. I would round off my argument by highlighting the sociological points of similarity between Karl Marx and Sri Aurobindo notwithstanding their philosophical differences. It may be mentioned in this connection that I use the term *sociology* in an extended sense.

To understand a thinker and his ideas one must know his method. Every man has his character, style and method. The method of a thinker reveals his perspective, indicates his field of interest and also its contents. The fact that a man chooses a particular field of study rather than another indicates further a personal-cum-valuational component of his character. There is nothing wrong or surprising in the personal factor being present in the choice of a thinker's field of study.

Sri Aurobindo is against the method of trying to understand and interpret human nature primarily in terms of external factors. He prefers what he calls the psychological and integral method. By *psychology* he does not mean ordinary empirical psychology. He is in favour of a different sort of psychology, a depth psychology or spiritual psychology which includes introspective or phenomenological studies both of the individual mind and the group mind. Secondly, by *integral* he means, negatively speaking, nothing partial or fragmentary. The integral method demands that a subject, be it a person or field of study, should be studied against its appropriate background, both historical and contemporary, both from within and from without. But Sri Aurobindo would perhaps like to add and insist that the objective is to be understood and interpreted in terms of the subjective. Kant said that objectivity is nothing but inter-subjectivity.[2]

## Theoretical Background

Concerned as we are with the sociological theory of Sri Aurobindo, we have to study it in its proper context. Broadly speaking, his leading ideas, though metaphysical in origin, are sociological in formulation. He characterises one of his major works, *The Human Cycle*,[3] as the Psychology of Social Development. Whatever term he may use to designate the ideas of his sociological theory, there is no doubt that they are subsumable under the discipline of sociology.

The origin of sociology may be traced back to four subjects—Political Philosophy, Philosophy of History, Biological Theories of Evolution, and the Movement for Socio-Political Reforms. Except the third one, all other subjects are fairly old. These subjects, though distinct, have influenced one another all along.

Auguste Comte, known as the founder of Sociology as a distinct discipline, approaches the ' science ' from the angle of Philosophy of History. In the model of other positive, i.e., natural sciences, he proposes to fashion this new discipline, the task of which would be to find out the causal inter-connections of human relationships and explain social dynamics. Obviously this approach is inconsistent with Hegel's. For Hegel is admittedly against approaching history by way of Nature. Nature, he says, has no history; it merely repeats its cycle. The historical process is spiral and creative, or dialectical, as he put it. For Hegel the difference between higher and lower organisms is merely logical and not temporal, and thus he does away with the idea of evolution. The positivist's revolt against Hegelian idealism was strongly supported by John Stuart Mill, a consistent and life-long admirer of Auguste Comte.

Before the Social Darwinians, who exploited most the notion of natural evolution, came Herbert Spencer. Spencer defines sociology as ' the study of evolution in its most complex forms '. In points of change from homogeneity to heterogeneity, increasing integration, definiteness, multiformity and coherence, social evolution is fulfilling the formula of evolution at large. Sociology for him is the ' science of super-organic evolution ', engaged in the empirical study of the growth, structure and functions of human society. True, Spencer follows Comte in doing away with the Hegelian distinction between the processes of social and natural evolution, but he perhaps lacks the latter's insight into the Philosophy of History. While Comte approaches sociology from the standpoint of Philosophy of History, Spencer does it from the evolutionary viewpoint.

The publication of Darwin's *The Origin of Species* in 1859 marks the beginning of the gradual disappearance of the difference between the static or scientific and the changing or historical view of nature. Darwinian notions of *natural selection* and the *struggle for existence* had been extensively and often extravagantly used by Social Darwinians like Ludwig Gumplowicz, Gustav Ratzenhoffer and Franz Oppenheimer. All of them think that social conflicts are the analogue of the struggle for existence in the sphere of socio-cultural life. They attribute a sort of causal role to it. Conflict is said to be the cause of social development. The implication of this view is obviously dangerous. Certainly all conflicts are not conducive to social development and, therefore, positive encouragement of conflict should not be accepted as a matter of policy.

Darwin's scientific method in general and his notion of the struggle for existence in particular had an important influence on Karl Marx. But the latter never accepted the former's belief that human society is an extension of biological evolution, nor did he accept the Hegelian contention that social development is autonomous and has nothing to do with the natural process. The biological pattern of man's nature is only one constituent of his character, which has in it other equally important constituents. The factor which shapes human character most decisively is said to be economic. Quite unlike the unintelligent animal, man is not helpless against the biological conditions and the physical forces of nature. But his freedom has its limits and the limit is set by his historical conditions. For man is essentially an historical agent. Marxists study the inter-relations of the different productive forces working within a definite historical context and try to lay bare the laws of socio-economic development. The non-economic factors are said to be relatively unimportant and have to be explained in terms of the economic ones.[4]

In spite of Hegel's strong and unmistakable influence upon him, Marx's sociology is largely based on his own independent study of history, classical economics and contemporary industrial society. Vico also influenced him through Hegel and other German idealists. But while he accepted the historical kernel of the Vician and Hegelian theories he rejected most of their ideas on the ground that they were highly speculative and not borne out by historical facts. Every hypothesis, he insisted, must be verified in the light of facts. Marx attached great importance to the unity of theory and practice. It was from Comte, Saint-Simon, Fourier and Owen that he inherited his practical zeal for social and political reform.[5] His insistence on the *practical test* of theoretical truth can be traced to the positivist tradition of Comte and Mill. But it has to be admitted that he was neither an ideal visionary nor a utilitarian as Mill was.

## Sri Aurobindo's Approach

Sri Aurobindo's concept of sociology is in a sense very unorthodox. True, many of his conclusions are strikingly similar to those arrived at by other contemporary sociologists, but his method has a striking originality of its own. Consistent with his philosophical position of *Integral Monism*, he develops what I propose to call a system of *Integral Sociology*.[6]

Sri Aurobindo speaks of the necessity of avoiding two extremes. In the name of spiritualism one should not ignore empirical findings and soar to the height of empty speculation or transcendental abstractions and in the name of empiricism one should not resort to fact-fetishism. A proper understanding of social life demands that one should shift the emphasis from the external data to the internal data of social life.

He differs from objectivists and materialists who affirm that social existence is based on our natural existence and that it has to be explained in terms of the economic environment. Sometimes he goes to the length of suggesting that economic, historical, institutional and other approaches to society are indeed very 'futile.' These hypotheses can at best successfully arrange, classify and organise social facts but cannot produce valid theory. The rationale of evolution lies deep in the process, and is not generally exhibited by its surface movements and is to be therefore discovered by a sort of subjectivist method. To understand social development we are advised to take proper account of the influence, importance and modes of working of the human mind. Thoughts and ideas of man mould his history more than anything else. We have to lay bare 'the potent secrets and all-determining laws of social life'. But this is not an easy task. And, therefore, we are generally found to be engaged in a relatively easy task, i.e., collection and classification of superficial sociological data. It is on the basis of external data that 'we advance hasty generalisations and make absolute systems which are positively announced today to be abundant perforce tomorrow.' Collection and classification of external facts of social existence yield at best certain generalisations which are only 'secondary rules and practical bye-laws (and) which help us tide over the difficulties of the moment and to organise empirically without understanding them.' Organisation of facts is *not* understanding them. This inability on our part to go deep into the laws of social evolution is attributed by Sri Aurobindo to the incapacity of our main instrument, *reason*. Reason works with commendable facility and rapidity. But it lacks profundity and therefore has to remain satisfied only with the *whats* and *hows* of the surface movements of society and cannot get to their *whys*.

> Sociology does not help us, for it only gives us the general theory of the past and the external conditions under which communities have survived. History teaches us nothing, is a confused torrent of events and personalities or a kaleidoscope of changing institutions. We do not seize the real sense of all this change and this continual streaming forward of human life in the channel of time. What we do seize are current or recurrent phenomena, facile generalisations and partial ideas. And all this happens because of our whole thought and action with regard to our collective life is shallow and empirical; it does not seek for, it does not base itself on a firm, profound and complete knowledge.[7]

The very idea of *complete knowledge* is extremely vague. It becomes even more vague in the context of collective life. Every piece of knowledge is a sort of answer to a given question or an attempted solution of a problem. It has its limit and is *partial*. Sociological hypotheses are framed in order to explain or tackle *specific* social problems. Because of its relation to specific problem or difficulty, theoretical or practical or both, a hypothesis is bound to be sketchy or partial and cannot be exhaustive or complete. Social phenomena are of interest to us in between their ends, the past and the present, and have to be explained in terms of both, to what they are due and what will be due to them. Both cause and consequence are of importance for the proper understanding of social phenomena. A distinction is often drawn between understanding and explanation.[8]

What Sri Aurobindo means is the inadequacy of *causal explanation in history and sociology*. What we really need in Integral Sociology is teleological or purposive explanation. Unless we know the purpose of man in the world, we cannot fully understand his thoughts and actions, which are being continuously influenced, either consciously or unconsciously, by it. The concept of the human purpose itself may be understood in two different but related ways, i.e., in a secular way or in the larger context of the divine purpose. The human context is said to be an open context—open to the larger context of the divine itself. That is how Sri Aurobindo takes it. For methodological convenience some sociologists study the complexity of the human phenomena within a closed context as if it can be satisfactorily understood without reference to the distant past and the distant future and what lies deep into it. The facile generalisations of sociology ignore the complexity of the human situation, and that exposes sociological theories to easy falsification.

## Beyond the Data

Broadly speaking there are two different methods of reasoning. One is called deductive, or, more accurately, *hypothetico-deductive*, and the other *inductive*.[9] The latter has its different forms—enumerative induction and induction per simple enumeration. On the basis of a careful study of a set of data obtained in a closed system, it has been argued that we may go well beyond the system and tentatively formulate some general principles which will hold good in other closed systems *of the same type*. This method of enumerative induction is not to be confused with the method of induction per simple enumeration. While the latter is a sort of summary of some things and/or properties and does not enable us to go beyond the given, the former, however limited might be its scope, provides a reliable inferential passage from the known to the unknown. It has often been argued against induction in general, and enumerative induction in particular, that either it is summative and therefore extremely restrictive in its scope or it is not inductive at all. Without a non-inductive postulate, induction cannot help us to go beyond the limits of observation. Induction, strictly speaking, is an aimless summary and is of little intellectual or scientific significance. Observation or experience assumes significance only in the light of some hypothesis or theory. It is only in terms of a general truth that particular pieces of information become *meaningfully* related and *testable*. Individual and isolated bits of observations are neither testable nor of any scientific worth. To surmount the difficulties of enumerative induction, logicians have often spoken of and emphasised the superiority of eliminative induction. While enumerative induction relies mainly on the method of agreement, eliminative induction is based on the method of difference. In scientific investigation *dis*confirmation is more important than confirmation. Exclusive reliance on confirmation encourages the development of only those theories which hold good within a *closed* system. The search for disconfirming instances tends to take a theory beyond the bounds of a closed system. The notion of scientific 'induction' is more closely akin to elimination than to enumeration. Scientific inference has always a non-inductive or theoretical component in it and is not inductive as it is ordinarily understood.

Another method which has often been resorted to in sociological research to surmount the difficulties associated with closed-system theories is known as the *comparative method.*[10]

An *incidental* character of the comparative method is its emphasis on a *genetic approach*. By the genetic approach we mean the attempt to explain the subsequent phases of the human cycle by its antecedent ones. One should not lose sight of the limits of the genetic method. Nobody denies the importance of *origin* in sociological study. On the contrary, most of us agree that different forms of primitive society throw light on the obscure beginnings of subsequent developments of different socio-political forms, but to insist that all types of society, modern and medieval, must be explained in terms of the earliest forms of society is to ignore the *qualitative characteristics* found in the relatively modern forms of society. Secondly, the proponents of the genetic approach forget that we cannot adequately explain a form of society or an institution merely by tracing its origin. The past *whats* of a form of society do not necessarily provide its *why*.

One uncritical reaction to this criticism of the genetic method is the view that every form of society is to be explained in terms of its *attending* circumstances and *not* by relating it to its antecedents. If the genetic method encourages a sort of reductionism, one might say that circumstantial explanation tends to make history worthless. The present cannot be reduced to the past nor can it be completely isolated from that. Highlighting this point as a criticism of both the genetic mode of explanation and the circumstantial one, evolutionists like Sri Aurobindo claim that explanation in terms of evolution can steer a clear way in between the two.

But this approach may not commend itself to many modern sociologists. They would say, if the comparative-genetic method commits us to invalid and ambitious generalisations and if circumstantial explanation encourages a sort of static and insular outlook, there is still another method different from the evolutionary one to avoid the difficulties. If *abstraction* is combined with *comparison*, then, it is claimed, we may scientifically compare different forms of society in their respective cycles without being landed in indefensible and highly general laws of social evolution. Morgan's analysis of *The Ancient Society* is cited as an example of what may possibly be achieved by a judicious combination of comparative and abstractionist strategies.

It is well known that Marx was deeply impressed by Morgan's research findings and conclusions and believed that his general theory of materialistic interpretation of history is corroborated by Morgan's works. Engels tells us that Marx 'planned to present the result of Morgan's researches in connection with the conclusions arrived at by his own'. Morgan's view that social relations are chief determinants of human history has been highly commended and gratefully acknowledged in Marxist quarters.

Social relations, says Marx, are expressive of the relations obtained in between the conflicting classes of a particular system of production. The relations of production are stated to be the foundation of all other relations—legal, political, cultural, and so on. The basic structure of society consists of inter-class economic relationships which operates more or less independently of the will of the people concerned. Consequently, it is argued, the super-structural phenomena and processes are to be explained in terms of the basic structural relationships and not the human ideas or ideals. To put it in Marx's own language: 'it is not the consciousness of men that determines their existence, but, on the contrary, their existence determines their consciousness.' Those who, like Sri Aurobindo, take the trouble of tracing 'the so-called general progress of the human mind' in order to explain social phenomena are regarded by Marx as essentially mistaken. He criticises them for taking an upside down view of historical explanation. Social progress is due neither to the human mind, nor to the divine mind, nor even to the combination of both. Society is a network of productive relationships. 'The anatomy of the civil society is to be sought in political economy.' And it is for the political economist to study the contradictions involved in productive relationships which account for conflict, movement and change.

Marx's method is marked by abstraction. The first step of abstraction is betrayed by his aim to study the *anatomy* of society rather than the society itself in which he is obviously more interested. The second step of abstraction is clear from the fact that in spite of his interest in different fields or levels of history, he concentrates on economic history or, to be more precise, on capitalism and that too mid-nineteenth century English capitalism. Further, it may be pointed out, Marx implicitly assumes that the conditions of the capitalist mode of production of that time and of that place would remain more or less constant over a long period of time and in different societies. And this assumption has been repeatedly questioned and criticised later on. Thirdly, from a variety of productive relationships Marx chooses only the capital-labour relationship and decides to explain the others in terms of it. Seen through these levels of abstractions, human beings appear to have lost their *basic* identity in the world of Marx's theory. 'Individuals are dealt with', he writes in the preface to *Capital*, 'only in so far as they are the personifications of economic categories, embodiments of particular class and class interests.' Marx is of course aware that individuals are not how they are *dealt* with in theory. To classify and organise the many and extremely complex facets of social life, abstraction is indeed necessary. But the point is that excessive abstraction projects a distorted picture of social reality. In fairness to Marx, it should also be admitted that his abstract economic categories may at least be partially corroborated by historical and sociological findings. He does not borrow these categories *a priori* from some speculative social philosophy. But his belief in the constancy of class antagonism down the epochs of history is nothing more than a speculative hypothesis and has been repeatedly falsified by the historical findings of different times and places. It must be remembered that this belief is essential to the tenability of his theory of history. Partly discounting Marx's claim that the class struggle is a universal character of history the critic may point out that he was over-impressed by *some* particular phases of European history. History may be *interpreted* in a very general way in terms of class-struggle, but this key concept of Marx does not help us explain all phases of human history. There is a clear distinction between *interpretation* and *explanation* and it seems that Marx is either not adequately aware of it or does not attach sufficient importance to it. The result is confusion.

To understand Marx's abstract approach and speculative sweep one should bear in mind his grounding in classical economics in general and Hegel in particular. Hegel wrote in his *Philosophy of History*: in the ' process of scientific understanding, it is of importance that the essential should be disentangled and brought into relief in contrast with the so-called non-essential. But in order to render this possible we must know what is essential.' For Marx the ' essential ' is capital-labour conflict which is a constant dialectical process and he tries to explain all other less essential and non-essential social processes, phenomena and relationships within this framework. In defence of Marx it has often been said that Marx is *not* a reductionist and that he does not propose to encompass all non-economic factors within the economic ones. Marx never asserts that the relation between the economic categories and other categories is unilateral; on the contrary, he speaks of a dialectical relation between the two, one influencing the other in turn. But Marx is never tired of asserting that the economic factors are more influential than the rest.

A careful Marxist would not deny that individuals are partly responsible for creating the social circumstances under which they are obliged to live. This is what Marx has in his mind when he says that the *forms* of economic relations of today become our *fetters* tomorrow. Obviously the fact that man does not like to find himself in fetters shows that social relations are to a great extent independent of his likes and dislikes and determined by certain *laws of history*. This is *historical inevitability*, an important corollary of economic determinism and the economic interpretation of history.[11] The *form-fetter contradiction* is being continuously created and resolved by the *necessary* and dialectical process of history. Whatever might be a Marxist's argument in defence of the role of man in history, it cannot be denied that he does not quite see how and to what extent human ideas shape the course of history. However impressive might be the Marxist's frequent reference to history and sociology, it is difficult to admit that this is enough to undo the miseffects of his extravagant use of abstract and over-simplified economic categories.

It is not my intention to play down or deny Marx's undeniably great contribution to human thought. He was perhaps the ablest spokesman of his times. I do not know of any other social philosopher who was able to understand the anatomy of the capitalist economy as clearly as he did. Extending the analogy of anatomy I would like to add that it is not necessarily expressed in physiology or body of the society. As our dress does not necessarily express our body, and our body does not reveal the bones and their inter-relations within, it would be partly incorrect to claim that there is a sort of definite correspondence between fashion, physiology and anatomy. Eager to get to the anatomy of capitalism Marx relatively ignored a lot of other very related and important topics, especially the influence of human ideas in history. Even the broad sweep and wide sympathy of his mind could not apparently save him from his abstract economic bias. Whitehead says:[12]

> Every age produces people with clear logical intellects and with the most praiseworthy grasp of the importance of some sphere of human experience, who have elaborated, or inherited, a scheme of thought which exactly fits those experiences which claim their interest. Such people are apt resolutely to ignore, or to explain away, all evidences which confuses their scheme with contradictory instances. What they cannot fit in is for them nonsense. An unflinching determination to take the whole evidence into account is the only method of preservation against the fluctuating extremes of fashionable opinion. This advice seems so easy, and is in fact so difficult to follow.

Following Aristotle it has been often said that the truth of a thing lies somewhere in between the extreme views about it. Ordinarily I take this adage to be true. But I doubt very much whether it is always the case. The Marxist says that the propellant force of history is *contradiction* or *struggle*. Some others, like Hobhouse, have struck a quite different note when they assert that history moves through a series of syntheses and that the main trait of history is *harmony* and not contradiction.

## Value, Fact and Harmony

At this stage we may perhaps profitably look into Hobhouse's concept of sociology. There are two important aspects of sociology, social philosophy and social science. The former is mainly concerned with an analysis of *values*, and the later with a study of *facts*. Whether fact and value are independent of one another is a perennial problem in philosophy[13]. Evolutionists like Hobhouse, in their bid to reject value-fact dualism, speak of a sort of purposive harmony between the two. It is said that values are being realised in facts through social evolution and by human instrumentation. Social and ethical developments are identical at bottom. The investigation of a social phenomenon should properly be carried on at two levels, factual and valuational. Both philosophy and science are necessary methods for the investigation of social phenomena. So far as the factual component of a social phenomenon is concerned there is no methodological problem for the pro-naturalist. The problem arises in respect of the valuational component. The pro-naturalist points out that value as understood (*not* defined) by the anti-naturalist or idealist is not amenable to scientific methodological treatment. If the so-called scientific methodologist does not know how to deal with value, one wonders whether that in itself may be regarded as a good reason for excluding the question of value from the domain of sociology.

The consideration of value or purpose in Marx's writings is conspicuous by its absence. Whenever they are discussed, they are viewed as external adjuncts or characters of a fact, physical or mental. In Marx's theory man is an ' ensemble of social relations ' subordinate to the productive technique and more a creature than a creator of his circumstances. In other words, man, according to him, is a product of the social environment marked by certain definite productive relationships.

## Integral Sociology

About the obvious objects of experience philosophers generally do not quarrel. Their controversy centres on or around some subtly formulated issues regarding the relative status, meaning and value of things which we take for granted on the basis of our pre-reflective experience. No sensible philosopher would deny, for instance, that conflicts and contradictions exist in social life. The controversy is over the question: whether contradiction is incidental or essential to the process of social evolution.

Sri Aurobindo has his own answer to the question. His emphasis is neither on contradiction nor on harmony. He does not subscribe to the Hegelian theory of dialectics either. He is an integralist and his method is called the *integral method.* According to him, both elements of harmony and contradiction are integral to the process of evolution. The scale of evolution, from the material and the vital to the mental and the spiritual, is marked by a gradual increase of integration and a progressive decrease of contradiction. The traits of opposition, differentiation and contradiction are very clear in the natural world. The same is not the case with the human world. The socio-political evolution of man is an integral part and extension of natural evolution.

*Nature* is said to be secret *God.* And *Man* is the middle-term in between God and Nature. That is how Sri Aurobindo defines the relation between the three main terms and stages of evolution. Man is both drawn towards Nature and withdrawn from it due to divine forces. Man is certainly natural, the conscious part of Nature, yet ' he possesses a power of turning his mind and will upon Nature and a possibility of governing her movement, even of varying from the course she dictates to him.'[14]

Man is integral to (but not supreme in) the Divine scheme of things. He is here to realise the purpose of the Divine. He is engaged in realising ' the ideal of human unity ' through association and union, and strife and opposition. Social evolution is the development of the integral relation between three terms—*individual, community* and *mankind.* ' Each seeks its own fulfilment and satisfaction', but Nature requires them to follow 'the law of liberty and harmony rather than the law of discord and regimentation, compulsion and adjustments and strife'. To follow correctly the law of liberty and harmony and avoid that of conflict and contradiction man must know his *destiny* first and should also master the means to realise it freely. The more he is conscious of his social self the more he knows the aim of his own life and gets the power to realise it.

Sri Aurobindo raises the question: how best can man know and realise the aim of his life? Should he rely on *reason*, which is almost universally glorified as a supremely necessary instrument for the discovery of truth, or should he fall back upon *intuition*? While Sri Aurobindo gives reason its due, he is never tired of exposing the hollowness of its lofty claims.

Reason is stated to be incapable of appropriately grasping and tackling the object of knowledge, for, it is intrinsically *differential*, while the object we seek in knowledge is *integral*. His critique of *reason as a method* is a moving plea for integral knowledge, pointing out the inadequacy and shortcomings of rationalism. 'The coils and zigzags of Nature are too deep to be fathomed by the plummet of reason.'

Sri Aurobindo favours the psychological approach to sociology. It is to be remembered in this connection that by *psychology* Sri Aurobindo does not mean ordinary *empirical psychology*. His notion of *integral psychology* is quite different in character. It is based on introspection, insight and intuition and not on experiment and observation. It is not by looking *at* things but rather by looking *through* them that he wants to get to the truth or rationale of the problems to be explained. In the name of science he is not in favour of following the 'objective' approach, which is capable of studying and explaining only what is observable or presentable to sense-experience. The objective approach leads to a sort of crass empiricism or positivism. Deeper truths elude the inspection of the eyes and lie beyond the reach of the senses. It is on this ground that he strongly advocates the 'subjective' method. Here again he cautions us against being misled by a false sort of subjectivity—a subjectivity which is fed by and is based upon sense-data. True subjectivity is spiritual and at that level the mind can work and carry on its search for truth more or less independently of what is sensible and in the sense-mind.

Sri Aurobindo's subjective-psychological approach towards human history and its main elements, individual, community and mankind, remind one of the phenomenological approach of Dilthey[15] and Lamprecht. Sri Aurobindo has evidently been influenced particularly by the latter. Anti-naturalist philosophers draw a line of distinction between what is natural and what is historical and they attach great importance to it. Those who deny it profess a sort of empiricism or naturalism, trying to reduce everything to the terms of sense-experience or to the mechanical laws of Nature. In Sri Aurobindo's integral sociology the concept of Nature occupies a very important position. But it clashes both with empiricism and naturalism as ordinarily understood. He rejects the dichotomy between Nature, on the one hand, and society and history, on the other. We cannot properly understand our socio-political life unless we get to the rationale of the forces of Nature working in and around us.

In other words, circumstantial and objective analysis and explanation of social events are not very illuminating. The proper *meaning* of an event cannot be fully grasped in terms of its relations with its *actual* circumstances or conditions. Most sociological theories about the place of man in society are found to have been offered mainly in terms of the physical, vital and intellectual conditions of his life. Sri Aurobindo thinks that these approaches are unsatisfactory on several scores. First, as it has been already pointed out, this approach is superficial and external and does not get us to the truth. Secondly, it does not tell us how the *potentiality* of a particular event or phenomenon shapes its *actual* perceptible characteristics. This unsatisfactoriness is attributed by Sri Aurobindo to the inherent limitations of the role of reason in our life. Preoccupied with the actualities of our social life, reason, because of its mechanical character, cannot inform and intimate to us correctly the immense *possibility* that lies within us and ahead of us. Our understanding of *man-in-society* cannot be satisfactory unless we can grasp his spiritual destiny in the future cycles of Nature. Placed in between the natural base and spiritual destiny, *man-as-a-phenomenon* should be studied with reference to what is behind him and particularly to what lies ahead of him. Nature's natural, man, to use Sri Aurobindo's language, is a growing God.

Like Hobhouse, Sri Aurobindo also maintains that social evolution represents a ' progressive self-realisation and self-fulfilment of the values and potentialities ' of the individual. Man is a sort of evolving value. He is more a promise than an achievement. His true significance cannot be adequately brought about only by analysing and classifying the factual conditions of his life. In this respect Sri Aurobindo's approach to man and what is human is quite different from Marx's. Sri Aurobindo seems to have accepted Hobhouse's basic position that society moves forward mainly through syntheses and that contradiction and conflict are only incidental. In this respect too, his difference from Marx is very clear.

Sri Aurobindo's method of sociology has a peculiarity of its own. It differs not only from the dialectics of Hegel and Marx, it clashes also with structuralism, functionalism, structural-functionalism and other methods of sociology and anthropology.[16] His main argument against structuralism may be developed somewhat along the lines of his opposition to the external-objective approach. One cannot satisfactorily explain a social phenomenon or an institution just by correlating it to its *actual* structure or theorised frame of reference. Structural relations reveal at best some prominent and actual traits of what is to be explained. He points out further that merely by indicating the function performed by an institution in a particular context we cannot rationally claim to have explained it adequately either. After all *function* is not *purpose.* The distinction between the two must not be overlooked. Function has a distinct positivist connotation and is more or less indifferent to the human purpose which, the idealist says, is being progressively realised in history and society. Even a judicious and careful combination of structuralism and functionalism is not enough to meet Sri Aurobindo's objections to the external-objective approach to sociology, which minimises the influence of ideas and ideals on history and ignores the significance of the spiritual destiny or potentiality of man.

Sri Aurobindo is consistently against misplaced concreteness and wild historical analogies. He says that the modern age should not be understood through old ideas,[17] nor the old age through modern ideas.[18] One age must not be telescoped into another. To support a particular theory of history or sociology we are not entitled to refer to events and trends out of their context. The individuality of historical perspectives should be borne in mind. The deeper we get involved in a social phenomenon and its human roots, the more difficult it becomes for us to tear it off from its appropriate context and use it as supporting evidence for a theory based on things of other times and other places. Sri Aurobindo is in favour of studying *society* mainly through *man*. For he regards the former as an expression of the latter. To him depth psychology is the key to the understanding of sociology and history. Here again his difference from the Marxist approach is unmistakable. While Marx thinks that man is more a creature than a creator of society and that he is to be explained mainly by his social circumstances, Sri Aurobindo takes pains to rebut this thesis and establish the view that man is destined to orient, regulate and progressively establish his control over the attending circumstances of his life.

Looking at the divergence of views expressed by Karl Marx and Sri Aurobindo one must not think that they have nothing in common. They share many fundamental ideas. First, they have expressed in different ways their profound and studied *concern for the alienated man* in an age dominated by matter, machine and money. Humanism and a profound moral appeal lie at the core of their social philosophies. Secondly, their approach is *essentially historical*, based of course on their own interpretation of history. Thirdly, both of them are *historical determinists* and have tried to show that the history of a society exhibits a general pattern marked by certain predictable rhythms. Fourthly, they subscribe to the doctrine of *methodological holism*. Finally, both of them, profoundly impressed by the doctrine of *anarchism*, have visualised the future of the human society in terms of statelessness and ' complete ' individual freedom. It goes without saying that the formulation of their views, the arguments used to establish their points and the method of deriving conclusions are quite independent.

One may or may not agree with what Sri Aurobindo has said on man and his spiritual destiny, but one who has gone carefully through his works is bound to be impressed by the sweep of his integral outlook, the perceptiveness of his mind, style and subtlety of expression, and the broad conclusions some of which are being borne out today. In spite of the fact that some of the disciples of Marx tried to portray him as a prophet of the doom of capitalism, and in spite of all that has happened in the world in the last hundred years or so, a critical thinker cannot accept the Marxist claim that history has consistently corroborated Marx's theory. Nor can he accept the view advocated by some of the devotees of Sri Aurobindo, viz., that he is a prophet. Personally I do not believe in *prophecy*. Man being finite as he is can only *predict* what is likely to happen, but cannot prophesy the future course of events.[19] Finite and fallible man cannot usurp the role and power of the God who never fails. A sound and scientific method should be based on this basic truth regarding human nature and ability.

# 2

# The Concept of Nature

## Nature and History

In this chapter I propose to delineate Sri Aurobindo's concept of Nature, indicating the purpose and planes of terrestrial existence as he understands them. For a correct appraisal of his socio-political theory let us start with 'the deep and complex truth of Nature' which, as he himself recommends, 'should be our light and guide'. Other relevant and comparable concepts of Nature will also be referred to in the course of expounding and examining his view.

Concepts such as evolution, development and history are all apparently meaningless. They are all somehow related to the process of time which, taken by itself, is a physicalistic concept and has little to do with the above concepts. What animates the process of time and relates it to evolution, development and human history is the purpose common to them all. To Sri Aurobindo, Nature is a she-principle and in this respect he has been influenced by the Sankhya doctrine of *prakriti*. Nature is the mover of this significant time-process and she is also being continuously moved along with the process. 'Apparent Nature is secret God.' Strictly speaking, Nature has no purpose of her own; the purpose she realises at different planes of existence is all God himself. Our social existence is an expression of that divine purpose.[1] In this connection what Sri Aurobindo asserts apparently clashes with the materialist conception of history.[2]

> Mankind has a habit of surviving the worst catastrophies created by its own errors or by the violent turns of Nature, and it must be so if there is any meaning in its existence. If its long history and continuous survival is not an accident of its fortuitously self-organising chance, which it must be in a purely materialistic view of the nature of the world.

Every step of history is a deliberate measure of Nature and has its reason behind it. What man has become is out of harmony both with the world he lives in and what he himself should be and *is* to be. The contradictions of his environment are 'not the punishment of a fall, but the conditions of a progress'.[3]

## The Steps of Nature: Matter, Life and Mind

Nature is the foundation of and sustains all human relations, actual and possible, trying to achieve a progressive harmony in them, and giving fullness and significance to them. Her passage to harmony and unity is marked by strife and opposition and is not at all smooth. Nature starts from Matter and there consciousness is in an inconscient state. 'An evolution in the Inconscience is the beginning, an evolution in the Ignorance is the middle, but the end is the liberation of the spirit into its true consciousness and an evolution in the Knowledge.'[4] The second term in evolutionary Nature is Life. In the plane of Life, consciousness subsists in an ignorant state. Ignorance, inertia and division are what the forces of Matter impose on the vital and the mental existence of man, causing pain and suffering and the unrest of dissatisfaction. Life is a creation of Conscious-Force acting sub-consciously on and in the Matter and has three stages in it—entirely sub-conscious and almost mechanical, sub-mental, and sense-mind and intelligence. The subtler powers of sensation and response assume a more coherent and organised form in Mind. Mind stands in between super-conscience and inconscience and is impressed by what it experiences around it and inspired by what it feels or intuits within. Nature creates man, the *manomaya purusha*, possessing intelligent will, at the fourth plane of her evolution, utilising all the potent forces of the preceding sub-human planes.

The development of Nature is distinctly methodical. She moves from simplicity to complexity, rigidity to plasticity, from inconscience through ignorance to self-consciousness, from lower to higher harmony and smaller to larger unity. This movement is characterised by and being carried on through a series of syntheses which are apparently but significantly opposed and sought to be frustrated, especially in the lower planes. In every plane there are two aspects which are seemingly antithetical but actually, in the words of Sri Aurobindo, 'elements of a harmony'. Nature maintains a balance between them but is not monotonously linear in the process. Sometimes she leans this way, sometimes that way, but generally treads the middle way. However, the mid-way balance never proves permanent. It is purely a temporary home of opposite forces; to correct their excess and imbalance they are brought back to a state of poise for the time being. Each aspect of the harmony tries to preserve itself, often at the cost of its opposite. The attempt at preservation proves successful only in proportion to its actual exerciseable power. Although engaged in realising the goal of spiritual harmony, Nature is not quite conscious of it in her sub-human planes of strife and contradiction. 'In effect swallowing up, not of one by the other, but of each by the other, so that both shall live entirely in the other and as the other, is our highest ideal of oneness.'[5] Nature is working in her characteristically slow fashion to realise this ideal in mankind.

Matter is the starting point of the evolutionary process, and the inconscient surface substance of Nature. It does not respond to the light within. And that accounts for the long struggle of Nature in the material plane to liberate herself from it. Because of its inconscient surface we must not think that Matter is absolutely dead and inert and incapable of a response to any sort of stimulation or light. In fact it is a status of being of the Spirit, and made an object of sense-experience. Life appears on the basis of and also within Matter as partially liberated Nature, the builder of forms which are energised, disintegrated and preserved by it. It is in Mind that Nature becomes not only liberated but also conscious of its liberation. From the other end, Matter may be characterised as an inconscient Spirit and Life, as an action of Conscious-Force. Mind itself is an inferior power of Supermind, a power to which Life acts as an instrumental energy. ' Mind, by its separation from its own higher reality in Supermind, gives life the appearance of division and, by its further involution in its own Life-Force, becomes sub-conscious in Life and thus gives the outward appearance of an inconscient force to its material workings.'[6]

To understand the secrets of Nature we must follow the light and guide of Nature and her own slow steps. There is no hiatus, no room for sudden change or revolution in the process of Nature. Everything happens according to some definite laws but the operation of which is not always very obvious or evident. Even at the level of self-conscious man the process of Nature cannot be expedited unnaturally. But the more man gives himself up to the will of Nature, which in fact is the will of God Himself, the faster becomes the pace of her advancement. However, the possibility of a faster pace in Nature's advancement encounters several difficulties. First, even if exceptional individuals and communities or nations who can well grasp the goal of history and are ready to work for it and to realise it, mankind as a whole, interested more in conserving the past rather than creating the future, is not likely to progress rapidly. Sri Aurobindo tries to establish this point by referring to the defeats suffered by the more gifted nations like Greece, Rome, Persia, India and China in the ancient world at the hands of the less civilised, sometimes even barbaric, communities. Secondly, sometimes enlightened individuals and nations themselves commit serious errors of judgment and take steps clearly inconsistent with their reason and experience. This point may be illustrated by the rise of Nazism in Germany and Fascism in Italy. From time to time and at different stages of history Nature takes stock of her past attainments and achievements and tries to see that they are not petrified and fossilised. She vivifies and resuscitates the past in different creative forms. This point may be illustrated by the Italian Renaissance, the Celtic Renaissance and the Indian Renaissance. Finally, it is at the end of all these difficult steps that Nature ' reaches the point when all immediate danger of relapse overcome, she can proceed to her next decisive advancement in the cycle of social evolution.'

No man or community can exist and progress in an isolated way. Everything in Nature has two aspects—self-affirming and self-exceeding. In one sense everything in the world is unique, but in another sense everything in its essence is at one with the rest. The aim of Nature is to preserve the unity without impairing the uniqueness of its diverse elements. ' The real aim of Nature is a true unity supporting a rich diversity.' True unity does not stand on the way of interchange, but requires each to develop its own character. This general truth of Nature holds good in all levels of life, animal, human and social. Sri Aurobindo says:

> all things are one in their being and origin, one in their general law of existence, one in their interdependence and the universal pattern of the relations;

but each realises this unity of purpose and being on its own lines and has its own law of variation by which it enriches the universal existence.[7]

## From the Natural to the Social

Sri Aurobindo thinks that in the light of this general law of existence we must shape our social life. The unity should be given expression in the form of law and the diversity in the form of liberty. Liberty is the freedom of diverse beings to realise the law of their own inner being and potentiality. In this connection he highlights the distinction between uniformity and unity. To achieve harmony in different social aggregates, Sri Aurobindo insists, we must follow the law of unity and reject that of uniformity which curbs liberty and leads to regimentation. The law of uniformity is the work of Reason which is more or less mechanical in its function. When Reason is allowed to govern our life, the resulting laws and formulae prove very rigid indeed. Our social ideal is not uniformity as envisaged by Reason; it is a spiritual unity which is being progressively worked out by Nature. Rigorous uniformity of Reason in society is inconsistent with the aim and method of Nature, for it crushes 'Nature's initiative and habit of intuitive self-adaptation'. But, Sri Aurobindo reminds us, man's freedom to crush Nature's initiative is only relative and temporary; finally, she must realise her purpose, and in order to do that, if necessary, she is disposed to overrule the workings of individuals and communities which prove inconsistent with the said purpose.

One notes two seemingly incompatible lines of thought in Sri Aurobindo's integral sociology. He is found to be an unwavering defender of human freedom, on the one hand, and emphasises the pre-determined purpose of God's working in Nature, on the other. Individuals and institutions are all stated to be manifestations of an all-comprehensive Existence. Sri Aurobindo often speaks of our *destiny* in Nature rather than our *freedom* in it. And he could easily anticipate the objection against it and has in fact tried to meet it from his point of view.

While Nature realises the purpose of the Spirit in an integral way, we, the human beings, do so only in a disjointed way. *Nature's destiny defines our freedom.* We cannot be more free than the scheme of Nature allows us to be. Our freedom depends upon our consciousness of the spiritual purpose operative in Nature. Human society progresses 'in proportion as law becomes the child of freedom' and also in proportion as freedom becomes the expression of its inner law. Though we are constantly told of an essential and secret harmony pervading all things and beings in Nature, the strife and contradiction of our common experience presents a somewhat different picture of life and God. Torn and tossed in his practical life, devastated or affected by repeated wars, global or local, hot and cold, the ordinary man of the world fails to understand and refuses to believe in an absolutely strifeless ideal of human unity. When he is told of the stateless ideal of human unity he feels sceptical about it and to him it appears to be the vanishing point of the human cycle. His experience of pain and suffering is often attributed by him to the step-motherly attitude of Nature, but Sri Aurobindo does not attach much importance to these pronouncements of the ignorant human mind. He rejects the dualism between Mind and Nature. He does not deny the opposition between the two, but refuses to accept it as an ultimate truth of the nature of things. The different principles of Being, Matter, Life and Mind follow their separate lines of development, and their independent self-assertion often renders their underlying unity obscure to us. Sri Aurobindo assures us:

> Yet there is still the unknown underlying Oneness which compels us to strive slowly towards some form of harmony of interdependence, of concording of discords, of a difficult unity. But it is only by the evolution in us of the concealed superconscient powers of cosmic Truth and of the Reality in which they are one that the harmony and unity we strive for can be dynamically realised in the very fibre of our being and all its self-expression and not merely in imperfect attempts, incomplete constructions, over-changing approximation.[8]

Rightly understood, then, the course of Nature, which appears to be blind and mechanical, and the destiny of man are marked by a gradual realisation of freedom and are integrally related, ' elements of a harmony ', and not antagonistic in character.

Sri Aurobindo's idea regarding the relation between Man and Nature has evidently been influenced by the Sankhya concepts of *purusha* and *prakriti*. While in the philosophy of the Sankhyas these two principles are presented as eternally separate entities, Sri Aurobindo interprets them differently. *Prakriti* is an executive power, blind and mechanical in character; *purusha* is consciousness, and without *prakriti*, i.e., in itself, static and motionless. Sri Aurobindo does not deny the truth of the duality of the experience of Soul and Nature.

> But the experience of their unity has also its validity. If Nature or Energy is able to impose its forms and workings on Being, it can only be because it is Nature or Energy of Being and so the Being can accept them as its own; if the Being can become Lord of Nature, it must be because it is its own Nature which it had passively watched doing its work, but can control and master; even in its passivity its consent is necessary to the action of *prakriti* and this relation shows sufficiently that the two are not alien to each other.[9]

Extending this principle of spiritual unity Sri Aurobindo also tries to overcome the apparent dualism between Body and Soul. In its moments of ignorance Soul may identify itself with Body, but that does not mean that it cannot master and control the latter. Occasionally Soul is subject to Body, but the subjection is not a *necessary* expression of the inner relation. *Purusha* and *prakriti*, Soul and Body, are not alien to one another but different modes of expression of one and the same spiritual reality. And it is in this way that

Sri Aurobindo tries to reconcile the *determinism* of Nature with the *freedom* of Spirit. But whether the ghost is really there in the machine is of course an open question. Sri Aurobindo would argue that the apparent machine is itself ghostly.

## Diverse Concepts of Nature: Divine and Secular

The concepts of Nature and particularly its adjectival derivative, the natural, are not free from ambiguity. These have been understood and interpreted differently by different thinkers. Sometimes Nature is taken to be a synonym of the physical universe. Sometimes *natural* is regarded as an antithesis of what is artificial, deliberate or willed. *Natural* and *spontaneous* are often used as interchangeable terms. Nature is also used to denote a realm which is quite different from the supernatural and the revealed realms. In Natural Theology, for instance, we find secular and scientific treatment of the supernatural and revealed phenomena and theories. Further it may be pointed out that sometimes a thing is characterised as natural only to contrast it from some other thing or things, which are acquired or civil. It is interesting to note that in the integral philosophy of Sri Aurobindo most of these connotations of Nature and natural interpenetrate and are found to be interdependent. The natural and the supernatural, the natural and the deliberate, the natural and the revealed and the natural and the civil are *essentially* connected and continuous.

But the question arises regarding the exact meaning of the *essential*. The materialist, the nominalist and the existentialist attack the notion of essential from different points of view. They have one common criticism against the essentialist, i.e., the essentialist does not discharge the epistemological responsibility of establishing and proving the connection between the pairs of concepts referred to above. For example, he does not show how the natural is related to the supernatural. To meet this criticism essentialists like Sri Aurobindo refer to their own theory of knowledge which attaches more importance to super-sensuous experience and less to sensuous ones and tries to show that the latter is a degenerate form of the former. In the final analysis the ontological controversy tends to boil down to an epistemological controversy over the rival claims of intuitionism as a theory of knowledge on the one hand, and empiricism and pragmatism on the other.

The relation between man and nature, Marx affirms, is also to be understood dialectically and not metaphysically. Neither man nor Nature completely determine either. Man knows the necessity of natural laws and by practical activity turns that necessity to his own use. Man and Nature, Thought and Being, are indeed distinct yet also form a unity. This unity is made possible by the social and practical activities of man, and does not owe its origin to what Leibniz calls pre-established harmony or the divine design. Nature is of no significance to man unless the latter is social. 'Society', says Marx, 'is the accomplished union of Man with Nature, the veritable resurrection of

Nature, the realised naturalism of man and the realised humanism of Nature.' It is a materialistic way of putting what Sri Aurobindo means by saying that it is in the human mind that Nature becomes self-conscious.

Aristotle says that man is social *by* nature, but Marx points out that man is social *in* Nature. Unknown and uncontrolled Nature stands in the way of the social mind's self-affirmation. Like religion and private property, uncontrolled Nature alienates man from his positive and social self-affirmation. This self-alienation or self-negation is overcome only when other factors such as uncontrolled Nature is itself negated. To bring Nature into an organic unity with man it has first to be grasped, then controlled, and finally socialised and humanised. And that is possible, Marx believes, only under Communism.

> Communism is the positive abolition of the private property of human self-alienation and thus the real appropriation of the human nature through man and for man. It is therefore the return of man himself as a social, that is, really human being, a complete and conscious return which assimilates all the wealth of the previous development. Communism, as a complete naturalism, is Humanism, and as a complete humanism, is Naturalism. It is the definitive resolution of the antagonism between Man and Nature, and between Man and Man. It is the true solution of the conflict between Existence and Essence, between Objectification and Self-affirmation, between Freedom and Necessity, and between Individual and Species. It is the solution of the riddle of History and knows itself to be the solution.[10]

## Back to the Paradigm: Sri Aurobindo on Nature and History

While Sri Aurobindo speaks of the necessity of following the lead and guidance of Nature, Marx speaks of the necessity of humanising it. Left to itself, Nature is of no human significance to Marx. Sri Aurobindo finds that humanity is already there in Nature in the form of a promise and that Nature in the course of her evolution fulfils that promise.

Material nature is devoid of any ethical significance. It is governed by those laws which co-ordinate our fixed habits and take note of the forces which create, arrange and preserve natural phenomena and processes according to the secret Will of Nature and ' according to the mute satisfaction of that Will in its own self-formations and self-dissolutions '. Animal or vital nature is also without ethical significance. But it has in it the stuff out of which the ethical impulse of man evolves.

> We do not blame the tiger because it slays and devours its prey any more than we blame the storm because it destroys or the fire because it tortures and kills; neither does the conscious-force in the storm, the fire or the tiger blame or condemn itself Blame and condemnation, or rather self-blame and self-condemnation, are the beginning of the true ethics.[11]

In brief, Nature, according to Sri Aurobindo, is infra-ethical in its beginnings and supra-ethical at its summit. In both these respects, his position, as we find it, is different, for instance from Plato's. While Sri Aurobindo thinks that the infra-rational plane of Nature, though in itself unethical, is mute preparation for the ethical, Plato asserts that it is not only unethical but also anti-ethical. Further, Sri Aurobindo points out, the life of the self-realised spiritual man, in which all is determined by truth of consciousness and truth of being, is supra-ethical, for there is no standard, no conflict necessitating a standard or criterion to use, no virtue or merit, no sin or demerit of Nature. The ethical domain is to be defined mainly in terms of *rational* human nature. Pressed by practical difficulties and guided by habits and impulses, the rational man is not his own master in the truest sense. He needs some laws or code and norms to guide him out of his practical difficulties. If, however, by dint of his superior spiritual evolution he succeeds in raising his consciousness above the level of strife and conflict and realises the essential oneness of things and beings, he does not need any law or morality to shape his life. Sri Aurobindo does not believe that Good, in the ethical or axiological sense, is ultimate or supreme. In this respect he will not endorse the identity of Good and God as proposed by Plato.

When Sri Aurobindo says that man is to be guided by the law and light of Nature, it is not to be understood in terms of the Stoic view that Nature provides us with the best possible guidance in all spheres of our life. Nature *qua* Nature cannot lead us either to a moral life or to a sane society. It is only because Nature embodies the Will of God that her guidance is of help to us in our quest for the ideal of human unity and strifeless morality. Nature creates for man favourable external circumstances and happenings or finds them created by man himself for his further evolution and development. Different forms of social aggregates found at different phases of the human cycle, from commune and tribe to the State, answer and fulfil the evolving and the growing needs of human nature.

Sri Aurobindo is a naturalist in a special sense. He rejects not only the mechanical-materialist view of Nature, but, as we have seen, also the Stoic view of Nature. Even then, he insists, we have a lot to learn from Nature. Our statutory laws, says he, should be in accord with the 'natural or organic life of society' which alone can ensure their 'spontaneous freedom of variation'. Otherwise these laws go against the requirements of the progress of society. We need an *avatar* (or a prophet), like Manu or Moses, 'who comes on earth in a millennium and speaks with a spiritual voice to formulate and codify our social laws without stifling their growth'.[12] Law must be 'a formulated expression of our nature and based on national will and consciousness rather than on the reason of a small legislative party'. One may well presume that Sri Aurobindo would reject the positivist view of jurisprudence advocated by thinkers like Austin and support up to a point the sociological view of law defended by jurists like Savigny. Those forms of law and morality facilitate social growth which are in accord with the basic impulses of Nature like spontaneity and variation. Freedom is the voice of God in Nature.

The Spirit is then the central secret of Nature. Life is the outward indication of the Spirit's power in Matter marked by spontaneity and organic variation in unity. Imperfect life evolves through the growth of consciousness. Man is the latest, but not the last, evolute of Nature. 'But not last', because 'mind is not native dynamism of consciousness of the Spirit; supermind, the light of gnosis, is its native dynamism'.[13] Man is the first of the three constant factors of social evolution, the other two being Community and Mankind. Nature has a double motive in her human purpose.

In man two ends of Nature, the enlarged animal sector and the arc of the divine circle, meet supplementing and complementing each other. Man 'has to turn Mind not only on itself, but on Life and Matter and the material existence; that is very clear not only from the law and nature of the terrestrial evolution, but from his own past and present history.'[14]

# 3

# The Concept of Man

## Man is an Ambiguous Phenomenon

Man can neither altogether reject his infra-mental past nor can he be completely aware of his supra-mental future. Caught in between the forces of Nature and the Spirit, man is evolving, growing and moving towards a definite goal. Man is a super-normal phenomenon in the normalcy of Nature, a mental being placed in, purposively related to, and influenced but not completely guided by, Nature. Nature poses a sort of spiritual challenge to man and does it with a purpose, which she only partly reveals and mainly conceals, and of which man is peculiarly equipped to be conscious of on reflection.

Man is a thinking instrument of Nature. To put it in other words, Nature becomes self-conscious in Man. At the level of Matter, consciousness is in the form of nescience, or thick darkness, at the level of life it is in the form of ignorance, or melting darkness, and at the human level it assumes the form of Reason, a sort of twilight area. The ambiguity of human nature is accompanied by the twilight faculty of mental reason. The bright light of the Spirit is yet an unachieved ideal for man which leads him upward to the supra-mental plane of existence and consciousness. Man, the mental being, is a complex of different kinds of knowledge and power. ' In mind itself there are grades of series and each grade is again a series in itself; there are successive elevations which we may conveniently call planes and sub-planes of the mental consciousness and the mental being.'[1]

## The Dimensions of the Human Being: Physical, Vital and Rational

True, all men are not equally developed, but humanity as a whole, says Sri Aurobindo, has arrived at no higher plane than the physical-mental, the lowest sub-plane of the intelligence. Generally we take our stand on any plane or sub-plane, depend on the lower stages and occasionally respond to the light from above. Usually we try to adjust ourselves to the requirements and forces of Nature and that explains why conformism and positivism are proving so popular and effective. From this it would be rash to conclude that there are no exceptional and creative human beings among us. Nature has her own plan in shaping the destiny of mankind, and sustains her initiative through relatively more gifted individuals among us. We are mutely desired by Nature to help her in her endeavour to realise the higher planes of the Spirit. The physical man proves of little help to Nature in her work to take us upward to the planes of overmind and supermind. For physical man works with the physical brain, the physical sense-mind and the physical sense organs which are said to be incapable of going deep into the secrets of Nature, and can give us only, what Sri Aurobindo calls, a physical sense of reality.

The physical man has a vital plane in him which is dominantly instinctive and impulsive. These impulses and instincts are hereditary and customary, forming no disciplined order. Sensations, desires, hopes, feelings and satisfactions are all impulsive formations of life-consciousness, stimulated by and dependent on external things and contacts. These are all unmistakable characteristics of the vital man who is engrossed in the practical, the immediately realisable and possible, the habitual, the common and average mode of life.

The physical man has also his mental part concerned as it is mainly with the physical nature and its images. Objective, customary, practical and traditional are his ideas and activities. The superior values of life are, from this point of view, superfluous or at best helpful adjuncts. Strongly influenced and dominated by an immediate sense of utility or pragmatism, the mind of the physical man is more or less indifferent to the higher modes of thought and action and unresponsive to the finer activities and movements of imagination and feeling. To him whatever is not immediately useful is either a pleasant luxury or an abstract fancy. Whatever falls below or passes over the physical mind is regarded by the physical man as dispensable addenda to his life. Unaware of the deeper unity and continuity of the different natural planes and sub-planes and yet called upon by practical reason to account for them, often he resorts either to physical laws or to traditions and customs. He always tries to explain the unknown in terms of the known, and in the process of doing so he commits the fallacy of *reductio ad absurdum.* Unfortunately, this mode of explanation is often uncritically represented and / or accepted as the scientific mode of explanation. We are advised by Sri Aurobindo to remember that the laws and possibilities of physical Nature cannot be entirely known unless we know the laws and possibilities of supra-physical Nature. A critic of the 'lower' scientific outlook, Sri Aurobindo does not deny the provisional necessity of this outlook as a starting point. But he believes that, sobered by its experience, science in its more developed form would leave behind its positive and pragmatic craze and be influenced by systematic reasoning and philosophical speculation, which may not be of any immediate use and yet would successfully anticipate many future observations and experiments.[2]

Above the physical mind and deeper within the physical sensation, there is, what Sri Aurobindo calls, an intelligence of the life-mind. This is said to be more open, more than the physical mind, to the psyche (*chitta-purusha*). It is an obscure life-soul, a frontal formation of the vital being (*prana-purusha*) and not the psychic being as such. The vital man is concerned mainly with the life-being and the life-force. To him the world is a field for the fulfilment of life-power, impulsion, ambition and adventure. Physical existence is an inert form of the life-force and its significance is only instrumental to the expression and satisfaction of Life which is based on the 'secret subliminal vital being'. The vital man may realise that subliminal vitality which considerably helps the working process of evolutionary Nature. Partly free from the bondage of the blind physical universe, he can understand the inner Life of Nature within and without him, 'independent of the body and of the symbols of the physical world'. The vital man betrays two very important characteristics, passion and the instinct of possession. The vital man, the *rajasica purusha*, is interested mainly in a life of action and not in one of contemplation.

As the physical plane of human evolution has sub-planes in it, the vital plane has also sub-planes within its fold. The first sub-plane is 'a dumb inconscient drive or urge', an imprisoned will, an extremely rudimentary form of consciousness which is unconscious of its own consequence and prospect and completely under the influence of the Universal Will. This sub-plane contains the seed of individuality in an obscure and unformed state. The second sub-plane may be characterised as the ground of desire. It is at this plane that the completely imprisoned Will of the previous sub-plane partly raises its head, becomes partly liberated, but being limited as it is in its capacity cannot possess all that it is eager to. In the third sub-plane the eagerness to possess ceases to be blind and dumb. Being partly conscious of its potentiality and prospect, Life now knows that to get more it has to forget something which is immediate and grossly sensible and accordingly becomes prepared to sacrifice the present for the future. It is out of this knowledge and preparedness that a new power emerges. This is the power of Love: 'The bud of the third (vital sub-plane) is Love', as Sri Aurobindo puts it. It is in and by love that life goes beyond itself, comes in communion with other forms of life and thus becomes more adequately conscious of itself. In the fourth plane, the bud of love blossoms into a flower of perfection. Here the original Will of Life emerges in its fullness and with purity. At this plane the aspirations and desires of life are truly illumined and fulfilled.

Whatever might be the graded achievements of Nature in the plane of Life is not quite aware of the light and potentiality which it carries within itself. The object of life is not simply living; it has to outline what it immediately finds around itself. Paradoxically enough, to be full and perfect, Life must go beyond itself. Matter for its own apparent-inherent inconscience and Life for its own apparent-inherent ignorance confuse their autonomy with the sovereignty which belongs only to the Spirit. As the potentialities of Matter cannot be realised with the materials readily found within itself, the potentialities of Life cannot be fully realised with the means and mechanism supplied by it in its pre-reflective stage. It is to be remembered in this connection that every plane of Nature has a double purpose to realise. First, it realises its own potentialities together with those of Nature as a whole. But in its pre-reflective stages Nature is not conscious of its simultaneously operative double purpose. Strictly speaking, no plane has its own exclusive potentialities. The actualities of one plane are correlated to the potentialities of another and the converse. It is only from the Spirit's point of view that all potentialities are truly his own. The process of their actualisation is spread over all the conceivable planes and sub-planes of evolution. Sri Aurobindo points out that Man, remaining as he is almost exclusively confined within a less dark veil, is under the wrong impression that the different planes of Nature are completely independent and secular. Like every plane of existence, Man must exceed his individual bounds to realise his great inward potentialities. Man must affirm and exceed himself to realise what he really and essentially is. The Universal Will is engaged in preparing the grounds for man's ultimate self-affirmation. And that constitutes the rationale of the whole evolution of Nature—sub-human, human and superhuman.

Above the level of vital mentality there is 'a mid-plane of pure thought and intelligence to which things are the most important realities'. The philosopher, scientist, intellectual, idealist and dreamer are at the top of this mid-plane. They are not necessarily fascinated, captivated and misled by the 'thingish' character of things and have the power to be aware of their potent and subtle ingoings. In the man of pure thought and intelligence Nature is partly conscious of her own goal—the goal of which she is more or less unconscious at the sub-human levels. In these sub-human levels, there is no doubt physical and vital struggle and strife, but it is only with mental conflict that Nature inaugurates the human stage of her evolution. Man is the thinking instrument of Nature, relatively free from the rigid grip of vital laws, free enough to bring about an adjustment in those laws and to control them in a way that would be helpful for him in his quest for the highest ideal. If we remember the double purpose of Nature's evolution, we must admit that Man's ideal is at the same time also Nature's. That explains why man is not completely free to impose his own ideal on Nature's working process. Man may control the conflicting tendencies of his own nature but cannot totally transform their inner drift. Nature has not yet given a free hand to mental man who is still partly under the laws of Matter and Life. Though not so obstinately and insistently as Matter and Life, yet Mind in Man, under the influence of the first two planes of Nature, wrongly supposes itself exclusive and independent, and on the basis of this wrong supposition tries to realise its (great) ideal within the (narrow) limits of its physical-vital existence. Interested in evolving the higher planes of existence, including the Supermind, Nature cannot remain long an indifferent spectator and a silent witness to the defective and myopic endeavour of mental Man. Man is under an intrinsic, i.e., natural, obligation to discover the inner harmony underlying the struggle and strife of the material and the vital planes of existence, and to shape his own life in the light of that harmony. If man becomes exclusively concerned with his own mental or rational conflicts and fails to see the light of harmony and to be guided by it, Nature intervenes. The sovereign rules of Nature ultimately over-rules the autonomous rules of Matter, Life and Mind.

Man is the middle-term of Nature's evolution. The more he realises his own ideal, the more he upgrades his own status. But he has not yet discovered his own natural truth. He is still the abnormal in the normalcy of Nature, an imperfect apostle of a perfect ideal. But 'this imperfection', to use Sri Aurobindo's own words, 'is not a thing to be at all deplored, but rather a privilege and a promise, for it opens out to us an immense vista of self-development and self-exceeding '.[3] The process of self-development and self-exceeding is tortuous and full of difficulties. The blind and dumb, obstinate and self-affirming laws of Matter and Life are not ready to open themselves to the twilight of human reason. On the contrary, they materialise and vitalise, i.e., try to downgrade and weaken the influence of human reason. Matter is comparatively simple in its organisation and therefore it is with less difficulty that Reason can tackle it. But the opposition that Reason faces at the level of and from Life is rather stiff and persistent. In the struggle between Matter and Life on the one hand, and Mind, as we find it in the mental-rational being, on the other, the former slowly but inevitably lose their ground in favour of the latter. Of this silent struggle and its results, man may be (but is not necessarily) conscious. The more he becomes conscious of his higher purpose and opens himself up to the light above, the faster becomes the pace of his progressive march towards the goal of spiritual evolution. As every plane of existence is eager to maintain its *status quo*, Man's spiritual journey cannot be linear and easy. A proper understanding of this non-linear movement of Nature demands of us a thorough probe. The *dynamics* and *rationale* of this movement provide the spiritual silken thread connecting the different planes of existence cutting across their sensible boundaries and leading them to their common spiritual goal.

## A Critique of the Concept: Scientific and Metaphysical

Sri Aurobindo's concept of man, particularly his account of man's position in the scheme of Nature, may be criticised on various grounds. In fact a charge of determinism has been levelled against his views. Sri Aurobindo himself is aware of the fact that this theory may be challenged on the ground that it does not have sufficient foundations or that it is highly speculative or metaphysical, and that its account of different planes of existence is superfluous. One may question the very usefulness of the idea of purposive evolution, and point out further that the ideal of human unity that Sri Aurobindo speaks of may be defended on a different ground—different from the one offered by him. Sri Aurobindo admits that the fact of the past and present regarding human and sub-human grades may be interpreted without making use of the concepts of teleology and evolution. Sri Aurobindo does not deny the relevance of the critic's point. In self-defence, he replies that his account of man in the process of evolution is based on true and infallible knowledge and *facts* of reality and that there is nothing *theoretical* about it. Theory being a product of human reason and often based on inadequate acquaintance with reality may be questioned, corrected and even refuted, but fact is either to be recognised or ignored and cannot be manipulated according to our sweet will. The matrix of all our doubts, questions and confusions regarding the bona fides of the evolutionary and teleological interpretation of history and pre-history of man is our relative ignorance, our lack of intuitive knowledge.

Sri Aurobindo is prepared to admit that even those who share all his fundamental views may refuse to accept his conclusion, namely, that there is a teleological purpose in creation. One is quite within one's right to argue that 'The Divine has nothing that he needs to gain or that he has not,' and that 'if there is creation and manifestation, it is for the delight of creation, of manifestation, not for any purpose.'[4] The teleological view of evolution has been sought to be countered also by the materialist. The materialist assumes that the whole evolutionary process is the work of an inconscient energy which acts automatically and mechanically and cannot have any conscious purpose in it.

While Sri Aurobindo recognises the 'considerable cogency and importance' of the scientific or materialist objection, he clearly asserts that this 'view of things is not complete and its cogency is not conclusive'. He is not prepared to accept the Darwinian thesis that the evolution of man may be satisfactorily accounted for in terms of a series of variations. The evolution of species or forms does not shed light on the very necessity of evolution. Evolution may be better explained if the cause of variation can be ascertained, for it is the cumulative result of variation which accounts for the evolution of species. Darwin's account does not enlighten us on the matter. Darwin frankly admits his ignorance about the cause of variation. If he is pressed further he ascribes it to chance. As against Darwin, Sri Aurobindo argues:

> Even in the inconscient, there seems to be at least an urge of inherent necessity producing the evolution of forms and in the forms of developing Consciousness, and it may well be held that this urge is the evolutionary will of a secret Conscious Being and its push of progressive manifestation, the evidence of an innate intention in the evolution. This is the teleological element and it is not irrational to admit it; for the conscious or even the inconscient nisus arises from a truth of Conscious Being that has become dynamic and set out to fulfil in an automatic process of material nature . . . .

Sri Aurobindo finds that it is relatively more difficult to meet the metaphysical objection for it is 'more serious' than the scientific objection. Logically it is undeniable that the Absolute, which is complete and perfect 'by definition', can have no purpose to realise in and through the process of evolution. And in that case, evolution turns out to be a mere expression of Divine Delight and absolutely objectless. Though this is a serious objection, Sri Aurobindo refuses to accept it. His first point is that material world is not absolute. Secondly, it is not complete. And, therefore, it is quite conceivable that the evolution of the material world has something to gain through the process of evolution. Besides, when Sri Aurobindo speaks of purposive evolution, he does not use the term *purpose* in the ordinary human sense. The purpose that guides the process of evolution is 'the urge of an intrinsic Truth necessity conscious in the Will of the indwelling Spirit'. Against the objection that all this evolution is a game or *lila* and therefore objectless, Sri Aurobindo argues that even a game has an object or purpose and without the fulfilment of that object, it lacks in the completeness of significance.

> ... The material world is not an integral totality, it is a part of a whole, a grade in a gradation; it may admit in it, therefore, not only the presence of undeveloped immaterial principles or powers belonging to the whole that are involved within its matter, but also a descent into it of the same powers from the higher gradations of the system to deliver their kindred movements here from the strictness of a material limitation.[5]

Disposing of the more serious metaphysical objection against purposive evolution, when Sri Aurobindo turns to the scientific objections he finds that it is ' concerned ' only with the outward and visible machinery and process, with the detail of Nature's execution, with the physical development of things in Matter and the law of development of Life and Mind in Matter. However important the machinery or the exact genealogy or chronological succession of time may be, it is after all secondary—secondary to the plan or purpose which lends significance and direction to the process of evolution.

Sri Aurobindo's position on evolution clashes with that of Darwin and Lamarck. While Darwin thinks that the cause of variation is mechanical, Lamarck thinks that it is due to the conscious effort of the individual being to adapt himself to his environment. Darwin attaches supreme importance to the almost blind operation of mechanical laws. Lamarck believes that the cumulative results of the individual's conscious efforts are transmitted through heredity. Modifying Lamarck's position some of his followers have argued later on that the change in the individual is effected not so much by his conscious efforts as by ' his ' unconscious response to the environment and the laws under the influence of which the environment itself changes.

The teleological account of the evolution has been rejected not only by Darwinians and Lamarckians but also by Marxists. On the nature and evolution of Life the Marxist's position is a compromise between Vitalism and Mechanism. In common with the Vitalist the Marxist rejects the Mechanist's view that life may be deduced from mechanical and chemical laws. He also rejects the Mechanist's view that the origin of life is due to chance. The Marxist accepts at least a part of the Mechanist's thesis when he denies the existence and operation of any ideal principle (like ' entelechy ', ' soul ', and ' life-force ') in living creatures and organisms. He thinks that life represents something quite different from, and higher than, inorganic matter. He draws a line of qualitative distinction between ' material form of motion ', and ' biological form of motion '. In this connection he refers to Engel's notion of Life: ' *Life is the mode of existence of albuminose bodies* and this mode of existence essentially consists in the constant self-renewal of the chemical constituents of these bodies.'[6]

The Marxists share the Darwinian denouncement of teleology. But they themselves differ on a very important point. While the Darwinian lumps ' natural selection ' and ' the survival of the fittest ' together, the Marxist thinks that they are entirely separate. The latter argues, to illustrate his point, that selection by the pressure of over-population, where perhaps the strongest survives at the initial stage, may result in weakness of the survivors in many respects. Secondly, selection by greater capacity of adaptation to altered circumstances may well mark a sort of regress or degeneration of the survivors in some respects. At times we survive by downgrading ourselves.

Sri Aurobindo rejects the materialist accounts of the evolution of Man offered by the Darwinian and the Marxist mainly on the alleged ground that they do not adequately recognise the importance of human phenomenon in the scheme of the Universe. Apart from his general objection that Darwin and Marx have failed to see the deeper significance of teleology, he points out that their main principle of explanation, matter-in-motion, itself is not self-explained and therefore begs explanation. 'Matter itself can no longer be explained by Matter alone, for it does not appear to be self-explained.'[7] The materialist's substitute for teleology is chance. If teleology does not suit his reason, one wonders how chance or accident can be accepted by him as reasonable and satisfactory. Teleology explains evolution from within the process as its internal dynamism; but the materialist theory approaches evolution from without and therefore goes deep into the process and accounts for its rationale. Sri Aurobindo does not deny the limited relevance of scientific explanation of the exterior phenomena and features of the process of evolution. The scientific theory of evolution is concerned only with the outward and visible machinery of the process of evolution. Matter and Life are indeed transitional terms facilitating the appearance of Man in the universe. But simply because Matter and Life are prior in point of time to Mind or Man, they cannot be regarded as superior in point of quality and reality to the latter.[8]

Sri Aurobindo acknowledges the principle of hereditary variation. 'Heredity upon which science builds its concepts of life evolution, is certainly a power, a machinery for keeping type or species in an unchanged being'; but he questions the adequacy of this principle in accounting for persistent and progressive variations. For, he thinks that the tendency of the principle of heredity is conservative or preservative rather than evolutionary.[9] Some biologists are of the view that each grade of Being is true to its type, exists in itself and by itself and has nothing to do with what precedes it or what succeeds it. This view is not acceptable to Sri Aurobindo. All that these biologists can claim on the basis of their findings is that the variability and actual variation of a type are confined within its own specification of Nature. And they have nothing to disprove the possibility of self-transcendence by a type of species. Sri Aurobindo is not in favour of regarding the existence of different grades or types of Being as the different resultants of the cumulative influence of hereditary variation. They are all due to the Force of Consciousness in the material universe. The practical or physical method of operation varies from grade to grade. But underlying the difference in the modes of operation there is a basic unity of Nature.

Nature starts her work in Matter with infinitesimals charged with immense energy associating them by design and number. Energised infinitesimals are grouped together by the operation of the laws of Nature; group infinitesimals are the sensible objects of our knowledge. In the process of life formation, what consciousness-Force produces first are infinitesimal forms of life and infinitesimal animalcules.

> It creates an original plasm and multiplies it, creates the living cell as the unit, creates other kinds of minute biological apparatus like the seed or the gene, uses always the same method of grouping and association so as to build by its various operations and various living organisms.[10]

The creation of various types as such does not prove the case of evolution, for what is needed is an evolving and conscious purpose working in Nature. Sri Aurobindo holds that types vary within their respective boundaries; typal variation is not specific evolution and a satisfactory explanation of specific evolution cannot be framed and offered exclusively in terms of heredity. Besides heredity, the forces which pave evolution are physical forces, such as food, light-rays and also perhaps some invisible forces of which our knowledge is still at a very rudimentary stage. The fact that some species under the influence of sub-conscious energy answer to the needs of environment, while others under the same influence remain unresponsive and fail to survive, is 'the sign of varying life energy and psychology, of a consciousness and the forces other than the physical at work making for variation in Nature'.[11] Typal variation, which is a symptom of a bigger internal movement, and trans-specific evolution are all being designed, engineered and successfully brought about by the force of consciousness. In other words, there is nothing blind and mechanical in the process of evolution.

Of course the evolution of Man may be explained without teleology, but, as Sri Aurobindo points out, in that case the supreme significance of man is denied. Teleology is generally abandoned in favour of two other possible modes of explanation. First, one can say with the materialist that 'all is the work of an inconscient energy which acts automatically by mechanical processes and have no element of purpose in it'. Secondly, we may suppose that the Infinite and the Universal have everything in them already and that they have nothing more to realise, to accomplish or to work out. As we have already seen Sri Aurobindo rejects both the scientific and the metaphysical denials of the teleological account of evolution. The scientific account of evolution is discounted by Sri Aurobindo mainly on two scores. First, it fails to explain how evolution is different from involution; and, secondly, how specific (or in species) variation leads to the emergence of a superior type of being, and of an ideal form of human unity corresponding to that superior type of being. The positivist-minded scientist always seeks to explain *ought* in terms of *is*, ideals or possibilities in terms of actualities. His reductionist bias makes him suspicious of everything which is not immediately given or testable by what is given. He distrusts transcendental entities and even higher level scientific theories which have no verifiable empirical correlates. This sort of pseudo-scientific attitude towards science lands one in an uncritical pragmatism, makes one a worshipper of whatever is given and sceptic about whatever is not given.

## The Ascent of Man and Progress

Sri Aurobindo reminds us that man is not a one-dimensional being. In our actualities we are true to our past and present and through our possibilities we project ourselves to the infinite future. Man is indeed a *project.*

> Our actualities are the form and value or power of expression to which our nature and life have attained; their norm or law is the fixed arrangement and process proper to that stage of evolution. Our potentialities point us to a new form, value, power of expression with the new and appropriate arrangement and process which is their proper law and norm.[12]

In spite of this significant distinction between his actuality and his possibility or project, man under the influence of his conservative reason is disposed to confuse the law of the future with that of the past and present, taking the latter as a sort of non-creative repetition of the former. He is more faithful to his actualities than to his possibilities, and that is why he is guided mostly by the actualities of his experience and environment, and that is why he even at his best can think only of that future which, in substance, is a mere reproduction of the past and the present. Man does not follow the spirit of the integral totality; he is not conscious of his heritage of the moving integral totality.

Creative consciousness is both integral and historical. The past is re-lived or is re-enacted in creative human consciousness. True historical consciousness does not mean the mere revival or repetition of what is past. If mankind partly forgets its past and gains new experience, that does not mean either the poverty or bankruptcy of modern culture. Similarly, if modern man lacks the integral outlook and the vision of the ancient seer, that does not mean that the modern outlook is necessarily inferior to the ancient one. In the place of epic vastness and classical grandeur ' there has been in later developments an increasing subtlety, complexity, manifold development of knowledge and possibility in man's achievements, in his politics, society, life, science, metaphysics, knowledge of all kinds, art, literature.' It is a new way of getting back to the past and exploring the future. Even in man's spiritual endeavour, Sri Aurobindo observes, ' this increasing subtlety, plasticity, sounding of depths and extension of seeking '[13] are becoming more and more evident.

The process of evolution is then marked by a movement from simplicity to complexity and subtlety, from flexibility to rigidity and again back to plasticity, from inconscience through ignorance to knowledge. This movement encounters opposition and obstruction in its way and, as we have said before, is never linear. Even regressive or backward movement is not unknown in the course of evolution. Backward movements are only ' temporary descent ' or at worst downward curves of the spiral of progress. Ultimately, Nature must move forward. Self-conscious man is the main agency and instrument of that movement. The evolution of man is destined to be progressive under the necessity of the Will of the Spirit. Through ups and downs Nature has a definite goal to realise in and through Man, transforming Man into Superman, transforming Mind into Supermind. 'For (man's) cycles are circles of a growing, but still imperfect harmony and synthesis, and (Nature) brings him back violently to her original principles, sometimes even to something like her earlier conditions so that he may start afresh on a larger curve of progress and self-fulfilment.'[14]

Progress in fact is of two types—radical progress and adaptive progress. In the case of adaptive progress there is no sharp departure from the past to the present; tradition, history and modernity are well balanced and preserved in it. In the name of radical progress, mankind in different times and places arrogated to itself the impossible task of making a clean sweep of the past, of starting from scratch, with an empty canvas before its eyes and a blue-print at its disposal. One may think of a man with no history behind him and society around him to determine and influence; but such a man is a theoretical abstraction and a practical impossibility. Because of an inner necessity progress proves always adaptive, interpenetrative and rhythmic. These are all unmistakable expressions of the presence and operation of a purpose operative in history. The uniform rhythm of human cycles is a truth of the Spirit and being worked out by Nature. Disposing of the scientific and metaphysical objections against the teleological philosophy of evolution and history, Sri Aurobindo emphasises the inescapable necessity of studying the human cycle from within, from the side of inner psychological forces and not from without, from the side of the outer material forces.

Sri Aurobindo does not believe in the autonomy of sociology, in the independent existence, action and reaction of social forces. According to him, they are all related to, influenced and supervened by, the inner psychological forces. Spiritualist and teleologist as he is, he thinks that there is an inner harmony and synthesis between the two segments of social reality—psychological and material. While the material forces are not conscious of their origin, operation and direction, the psychological forces are, however, vaguely so.

## The Marxist Objection: A Review

Sri Aurobindo's teleological philosophy of evolution and history is basically incompatible with the Marxist's account of the same. Marx says that 'all historiography must begin from . . . natural bases and their modification in the course of history by men's activity.' By the 'natural bases' he means the geological, oro-hydrographical, climatic and the life conditions of living human individuals. Sri Aurobindo tells us that the modification of natural bases referred to by Marx is brought about both in the human and in the sub-human grades, particularly in the latter by the conscious design of Nature. Even when man is found to be an active agency in bringing about modification and transformation in the natural bases, he is acting knowingly in consonance with the purpose of Nature. This view is obviously unacceptable to Marx. After the *natural* bases what a scientific historiographer must take into account are, says he, the sum of productive forces, capital and social relationships; and all these taken together form the real bases of human history. Extending this line of argument Marx affirms that the true conception of history ' rests on the exposition of real process of production, starting out from the simple material production of life, and on the comprehension of the form of intercourse connected with and created by this mode of production '. The natural bases of history are transformed into real bases by man's own activity; and of the different forms of activity Marx attaches greatest importance to the productive activity. He finds nothing divine, no design in this gradual and human transformation of Nature into social reality.

But, I think, it would be wrong to suggest that the materialist account of evolution as represented by the Marxist is concerned only with the external process, machinery and attending circumstances of evolution. To regard the human organism purely as a machine would perhaps be rash. And many Marxists would denty he criticism. Man is perhaps neither entirely a machine nor completely an individual. It is very difficult to substantiate the Vitalist's claim that human life is shaped and therefore explainable without reminder by its internal properties. In fact, we cannot isolate any system completely from the rest of the universe and definitely ascertain if it is completely mechanical or not. There is always an element of residue or uncertainty in the explanation offered exclusively either in terms of internal properties or in terms of external environment. It seems to be a part of the very nature of every form of life to interact with its environment. It not only adjusts and adapts itself to the environment, but it also tries to adapt the environment to itself in some respects. It is very difficult to draw a sharp line of demarcation between an organism and its environment. It is undeniable that organic evolution is marked by a progress towards more and more complete individuality, both in the development of the individual and in the evolution of the race.

The Cartesian tradition is not yet dead. Descartes thought that the human body is a complex machine. Even those who, like Haldane, accept this mechanistic outlook deny that the behaviour and responses of the organism as a whole confirm the mechanistic hypothesis. They would rather say ' that the organism is something more than a machine, in the sense that it has a unity of a type which the machine lacks '.[15] Unlike the machine, there is something in the organism which enables it to repair itself and bring itself back to a normal state if it is not too seriously injured. But the ultimate subjection of all forms of life to death unmistakably indicates the superiority of the laws of material motion over those of biological motion.

Further, perhaps it would not be quite correct to mention the shortcomings of the Darwinian principle of Natural Selection in order to prove the untenability of the general materialist theory of the evolution of man. Perhaps we should remember that to justify his theory of evolution Darwin spoke not only of Natural Selection but also of the inheritance of the effects of the use and disuse of organs by the organism. True that the latter view has not been as strongly defended by Darwin as Lamarck and Herbert Spencer, for example. Consistently with his dialectical approach, Engels was more influenced by Lamarckism than by Darwinism. Darwin took variation, or rather heredity variation, for granted, and he did not seriously search for its origin. Over-impressed by the principle of heredity, he did not take serious note of the principle of mutation, which partially opposes and negates the work of heredity. Mutations generally disturb the normal relations between an organism and its environment and are, therefore, often regarded as harmful from the evolutionary point of view. Because of this, many biologists refuse to regard mutation as an evolutionary agency. But the problem is that qualitative novelty cannot be satisfactorily accounted for purely in terms of natural selection which is a negative process. Natural selection may at best account for the appearance of what is qualitatively new. But what makes qualitative distinction actually possible is something other than natural selection. It is on this ground that in Marxist's quarters there has been a reaction against Darwin and a tendency to veer round to Lamarckism, a tendency to explain qualitative distinction exclusively in terms of the influence of the environment and its creative interference. It is to be remembered that Lamarckism itself has been interpreted in some cases very mechanically, and of course sometimes also in a creative way. Some Marxists, including Engels, betray the rather mechanical Lamarckian view that changes produced by the organism in response to a change of environment are directly inherited.

Haldane offers a different theory which tries to explain evolution in terms of a dialectical opposition of mutation and selection. And he claims that this is a Marxist interpretation of evolution, supported by modern researches in the field of biology.

Lysenko, the well-known Soviet scientist, also rejects the Darwinian theory of evolution criticising the principle of natural selection as 'flat' and pointing out its inconsistency with the conclusions of modern science. To him the classical theory of heredity (associated with the names of Mendel and Morgan) is also unacceptable. According to Mendel and Morgan, the bearers of inheritance are constituents of the cell nucleus, the chromosomes, or the genes contained in them. They explain changes of heredity, or mutation in terms of change that occurs in the constitution of the genes or chromosomes, which may in fact be achieved artificially. Lysenko does not believe that there are necessarily specific carriers of inheritance in the organism itself. His starting assumption is that organism and environment constitute a dialectical unity. A change in the environment offers man the opportunity of bringing about a change in the organism which can be passed on by inheritance to its descendants. To Lysenko heredity itself is not an abstract or a static principle. It is a concentrated form of the environmental conditions assimilated by the organism in a series of preceding generations. Usually the organism with a conservative heredity does not assimilate the conditions that are not native to it. But the organism with a de-stabilised or 'liberal' heredity accepts and assimilates the environmental conditions which environ it, with less discrimination, promoting greater intake and growth.

Lysenko criticises the Darwinian theory.[16] He claims to have scientifically established the possibility of transforming one species into another. Unless the intra-specific composition of the organism is known, the desirable mode of inter-specific relation and the ideal unity between organisms and the environment cannot be correctly ascertained and established. The Marxist tries to prove that there is something in the organism which enables it to accept and assimilate some conditions of the environment and reject some others. But he refuses to characterise or identify this native 'something' of the organism as spiritual. Further, the Marxist tries to give the impression that his dialectical approach should not be confused with the mechanical approach. While on ultimate analysis he defends mechanism and determinism, he takes pains to point out that they do not clash with the spontaneity, initiative and creative response of the organism. In other words, the Marxist claims that the scientific determinism and creative enterprise of the organism are not at all incompatible.

Whatever might be the liberal interpretation of Marxism, one can hardly deny that the Marxist is very much concerned with the practical, particularly political, implications of his theory. Certainly one of the main reasons of his opposition to Darwin's theory of evolution is that in its sociological counterpart he finds an eloquent plea for unbridled economic competition. Influenced by Malthus, Darwin portrayed the struggle for life as an external struggle, a struggle between individuals rather than as a struggle between individuals and their environment, and as a struggle for external adaption rather than an internal struggle. Secondly, the Marxist rejects the Darwinian assumption that evolution is an uninterrupted and continuous process, believing as he does in a ceaseless class struggle climaxed by revolution.

Sri Aurobindo's theory also has a pronounced political implication. While Sri Aurobindo would claim that it is more or less a true statement of the unfolding of the Divine design in human history, the Marxist reiterates his position that there is nothing like Divine design and that human history is being created and modified by man himself. Yet, man himself being subject directly to economic laws and indirectly to those of Nature, his freedom to create and modify history is always a matter of degree and never absolute. Regarding man's position *vis-à-vis* the Divine design, Sri Aurobindo points out that there is nothing which might suggest that man is not free to shape his own destiny. His place in Nature does not stand in his way of a search for greater ideals and larger freedom. Man wants to be wholly conscious of his being. Self-consciousness is what is meant by spiritual knowledge and its essence is an intrinsic self-existent consciousness. But here again man's subjection to the laws of Matter and Life enables him only to be partially (and not integrally) conscious of his total being. Both Sri Aurobindo and Marx agree, in different ways of course, that man is the author of his socio-historical destiny, but not solely.

But the point of agreement must not make us blind to their fundamental differences. The Marxist thinks that the metaphysical pre-suppositions of Sri Aurobindo's sociology are not only superfluous but also scientifically untenable. An Aurobindite argues that the Marxist account of the human cycle is superficial. Despite his denial of the existence and operation of an intelligent principle underlying the process of history, the Marxist admits that the histories of different societies, separated from each other by Time and Space, exhibit certain definite rhythms, indicating thereby that there are some general laws of history. Sri Aurobindo also finds definite rhythms in history; but believing as he does in the existence and operation of an intelligent principle in history, it is with greater theoretical plausibility that he can speak of universal patterns or rhythms of history. According to him, the materialist conception of history is superficial and reveals empirical trends sustained by a deeper teleological movement of Nature. He finds no incompatibility between the deeper natural laws of history and superficial empirical trends. In defence of his own view he argues that the Marxist's commitment to the empirical (' dialectical ') theory of knowledge makes it impossible for him to go deep into the workings of human history and discover its persistent inner laws.

# 4

# Rhythms of the Human Cycle

## Are the Rhythms Universal?

Sri Aurobindo welcomes the modern movement of emancipation from what he calls the obsession of physical science, the pseudo-scientific effort to prove the all-sufficiency of Matter to explain Mind and Soul. He is aware of the fact that this movement has not gone beyond a few awkward and rudimentary stumblings. Still he welcomes the new realisation that 'behind the economic motives and causes of social and historical development, there are profound psychological, even perhaps soul factors'.[1] In this connection he refers to Karl Lamprecht and his 'luminous idea' that every nation or civilisation passes through some definite rhythms of the psychological cycle,—symbolic, typal and conventional, individualist and subjective. In spite of his belief in the deeper psychological laws of history, Sri Aurobindo does not appear to have accepted the view that *every* cultural unit, society or nation, must necessarily pass through some uniform rhythms. He admits that it is very difficult indeed to rigidly classify the pathways of social evolution, and points out that its empirical analysis cannot exhaust all the possible curves, turns and twists which its process may exhibit. 'The psychology of man and his societies is a too complex, too synthetical of many-sided and intermixed tendencies to satisfy any . . . rigorous and formal analysis.' Further he admits that this theory of a psychological cycle fails to disclose the inner meaning of its successive phases or the necessity of their succession or the goal towards which they are moving. Yet, Sri Aurobindo seems to have found Lamprecht's psychological schema or theory very useful for the purpose of his own theory. While Lamprecht tries to substantiate his theory by the developments of European and particularly of German History, Sri Aurobindo tries to show that it may be confirmed by the cultural and political history of India as well.[2] The human cycle begins at the fourth stage of the evolution of Nature, when man becomes self-conscious.

## The Symbolic Period

Every civilisation in its early stage is said to be pervaded by a strong symbolic mentality. Symbolic mentality develops from intuitive and imaginative power in man. Human ideas, customs, religion, institutions and other forms of culture bear the stamp of the symbolic mind and its intuitive capacity.

The symbolic mind feels a very intimate kinship with the wide world around it and keenly responds to its calls and stimulations. Man with the power of intuition feels the mysterious depth of the nature of things which, however, he fails to express adequately in language. He is also conscious of an overwhelming power dwelling in Nature which he tries to utilise in shaping all aspects of his life, personal and social. Having realised the inadequacy of ordinary language in giving expression to his experience of the mysterious depth and overwhelming power of Nature, he makes increasing use of signs and symbols, similes and metaphors in his language.

Symbolic society was quite different from the sort of society we see today. It was then ' a free and fluid association ', in which the man of the period ' not bound by (outer) laws or institutions ' used to follow the inner law of living, needing neither to prey on his fellows nor to be restrained by ' the iron yoke of the collectivity '. It was indeed a ' natural state of society '. Human life at this stage was not, in Hobbes' words, ' nasty, brutish and short '. And in this respect Sri Aurobindo's position is definitely opposed to Hobbes'. Human relations, according to Hobbes, are all governed by covenants, and covenants without swords are but words. To put it otherwise, Hobbes rejects the theory of symbolic mind and society and discounts the possibility of a ' free and fluid association '. But Sri Aurobindo seems to be a firm believer in the existence of a Golden Age in which man was ' freely social without society '.[3] One of the reasons why most of us do not subscribe to the theory of a Golden Age is said to be that our intellect is discursive and devoid of intuitive and imaginative power. ' We read always our own mentality into that of (our) ancient forefathers and it is therefore that we can find in them nothing but imaginative barbarians.' In fact, they were insightful seers and not barbarians with a prelogical mentality.[4] To justify his theory of primitive symbolism Sri Aurobindo refers to the earliest account of Indian society. The religious institutions of sacrifice (*yajña*), the social institutions of marriage (*vivāh*) and the fourfold caste order (*caturvarna*), were all pervaded by symbolism and mysticism. He takes up the *Ṛg-Vedic* hymn of marriage to illustrate his point. It was originally purported to express the successive marriages of *Surya*, daughter of the Sun, to different Gods, but now it is supposed to be a marriage hymn for the union of a human couple. Also he cites the case of *caturvarna* which is now believed to be the result of an economic evolution complicated by political causes. But that was not the idea of the people of that Golden Age.

The bent of mind of the modern man is generally very utilitarian or pragmatic. It is interested only in the external, material and human factors of a cause to explain its effects—social, moral, or religious. This mode of explanation can at best acquaint us with the superficial features of the phenomenon. It does not disclose its inner significance or spirit. To understand the inner spirit of the *caturvarna* one should study the *Purusha-Sukta* of the Veda where the four orders are described as having sprung from the body of Brahma—*Brahmins*, the priests, from the head; *Kshatriyas*, the warriors, from the arms; *Vaishyas*, the merchants, from the thighs; and the *Sudras*, the servants, from the feet. Sri Aurobindo writes:

> To them (the ancient people) the symbol of the Creator's body was more than an image, it expressed a divine reality. Human society was for them an attempt to express in life the cosmic *Purusha* who has expressed himself otherwise in the material and the supra-physical universe. Man and the cosmos are both symbols and expressions of the same hidden reality.[5]

However desirable the symbolic age might have been, Sri Aurobindo knows it will never return, for history never repeats itself.[6]

Sri Aurobindo firmly believes that the future prospects of human civilisation lies in our success in rediscovering the past symbolic truth of the Spirit. We have to get rid of social stagnation with the help of intuition and imagination. We have 'to resuscitate the ancient free force and truth and vigour or permanently revivify a conventionalised and stagnating society.'[7]

Sri Aurobindo's concept of the symbolic age has many historical parallels. Herder, for example, speaks of the *infancy* of the human cycle. According to him, there are five stages in the cycle—infancy (Oriental), boyhood (Egyptian and Phoenician), youth (Greek), manhood (Roman) and old age (the Christian world). Sri Aurobindo also uses the terms *boyhood*, *manhood*, etc., to denote the different phases of history.[8] Fichte divides human history into five periods—the period of 'innocence', of 'commencing sin', of 'complete sinfulness', of 'commencing justification', and of 'complete justification and scientification'. In the 'innocent' period of early human civilisation, Fichte tells us, man used to adhere impulsively and unconsciously to whatever was rational and just. Fichte's notion of the age of innocence corresponds to Sri Aurobindo's symbolic period. As 'infancy' passes into 'boyhood' and the state of 'innocence' into that of 'commencing sin', the symbolic stage naturally passes into the typal stage. The first stage is predominantly religious and spiritual; all other factors—ethical, psychological, economic and the like—are subservient to the religious and spiritual ideas of the Time.

## The Typal-Conventional Period

The second stage, which we may call typal or conventional, is 'predominantly psychological and ethical; all else, even the spiritual and religious, is subordinate to the psychological idea and to the ethical idea which expresses it'.[9] At this stage we see a growing power of reason, an increasing tendency to intellectualise the intuitive, impulsive, instinctive and subliminal modes of understanding. Reason does not work well with ambiguous symbols: it prefers concepts with a definite connotation. The free and dynamic idea of Nature is replaced by a new mechanical one. Used to moving in predetermined grooves, Mind steers away more and more from the vast unchartered world of symbolised truth. With the growth of intellectual sophistication, one observes a new process and a new tendency in the different spheres of culture: man bids farewell to everything but creed, institution, formal practice and ethics. The old mystic and occult elements are generally forgotten. When they are preserved, they are preserved only in the form of rituals and myths, forgetting their inner spiritual content. The living spiritual experience gives way to faith, emotional fervour and ethical conduct. Religion becomes an other-worldly affairs; ethics assumes the position of religion. *Shastra* replaces *dharma.*

> A complete denial of religion, occultism and all that is supra-physical is the last outcome of this stage, a hard dry paroxysm of the superficial intellect hacking away the sheltering structures that are the refuges for the deeper parts of our nature. But still evolutionary nature keeps life as her ulterior intention in the minds of a few and uses man's greater mental evolution to raise them to a higher plane and deeper issues.[10]

The average human mind of the period is detached from the living and moving symbols and, in order to fill up its rational vacuum, accepts and follows some dead types and formulae. In spite of this mechanical turn of the human mind, Sri Aurobindo never denies the superiority of the typal stage over the symbolic stage. But he rejects the intellectual notion of religion of the symbolic stage; he refuses to accept the view that the religion of that period is only a mass of animism, fetishism, magic, totem, taboo, myth and superstitious symbols.[11] This distorted and highly theory-laden view of religion is attributed by Sri Aurobindo to the insightless mechanical cast of the modern positivist-minded anthropologist. In spite of all the petrified characters of the religious institutions and practices of the typal period, Sri Aurobindo observes that the religion of the typal period is moved beyond the religion of the previous period. This advanced type of religion is ' composed of a polytheistic belief and worship, a cosmology, a mythology, a complexus of ceremonies, practices, ritual and ethical obligations interwoven sometimes deeply into the social system '. This is the stage of a national or tribal religion unknown of before.

The typal stage of society and civilisation is not fundamentally different from its immediate next stage, the conventional stage. Also, the difference between the individualist and the subjective stages is not very pronounced either. Perhaps because of this fact Sri Aurobindo sometimes speaks of three stages or rhythms of the human cycle.[12] At the moments of discernment, of course, he speaks of five stages: ' symbolic, typal and conventional, individualist and subject '.[13] After ' symbolic ' he puts a comma, and also after ' typal and conventional ' he puts a comma, but not between ' typal ' and ' conventional ', nor between ' individualist ' and ' subjective '. In between ' typal ' and ' conventional ', and ' individualist ' and ' subjective,' he puts ' and ' and not comma. From his detailed analyses it is clear that he draws a distinction.' however subtle and fine that might be, between ' typal ' and ' conventional ' on the one hand, and ' individualist ' and ' subjective ' on the other. But in *The Foundations of Indian Culture* he repeatedly speaks of three stages and not five.[14] In tracing the development of the Indian polity he speaks of four stages.[15] One need not spend too much time in ascertaining the exact number of stages or rhythms of the human cycle. It is enough for our purpose to bear in mind that after all there is only a distinction and not a division between any two successive stages and that the stages are only ideal types or classificatory concepts and not concrete descriptions of empirical situations.[16]

In the typal stage the people generally forget the advantage and the significance of fluid and flexible associations of the previous stage. The spiritual ideals of the *caturvarna* are gradually substituted by some relatively rigid socio-ethical ideals. The social ideal of honour becomes very popular. The honour of the Brahmin consists in his purity, piety and spirituality, and that of the Kshatriya in chivalry, strength and nobility of character in action. The social honour of the Vaishya lies in business ethics, while it is the rendering of faithful service that makes the Shudra honourable.

Another important characteristic of the typal stage is gradual degeneration of symbols into signs and types. Symbols begin to lose their vast world of suggestion and settle themselves into a social mould of ethical ideals. True ethical ideals are inferior substitutes for spiritual symbols: yet they are flexible and supple enough to adjust themselves to the diverse callings of practical life and to be in accord with different views of life. The early period of Buddhism represents the typal stage of Indian civilisation, when old symbolic ideals of spiritual life had been slowly disappearing under the growing influence of the teachings of the Buddha and Mahavira. Neither the Buddha nor Mahavira are intellectual in their approach to the problems of life, society and religion. But the religions founded on their teachings assumed an institutional character and started exhibiting a tendency of rationalisation and ratiocination. And the simple and supple truths of the masters were almost buried under the weight of the logical logomachies of their disciples. The seers were followed by thinkers, the symbols by types.

The cultural movements of the typal period culminate in the cult of cold reason and fixed ideas.[17] This period is called the conventional stage. It is marked by the rigidity of social and ethical orders and fixity of ideas and norms. Society lives more in its external supports than in its inner essence. For example, in the symbolic period birth is not the sole factor in determining one's position in social order; for quality counts as well. But in the conventional period the convention of preserving the old social honour through hereditary grooves is firmly established and maintained through jealously guarded sectarian education and tradition. Naturally education tends to become highly specialised and at the same time monopolised by a select few. People in general suffer a slow and unconscious decay in their cultural and ethical attainments. Old types are now new conventions. The task of determining the application of ideals and connotation of ideas is now being enjoyed and exercised by the orthodox pundits. Flexible social customs and free ethical obligations are gradually codified. Religion loses its spiritual depth and intimate contact with the people at large and becomes highly institutionalised. It is true that highly organised preaching and widespread institutional networks of religion prove of considerable help in popularising the ethical ideals of the time, but even then the previous inner appeal of it to move the heart of the masses becomes weaker and weaker. Social orders of the typal stage are transformed into the archaic ideas of the occupational caste system.[18] A rigid social stratification prevents social mobility and this results in economic stagnation. Sri Aurobindo writes:[19]

> In the full economic period of caste, the priest and the pundit masquerade under the name of the Brahmin, the aristocratic and the feudal baron under the name of the Kshatriya, the trader and the money-getter under the name of the Vaishya, the half-fed labourer and economic serf under the name of the Shudra.

In brief, in the conventional period social position comes to be determined by ascriptive and not achievement criteria.

With the waning away of the symbolic age the psychological forces of the time also betray the signs and symptoms of decline. The forces of life usurp the position of the psychological forces of the Golden Age and here we experience a paradoxical situation. The strong life-impulse of a vigorous people can hardly be accommodated in the fixed stratified society of the typal and conventional period. Stratification, once fixed, cannot be easily unfixed even on social demand, and that is what breeds stagnancy and thwarts progress. Being poor as it is in spiritual and religious content, the conventional age has to try hard to maintain its *status quo* and therefore resorts to the oppression of the masses, setting up inflexible organisations and putting up fortifications of power—academic, military and commercial. When reforms do not pay or become impossible, repression becomes inevitable.[20] The irrational and disproportionate concentration and organisation of power in a privileged class, constituting only a thin layer of the total population, gives rise to authoritarian rule. Free thought and action are seriously threatened.

> The tendency of the conventional age is to fix, to arrange firmly, to formalise, to erect a system of rigid grades and hierarchies, to stereotype religion, to bind education and training to a traditional and unchangeable form, to subject thought to infallible authorities, to cast a stamp of finality on what seems to it the finished life of man.[21]

From the above characterisation of the typal-conventional stage of the human cycle one might think that nothing important and valuable happened at that time. But that would be a totally wrong impression. On the contrary, much of what we are proud of today is to a great extent a gift and contribution of that period. The typal-conventional period appeared in the post-Vedic civilisation of India with a large-lined advance. The socio-cultural achievements of the time are extremely significant and have proved of lasting value. One of the acutely felt problems of the typal-conventional period is the relative weakness of the spiritual basis of life inherited from the symbolic period. As this basis is not broad enough to support the increasing pressure and forces of practical and rational life of the later period, impatient critics start questioning the very worth of the spiritual basis of practical life. In fact the heritage of the symbolic period, or the period of 'dream-heavy consciousness' as Spengler calls it, appears mysterious and nearly unintelligible to the intellectual of the typal period.[22] For the time being let us leave aside the intellectual critic's view about the Golden Age. It is perhaps true that the spiritual basis of the symbolic age is not strong and broad enough to support the structure of a growing intellectual self-conscious nation-soul. While in the Golden Age human development is mainly brought about by *individual* efforts, in the later period it is the drive and initiative of the aggregate or *group* which counts most.

People first shape all parts of their life in the light of developed intelligence and then by the power of critical and constructive reason. This is the age of intellectual, aesthetic and ethical culture. Social structure accordingly becomes more complex and less flexible. Small socio-political units of the previous age begin to lose their original vigour and spontaneous vitality. The idea of order displaces the ideal of liberty. The democratic and republican features of government are succeeded by fully developed royalist politics. It is a very grand age.

> The second or post-Vedic age of Indian Civilisation was distinguished by the rise of great philosophies, by a copious, vivid, many-thoughted, many-sided epic culture, by the beginnings of art and science, by the evolution of vigorous and complex society, by the formation of large kingdoms and empires, by manifold formative activities of all kinds and great systems of living and thinking. Here as elsewhere, in Greece, Rome, Persia, China, this was an age of a high outburst of the intelligence working upon the life and the things of the mind to discover their reason and their right way and bring out a broad and noble fullness of human existence.[23]

The typal-conventional period, though rigid in its outer structure, does not stifle all that it inherits from the past. The luminous ideas and inspirations of the symbolic age receive new rational interpretations, of course within the bounds of time. The chief characteristic of the age is to formalise everything in the name of stabilisation and preservation. The process of stabilisation and preservation is undeniably necessary to impart a definite character to the fluid ideas and ideals of the symbolic past. But the craze for stabilisation and formalisation instead of being a promoter of social progress turns out to be its fetter in practice. And this happened not only in India but also in the West. The old knowledge of the Homeric period was systematised and codified in different forms, philosophical, ethical and social in the post-Periclean era. It became less inspired, less dynamic and more intellectual. This proved to be the age of system-building; Greece leading the way in Europe. The intellectual and ethical systems of the Pythagoreans, the Stoics, of Plato, Aristotle, of the neo-Platonists and the neo-Aristotelians bear the unmistakable stamp of the spirit of that period. Human civilisation lives in this period more in its outer structure than in its inner Spirit. The achievements of the time are, therefore, predominantly structural, while the Spirit languishes within the dark interior of the brightly illumined chamber of logical reason. Easily fascinated by the outer glamour and grandeur of the cultural life, the rationalist mind of the period tends to forget the inner truth and spirit.

Strictly speaking, every period is more or less ambiguous. The dark ages were not quite dark nor was the age of Renaissance full of light and lustre. Medieval Europe was actually under a mixed influence of history—it had its dark as well as bright sides. But because of our modern bias many of us uncritically concentrate on its outer structure and silver linings, forgetting the inner truth for the time being. The modern litterateur, the artist and the thinker often look back to the Middle Ages with a sentimental longing. Swayed by romantic imagination, they think only of the poetry and art, nobility and spirituality of the time and forget the folly, ignorance, inequity, cruelty and oppression of that harsh age. The splendid facets and fine surfaces of the time conceal from the uncritical eye the suffering and revolt, the misery and squalor of the people. Similar is the attitude of the Hindu orthodox idealist towards his so-called golden past. He 'looks back to a perfectly regulated society devoutly obedient to the wise yoke of the *Shastra* . . . his golden age—the nobler one than the European in which the apparent gold was mostly hard burnished copper with a thin gold-leaf covering it, but still of an alloyed metal, not the true *Satya Yuga*.'[24]

Due to the steady weakening of the psychological basis of society and the growing pressure of its outer structure, the gulf between the truth of social life and convention becomes gradually too wide to be bridged over by the materials available within the period itself. In order to get rid of this intolerable state of affairs society seeks a new opening and tries to come out of its dead shell. The old economic system proves inadequate to meet the demands of the fast changing time and begins to disintegrate. Heredity ceases to be the most important factor in the choice of profession. The feudal economy starts yielding its ground to the industrial economy. Religion loses its spiritual touch and often assumes the perverse form of what is called religionism. The living communion between God and his children is lost. The interest of the intermediaries, priests and pundits becomes supreme. God finds himself imprisoned within the walls of Church and Temple.

Whatever might be the excellence and stability of the typal-conventional period, its main defect is that it cannot meet the deeper demands of the *individual*. The perfection or otherwise of a society is to be judged always in terms of the demands and aspirations of the individuals concerned. In hours of trial and tribulation individuals may not assert their individuality and may conform to social demands; but as soon as they return to their own individual nature, they feel the gap between what they are and what they can be. The end of the typal period is marked by the rise of the questioning spirit. Individuals questioned the rationale and bona fides of the types and conventions around them. And this was the beginning of the age of Protestantism, the age of Reason, the age of Enlightenment.[25] People protested against dogma, types and conventions. Authority and tradition were being openly questioned. The European mind, illumined by the light of the Renaissance and the Reformation, was trying to discover a new ideal for itself and for society as well.

People were not at all happy with the *status quo*. They were badly in need of a new ideal, an ideal society in which they could grow and create freely. The period witnessed the revival of classical learning and letters. The age of individualism in Europe was rational in its inspiration and critical in its outlook. The people began to follow the new path of individualism with a passion and seriousness unknown to the Graeco-Roman mentality and traceable only to the Judeao-Christian period.

Protestantism piloted the age of individualism with its loud protest against the religious monopoly of the Orthodox Church which denied the individual his right to determine the true meaning of the holy scriptures.[26] Intermixed with the spark of revolt against the Church, the bright light of the Renaissance religion was transformed into a white heat of fury. The Protestant philosophers of Germany and France were deeply inspired and influenced by the social and political thinkers of the age. The Theory of the Divine Origin of the State and the Divine Right of Kings came under heavy fire. While on the continent the age of individualism laid emphasis on the power of *reason*, in England the emphasis was shifted to empiricism. The spectacular scientific progress of the period is to be understood in terms of the co-operation between reason and experience.[27] The self-affirmation of man found its expression in the doctrines of constitutional and popular sovereignty. Aristocratic, privilege and monarchical absolutism began to face growing popular disapproval. The sophistry and casuistry of the 'typal' scholars provided no impetus to the advancement of learning. It is against ancient privilege and dry scholasticism that the age of individualism raised its banner of revolt. Of course it was not interested only in destruction and revolt; under the sobering influence of reason and experience it realised the necessity of organising the gains of revolution. Above all, the people wanted to establish a just and free social order. The quest for truth continued till the nineteenth century, when the discoveries of physical science offered Western man a rational view of life, and encouraged him to reform society on a scientific basis. Science was at last successful in its search for the supreme desideratum. Europe arrived at the culminating movement of our civilisation. Thus, curiously enough, we find that 'in seeking the truth and law of his own being the individual', after a five-hundred-year journey, 'seems to have discovered a truth which is not of his own being at all, but the collectivity, the pack, the hive, the mass'.[28] Sri Aurobindo does not favour this form of social uniformity and collectivity, for it does not encourage the flowering of human personality. If the very dynamo of social progress, the individual, is crushed under the yoke of the collectivity, progress gradually becomes impossible.

In the context of evolution Sri Aurobindo is a determinist, but in the context of socio-political organisation he is an apostle of individual freedom. He finds no incompatibility between the two. If we go deep into the scheme of Nature, Sri Aurobindo assures us, we would discover an all-pervading spiritual harmony in which man is really free, both in the synchronic and also in the diachronic ways. Although he critically refers to the 'inevitable' collectivistic end of the age of individualism, Sri Aurobindo does not deny that the Western world owes its strength, enlightenment, progress, and expansion to it.

The broad features of the European age of individualism may be found also in the corresponding age of Indian history. The typal-conventional age lingered long in India. Starting from the early years of Buddhism, it covered even the first few decades of the nineteenth century. It is like the long Indian summer. Here also we have witnessed the spate of formalisation, systematisation and codification. The great works of the period, the six systems of philosophy, for example, lack the mystic intuition of the seer. A steady decline is evident in the different spheres of culture and civilisation. From the Vedic hymns and the classical poems of Kalidas, Bharavi and Magha, to the *Mangal Kavyas*—what a decline one witnesses! One comes across a similar decline in the history of the Indian polity as well. Starting from the simple and free Aryan community (*Kauma*), passing through a very long period of experimental formations of diverse political structures and then the period of definite formations of monarchies comprising imperial and regional aggregates, the Indian polity suffered an internal arrest and stagnation under the imposed and alien cultural systems of Central Asia and Europe. In religion and spirituality also we may trace the same evolutionary course and character. The spiritual glory of the Vedic-Upanishadic stage was nearly lost in the Purano-Tantric stage.[29] Though deep spiritual insight is evident in the systems of great thinkers like Shankara, Ramanuja, Gautama, Patanjali, etc., it is not as living and moving as the steady and boundless spiritual realisation of the Vedic seers was. It is interesting to note that in Indian history, as in European, there are occasional movements of protest against codified ethics and formalised religion. The teachings of Nanak and Chaitanya were both protestant, reformative and liberal in attitude and inspiration. In spite of all these occasional protests and reforms, it is undeniable that a spirit of conservative stability and continuity permeated all these spheres of Indian culture. There was constant interaction between the old and new creeds or cults. The religious movements of the nineteenth century also testify to the general character of Indian culture; even the strong contrary influence of Europe could not render it obscure.

## From Individualism to Socialism

The age of Individualism and Reason appeared first in Europe. Contact with Europe awakened the inert masses of India from their ' long contented slumber in the cramping bonds of a mechanical conventionalism '. The impulse of the Indian Renaissance was neither original nor native. It was due mostly to Western influence. Every cultural system, whatever might be the form of its identity, is open to foreign influences. When at the end of the long typal-conventional period India was groping in the dark, trying to realise its inner truth, Western influence supplied the light. The beginning of the age of Individualism and Reason is always marked by scepticism. India proved no exception. The age of Individualism in the East is not more than a hundred years old. But in the meantime a new force appeared in the West and its impact did not allow the East to travel in her own leisurely way the full length of the age of Individualism and Reason. And this new force was Socialism.

In fact, two very distinct ideals of society are found to have influenced the human mind and history—one is the ideal of liberty and the other that of uniformity. One advocates more opportunity, and the other more equality. In spite of their diverse ways of social life, thought and action, the adherence of nations to the above two ideals is common and very significant. It indicates that we have not yet been able to come out of the domain of the limited and unrealised possibilities of the age of individualism, rationalism and freedom and that, at the same time, notwithstanding the limitation, we all are demanding some sort of socio-political uniformity and equality. Spengler is perhaps right in affirming that ' we are all socialists, wittingly or unwittingly, willingly or unwillingly. Even resistance to it wears its form.'[30]

## The Advent of the Subjective Age

Although mankind has to its credit the spiritual legacy of the symbolic period and the spectacular achievements of the typal-conventional period and progressed well beyond the frontiers dreamt of by our forefathers, no serious thinker of the day seems to be happy with our present state of affairs or hopeful about the future. The necessity of a new mode of human life, thought and society has made itself felt in the more perceptive minds. So far man has not been able to discover a way of life which will promote human unity. This is the supreme need of the subjective age, the last rhythm of the human cycle. Sri Aurobindo believes that the consummation of this rhythm would take man beyond manhood and a new vista would be opened before him. The objective ages of typalism-conventionalism and individualism-rationalism are now matters of the past and cannot be repeated. Though they could not fulfil all that man required, their importance must not be minimised. With the passage of time human nature and its requirements change. The form of the symbolic age is now useless; but we require the spirit of that age in a new form. We need a subjective approach for the solution of our problems, an affirmation of all valuable and useful things of the past and present, and the rejection of all dead types and conventions, harmful angularities, injustice and inequality, and, above all, transformation of all forms and transvaluation of all values. Unless Man as the main instrument and agency of change is himself sufficiently transformed and made equal to the task, our ideals would remain empty impossible dreams. The common man of the day is very poor in self-consciousness and unaware of his own inner nature (*swadharma*) and the demand of the age (*yugadharma*). Sri Aurobindo thinks that with this sort of human being we cannot bring about a radical transformation and a fundamental transvaluation. Man must rise above every sectarian affiliation. Class, caste, religion and the like do not disclose the true identity of man. Even the national identity of man is imperfect and has to be outgrown. Man has to try to enlarge the area of his freedom and deepen further the depth of his existence. Unless man feels the unity of mankind in the depth of his being, he will not believe that the establishment of a global society and the world government is a real possibility.[31] And man cannot work earnestly for an ideal unless he is convinced that it is both possible and desirable.

In this connection Sri Aurobindo points out the inadequacy of the socialist ideal of social uniformity and that uniformity imposed from without and not answering the needs of the inner human nature cannot make man ultimately happy. For the fulfilment of some limited purposes and immediate needs the socialist order is perhaps unavoidable. Sri Aurobindo recognises the importance of socialism and also anticipated its inevitability as early as 1916. According to him, socialism is an expression of the cult of State, a hang-over of the typal-conventional age, notwithstanding the protest of the age of individualism and rationalism. The cult of State is mainly due to the quickly developing influence of science and technology, shaping all spheres of our life. The individual man is nearly lost in his collective identity, class, race, religion and the like. The cult of State is, therefore, to be understood mainly in terms of science and technology and not in terms of socialism and communism. The socialist and communist ideologies are more a product than a producer of the scientific and technological world-view.

Sri Aurobindo is of course an ethical positivist in a sense. Whatever happens has a reason behind it. Whatever appears in or disappears from history does so according to a design. Even the features of this or that age of the human cycle which he criticises are, on his own admission, necessary and inevitable. The ambiguity and many-sidedness of history has to be accepted at one time and rejected at another.

Sri Aurobindo thinks that the time has come for the rejection of the ideal of social uniformity. Man needs more freedom than what possibly could be provided by the Nation-State. In fact the self-conscious and serious-minded people of the world today do feel the necessity of a larger human order, some form of world government. In and through the creation and dissolution of the League of Nations and in the establishment of the United Nations Organisations, Sri Aurobindo perceives the beginning, a very feeble beginning indeed, of the subjective age, which is still more an ideal than actual.

A careful appreciation of different forms of art, music and finer aspects of culture would confirm the advent of the new age of the human cycle. The beginning of an age is to be perceived first in the sphere of culture and then in that of polity. When fulfilled, the subjective age would be the age of complete freedom and spiritual unity, the fulfilment of the dream of the millennium.[32] Sri Aurobindo is aware that his view may be criticised as utopian and that it is open to other objections.

# 5

# The Subjective and the Objective in History

## Prefatory

History may be interpreted, and in fact has been, in very many ways. Broadly speaking, these interpretations may be classified under two heads—the subjective and the objective. Some contemporary philosophers of science like Polyani, Popper, Hanson and Feyerabend have tried to show that all factual accounts, including the scientific ones, are very much value-oriented, subjective or even ' personal '.

## Possible Criticism of Sri Aurobindo's Theory of History

The whole account of Sri Aurobindo's theory of the process and *meaning* of social evolution is open to question on several grounds. It may be questioned, to start with, on the ground that it is not clear enough and its foundations are unverifiable and weak. Moreover, one may challenge the very basic assumption of Sri Aurobindo, namely, that social evolution, the human cycle, is proceeding towards an ideal state of society based on the spiritual unity of mankind. In this connection, his notion of the natural dynamics of social evolution may also be criticised as purely speculative. Sri Aurobindo is not unaware of the objections which may possibly be raised against his view. But he thinks that these objections rest on the incomplete understanding of the process of evolution which is ' still half-way on its journey '. A part of our mental being recognises incompleteness; there is a part which rejects it; and it is the spiritual part which accepts it and then tries to transform it into its spiritual completion. Incompletion and imperfection are all said to be pre-conditions of a greater perfection to which this evolution is an approximation. There is an inexorable necessity in the law of evolution.

Man is a part of natural evolution and bound by its necessity. His responsibility and capacity for influencing the course of evolution depends upon the depth of his own self-consciousness. Human freedom is defined by natural necessity, and that in turn is determined by the Divine design. The truth of the Divine design and the mysterious mechanism and its execution in the course of human history are not revealed to the positivist historiographer. It is said that, fascinated by the surface phenomena of history, man fails to follow the psychological laws of history and misses its inner truth. It is for this reason that Sri Aurobindo is primarily interested in the *psychology* of history and not in the *sociology* of it.

Sri Aurobindo's spiritual and teleological theory of history is likely to be criticised for its allegedly unnecessary mystification of some plain facts and phenomena of history which, the critic thinks, could well be explained without using any transcendental hypothesis. Sri Aurobindo anticipates the criticism and his reply is clear: 'The mystery of things is the truth of things; the intellectual presentation is only truth in representation, in abstract symbols, as if in a cubist art of thought-speech, in geometric figure.' Secondly, Sri Aurobindo's theory of history may be criticised also on the ground that it is over-ambitious. It wants to bring everything that has happened in the past into a very neat order. This search for orderliness is perfectly acceptable and it is there perhaps in the very nature of man. But the question is whether there is *really* an all-comprehensive order in human history or whether it is an achievement of the inspired scholar's historical imagination. Sri Aurobindo frequently speaks of the *meaning, the inner meaning of history.* It is not quite clear what precisely he means by these terms. It has often been doubted whether there is at all anything like a *general* history of mankind as a whole. The intrinsic meaningfulness of a general history of mankind has also been questioned. Some philosophers of history have very definite and contrary opinions on these points. They think that there is no general history of mankind at all, and the meaning which we often claim to have discovered in history is more an ascription or attribution of our mind than an objective thing discovered by us. Popper writes:

> There is no history of mankind, there is only an indefinite number of histories of all kinds of aspects of human life . . . a concrete history of mankind, if there were any, would have to be the history of all men. It would have to be the history of all human hopes, struggles, and sufferings. For there is no one man more important than any other. Clearly this concrete history cannot be written. We must make abstractions, we must neglect and select. But with this we arrive at . . . many histories.[1]

The question of historical meaning is also full of difficulties. Different thinkers find different meanings in history. Different thinkers offer different interpretations of history according to their own theoretical or practical pre-suppositions.[2] History is often used also for didactic or educative purposes. There are thinkers who regard history as the supreme dispenser of justice. Some theoreticians of history like Toynbee think that history is moving towards the goal of realising the supreme significance of the crucifixion of Christ. Sri Aurobindo tells us that the goal of history is the descent of the Supermind on the earth. Popper warns us, 'History has no ends, we can impose these ends of ours upon it; and *although history has no meaning, we can give it a meaning.*'[3]

## THE MARXIST CRITICISM AND SRI AUROBINDO'S ANSWER

The problem of meaning bedevils not only the teleological historiography of Sri Aurobindo, but is also present in Marxist historiography which totally rejects the idea of teleology. Marx turns the idealistic historiography of Hegel upside down.[4] As is well known he wants to show that it is neither God's idea nor human idea which shape the course of history. On the contrary, he claims that it is the material factors, including the economic ones of history, which directly or indirectly determine the forms, formations and transformations of human ideas. The Marxist thinks that the best way to attack and demolish a subjective interpretation of history is to point out the parasitical or derivative character of human ideas themselves. All past history, according to him, is the history of class struggles. The concepts of teleological Nature and Divine design are said to be mere ' pious wishes ' which are conveniently ' smuggled ' into the so-called conscious plane of Nature. Thus, the Marxist alleges, the clear law-governed Nature is first mystified and then that mystified Nature is supposed to mirror itself in human consciousness. This teleological-*cum*-spiritual interpretation of history projects a passive picture of man; man is a passive mirror in which Nature comes to consciousness on its own.

Marx does not deny that man is natural. But by ' natural ' he means something else, not something mystical or teleological. Nature has no consciousness of its own, nor does it become conscious of itself in man; it is man who through his *acts* (not passively) becomes conscious of Nature and *through it of himself*.[5] Man's consciousness of Nature is determined and measured by his understanding of the laws governing Nature. Man is always subjected to the necessity of ' objective nature ' which includes everything from the physical-geographical environment to socio-economic relations. The physical-geographical conditions of a society constitute only the *natural* basis of its history; the *real* basis consists of the modes of production and the resulting economic relationship. Plekhanov writes:

> Marx says in explaining the *subject*, let us see into what mutual relationship people enter under the influence of *objective* necessity. Once these relations are known, it will be possible to ascertain how human self-consciousness develops under their influence. *Objective necessity* will help us to clarify the *subjective* of history.[6]

Every age of history has a definite social structure corresponding to the productive relations in the economy. The character and necessities of the social structure are mirrored in the psychology of the people, in all their habits, manners, feelings, views, aspirations and ideals. ' The psychology of society is always expedient in relation to its economics, always corresponds to it, and is always determined by it.'[7]

Thus, if the psychological forces of society are subordinate to its economic forces, then it is difficult to defend Sri Aurobindo's comprehensive theory of psychological historiography.

The economic determinants of history to which the Marxist frequently refers are, according to Sri Aurobindo, superficial but not altogether unimportant factors of history. If we think that they are ultimate forces shaping our historical destiny, then our role in shaping the course of history becomes itself very unimportant and secondary in character. The Aurobindite might argue that it is very curious to note that Marx, who tried so much in theory and practice to save human freedom from the totalitarian and teleological rational necessity of Hegel, is himself offering an economic interpretation of history which may well be cited in justification of abridgement and curtailment of individual liberty.[8] Another unfortunate consequence of the Marxist view is the relatively unimportant role assigned to man to shape his own destiny. The Aurobindite may further point out that, like Hegel, Marx also defines freedom in terms of objective necessity. Marx's *economic necessity* takes the place of Hegel's *rational necessity*, and a change of phraseology does not improve the situation insofar as it relates to human freedom. As for himself, Sri Aurobindo does not deny that human freedom, the freedom of the mental being, because of its very nature, is bound to be limited, derivative and secondary. The necessity which really defines human freedom is spiritual—neither economic nor rational. The physical and empirical propensities of the mental being stand in the way of his realising the highest form of freedom. Insofar as man is guided by his physical sense of reality or confuses his restricted psychological autonomy with the sovereignty of the Spirit, he postulates a non-existent antithesis between *liberty* and *necessity* and does not know what true freedom is like.

'The two principles of freedom and order, which in mind and life are constantly representing themselves as contraries or incompatibles, though they have no need to be that if freedom is guarded by knowledge and order based upon truth of being, are in the supermind consciousness native to each other and even fundamentally one.'[9] In other words, freedom is native to spiritual consciousness. The sort of freedom we may and do enjoy in the process of history is bound to be more or less limited. But this limitation is not externally fixed. By 'inwardising' our consciousness, going deep into our *being*, we may *be* more free than we ordinarily are.

## Law, Order and Liberty in History

Some zealous champions of *liberty* and *progress* overemphasise the principle of *orderliness* in history. To defend a theory of individual liberty with social progress, they speak of the law-governed character of history (i.e., of *historicism* as Popper calls it), as if the freedom of the individual and the uninterrupted progress of mankind are guaranteed by some *laws of history*. This didactic overtone of historiography has been seriously questioned by some professional historians and thinkers in recent times.[10] In a famous passage H.A.L. Fisher writes:

Men wiser and more learned than I have discerned in history a plot, a rhythm, a pre-determined pattern. These harmonies are concealed from me. I can see only one emergency following upon another as wave follows upon wave, only one great fact with respect to which, since it is unique, there can be no generalisations, only one safe route for the historian: that he should recognise in the development of human destinies the play of the contingent and the unforeseen. This is not a doctrine of cynicism and despair. The fact of progress is written plain and large on the page of history; but progress is not a law of nature.[11]

Whether the nature of history permits the historian to indulge in *generalisation* is a very old and controversial question. But it seems pretty clear that the questions of individual freedom and social progress have no necessary relation with the belief in, or denial of, historical laws. The questions are separable and should be discussed separately. Simply by denying the law-governed character of history one does not successfully defend the cause of human freedom. In this respect one wonders whether Fisher's well-meaning attack on historicism serves the purpose. Many of us will agree with Fisher that history is not a generalising science but it is difficult to 'recognise' with him that the development of human destiny is the random play of the contingent and the unforeseen. There are thinkers like Sri Aurobindo who discern in history a plot, a rhythm and a harmony, and yet stoutly defend the cause of individual freedom against every form of collectivism.

*Prophecy* may be impermissible in history, but there is no valid argument against rational attempts to *predict* the future course of history. By over-emphasising 'the role of the contingent and the unforeseen' the historian should not give the impression that even in terms of modifiable and revisable concepts we should not try to connect and organise historical details.[12] To make the details of history intelligible we do need and use concepts, without which history would degenerate either into a shapeless heap of facts or, at best, chronology. The historian is advised to avoid two extremes, crass positivism or *fact-fetishism* and blind historicism or *law-craze*. In fact the professional historian, unless he is very much influenced by some set of presuppositions or a predilection, generally avoids these extremes. History does not either drown us under its boundless and numberless particles of water (i.e., the sea of facts) or wash away by its waves (i.e., laws). If Ranke is accused of fact-fetishism, Lamprecht is to be criticised on account of his law-craze. 'Lamprecht demanded that all historical study should lead to the formulation of general concepts in which the knowledge of the specific facts was assimilated and lost all independent significance.'[13] The necessity of general concepts for the organisation of historical details is quite understandable, but Lamprecht's attitude of 'away-with-the-rubbish-of-details' is unfortunate and uncritical. If the individuality of facts is ignored or even underestimated, historical criticism or corroboration becomes useless. If details are forced to fit *a priori* with general concepts, history loses both its charm and value.

## Different Forms of Subjective Interpretations of History

The subjective interpretation of history has very many forms—*psychological, phenomenological* and *spiritual.* These forms are not necessarily exclusive. Mill, Dilthey, Nietzche, Bergson, Lamprecht, Barth, Ravaisson and Spengler are all believers in the subjective interpretation of history. But they certainly do not belong to the same philosophic fraternity. Karl Lamprecht, who influenced Sri Aurobindo most in his general psychological approach to history, was himself influenced partly by the psychological ideas of Wundt and the economic theories of Marx. The generalising tendency of Lamprecht is clearly evident in Sri Aurobindo's thought. But he cannot be 'accused' of being influenced by Wundt's experimental approach to psychology. Sri Aurobindo's 'psychological approach', as we have said before, is quite different from that of the rest. His approach could better be characterised as *integral and spiritual.* He thinks that there is a sort of structural similarity between the operation of mentality and of society. In other words, there is an isomorphic relation between the development of the human mind, on the one hand, and that of human society, on the other. One influences and in turn is influenced by the other. This *integral interaction between mind and society* marks the gradual release and liberation of the mental powers, including *freedom,* of man and more and more *orderliness* and *harmony* of society.[14]

Although I do not propose to deny the originality and insight of Sri Aurobindo's subjective interpretation of Indian history and its different cultural facets, one can hardly miss the pro-idealist character of his approach. For the integral monist in Sri Aurobindo the traditional distinction between idealism and realism is not of much consequence. Using standard philosophical jargon one might say that Sri Aurobindo is empirically a realist and transcendentally an idealist. True, he will insist that in the mind-society dialectic mind supervenes on society, but for that he will not deny that society also shapes human mind. Then the question is: which of these two factors is more influential and what are their relative status?

To understand Sri Aurobindo's subjective interpretation of history more clearly we may profitably look into other theoretically comparable psychological interpretations of history.

Mill, for example, thinks that 'all phenomena of society are phenomena of human nature' and that 'the laws of the phenomena of society are, and can be, nothing but the laws of the actions and passions of human beings'.[15] The sort of psychological interpretation of history and society which Mill proposes to defend is purely reductionist in character and seems indefensible on that ground.[16]

The psychological interpretation of history is often criticised also on another ground. The laws of psychology which are proposed to be used for explaining social phenomena are empirical in nature and, therefore, refutable and modifiable. The laws of psychology which are accepted today may well be rejected tomorrow. So it would be unwise on our part to defend that sort of historiography which is thoroughly dependent on the theoretical or experimental fortune of psychology.

Dilthey thinks that history is the expression of our psychical life. But he takes ' psychic life ' in a very comprehensive sense. Our psychical or psychological phenomena *in themselves* are not clearly *meaningful*. To understand their meaning we have to *review* them in their proper and comprehensive context. He thinks that historical life is a part of the whole of life which is given in experience and understanding. ' Life in this sense... extends over the whole range of objective mind accessible to experience.' Starting from the ' subjective ' pole of life, we may pass over to the objective one because of the *meaningful* or, to use phenomenological jargon, *intentional* correlation between the two. It is in terms of *meaning* and *interpretation* that mind breaks through its psychological privacy and gets into other minds, and recaptures objects of other times and places. Dilthey says:

> The development of the human (and historical) studies depends on the deepening of experience and on the increasing tendency to bring their content to the surface; at the same time, it is dependent on the spread of understanding over all the objectifications of mind (viz. books, laws and institutions) and on the increasingly complete and methodical extraction of the mental content from the different expressions of life.[17]

In terms of the concepts of *structure*, *meaning* and *interpretation*, Dilthey has made a very serious (but not necessarily logical) attempt to do away with the defects of the phenomenalistic type of psychological or subjective interpretation of history.[18] Because his writings lack logical rigour his ideas have not been well received in many quarters. One might even feel that what Dilthey writes, using a lot of philosophical jargon, is plain common sense.

There is nothing wrong in trying to defend and argue in support of what is plain common sense. The only question is whether it is philosophically defensible and valid. It is not quite clear to me what Dilthey means by the *structural correlation* between the mental world and what he calls the objectifications of mind like books and institutions. It is obvious that institutions or books written by human beings would bear the imprint of the concerned human experience and understanding. Human institutions are cumulative results or silted forms of human experience and action. What I am now saying appears to me to be plain common sense. And this view, I believe, may be defended without invoking what is called objective idealism in professional philosophical quarters or even without using such philosophical concepts as meaning, intention and interpretation.

## Croce's Subjective Interpretation of History

Much of what Hegel and Dilthey said can be found in Croce's philosophy of history. Following Hegel and Dilthey, Croce also maintains that nothing exists outside mind. History is also mental or an act of thought. It is a matter of appreciation, imagination and construction *analogous* to the creation of the artist. Historical truths are not really historical if they do not arise out of intimate human experience. It is a *peculiar* sort of experience in which the individuality of past events is revived and recaptured. Historical experience is analogous to, but not to be confused with, art experience. In the case of art we *intuit* the individual object or event. But in the case of history we *judge* it. Judgement involves thought and therefore universality—an *a priori* component. The historian recaptures the *real* individual. The artist is contented with the possible individual. The latter is a dealer in the realm of possibilities which may or may not be actually individuated in space and time, in society and history. The subject-term of historical judgement is individual and its predicate-term universal. The historian is always a philosopher, for he thinks and by thinking finds out the *universal meaning* of the predicative concept. Reality, according to Croce, consists of universal concepts expressed in particular events or objects. History is reality incarnated.

> What constitutes history . . . is the act of comprehending and understanding induced by the requirements of practical life. The requirements cannot be satisfied by recourse to action unless first of all the phantoms, doubts and shadows have been dispelled . . . by an act of thought.

History is thus a type of spiritual, i.e., thought, activity.

## Historical Scepticism and the Marxist Answer

Those who reject the pro-idealist view that thought is a mode of spiritual activity are also critical of the thesis of historical autonomy and Croce's method of combating historical scepticism. According to Marx, the relation between thought and thing is mediated and defined by human action. The relation between Mind and Nature is not defined by any common purpose underlying them. It is to be understood in terms of the laws of the physical universe and the social universe. It is in this way, the dialectical way, that the Marxist tries to do away with the problems of defending the idea of structural correlation between the subjective and the objective, between Mind and Nature. To him there is nothing spiritual in human action. To him action is something material or, at best, a complex physiological movement.[19]

Sri Aurobindo claims that ' our individualisation is only a superficial formation, a practical selection and limited conscious synthesis for the temporary utility of life in a particular body '.[20] In the spiritual depth of our being there are three inter-related aspects—individual, universal and transcendental. The individual historian, without ceasing to be what he is at a particular time and place, by his thought (or spiritual) activity can participate in a sort of universal life. But even then there is always a life beyond. Time-bound history cannot be the true story of the spiritual journey of our thought-life. For it is almost exclusively dependent upon what we observe and what we get from deciphering our observational findings in terms of some readily available formulae. Since 'time', as Sri Aurobindo puts it, 'is only our means of realising things in succession... a condition and cause of conditions, (and) varies on different planes of existence, varies even for beings on one and the same plane', time-bound history cannot be absolutely free from 'phantoms and problems and doubts'. It is on this and related grounds that Sri Aurobindo concludes: 'history teaches us nothing'.

Like Sri Aurobindo, Bergson also subscribes to a radical form of historical scepticism. Quite unlike Sri Aurobindo, he thinks that time is very much real and yet he thinks that what passes by the name of history is a mere story constructed by our intellect to help us in action or practice.[21] Thinkers like Sri Aurobindo and Bergson highlight the point that whenever a particular mode of human knowledge, the historical mode in this case, is tied down to practical needs and influenced by the discursive operation of the intellect, its results are bound to be doubtful. This critical or negative side of their doctrines is, to some extent, inconsistent with what Croce says about history. I say 'to some extent' deliberately because I think that the difference between Sri Aurobindo's view of history and Croce's is one of emphasis. Croce does not reject the considerations offered by Sri Aurobindo in support of historical scepticism, but emphasises how by our thought, the reflective activity of the Spirit, we can get rid of historical scepticism. On the positive side their views seem somewhat similar. It is by deepening our consciousness that we may get to a level of thought where we can successfully rediscover the past and relive it in the present.

## The Role of Heroes and Ordinary Men in History

It is often claimed by the subjectivists that there are some extraordinarily gifted people who can play a more effective and influential role in history. The great man or the hero is said to be the pathfinder and the pathmaker of history.

Whether the heroes or the common people are the real authors of history is a very vague and general question. And, therefore, it is very difficult to answer it in an acceptable form.[22] The question does not seem to be one of 'either-or', i.e., disjunctive, it is one of 'and', i.e., conjunctive. The story of history is full of ideas and actions of all sorts of human beings, heroes and common men, without (necessarily) identifying them by name or address. If the names of great men are frequently mentioned in history, the reason is simple and obvious. They are the foci of intelligibility. Because of their influence and impact, either as thinkers or rulers or both, the great men are given prominent places in history. This does not necessarily mean that they are the real or the only authors of history. Sometimes some people are given prominent places in history not because they did in fact occupy positions of importance or prove very influential in their own time but simply because the concerned historian for some reason or unreason thinks that they did.

As we all know, common people are guided mostly by custom, tradition and conventions. Unless these are changed or transformed, we do not see any significant or creative turn in history. Only a few people, who are quite alive to what happened in the past and also to the demands of time and place, can build up a new future. It is these great men, combining the spirit of the time (*yugadharma*) with their own spiritual realisation (*swadharma*), who prove themselves the main architects of history. Sri Aurobindo calls them the 'swallowers of formulas'.[23] They are not guided by stereotyped ideas and conventions. They are found to possess a deeper understanding of the mind and aspirations of the people, a rare power of anticipation of the future and an unflinching determination to act accordingly. Sri Aurobindo thinks that Manu, Moses, Lycargus and Mohammed, for example, are persons of a rare kind. Because of their spiritual insight they can easily follow the spiritual, deeper and subtler forces operative in history.

The common man, who works with the help of his sense-based intellect, can hardly rise above the influence of contemporary thinking and conventions and, therefore, is unable to see the movement of history in its integral perspective.[24] He takes a piecemeal view of his time and place. He cannot see the spiritual connection between the individual and the universal, what unites 'the logic of the situation' with 'the logic of the infinite', and 'epochal necessity' with 'eternal freedom'. Sri Aurobindo points out that only the rare individual, Manu, *avatar* or prophet, who comes on earth perhaps once in a millennium, can speak truly about how a group of men should organise itself, and that the secret of this sort of men is not political but spiritual. It may be mentioned in this connection that for Sri Aurobindo, Manu or Moses are *not* historical individuals. They are more a symbol than anything else. 'His (Manu's) name means man, the mental being... who fixes the lines upon which the race or people has to govern its evolution.' He can fix the lines because he has correctly grasped the necessary principles for fixation. He possesses both spiritual insight and empirical outsight. Referring to Mohammed, Sri Aurobindo observes that 'he developed the existing social, religious and administrative customs of the Arab people into a new system dictated to him often in a state of trance, in which he passed from his conscient into his superconscient Self, by the Divinity to his secret intuitive mind'.[25] The secret of the success of the heroes in history is claimed to be spiritual and intuitive.

The Marxist is generally credited with the view that the real author of history is the working class. Those who attach too much importance to outstanding personalities offer in fact an elitist conception of history. Whether Marxism itself is inconsistent with the elitist conception of history is not beyond controversy. Stalin, for example, tells Emil Ludwig that 'Marxism has never denied the role of heroes. On the contrary, it admits that they play a considerable role.'[26] Human beings, whether they are heroes or not, are obliged to think and act in a social milieu and within some definite constraints or conditions. The Marxist points out that 'great people are worth anything at all only to the extent they are able correctly to understand these conditions to understand how to change them'.

This view is not incompatible with what Sri Aurobindo or, for that matter, any objective idealist would say. Sri Aurobindo would not hesitate to endorse the view that the greatness of a man consists in his ability to understand his contemporary conditions and anticipate future ones. He also believes that there is an intimate relation between action and knowledge. Clear knowledge of a given situation is of course an aid to the correct mode of action called for in that situation. But it has to be mentioned in this connection that Sri Aurobindo is not a pragmatist in any ordinary sense. He for one will never insist that the validity of knowledge has to be established in terms of some definite practical success. Knowledge is truth-seeking and not success-seeking. Although the materialist and the spiritualist fundamentally differ on the nature of knowledge, they agree on a very important point, viz., the great men of history, because of their deeper understanding of the process of history, can more effectively mould its course. But on the question of how they do it, the difference between them becomes very clear. While the Marxist tries to show that the objective conditions, particularly the economic ones, are supremely important in shaping the course of history and that the subjective side is more or less derivative in character, Sri Aurobindo, without trying to reduce the former to the latter, seeks to show the more developed form of the latter as the end of the former. The spiritualist believes that whatever we see, including social and political institutions, are all works of the Spirit and are realising a definite purpose. Everybit of existence is permeated and oriented by a definite purpose, of which one may or may not be aware.

## The General and the Individual in History

A general and highly philosophical view about the nature of things enables the philosopher of history to connect everything with whatever he likes. Consequently, historical generalisations and hypotheses become too comprehensive and vague to be tested and corrected. In that case any and every thinker may come forward with his own interpretation of history, historical events and processes of relatively limited durations; and history ceases to be an empirical discipline. If history is an empirical discipline, then, Sri Aurobindo alleges, it 'teaches us nothing'. If, on the other hand, history becomes an expression of spiritual truth, it is hardly testable and corrigible. One may point out that both the spiritualist and the materialist interpretations of history, in spite of their basic difference, are open to one common criticism—they are untestable and incorrigible. Referring to Hegel, Professor Dunning writes:

> With benumbing legerdemain, the philosopher makes the commonplace facts of familiar history fit themselves nicely . . . into the categories and relations of his logic, and shows us mankind through all the ages marching steadily, but unconsciously along Hegelian lines towards Germanic perfection of the nineteenth century.[27]

Similar criticism has been raised against the sweeping Marxist's generalisation that all history is a history of class-struggle. This interpretation of history turns out to be a dangerous *definition* of history. Those who believe in this definition of history try uncritically to transform, portray and interpret every phase of human history in terms of class-struggle and class-contradiction. In that case even the history of co-operation between different classes is distorted and interpreted otherwise. For the Marxist and the spiritualist, history ceases to be a matter of *description* and becomes essentially a matter of *interpretation* and *definition*.[28] And this is due to their uncritical generalising tendencies.

Sri Aurobindo's main criticism against the objectivist's interpretation of history is that it attaches too much importance to the facts and forces witnessed by our *physical* sense of reality and too little to our subjective movements and experiences. No sensible person would possibly deny that many of our mental phenomena are objectively conditioned. But to assert on that ground that all facets of our mental phenomena and all cultural products of different periods of history are objectively determined and, therefore, to be understood in terms of objective factors like the economic ones is patently a very one-sided view. Any careful student of history would admit that social phenomena and historical forces are so complex and many-sided that they admit different and almost equally plausible *interpretations*. For example, one historian may glorify the city-state of Athens of the Periclean age as a cradle of democracy, 'showing mankind many things, and, above all, the most precious thing in the world, fearless freedom of thought' [Bury]; another historian, with comparable plausibility, may point out that the fearless freedom of thought in the upper strata of society was possible because of the fearful bondage of the slaves in the lowest stratum [Thompson].

Every historical phenomenon has different facets. Which particular facet will be chosen by the historian for study, description or interpretation depends upon his interest and value-judgement. Lecky says: 'The predominating passion of every one (including the historian) colours the whole train of his reasoning, and in every subject he examines, he insistently turns to that aspect which is most congruous to his favourite pursuit.'[29] Perhaps it is to minimise this problem of historical subjectivism and relativism that Lord Acton said: 'Study problems, not periods.' Rightly speaking, the problems of subjectivism and relativism have to be faced and cannot be avoided. For, every human being is bound to have his bias and value-judgement. These human considerations are not necessarily incompatible with the end of rational objectivity. The real problem is not with the subjectivity but the subjectivism of the historian. By subjectivism we mean a psychological disposition which is uncriticisable, incorrigible and therefore makes it impossible for the historian, or for that matter any human being, to see things *as they are* related to their perspective. The questions, 'How are the objects of history in themselves?' and 'To what extent is their identity influenced by imagination and thought of the historian?' are the perennial problems to the epistemologist, the theorist of knowledge. Simply because these are difficult questions we must not think ourselves helpless in tackling them.

First, we have to avoid the generalising tendency as we find it in many historians and historiographers. We need a Huizinga or a Namier, and not a Toynbee or a Spengler. The historian should address himself to specific questions and issues. If instead of that he tries to capture 'the spirit of the Time', or 'the general tendency and character of the Time', he will be landing himself and as well as ourselves into a host of problems and difficulties. When I say this I for one do not mean to deny altogether the importance of the generalising approach to history. It has its limited utility and necessity for some particular purposes. But the charm and the main characteristic of history consists in bringing out the individuality of specific historical events and not in establishing general truths or formulas 'on the basis of' those specific events. Morris Cohen observes:

> Historians differ in their points of view, and accordingly in the question that they wish to answer, much more than they differ in answering even specific questions. The diversity of categories or perspective is (itself) an objective fact.[30]

Secondly, when we speak of the danger involved in the generalising tendency, we do not mean to say that laws, regularities or *trends* are unimportant in the social sciences. In fact the identification and correlation of the individual social phenomena are made possible, may be indirectly, in and through some general propositions. Presuppositionless correlation of social phenomena is a theoretical impossibility. To indicate the objective possibility of happening of certain events or phenomena in a certain situation we need certain laws. Laws have a prohibitive aspect as well. For, they also enable us to rule out the possibility of the presence of certain things and qualities in a given situation. In historical disciplines laws are of only indirect or heuristic importance. Max Weber writes: 'Wherever the causal explanation of a cultural phenomenon—and "historical individual"—is under consideration, the knowledge of causal *laws* is not the *end* of the investigation but only a *means*.'[31] The term 'causal laws' is to be taken in a weaker sense in this context. It is a sort of *adequate* correlation. If in terms of some general concepts or theories some phenomena are not repeatable (repeatable for the purpose of understanding), the correctness or otherwise of their knowledge can never be satisfactorily ascertained. The concrete individual phenomena cannot be grasped without some relatively general and abstract laws or theories. This may sound paradoxical, but on analysis it turns out to be true. To avoid the fallacy of subjectivism the limited use of general truths in history is unavoidable.

Thirdly, the pro-idealist or the anti-naturalist thinks that we can achieve objectivity without using generalisations at all. Sri Aurobindo himself anticipates the charge of subjectivism against his view. He speaks of two types of subjectivism, true and false. The false subjectivism is due to false identification of the Self. If the individual or a group takes its ego as its true Self, it is likely to commit a series of mistakes. The narrow, superficial and separated ego cannot get to the objective truth of the world. To avoid the fallacy of false objectivism, Sri Aurobindo argues, we need not fall back upon abstract laws or theories. There is another way out. If the individual deepens his consciousness and transcends his immediate Self, he realises 'that he is not only himself, but he is in solidarity with all of his kind'.[32] In his spiritual depth man *is* mankind. And at that level subjectivity, inter-subjectivity and objectivity become synonymous expressions. In fact Kant defines objectivity in terms of inter-subjectivity—the structural identity of different individual human minds. The theoretical purpose served by laws or theories on the one hand, and mental or spiritual structural identity on the other, is basically similar. In other words, in whatever way we look at them, either through laws or through our own mental structure, we cannot definitely say what historical events are in themselves. Their true identity is always a matter of corrigible imagination and criticisable conjecture. The historian's mind is engaged in a perpetual and critical dialogue with the concrete world of historical events.

## Demarcation between the Subjective and the Objective in History

The line of demarcation between the subjective and the objective cannot be drawn very rigidly. To be aware of what is going on even in my own mind I have to *objecti*fy my mind in some form or the other. One cannot possibly grasp what pure *subjecti*vity is like. Our subjectivity, as an object of knowledge, is bound to be conceptualised and objectified. Pure subjectivity is a limiting concept. The subject and the subjectivity which we can actually encounter in experience is always object-oriented. This is perhaps true also about object and objectivity. These are again ideal entities; we cannot actually apprehend them as such. Consequently, our knowledge of objects knows no limit or boundaries. And that explains the possibility of the limitless or boundless growth of knowledge, whether it is of object or of subject.

Sri Aurobindo says:

> In fact, subjectivity and objectivity are not independent realities, they depend upon each other; they are the Being, through consciousness, looking at itself as subject on the object and the same Being offering itself to its own consciousness as object to the subject.... Indeed, we have no means of knowing the objective universe except by our subjective consciousness of which the physical senses themselves are instruments; as the world appears not only to that but in that, so it is to us.[33]

Sri Aurobindo rightly admits the relativity and interdependence of the subjective and the objective. Consequently, he is also obliged to admit that whatever is subjectively determined is also objectively determined and *vice versa*. But even then he insists on the point that the subjective is not so dependent on the objective as the latter is on the former. Guided and fed by the physical sense of reality and working constantly under an egocentric attitude and predicament, we are prone to believe whatever is physical and objective and doubt whatever appears in subjective experience. Simply because subjective experience as such cannot be referred to the evidence of the external senses, we have a general tendency to challenge its validity. Our distrust of subjective experience, Sri Aurobindo argues, results from the fact that it is unverifiable in terms of standard scientific method. 'It has been implicitly or explicitly held as an axiom that all truth must be referred to the judgement of the personal mind, reason and experience of every man or else it must be verified or at any rate verifiable by a common or universal experience in order to be valid.'[34] Sri Aurobindo rejects this 'false standard of reality and of knowledge', for this means the sovereignty of the former or the average mind and its limiting capacity and experience. The sovereignty of the normal or the average mind leads to what Sri Aurobindo calls 'an egoistic illusion', 'a gross and vulgar error'. Sri Aurobindo admits that our pursuit of knowledge in the sphere of subjectivity is beset with many difficulties. Of course we may commit errors in our pursuit. But that is no reason why we should not attempt to explore the deeper depths and the vaster reaches of consciousness and experience. Sri Aurobindo thinks that the spiritual mind has its own method of verification, rather self-verification. Simply because it differs from the method of scientific verification, it need not be taken as less reliable than that. The determining power of consciousness, the subjective, particularly of spiritual consciousness, is claimed to be immensely superior to that of the objective world, the physical sense of the objective world. The objective as such does not and cannot determine or shape our mind, unless we are more or less open to it. But the point is we cannot shut ourselves forever within the bounds of pure subjectivity. We are not neither windowless nor atomic monad. An invisible but continuous commerce is going on between ourselves and other-selves. In fact we live in a community of selves.

It is true that the objective works in history through the subjective. But from that it would be wrong to infer that the value in operation of the objective is absolutely dependent upon the subjective, upon our minds. Truths or results of our knowledge and experience as embodied in ideas, propositions and theories are very much objective. Their validity or otherwise does not depend upon what we think about and how we feel about them. The world of knowledge and experience finds its institutional expressions in library, laboratory, language, university and other areas of cultural life. They are of course objective, do exist on their own right, and have varying life-spans of their own quite independently of the life of this or that individual man. These institutions and agencies certainly shape our lives, minds and even the patterns of our emotional responses. It is almost equally true that over the years, decades and centuries the reactions and responses of 'our mind' to what 'we' understand and experience, mould and transform the institutions and agencies of our cultural life. I say 'almost true' because a careful study of the inter-relation between the subjective and the objective unmistakably reveals that in the long run we human beings, including the heroes, are more influenced by the objective conditions of our life than we can possibly influence the said conditions.

# 6

# Smaller Human Aggregates: Family, Clan, Commune and Tribe

## Growth of the Human Aggregates

The process of social evolution is gradual and complex. The factors involved in the process are three in number—man, community and mankind. The individual man is not directly related to the totality of mankind. In and through smaller social aggregates man is related to mankind. If the character, composition and organisation of the smaller aggregates answer the growing needs of the developing human personality, then they justify not only their own existence but also help mankind in achieving greater unity. If, on the contrary, the function of these aggregates does not favour the growth of the individual, they prove themselves an impediment to the perfection of all the factors involved in the process of social evolution.

The social aggregates by their very nature are of mixed character. Consequently, they partly help and partly obstruct the process of the gradual and increasing unification of mankind. Even if one admits that there is an essential *unity* of mankind, that does not negate the possibility and necessity of *unification*. Because of various limitations—organisational, territorial, economic and intellectual—under which human beings are initially obliged to live and work, they can form only smaller aggregates like family, clan, commune, class and tribe. With the help of their growing capacities, they gradually remove the older conditions and constraints of living, develop new organisations—political and economic—expand territorially and from the city-state or the phratry come the nation and the empire. These aggregates may be ordered in a graduated way in the scale of social development.

Man, says Sri Aurobindo, is a growing God. He is the first self-conscious expression of the infinite existence, but the natural conditions under which he is placed determine his living to a great extent. Unless he realises the *essential* relation between himself and his attending conditions, he may feel at times stifled by the latter. But the more he realises himself and the inner significance of the objective conditions of his life, the more convinced he becomes of the necessity of community and society around him for his own perfection. The structure and functions of society answer his social needs and enrich his personality. So the conditions of life which once appeared to him as mere obstacles to his enrichment and enlargement now convince him of their necessity and value. The individual does not live within the bounds of his sense, nor even within the limits of his circumscribed *personal* individuality. In fact he has a greater social individuality of his own. His true individuality means not only his unique characteristics but also those of his race-type, his class-type, his vital-, mental- and spiritual-types. Within the group he resembles and differs from others more or less on various matters. But, Sri Aurobindo thinks, the group has a soul, its basic psychological unity. Because of the vaguely felt urge of that basic unity the individual tends to associate or identify himself with some social forms like the church, sect, community, class and association. Participating in the life and activities of the social forms he develops different aspects of his own nature, and by so doing he indirectly makes the multi-formed growth of his nation as a whole possible. The nation is said to be the highest psychological unit that has so far been evolved in the history of mankind. But the unity of mankind as a whole is an ideal yet to be realised.

## The Individual and the Group

The first self-conscious formation of life is man. 'From the individual, therefore, we have to start; he is our index and our foundation.'[1]

It is said that a group results from man's attempt to expand his soul. Group-soul is expanded human soul. In the course of his development man starts feeling limitations in and around him. To enlarge the domain of his freedom and undo the effect of limitations he tries to internalise those limiting conditions, not by widening a logical idea engulfing them all but by a living and concrete consciousness which brings them into the unity of the soul. Driven by a psychological necessity and conscious of a haunting negation, the individual soul makes use of external conditions of life and constitutes for itself an organised structure. And that results in the formation of a group.

This line of argument is open to objection on several grounds. It is not quite clear why we should think that man comes first and group next. One may argue as well that a man is not human at all unless and until he is the member of a group. If man by his very nature is social, he cannot be what he is without an essential group affiliation. Group structure is in the very being of man. The idea of enlargement of an individual soul into a group-soul is a sociological fiction. The group as an organisation cannot result from individual human consciousness unless in some or other structural form it is already there. The question of internalisation, incorporation or assimilation of his external conditions by man does not make any sense unless we believe that it is possible. This possibility means something really deep. In the depth of their being, humans and their group are isomorphic. Now this view may be dubbed as metaphysical, for it is very difficult to prove the structural identity of man and his group except in a very metaphorical sense as indicated before. If human personality is shaped, and we think it is, by some definite and necessary social institutions like language, traditional behavioural responses, conventions and customs, there is no reason for man to be surprised at the discovery of similarity between personality structure and social structure. But this account of individual-social isomorphism clashes with the view that man comes first and the group next.

Sri Aurobindo's own formulation of the relation between the individual and society is very careful and cautious. It is not opened at least to the objection that the individual is something quite independent of his group affiliation. Often he warns us against the opposite error, i.e., not to identify the individual *completely* with his group affiliation. At least in some respects the individual is something more than his group. True to his intuitive epistemology Sri Aurobindo thinks that we can never grasp the correct relation between the individual and the group in terms of reason.

It is through the mind of man that Sri Aurobindo tries to grasp the process and significance of the evolution of different socio-political aggregates. Man himself is a representative 'excerpt' of a hidden and great spiritual truth. In the give-and-take relation between man and society man *as an integral part of the great spiritual reality* gives society more than what he takes from it. Sri Aurobindo does not deny the importance of other factors in accounting for the formation and evolution of different human aggregates. 'Race, language, local relations and economic convenience of powerful factors, what he decides must be a dominant psychological element that makes for union.'[2] The subtle and invisible spiritual force that works through human agency is always restless and relentless and all other forces ultimately succumb to it.

The larger human aggregates result from the fulfilment of the purpose of smaller human aggregates. Sri Aurobindo speaks of 'a free and unsocial state'. And he thinks it is the earliest human aggregate we know of. He takes note of the sceptical attitude of some modern thinkers towards the very existence of such an asocial state of society—a free and fluid association. The sceptic argues that 'if such a state ever existed . . . it must have been not merely unsocial but anti-social.'[3] Sri Aurobindo is definitely against this pro-Hobbesian theory of the earliest form of human association. It is not a creation of any poetic or idealistic imagination. It is said to be a very natural expression of the instinctive spontaneity of the primitive mind. The people of that age knew the way to live by the inner law of love and natural righteousness. Tyranny, oppression, selfishness, corruption and the like were all unknown to that state of society. It seems that in their primitive mode of living they realised, at least partially, the high dream of philosophic anarchism. This 'original animal association' is marked by a natural uniformity which is not to be confused with the spiritual unity, the end of the human cycle. We start with natural uniformity and are destined to end up with spiritual unity.

Sri Aurobindo writes: 'Our destiny may be the conversion of an original animal association into a community of the gods. Our progress may be a devious round leading from the easy and spontaneous uniformity and harmony which reflects Nature to the self-possessed unity which reflects the Divine.'[4] It is quite likely that Sri Aurobindo's notion of Divine destiny as a central component of his theory of social evolution will attract critical comment from different quarters. He concedes that the available data of sociology and archaeology may not bear out his view of the spontaneous uniformity and harmony of primitive society. But he has his answer to this sort of criticism. First, the critics uncritically use some modern concepts to explain primitive human society where their relevance and application are indeed very limited. Secondly, they lack that insight and sympathy of experience which alone could enable them to get to the heart of the ' alien ' field of their study. And, finally, the methodology of most of the modern anthropologists, archaeologists and sociologists is defective, for they rely excessively on what may be called a mechanical and objective approach. It is because of this defective methodology that they try to trace the origin of the earliest human association to the gregarious impulse of man resulting from the necessity of survival. Sri Aurobindo is against any attempt to explain human aggregation or grouping in terms of any objective necessity. He sees in it the development of man's inner power, a subjective and psychological drive.

Tracing the course of human evolution and analysing the structures of different human aggregates Sri Aurobindo comes to the conclusion that Nature has been trying to strike a balance between the perfection of the individual and peace and security of the group. He contests the view that individual freedom was unknown in primitive society. The individual had to surrender his freedom to the artificial group interest represented by the State, which was of a degenerate form in primitive society. The freedom and fluidity of primitive society was not there in the State. The earlier and smaller social aggregates were relatively more free and flexible than the subsequent and larger aggregates. Primitive society and the smaller aggregates that we come across therein reflect the symbolic mentality and all its characteristics. Social development depends upon social mentality—the individual's realisation of his inner social affiliation and mooring. The individual is required to realise progressively his spiritual bond with others in the social context. The more he realises it the more he enlarges himself. The human cycle is marked by the progressive enlargement of the individual in relation to the society. ' The family, the commune, the clan or tribe, the class, the city-state or congeries of tribes, the nation, the empire are so many stages in this progressive and constant enlargement.' These stages are not necessarily exclusive. Often they are interpenetrative. And as a result the composition of the later and larger aggregates is very complex. The human cycle is marked by an increasing complexity, order and efficiency. In the name of order and efficiency, safety and security, the individual is called upon to sacrifice more and more of his early freedom.

Sri Aurobindo mentions another characteristic of the human cycle. It is the non-linear movement of Nature through the different aggregates of the cycle. Nature first leans this way, and then that way, and finally comes back to a temporary balance; it is again disturbed by the urge which is already there in her bosom for further progress. In the course of social evolution the smaller aggregates are never completely destroyed. The reason that one or two of them have totally disappeared is that they exhausted their utility. They are all preserved for the variety, richness and multiformity of social life. In the process of its gradual development society tends to become rigid. The man of the typal period lacks the flexibility and fluidity of the mind of the symbolic period. The family, the tribe, or the city, the *polis* were plastic group units. But the clan, the caste and the class were rigid group-units. The democratic freedom of the former was not there in the latter. The problems of indirect government of the larger aggregates were also successfully avoided by tribal society and the city-state. But the perfection of the individual necessitated the expansion and organisation of smaller social units.

> The primal law and purpose of the individual life is to seek its own self-development. Consciously or half-consciously or with an obscure unconscious groping it strives always and rightly strives at self-formulation—to find itself, to discover within itself, the law and power of its own being and to fulfil it....In the same way, the primal law and purpose of a society, community or nation is to seek its own self-fulfilment.[5]

Man fulfils himself gradually. The development of human society knows no hiatus in between the smaller and the larger human aggregates. On the contrary, as I said before, these aggregates inter-penetrate and overlap and are, therefore, very complex in composition. Human institutions together with the societies which environ them move from relative simplicity to relative complexity.

### Family

In the course of his self-development man formed at first the family. This formation is nowhere historically datable; it is to be taken in a conceptual sense. The necessity of family is both biological and sociological at the same time. The family relationship is associated with some definite obligations, the fulfilment of which is sanctioned by some ethical or religious beliefs. The family is not a mere reproductive unit, it has its larger and bilateral ramifications. Even in the tribal period the bilateral principle was recognised in the family life. 'The tribal family is a social unit which includes both parents and in a secondary sense, the kindreds on both sides.'[6] Patronymic or matronymic, whatever might be the form of the family, the most important trait which establishes its social character is the bilateral principle it embodies in its structure.

The family has been defined and classified in various ways. Some sociologists think that the basis of a family unit is conjugal and/or parental relation. Ogburn and Nimkoff write: 'When we think of a family we picture it is a more or less durable association with or without children, or of man or woman along with children.'[7] Murdock insists on the simultaneous existence of conjugal *and* parental relations as the foundation of family. According to him 'a married but childless couple or a widow or a divorced parent with children may form a household but not a family.'

But these views ignore the importance of a particular intra-family relationship obtained within the family structure. For divorce or some other reasons a cohort may find himself alone with or without children and meaning thereby the end of conjugal relation, but that does not mean either the end of actual or possible (in the case of an expecting mother, for instance) parental obligations or that of family life itself. We may conceive of family not only without conjugal relations but also without parental relations. If a spouseless cohort has not yet produced or adopted any child, that does not *ipso facto* make it impossible for him/her to be regarded as a unit *of a family*. The definition of family framed exclusively in terms of parental and/or conjugal is very narrow. The Hindu joint-family, for instance, is not covered by this definition. In such a family there are members who are not related to the rest either conjugally or parentally. The unity of the family is in fact multilateral. The relation of kinship or affinity between any two members in a family unit may be regarded under any one of the following five categories:

(*i*) *Conjugal*, between husband and wife, or man and woman;
(*ii*) *Parental-filial*, between father and/or mother, on the one hand, and son and/or daughter, on the other;
(*iii*) *Sibling*, between brothers and/or sisters;
(*iv*) *Lineal*, between those related by common ancestry as traceable through males and/or females; and
(*v*) *Affinal*, between those related through the spouses of one or both of them.

There are different types of families, simple and composite: 'The first and most basic . . . *nuclear family*, consists typically of a married man and woman with their offspring, although in individual cases one or more additional persons may reside with them.'[8] Murdock claims that the nuclear family is a universal human social grouping. But anthropologists like Linton have expressed a different view:

> It is hard for Europeans to realise a sharp distinction which exists in many social systems between the reproductive unit composed of mates and their offspring and the authentic, institutional family. It happens that in our own (American) society these two units coincide much more closely than in most . . . . Actually, such groupings play an insignificant role in the lives of many societies, while at least one society refuses to give them any formal recognition.[9]

In this connection Linton refers to the Nairs of South India. They provide no place for husbands or fathers in their social systems. It is true that their women used to formally marry an upper caste Brahmin (Namboodiri), but this marriage used to be terminated at the end of a few days by a formal divorce. The case of the Nairs is cited by Linton to prove that 'it is possible to eliminate from the functions of the social family the very items which brought the biological family into existence'.

The family has lost much of its past rigidity and unitary character. Still it is there and has not disappeared, for it has its continued utility. The mind of the individual man, particularly of those individuals who are very perceptive and gifted, evolve faster than the attending institutions. As the human mind is not completely determined by its *sociology*, it may successfully anticipate and even live the *psychology* of an aggregate which is yet to be formed structurally or outwardly.

## Enlargement of the Smaller Human Aggregates: One View

The institution known as the joint-family is not known all over the world. But almost in all social systems there are units whose membership is determined by descent through a male or a female line. Kin groups are generally based on two principles—one is of descent and the other of residence.

The family is of course a kin group, since each of its members is a relative of the others. The polygamous family is a kin group. Extended families, whether of the patrilocal, matrilocal, avunculocal or bilocal types, are also kin groups. Extended families include not only primary relatives but also tertiary relatives and even remoter relatives. The relation which binds the members to one another in a family is always partly affinal and never exclusively consanguineal. Besides their mixed consanguineal and affinal ties, they are also united by common residence. The *residential kin group* is to be distinguished from the consanguineal kin group. The latter is never characterised by common residence and includes only consanguineal relatives. While the residential kin group includes husband and wife but not brother and sister, the consanguineal kin group always includes both brother and sister but not both husband and wife.

The form of a residential kin group is mainly determined by the rule of residence, and that of a consanguineal kin group by the rule of descent. Descent is not to be confused with genealogical relationship. It is a cultural principle in terms of which a person is socially allocated to a specific group of consanguineal kinsmen, from whom he can expect support and help in difficulties. The ramification of consanguineal kinship may be almost endless, embracing all members of the local community or even of the tribe. So some discrimination and selection has to be made. On birth, an individual has to be affiliated to a particular group of relatives to the exclusion of others. This group affiliation is established principally by the three primary rules of descent—patrilineal descent, matrilineal descent and bilateral descent. *Patrilineal descent* assigns the child to the father's kin group, discarding the mother's kin group. *Matrilineal descent* establishes the affiliation of the child to his mother's kin group, excluding the father's kin group. *Bilateral descent* establishes the child in a kin group where some of the members of the father's kin group and some of those of the mother's are included and some of both groups excluded. Murdock speaks of *double descent*. Generally one of the rules of descent, patrilineal or matrilineal, is applied to establish the group affiliation of the child. But when patrilineal and matrilineal descent are applied together, their joint application is known as double descent.[10]

Most modern societies are characterised by bilateral descent. Our kin groups include and exclude some relatives of our parents on either side and they are popularly known as relatives and technically as the *kindred.*

Primitive societies are generally characterised by unilineal descent, either patrilineal or matrilineal. Their structure is, therefore, relatively simpler than the structure of kinship groups resulting from bilateral descent. Several terms are used to designate unilinear descent groups: clan, gens, lineage, moiety, phratry, etc. When a consanguineal kin group follows a particular rule of unilinear descent and its members can actually trace their common ancestry, it is technically known as a lineage. Thus, all persons bearing the surname Chattopadhyaya who claim that they can successfully trace actual descent in the male line from a common ancestry form a patrilineage. But there are consanguineal kin groups whose members are unable to trace the actual genealogical relations between themselves through the common ancestor, and these are called *sibs.* Sometimes the members of two or more *sibs* believe that they are related by a unilinear bond of kinship and constituted a *phratry.* By moiety we designate a society which has only two sibs or phratries and every person in such a society necessarily belongs to one or the other.

One of the most general characteristics of unilinear consanguineal kin groups is exogamy. In an exogamous kin group all members have to seek their spouses in some other group. Lineages are also found to be exogamous. Sibs are exogamous only to a partial extent. Moieties are often found to be endogamous.

In the order of evolution the sib or clan appears after the family. While the family is a bilateral kin group, the sib is a unilateral one. The mother-sibs are known as clans, and when a tribe is organised into mother-sibs every member of the tribe becomes a member of his or her mother-sib and assumes the maternal sib name. The father-sibs are known as *gentes* and when a tribe is organised into father-sibs every member of the tribe becomes a member of his or her father-sibs and assumes the paternal sib name. Morgan (L. H. Morgan, *The Ancient Society*, Bharati Library, Calcutta, no date) thinks that the family is universally preceded by the sib. But this view has been contested among others by Lowie and Swanton. The Sakai and the Somang of Malaysia and the Negrito Andamanese have their families but not sibs. Lowie and Swanton think that the sib organisation appears among the tribes only at an economically and politically advanced stage.

The *clan* is a compromised kin group, compromising unilocal residence and unilateral descent. A genuine clan is characterised by three things—a unilateral rule of descent which unites the central core of members, residential unity, and a positive group sentiment. Each and every group of individuals residing in a particular place, for instance, in a big apartment or barrack house, do not constitute a clan. This shows the importance of the third factor, a positive group sentiment, in the constitution of a clan. The clan is an expanded and diffused family unit. No doubt that it is primarily a biologically determined unit. But it has its *esprit dec orps* or, what Murdock calls, a we feeling. The functional potentialities of the clan are influenced by the group sentiment of its members. The sentimental and the emotional unity of the clan is itself dependent upon the techniques and norms of developing and regulating the correct attitudes and behaviour in the clan members. The density and distribution of the members over a territory has also an important bearing on the functional potentialities of a clan. If the members are distributed thinly over a large territory, it is natural that, in course of time, their psychological bond will be weakened.

There is no necessary relation between the clan organisation and primitive society. There are primitive societies which know no clan organisation. For example, the Eskimo have no clan organisation. Linton says:

> Although strong functional clan organisation cannot be correlated with any particular stage of cultural complexity and certainly is not a stage in the unilinear evolution of society, it does seem to be correlated, in a very general way, with stability of culture and fixity of residence.[11]

In spite of its extended character, the clan is undoubtedly a blood-determined social unit. It stands in between the basic family unit and the joint-family on the one hand, and *hordes, villages and bands* on the other. Hordes and bands are not universal social groups. To designate the intermediary social groups Linton uses the descriptive term *local group* while Murdock prefers the sociological term *community*. The community and the nuclear family are claimed to be the only universal social groups. The community organisation provides its members with increased opportunities to satisfy their demands through social intercourse, abundant food through cooperative food-gathering techniques, and security against illness, incapacity, or enemy attack through mutual aid and assistance. The community organisation is better equipped than the clan organisation in terms of division of labour and specialisation for the purpose of exploiting the natural resources of a territory. Because of its greater technological efficiency the chances of survival of the community organisation are higher than those of other intermediary groups. And this partly accounts for the universality of the community organisation.

Communities differ in types because of their different modes of production. Some nomadic communities depend upon gathering, hunting, or herding. This type of community, consisting of a number of families habitually living together in a camp, is known as a band. Every band claims a certain territory as its own and tries to defend it against trespassers. Within this territory and with more or less regularity it moves round the year, and if it succeeds in using and exploiting its territory over a number of years, it tends to settle down there. Permanent settlement becomes possible on the fulfilment of two conditions—when a territory can be defended for a reasonable length of time against enemy trespass, and when the territory can be relied upon as the source of necessary food supply.

The permanent settlement of the community does not necessarily mean that its mode of production is agricultural. Compared to the hunting communities it is even more difficult for the cattle-rearing communities or those who depend upon domestic animals to establish permanent settlement. This type of community is always in search of sure and sufficient pasturage within the territory which can be exploited from a single centre. It is true that the agricultural mode of production proves to be the single most important factor helping the community in establishing permanent settlement, but we know of hunting and cattle-rearing tribes who have achieved permanent settlement without knowing any agricultural techniques. The hunting tribes of British Columbia live on fish and wild berries and their settlement is permanent. The same may be said of the cattle-rearing Masai bands of Africa. Conversely, it has been pointed out that the development of the agricultural mode of production does not necessarily mean permanent settlement. The Iroquois tribes of North America are quite conversant with agriculture, but they move from one place to another at intervals of about ten or fifteen years, when they find that the corn lands are subjected to the law of diminishing returns and the locally available firewood has been exhausted. The same practice is observed also among some Borneo (Kalimantan) tribes, who, after a few years, dismantle their huge communal houses and carry them, together with other property and belongings, to new places.

The social life of the band, or for that matter of any other form of community, is governed by face-to-face relations. Whether it is settled or not, its isolated and exclusive composition necessitates social control and promotes local culture. It would be wrong to think that individuals are united in the intermediary groups only on the basis of economic necessity. The psychological and moral factors are equally important. To govern inter-individual relationships and preserve friendly relations between neighbours, some behavioural norms and modes are gradually established. To start with, the mechanism of social control is found to be flexible and plastic. But in course of time it becomes rigid and stereotyped. The operation of social sanctions, ideas and behaviour results in a relatively stereotyped local culture. In course of time the element of control and associated culture transform the community into a political group characterised by a rudimentary form of government. In order that the community can exercise its controlling power it evolves the offices of *chief*, *leader* and *deliberative bodies* with culturally defined powers and functions. Without these agencies and offices the community cannot order social life. But the power that is delegated or given to the leader or the chief is often misused by him or used for the purpose of self-aggrandisement.

It goes without saying that the points of contact in between the different bands are few and far between. But even then the belligerency and atomism of simple societies should not be over-exaggerated. Through trade, intermarriage, and other forces, primitive people belonging to different communities come close to each other and try to extend the area of peace and stability. Murdock writes:

> Primitive man is as capable as ourselves of perceiving the advantages to be obtained through peaceful intercourse with his neighbours, and of control-

ling his ethnocentric prejudices in order to reap these advantages. Even in regions where war is endemic, it is not waged all the time nor with all surrounding groups; at the worst, armed truces of temporary alliances occur. Far more commonly, however, peaceful intercommunication prevails as the norm over wide areas.[12]

It is through local exogamy, blood brotherhood, safe conduct, market peace and similar other cultural devices that personal relationships obtained between bands or communities are extended and larger social groups formed. The enlarged social groups cut across the lines demarcating different sibs, religious sects and social classes. The consolidation of the large groups necessitates and is brought about by political authority, by the organisation of a number of local groups under a unified tribal or state government.

But this is not necessarily the case. There are many societies which did not develop any genuine political integration beyond the community. Among other factors, it is perhaps the settled mode of living which favours most the wider political organisation and unification of the smaller human aggregates. By contrast it is generally observed that the bands of migratory tribes are politically disunited and are not inclined towards unification. The bands or the communities are said to be common in all human societies, whatever might be the size or the form of their government. The intimacy of inter-personal relationships is a common characteristic of the relatively simple form of societies. Even within the larger human aggregates like tribe and state, the face-to-face quality of human relationships, though diminished, is not entirely lost. Some modern anthropologists apprehend that with the development of faster means of communication and the mechanisation of human relationships, the community life, characterised by face-to-face relationship, will quickly disintegrate and be replaced by a new type of society marked by anonymity and narrowly defined positions and roles. Ralph Linton writes:

> In spite of its superficial differences from one culture to another, the band is the most constant of all social phenomena and, in many respects, the most uniform....Its disintegration is one of the most revolutionary results of the rise of modern civilization....The modern city, with its multiplicity of organisations of every conceivable sort, presents the picture of a mass of individuals who have lost their bands and who are trying, in uncertain and fumbling fashion, to find some substitute....Although the disintegration of local groups in our society may progress even farther than it has, the author is inclined to regard it as a transitory phenomenon. The sudden rise of the machine and of applied science has shattered Western civilization and reduced Western society to something approaching chaos. However, unless all past experience is at fault, the society will once more reduce itself to order.[13]

Whether band or community life will survive in some form or other is yet to be seen. But one thing seems to be definite and that is that every man has two distinct, but not unrelated, aspects in his life—personal and social. He stands in and lives through certain intimate personal relationships. And, at the same time, he needs and maintains certain other relationships which answer some of his less personal social requirements. Linton's emphatic assertion about the survival of band life is based on the former type of human relations. And I think, in spite of the mass character of the modern society, the community life, in some form or other, is sure to survive. It goes without saying that the character and behaviour of the community in a mass society is bound to be quite different from what it was in the primitive past, in the pre-tribal period, when the community was itself in the most developed form of social life.

At every stage of his life, whether he lives a family life or a community life, man increasingly feels the necessity of certain goods and services, which cannot be provided by his existing social unit. And that is the psychological basis of yearning for a larger and more resourceful social unit. There is no doubt that this psychological basis is itself nourished by some objective and institutional factors. When the population of a band increases beyond a particular limit, some members find it difficult to live within the original territorial boundary of the band and they move out to some adjacent territory. The inadequacy of food supply for an increasing population is the general cause of the splitting up of the original band life. The division of labour at times accentuates this process and often works also as an independent cause of internal division. It is only natural that, after the division, the individuals of the band who occupy and live in adjoining territories do not forget their original and numerous ties of personal acquaintance and family relationships. Even after the division, these groups remain attached to each other through common culture and language. The bands, bound together by a series of interlocking relationships, form the larger social aggregate, the *tribe*. The tribe has been defined by Linton as 'a group of bands occupying contiguous territories and having a feeling of unity deriving from numerous similarities in culture, frequent friendly contacts, and certain community of interest.' The tribe is a territorial unit. At the initial stage, the tribesmen maintain very intimate personal relationships with their fellow tribesmen and then share the memory and pride of common origin. But with the passage of time things change, the memory fades and culture and language undergo transformation. And, in the absence of a strong central authority, the unity of the tribal life gradually ceases to be functionally effective and becomes a matter of cultural psychology. Tribal solidarity is sustained through certain occasional ceremonies and assemblies. The tribesmen draw a very clear distinction between themselves and outsiders. Tribal unity is strengthened and tested by external warfare.

Anthropologists are not unanimous on the question as to whether the political organisation of primitive tribes was founded upon territorial contiguity or not. While Maine and Morgan think that the primitive tribe deals with an individual only as a member of a sib, i.e., of a kinship group, many modern anthropologists think that the sharp distinction drawn by them between kinship (tribal) and territorial (political) organisations is untenable. Lowie points out that in primitive society territorial organisation is often based on kinship relationship. He refers to some Australian tribes which comprise many kin-groups, but continue to function as territorial units.[14] He concludes that ' even at a very early time and in a very lowly environment, there was no necessity for disrupting the ties of kinship in order to found a political state'. This conclusion is obviously inconsistent with the Marxist theory of primitive communism, which intends to defend the Maine-Morgan idea regarding primitive tribal society *without* political organisation. I propose to take up this point later on.

The transformation of the *tribal* society into what may be called the *national* society is brought about by the joint effects of the institutional requirements of the people and their psychological development. Sri Aurobindo says that Nature supplies only the psychological nucleus of tribal life and society. And only the best people of the tribe can realise an inner drift of a larger and more perfect group-life and read its signs and symptoms in the workings of the existing institutions. The common man in primitive society also feels the same thing, but he does so under the pressure of circumstances. The general mode of transforming the existing society and of building new and higher forms of society is external and mechanical. Consequently, Sri Aurobindo argues, the larger aggregates suffer internal contraction and corresponding external shrinkage. If the external structure of a particular form of society is more heavy and cumbersome than what possibly could be supported and sustained by the concerned human nature, then the social process shows all the decaying features due to the lack of functional harmony and cohesion between them. Before an aggregate may develop freely and smoothly, it must live around and up to its own psychological centre. When the outer body of an aggregate is too big or too heavy to be supported by the power of its inner consciousness, either it dies a natural death under the pressure of its own body, as the massive Titan, or it stands still, ceases to grow, and looks within itself in search of that inner power which may ultimately save it from its own lethal mass. The motive-force of Nature working in the field of society is not equally obvious to the human agents who further social evolution. Because of their superior understanding and better technology some people understand it more clearly than the rest and accordingly try to dominate the latter. Therefore, ' the emergence of a dominant class is inevitable within the aggregate itself, just as in the constant clash between the aggregates the emergence of a dominant nation is inevitable'.

To illustrate his point that class dominated pre-national aggregates cannot survive for a long time Sri Aurobindo refers to the ancient histories of Greece, Rome and India. Democratic equality and cultural efflorescence existed in the early Greek, Roman and Indian city-states and clan-nations but could not prevent the inevitable decay and disintegration of those smaller aggregates. Sri Aurobindo offers the following reasons for their decline and ultimate disappearance. First, the slaves and women were not allowed to participate fully in the civic-cultural life of the community. Consequently, the burden of civilisation proved too heavy to be borne by the enlightened section only.

Secondly, the early forms of societies, the communities, the tribes and the city-states, could not envisage any appropriate institutional means for the solution of the problems resulting from the antagonistic relations between themselves. The communities failed to develop any form of free and stable federation. They knew no means of unification other than military conquest. War was the final arbitrator of all grave disputes but the larger needs and tendencies of the time necessitated some sort of unity of smaller aggregates. Some sort of mental and vital insularity developed by the people, especially of the powerful communities, resisted this movement towards larger unity. Ultimately, of course, the old and small aggregates and states had to dissolve and disappear into some or other gigantic bureaucratic or military and commercial empire. Those empires also did not last long as they were not based on healthy development of the intermediate aggregate, the nation-unit.[15]

## Enlargement of the Smaller Human Aggregates: Another View

There is another theory about the evolution of the smaller and larger human aggregates, from the family to the state, which has been developed mainly in terms of the dominant mode of production. It is almost universally associated with the names of Marx, Engels, and Lenin. But classical economists like Ricardo and anthropologists like Morgan have also directly and indirectly contributed to the development of this general theory.

According to this view, in the lower or middle stage of barbarism man developed a new mode of production which enabled him to produce more than what he required for self-sustenance. The surplus production gave him the purchasing capacity which he used to buy women and slaves and establish proprietary rights over them. Agriculture made private property possible. The family and slavery are said to be the outcome of the institution of private property. This view about the origin of private property and family has been generalised. And the Marxist claims that it is valid in all societies throughout the world.

During the period of transition between the middle and upper stages of barbarism, the monogamous family arises out of the pairing family. The pairing family is based on marriage between single pairs but *without* any exclusive cohabitation. The monogamous family is based on marriage between single pairs *with* an exclusive cohabitation. The evolution of the monogamous family begins to threaten the group life of the *gens*.[16] The gens, or the (Sanskrit) *gana*, ' embraced all persons who traced their descent from a supposed male ancestor, through males only, the evidence of the fact being . . . the possessions of a common gentile name'.[17] At the early stage, the gentile kindreds, according to Morgan, are linked together chiefly through the bonds of their maternity. For a considerable period the gens remain the unit of the social system. The gentile institution is based on three factors—the bond of kin, the pure lineage through descent in the male or family line, and exogamy.

The middle stage of barbarism comes to its end with the discovery of such instruments as the axe and the sword. Deforestation is carried out to extend the extent of arable lands. Agriculture becomes a stable source of livelihood, and an increasing part of a growing population comes to live off the land. A division of labour develops resulting in a class of slaves and one of masters. Commodity production starts, and it is followed by exchange. Commodity production and exchange taken together account for the gradual expansion of trade both within and without the tribal communities. Antagonism between the rich and the poor is added to that between free men and slaves. The unequal appropriation of the benefits of increased production widens the difference between the families belonging to the same gens or commune. The well-to-do families develop vested interests in preserving and even in increasing their family wealth. The old community-unit of society gives way to the family-unit, which has already been strengthened by this time by the institution of monogamous marriage.

The Marxist tries to show thus that the mode of production breaks up the internal structure of the gens and transforms it externally into a larger aggregate. The Grecian *phratry* and the Roman *curia* represent the socio-political ingenuity of the people of the upper stage of barbarism. The new political organisation of the time was a sort of military democracy; *military*, because war was the only arbitrator to decide the feuds between the different phratries; and *democracy*, because hundreds of autonomous *demes* or townships used to decide together the general affairs of those units or aggregates. The freedom of the *deemes* is adversely affected by the growth of the power of the ruling class. In order to plunder and oppress the neighbouring peoples the ruling class demands and receives more and more authority and power from the people. But subsequently it refuses to give the popular power and authority back to the people. The right to private property and the laws governing its creation, protection and enjoyment make the rich families of the ruling class richer and the poor people still poorer. 'This could not have happened', according to Engels, 'had not the greed for wealth divided the members of the gentes into rich and poor.' Marx observes that 'property difference in a gens changed the community of interest into antagonism between members of a gens'.

The second division of labour in the upper stage of barbarism increases production to an enormous extent much beyond the necessity of the people of the tribe or the phratry. The surplus production augments the exchange trade and the benefits arising out of that go straight into the hands of the rich class. To perpetuate this advantage the laws of inheritance are accordingly changed in favour of their class. The communal ownership of property is thus replaced by private and hereditary ownership. The earliest laws of Greece, Rome and India merely record and modify the usages and customs of the time.

The advent of civilisation brings a new class into the picture. The members of the new class, merchants, take no part in the process of production, stand midway between producers and consumers, and exploit both. Metal money and minted coins come into use to serve as the store of their benefits of exploitation. The appearance of the parasitical mercantile class marks the third and the most decisive division of labour. An enormous amount of the whole social wealth is quickly concentrated and centralised in the hands of this small class. The development of the mercantile economy demands the expansion of tribal society. Partly to fulfil the economic necessity of further expansion and partly to avert intra- and extra-tribal strifes, the coalescence of the larger tribes or communities becomes inevitable in the course of time. And this leads to the formation of the nation and the development of nationality.

The Marxist account of social evolution is unacceptable to Sri Aurobindo. He finds it defective on several counts. First, he does not accept the all-engrossing group character of primitive man. According to him, primitive society is free and fluid. Secondly, the state of society and culture cannot be necessarily connected with definite modes of production. Different types of societies are found to stem from the same mode of production. Social relations are not always determined by the productive system. For example, the Andamanese or the Vedda women, who contribute little to their hunting economy, are equal to their men in social status; but in the average Bantu village, the woman, though not a slave, does not enjoy the rank and rights of a man.[18] The dissolution of ' primitive communism ' is not necessarily followed by the slavery of woman. Evans-Pritchard assures us that ' the findings of modern anthropologists are in agreement that women's status among primitive people has been misunderstood and underestimated '. Thirdly, the Marxist theory is based on a wrong assumption about human nature. The subjugation of woman by man is not always economic, but psychological.

# 7

# Larger Human Unities: Empire and Nation

## FORMATION OF NATION: DIFFERENT FACTORS

In his study of social development Sri Aurobindo relies too much on and is consistently guided by the analogy of the natural process. He thinks that the process which works in the formation and transformation of natural aggregates and human aggregates is essentially the same. ' In the case of a natural aggregation a natural body is first created, and then a common life and a common interest are brought to the constituent elements of the body, and thirdly, a central organ is provided through which a common ego-sense can realise itself the body.'[1] Much the same principle is at work in making a human aggregation possible. For example, several groups coalesce to form a tribe. And, to start with, this means nothing more than a physical association. Because of its bare physical nature it fails initially ' to deliver, to manifest and to bring into secure working a supraphysical, a psychological principle latent behind the operations of the life and the body '.[2] But in course of time physical association imparts and develops a common way of life. Finally, this common way of life gives rise to a common ego-sense which permeates and tends to unify the constituents of the association.

The territorial unity of groups necessitates a common social life under some form of government. Living under the same government the groups gradually develop a unity among themselves. Once developed, the sense of unity turns out to be extra-territorial and non-physical to a certain extent. There are some nations who have national unity without any common territorial bond. The Jewish nation provides perhaps the clearest example in this respect.

Tracing the origin of nationalism Sri Aurobindo goes back to primitive society. He thinks that the coalescence of small primitive societies or their disappearance means two important things. First, the coalescence of the primitive tribes is the result of *economic development* and inner *psychological necessity*. Secondly, once the tribes come together, they are obliged to reorganise their governing or superintending apparatus. The rudimentary form of nationalism found in the early tribes is not based mainly on political unity. Tribal nationalism is predominantly a cultural phenomenon sustained by a distinct dialect or speech, observance of some common religious rites, a set of oral traditions, beliefs and ideas. The transformation of the tribal character of ancient social life is brought about by the development of agricultural and industrial techniques and the conquest and consolidation of tribes by military empires. This process of transformation is further accelerated by two other factors—the development of inter-tribal *languages*, like Sanskrit, Greek, Latin and Chinese and the appearance of inter-tribal *religions* like Hinduism, Buddhism, Christianity and Islam.

## Building up of Empire: The Ancient Period

While military power itself is enough for the purpose of establishing a tribal unity, many more things are necessary to establish an imperial unity. Rome, for example, had a psychological unity of its own, but it is very doubtful if the Roman empire as a whole had remained united always. Imperial aggregates were nothing more than mere aggregates. Their unity was more a myth than a reality. And that myth always used to originate from the metropolitan state or the central nation-unit, and the subjugated nation-units had to subscribe to it. The imperial aggregates superseded but did not fulfil the nation to preserve the feudal unity of the heterogeneous nations. The national ego had to be extended to the whole of the empire. The imperial extension had little or no depth dimension.

But this method of achieving imperial unity is neither desirable nor necessary. This becomes clear, Sri Aurobindo points out, when we look at the working processes underlying the formation of natural and human aggregates. In some respects these processes are similar, but there are other respects where their differences are obvious. First, in physical nature the component units, remaining distinct and external as they are to each other, try to arrive at a loose unity in which they exist by interchange with other units or partly by that interchange and partly by devouring others. Secondly, the processes of unification operative at the levels of life and consciousness and socio-political unification are in many respects different from the method of natural unification or aggregation. In the former cases the component units need not and do not maintain their distinctness detrimental to a mutual assimilation and reception of one's life energies by the other. On the contrary, these units may even consciously subordinate themselves to a general unity and in the process of forming that unity some of the units may suffer a natural decay or death but would not feel the strength of a particular dominant unit which is determined to remain ever at that position even in a way prejudicial to and disturbing the general unity. Lastly, Sri Aurobindo points out that the main problem consists in devising the ways and means for subordinating the component units to a new unity without causing their decay, death or disappearance. It is generally admitted that the majority of mankind has not yet been successful in evolving the best possible method of achieving human unification.

History abounds with the ill-effects of pursuing the *external-natural* method of imperial unification. Rome had to pay the penalty by having to watch her empire debilitated by invading barbarians. The vigorous barbarians, Goths and Vandals, invigorated the Roman world which before its ultimate fall became ' a huge, decorous, magnificently organised death-in-life '. Sri Aurobindo is a historicist and believes in the inevitability of whatever happens in history.[3] No step of Nature, nothing whatsoever that happens in history, is to his mind meaningless or useless. The decline and fall of the Roman Empire has left behind a profound lesson for us. Rome fell because it thrusted an iron uniformity over her colonies. These countries were robbed of their riches by Rome and in return received little or nothing of Roman culture and prosperity. This uniformity weakened the component units and developed a rebellious and breakaway tendency in them. A similar lifeless and iron uniformity resulted in the disintegration of the Assyrian imperial unity. The absence of imposed uniformity explains the non-emergence of a national unity in India before the beginning of the British domination of this sub-continent. The Maurya, Gupta, Andhra and Moghul empires were undoubtedly very powerful and organised, but never under them had India experienced the discipline which they experienced during the British period. Somehow the strongly independent life of the subordinate unities in India succeeded in withstanding the successive imperial pressures. And that partly accounts for how, in spite of their repeated political defeats, different regional or linguistic groups of India succeeded in saving, and even at times enriching, their cultural heritage and individuality. They escaped death but could not achieve a central national unity.

A somewhat similar thing happened also in the case of Rome. Under the Roman pressure the separative city-states declined, some even died, but they did not completely lose their individuality. When the pressure was removed, it was quite possible for each of them to develop in their own individual way, but instead of exploring that possibility again a premature attempt was made for the national unification of Italy. This new development, though otherwise ' an incalculable boon and advantage to the culture and civilization of the West ', was disastrous to the nation-life of Italy. This attempt proved indeed very premature as there was no adequate psychological unity to support a large Italian nation. But it should be recalled in this connection that this attempt, though premature, paved the way for the evolution of the subsequet national unity of Italy. The loose unity of the free or half-free municipalities of medieval France, Flanders and Germany afforded a sub-conscious basis for the establishment of national unity in those parts of Europe later on. This socio-political development was synchronised with bidding farewell to the medieval tendency to intellectual uniformity, stagnation and obscurantism.

## Empire-Building and Nation-Building

The parallelism between the ancient cycle of empire-building and the European cycle of nation-building is very interesting indeed. Sri Aurobindo takes pains to point out where and how the parallelism breaks down. First, the latter process of unification is marked by an attempt to meet the demand of the individuality of component units. Secondly, it moved much faster than the ancient cycle of empire-building. The first characteristic of the slow progression of the units towards unification finds its clear expression in the feudal order of the medieval period. To a certain extent this order is successful in striking a workable balance between the centripetal and centrifugal forces of society and in giving a loose but organic unity to it. In the second characteristic of this movement for national unification some features of the old imperial system of Rome are found to recur but not in the old ruthless form. The first feature of the second characteristic is the creation of the metropolitan centre. The second is the growth of an absolute sovereign power to establish a legal, administrative and linguistic uniformity and also to centralise the life of the nation as a whole. And the third is the establishment of a central spiritual authority whose duty is to impose spiritual and intellectual uniformity on the member units. The joint effect of these three features of the second characteristic of the process of national unification might have spoiled all the gains accrued to it but for the emergence and timely intervention of the third stage referred to before. This resulted in partial decentralisation of the excessive metropolitan power, higher freedom and justice to the subordinate governments, communes and provincial cities, and the beginning of federated nation of federal empire.[4]

When Sri Aurobindo refers to the three stages in the formation of the nation-unit in Europe, he seems to have had the history of medieval Italy particularly in mind. Like all historical generalisations it holds good only within limits.[5] The modes of appearance, operation and disappearance of the stages of history are not uniform all over the world. And this is to be understood in terms of the peculiarities of group psychology, historical past and attending circumstances. It need not be taken for granted that all nations owe their nationhood to a sort of iron uniformity imposed by an alien rule. There must exist some kind of looser yet sufficiently compelling order of society and a common type of civilisation. One should not be misled by superficial resemblances between widely different societies and civilisations.[6] For example, it is true that 'the feudal period of Europe with its four orders of the clergy, the king and the nobles, the bourgeoisie and the proletariat has a sufficiently close resemblance to the Indian four-fold order of the sacerdotal, military, mercantile class and the Shudras'. But one should remember that while in Europe these orders were mainly an expression of the social, political and economic patterns of the prevalent society, in India they had also a distinct ethical and spiritual significance. Sri Aurobindo does not tell us whether he undertook any enquiry into the psychology underlying the politico-economic hierarchies of the feudal society in Europe and why he regards them as secular and devoid of any ethical and spiritual significance. Sri Aurobindo refers to the history of Islamic civilisation to buttress the point that without an imposed uniformity the emergence of nations proves very difficult and is a long time-consuming process. The absence of a compelling social hierarchy and the presence of a strong sense of equality and brotherhood in the early Islamic civilisation account for its failure to evolve any nation-unit even after the disruption of the empire of the Caliphs. Islamic nationalism is a very modern development.[7] Sultan Abdul

Hamid, the Ottoman Emperor, tried to crush the sentiment by the cry of pan-Islamism. The Young Turks, who managed to overthrow imperial despotism in 1908, abandoned the idea of establishing the empire of Islam and wanted to fuse all the Arab nationalities in a common Ottoman nation. The Young Turks failed, but they tried to impose the Turkish language and pan-Turania-nism in place of pan-Islamism. After the First World War the Arab countries became the mandated territories of France and Britain. And that laid the foundation of what we see today of Arab nationalism. Even in the recent past we witnessed several abortive attempts to bring together different Arab countries under the common banner of Arab nationalism.

In the second stage of the development of the nation-unit the relaxed rigours of the social hierarchy paved the way for the establishment of a strong political and administrative unity. The part played by a powerful kingship in the evolution of the nation type is indeed very important. The Plantagenets and the Tudors in England, the Capets and their successors in France, the House of Castile in Spain and the Romanoffs and their predecessors in Russia provided the nuclei around which the concerned nations grew and attained their maturity. Monarchical absolutism proves undoubtedly successful in evolving a robust organisation, but the power-concentration stringency and uniformity which accompany it turn out to be inconsistent with liberty and free variation. The monolithic character of kingship in the second stage of the development of the nation-unit exhibits some of the worst features of the ancient empires.

The third stage of development appears as a reaction to and protest against these defects. The monarchical state tends to crush or subordinate the autonomy and privileges of the church, rob the aristocracy of its liberties, use the bourgeoisie against the nobles and then tries to minimise civil liberties. The common man has no liberties at all. Strong policies and measures are tolerated or allowed to continue so long as the people feel their necessity. As soon as they realise the unjust character of absolute monarchy, they become impatient to get rid of it. In its struggle against the feudal and spiritual aristocracy, the monarchy backs the bourgeoisie and in the course of doing so first weakens and ultimately loses its own foundation. The rise of the bourgeoisie and the fall of absolute monarchy mark the birth of a new age. The brain-child of the revolution is liberty. The highest of all ideals, the ideal of fraternity, is revived and, for the first time, mankind is told by a sincere voice to realise its inner oneness.

## The Psychological and the Institutional Aspects of the Human Aggregates

Sri Aurobindo thinks that the method followed generally by statesmen, politicians and people to build up the nation-unit has remained, even up to our own times, more or less external. This admission of Sri Aurobindo is particularly significant in the context of his persistent inclination to give a *psychological interpretation* to a phase of history which is satisfactorily explainable in terms of *institutional* conflict and development. He writes:

> The external method tries always to mould the psychological condition of men into changed forms and habits under the pressure of circumstances and institutions rather than by the direct creation of a new psychological condition which would, on the contrary, develop freely and flexibly its own appropriate and serviceable social forms.[8]

It is very clear from what Sri Aurobindo says that the ideal as well as the most durable method of formation of the nation-unit is psychological or subjective in character. Unless our social institutions are formed and transformed according to our psychological needs, their existence and function instead of promoting the growth of nation-unit prove to be a sort of fetter to the realisation of their ideal unity. The institutional products of the external method never answer the psychological or spiritual demands of developing human nature. Consequently, this leads to an imbalance between what we really are and our institutional environment. It is true that the external method may directly help us for the time being to build up an institution or organisation, but the ideal unity, both national and international, is much more than a mere institution. It is a living soul. Rightly understood nation or society 'essentially *is* a soul rather than *has* one'.[9] Psychological unity is not a mere attribute but the very substance of the nationhood. This nation-soul has to be realised directly and subjectively and not through external circumstances and the institutional framework, adopting the dubious and devious method of trial-and-error.

At this stage Sri Aurobindo draws an important distinction between the national ego and the nation-soul. The subjective age of the human cycle is marked by an increasing consciousness of the people. The subjective turn of the nation by itself is not enough for its sound development along correct lines. If the external method fails to get us to the nation-soul, the subjective method, unless it is correctly understood and applied, encourages an unwelcome kind of national egoism or chauvinism.

Sri Aurobindo speaks of two forms of subjectivism, true and false. True subjectivism makes us conscious of the psychical basis of our national unity, its historical genesis and growth, environment and inner deficiencies, and also of the means necessary to make them good from within. National egoism often encourages states facing internal difficulties or deficiencies to embark upon a career of external conquest. National egoism then tends to degenerate into a form of aggressive imperialism.[10] A truly subjective nation first looks within and tries to make good its defects or deficiencies utilising and subtilising its internal resources. It also solicits the free cooperation of its neighbouring nations. Sri Aurobindo observes, 'only that which lives in its own self-existence can endure'.[11] The aggressive and egoist nation may achieve some spectacular successes within a short period of time, quickly exhausting its vital powers, and is likely to die an early but natural death. Any great achievement or victory of lasting importance demands of us a lot of hardship, sacrifice and realisation of the inner law and unity of consciousness.

The right type of nationalism has to be established on the basis of true subjectivism and the realisation of our inner unity and solidarity with the people of other countries. We live not merely for our own selves; we have a secret unity with the whole of humanity. Of this profound truth most of us have a very vague idea. Practically there are very few among us who could see clearly the relation between self-existence and our secret unity with fellow human beings. What is true in our individual life is also true in the sphere of national life. Unless a nation can properly grasp the significance of *self-existence* and the spiritual character of unity, its practice of nationalism in politics is likely to create a lot of problems. Self-existence does not mean self-expansion at the expense of other selves. The ego-consciousness of a nation is not to be confused with its self-consciousness. Nazi Germany ignored this basic truth. And the type of nationalism it advocated and practised precipitated a global crisis. The egoistic self-vision of the aggressive nationalistic states creates certain problems. First, in order to make the individual efficient he is completely subordinated to the state. Secondly, the unquestioned submission of the individual to the state is said to be an ethical and divine duty. And, thirdly, the elimination of the unfit and the assimilation of the less fit are claimed to be in accordance with the principle of natural justice.[12]

This type of nationalism develops two important characteristics—the cult of the state and the cult of international egoism. This apocalyptic theory has been advocated, among others, by Fichte, Hegel, Treitschke and practised by Bismarck and Hitler. Sri Aurobindo, an ardent advocate of nationalism based on peace and spiritual unity, rejects this aggressive and perverse form of nationalism, which, according to him, crushes individual liberty and the freedom of the weak nations. He writes: 'The theory of inferior and decadent races was loudly proclaimed by other than German thinkers and has governed, with whatever assuaging scruples, the general practice of military domination and commercial exploitation of the weak by the strong.'[13]

The aggressive model of German nationalism has so deeply impressed some Western scholars that they are inclined to think that nationalism, whatever might be the difference in the attending circumstances of origin and development, is bound to assume the German characteristics sooner or later. The disastrous Nazi experiment has often been cited as a conclusive and an irrefutable proof of their theory.

## From Nationalism to Patriotism and Internationalism: The Marxist View and Sri Aurobindo

The Marxist believes that capitalism, being itself a decaying force, bourgeois-nationalism, imperialism, or whatever is parasitic upon it, is bound to decay and disappear. He prophesies the inevitable defeat of imperialism and the victory of internationalism. And to him it is merely a matter of course or question of time. Whether in the face of the modern developments in the world this theory of Marx is tenable is, of course, a different issue. The Marxist substitute for nationalism is *patriotism.* While the nationalist's vision is blinded by narrow class interests, the patriot, guided by the true and objective consciousness of the proletariat, can rise above the petty sectarianism of the bourgeoisie and refuse to identify himself with it. The nationalist's attitude is: 'Right or wrong, my nation.' The Marxist patriot's attitude is: 'If right, my Fatherland, but if wrong, I'll be with the toiling masses of the world.' It is only in this context that one has to understand the Communist view of patriotism *and* internationalism.

It may also be noted that the Marxist has in the recent past backslided from his previous attitude towards nationalism and Fatherland or Motherland. M.N. Pokrovsky, the most important of the early Marxist historians, denounced nationalism as a bourgeois device and asked fellow historians not to tolerate such bourgeois sentiments as nationalism and patriotism. But later on the notions of Soviet patriotism and the socialist Fatherland, supported by Stalin, gained respect. The war against Germany became known as the 'Holy War', and the 'Great War of the Motherland'. The orthodox Marxist is bound to feel uncomfortable because of the pro-nationalist propensity clearly evident in some socialist countries. Theoretically committed to proletarian internationalism and to the repudiation of nationalism, he finds it difficult in practice to define unequivocally his attitude towards the deep-rooted sentiments and forces associated with nationalism. He finds it impossible not to reckon with the fact of national differentiation. He refers to Lenin in this connection who said: 'One cannot refuse to recognise what is, one is forced to recognise it.' It is only after referring to the authority of a Lenin, Stalin, or Mao Tse-tung that he feels justified in according recognition to the peculiarities and sensibilities of different nations. Then he hastens to add as a sort of defence that the Marxist's recognition of nationalism is at once consistent and highly practical, serves the purpose of transition and facilitates the triumph of socialism. Oscar Janowsky writes:

> Bolshevik theory did not regard nationalism as an end in itself. It was neither rooted in human nature, nor inherently desirable, nor necessarily ineradicable. A product of historical evolution, nationalism flowered in the competitive era of the bourgeoisie, and would wither when the quality of all peoples had been achieved under socialism.[14]

One may not accept the Marxist theory of nationalism and internationalism and the critic may even point out the gap between his theoretical propositions and practical position, but that must not make one blind to the dangers and deformities mixed up with the forces of nationalism and the rationale of the Marxist's critique of nationalism.[15]

Sri Aurobindo's view on the matter seems to be very interesting and instructive. He is quite aware of the dangers of nationalism and the sufferings experienced by the people during the formative period of the nation. He also takes note of the unfortunate incompatibility between the *existing* forms of nationalism and the ideal of international unification. He writes: 'Undoubtedly, nationalism is a more powerful obstacle to farther unification than was the separativeness of the old pettier and less firmly self-conscious groupings which preceded the developed nation-State.'[16] He thinks that the relation between the true form of nationalism and internationalism is not antithetical, on the contrary, the desired and durable form of internationalism will emerge not by suppression but through the fulfilment of nationalism. It is here that the difference between Marx and Sri Aurobindo on the question of nationalism and internationalism assumes its most significant form. Sri Aurobindo takes pains to point out that the dangers associated with the existing forms of nationalism are not necessarily inherent in it. These dangers are there because people have not yet been successful in discovering the true psychological unity of the nation. Unfortunately, most of them take nationalism in the narrow sense of national egoism. This purely negative side of nationalism tends to separate and isolate one nation from other nations, creates an atmosphere of mutual distrust and suspicion, and leads it to a striving for superiority and domination. Consequently, the positive side of nationalism which seeks expression in the striving for national solidarity and freedom is often ignored and neglected. National solidarity is defeated by an unfortunate xenophobia and ugly racialism. But all these things are due to the practical deformity or perversion of nationalism and not due to nationalism itself. Nationalism, rightly understood, i.e., based on a true psychological unity of the people, has no necessary relation with the rise of imperialism.

Not only that. Sri Aurobindo goes a step forward. He claims that nationalism or patriotism, rightly understood, is not only consistent with socialism and internationalism but also a necessary step towards those ends. He writes:

> Patriotism is only a phase of that universal brotherhood, which humanity aims at. It is only the consideration of degree that puts patriotism second to the sentiment of universal love. The culture of heart cannot be finished with one single attempt. It has to undergo processes of varied degrees of completeness and depth. One cannot love all men alike and that at the very first stage of cultivating the social sentiments. We must rise by degrees.

Then he refers to the deliberations of the Stuttgart Socialistic Conference which considered the question whether socialism is consistent with or excludes patriotism. As for himself Sri Aurobindo has no doubt in his mind that socialism, which 'seeks to free human society from the tyranny of wealth' and aims to ensure equality of opportunities and conveniences of life for all the members of society, is not inconsistent with the object of nationalism. He observes:

> Patriotism which aims at the amelioration of the condition of the society in which we live, move and have our being cannot conflict with the object which socialism seeks to achieve . . . freedom is the end of both patriotism

and socialism. The all round well-being of man is the aspiration of both.[17]

Sri Aurobindo is a gradualist, an evolutionist. He does not believe that larger human aggregates or unities can be achieved suddenly by force or revolution. Internationalism in its genuine and durable form will emerge out of nationalism only when it fulfils its historical mission. Unless we can cultivate the larger sympathies and affections in our mind, our theoretical profession for internationalism will go ill with our practical actions. Fulfilled nationalism leads to internationalism, some sort of a world-union. And it has nothing to do with imperialism, which is an artificial political monstrosity created by gunfire and sword-edge. By implication Sri Aurobindo rejects the Marxist view that nationalism necessarily leads to some form of imperialism.

Obviously this view of Sri Aurobindo is not acceptable to the Marxist. For, he thinks that the most economically powerful class of the nation (if for no other reason, only in order to avoid its own early disintegration) requires expansion beyond the national territory. And that marks the beginning of imperialism. The empire proves to be both the cradle and the grave of the nation. Sri Aurobindo points out that imperial unity is basically artificial, because there is no common psychological consciousness underlying it, and its basis is physical power. But even then the empire has made its contribution to the formation and growth of nation-units and national unity. Imperial suppression and domination make the sleeping countries conscious of their national unity. Both pan-Germanism and pan-Slavism owe their origin, besides other factors, to the Napoleonic invasion and the havoc caused by it.

## Foundation and Character of Nationalism

Thinkers are not unanimous about the true basis and character of nationalism. Some, like Herder and Hegel, believe that nationalism is primarily cultural and only incidentally political. Toynbee particularly emphasises the importance of language in the formation of the nation.[18] Mao Tse-tung claims that the culture of the new democracy is national in character. 'China's culture should have its own form, the national form. The national form, plus the new democratic content, is our new culture today.' He also characterises this culture as scientific and popular. He writes: 'This national, scientific, and popular culture is the anti-imperialist, anti-feudal culture of the people, the culture of New Democracy, the culture of New San Min Chi I, the culture of the Chinese Nation.'[19] Some writers like Montesquieu exaggerate the influence of climate on the process of nation formation. Herder and Hume, among others, have rightly contested this view. And it has been rejected by human geographers later on. The romanticist lays emphasis on the organic and historical characteristics of the nation. C. D. Gobineau and H. S. Chamberlain are the champions of racial nationalism. The importance of common language and common territory have been generally acknowledged as the two basic factors responsible for the formation and growth of nationalism. While some thinkers stress the subjective aspect of nationalism, others highlight the objective and institutional character of it. Hans Kohn says: 'Nationalism is first and foremost a state of mind, an act of consciousness.' The Marxist points out that nationalism, although expressive of the inadequate consciousness of the bourgeoisie, is firmly grounded in the capitalist mode of production, the class-ridden society.

It is not easy to state clearly what precisely the term nationalism designates. Nor is it easy to neatly classify or categorise the activities, attitudes, assumptions and phenomena associated with nationalism. Various typologies and taxonomies of nationalism have been offered by different thinkers. Historians have offered *historical* taxonomies. Referring to the history of Europe it has been said that from 1815 to date we observe four phases, namely, *integrative* (1815–1871), *disruptive* (1871–1900), *aggressive* (1900–1945), and *contemporary* or *consolidative* (1945 to date). Obviously outside Europe this taxonomy has little application or relevance. For example, when Europe was passing through its disruptive phase India and China were in their integrative phase.

Carlton Hayes advocates a sixfold *ideological* taxonomy—*humanitarian* (Bolingbroke, Rousseau and Herder), *Jacobin* (Robespierre, etc.), *liberal* (Bentham, etc.), *traditional* (Burke, Schlegel, etc.), *economic-protectionist* and *integral-totalitarian.*[20] Analysis reveals that this typology is not purely ideological. It is a mixed bag of ideology and sociology. Moreover, these ideological types are not necessarily exclusive. There are some national movements, pan-Islamism and Ba'athism, for example, in which different strands of ideology—traditional, Jacobin and integral—are mixed up.

Hans Kohn has offered us a *geographical* typology. He draws a distinction between *Eastern* and *Western* nationalism. He incorporates chronological, intellectual and sociological elements in his otherwise geographical typology. In Western (i.e., English, North American, French, Dutch and Swiss) nationalism of the seventeenth and nineteenth centuries he notes the political aspirations of the rising *middle classes* and the spirit of the Renaissance. The nationalists of these countries were rationalist, pluralist, optimistic, and inspired by the Enlightenment's ideal of endless progress.[21] 'Eastern' nationalism (i.e., Central and Eastern Europe, and Asia) of the nineteenth century was more or less a cultural movement, sometimes reformist and sometimes revivalist, of the lower aristocracy and the masses. It was characterised by two things, an emotional and authoritarian consciousness of cultural inferiority in comparison with the educationally and industrially advanced West, and a Messianic sense of mission. This typology, however, does not represent the true situation obtaining in nineteenth century Europe and Asia. One may point out, for example, that socially backward Western countries like Spain and Ireland belonged to the 'Eastern' type of nationalism as defined by Kohn. Secondly, one is not clear where the Latin American and the developing countries of Africa are to be placed in the scheme of Kohn's classification of nationalism. Thirdly, it is perhaps not correct to suggest that in all cases of 'Eastern' nationalist movements the masses had a say or a significant role. Finally, this sort of omnibus and unwieldy classification nearly defeats the very purpose of classification itself.

The brief taxonomy offered by Seton-Watson in terms of *movement* seems to be more satisfactory.[22] He speaks of three types of nationalist movements—*independence-seeking*, *irredentist* and *nation-building*. A free and satisfied nation, according to him, does not need to be nationalist. By implication he says that a nationalist movement has only a means-value. This is perhaps partly true. After the achievement of independence only a few nations are historically found to remain interested in reviving the nationalist sentiments in the form of a movement. The few which do so are either territorially dissatisfied or to cope with some internal difficulties feel the necessity of diverting the popular attention and interest to some external issue often artificially cooked up. It is of course true that the nationalist sentiments may be fruitfully exploited also for the internal development of the country. All these contingencies and characteristics have been taken into account by Seton-Watson in the formulation of his taxonomy. But it is not easy to identify clearly the movements to be subsumed under the type of *nation-building*, because some secessionist and even accretionist movements are often claimed to be conducive to nation-building. However, this analytic scheme is free from the usual difficulties of the highly general approach of historical, geographical and ideological taxonomies.

Anthony Smith has worked out an elaborate *sociological* taxonomy of nationalist movements. He classifies nationalism firstly in terms of *movement* and applies two divergent sets of criteria, *formal* or external, and *substantive* or internal. The first set is intended to assess the degree of *intensity* of the *aims* and *achievements* of nationalist movements. The second set is concerned to identify the types of situations and assumptions which account for those aims. In terms of *intensity* the nationalisms may be graded as *primitive*, *developed* and *current*. *Developed* and *primitive* nationalisms may be further subdivided, in terms of the variable *achievement*, into *failed* and *successful*. Smith finds it difficult to predict the outcome of the *current* nationalist movements as obtaining in India and some Arab countries, for example. Although the initial aims of these movements are found to be liberation, integration or consolidation, the character of their final achievement, being dependent on various external and contingent factors, is more or less uncertain. Smith says, ' the " formal " criterion of achievement of independence is the province of the historian '.[23] The sociological taxonomy of Smith is very comprehensive and complex.

But Sri Aurobindo works with a very simple *descriptive* classification of nationalism. He classifies nationalisms under two types, *subjective* and *objective*. Then he identifies another sub-type within the subjective type, viz., *objectively subjective*. The objectivist tries to explain nationalism in terms of some economic, ethnic or religious factors. This sort of institutional approach does not commend itself to Sri Aurobindo. He produces several counter-examples to this type of theories of nationalism. He points out, first, that in France three different languages are spoken; secondly, Austria was a congeries of races and languages; thirdly, the people of Finland who speak the Swedish language have formed a different nation; and, finally, as we all know, in spite of the linguistic, racial and religious differences, we have succeeded in India in forming one nation. The nation-idea, according to him, arises from circumstances, from environmental evolution; it arises not from a vital but from a geographical and historical necessity. While the family, the clan and the tribe ideas grow out of a primary vital need and easily acquire the psychological motive-forces necessary for their institutional transformation, the nation-idea evolves out of a secondary or even tertiary necessity resulting from circumstances and environment and not from our vital nature, and, as a consequence of that, it had to rely on the physical force, the power of the king or the conquering nation, for converting itself into a State. Whatever might be the contribution of the circumstantial factors to the growth of the nation idea, the basic factor is psychological or spiritual. If the psychological or soul factor is missing, then there is no guarantee of the durability of the nation. 'Without it, what circumstances have created, circumstances easily will destroy.'[24]

Sri Aurobindo does not deny the historical fact that the political character of nations has hitherto rested on an almost entirely objective, i.e., geographical, commercial and military, basis. This physical and vital basis was good enough for supporting the smaller aggregates like clan and tribe. But for the foundation and durability of the nation idea, a stronger and deeper psychological basis is necessary. Sri Aurobindo writes:

> Nationhood found itself partly on (a geographical) association, partly on others which accentuate it, common interests, community of languages community of culture, and all these in unison have evolved a psychological idea, a psychological unity, which finds expression in the idea of nationalism .... The new principle (of self-determination), that of the right of every natural grouping which feels its own separateness to choose its own status and partnerships, makes a clean sweep of these vital and physical grounds and substitutes purely psychological principles of free will and free choice as against the claims of political and economic necessity. Or rather, the vital and physical grounds of grouping are only to be held valid when they receive the psychological sanction and are to be found themselves upon it.[25]

The objectivist understanding and explanation of the nation idea is bound to be superficial. For it relies almost exclusively on the visible institutional signs of unity, ignoring altogether the psychological cohesive force which holds the institutional factors together, sustains and nourishes them. Sri Aurobindo thinks that the realisation of the inadequacy of the objectivist idea of nationalism has led some thinkers to develop a sort of false subjectivism or what he calls objective subjectivism. Instead of identifying the nation in terms of its profound psychological character the objective subjectivist confuses it with its physical and vital aspects and superficialities. If the nation identifies itself with its physical body (territory), vital powers (commercial and military) and superficial ego (as represented by the industrial and military elites and the easily gullible public opinion), it is not possible for it to develop a pacific-democratic character and a durable form. The objective method of self-realisation adopted by the nation prevents it from getting to the depth of its own spiritual unity.

National egoism, like the egoism of the vital man, desires a total self-satisfaction, intensive and extensive or expansive. Every national ego wants its own cultural enrichment, more political and economic power, and the right of self-determination. But some national egos are interested in something more than this intensive self-satisfaction; they want other nations to accept their culture, to come under their rule or at least under their influence, political or economic. This national egoism tends to develop into imperialism unless this evil trend is resisted by the egoism of other nations. And that leads to war. War is the institutional expression of the psychological conflict between two national egos. The last two World Wars may quite plausibly be explained in terms of a conflict between some very powerful egoistic nations.[26]

Sri Aurobindo would treat the Marxist idea of nation as an example of the objectivist theory of nationalism, because it relies too heavily on economic-institutional factors and regards the psychological aspect as a mere parasite on the former. He also notes that this objectivist tendency is very common among the proponents of nationalism. He has his own explanation of this.

Modern nationalism originated in Europe. The technologically and commercially advanced European nations left the ports of Europe in search of new continents and colonies, reached different parts of the world, and established their rule by force, seeking an extensive self-satisfaction. They wanted to dominate the conquered countries not only militarily and administratively but also culturally. The motive of economic exploitation was of course present. But this domination and exploitation resulted in an unintended development. Foreign rule and circumstantial pressure roused a sense of unity in the mind of the conquered peoples. When the objectivist says that the sense of unity was a creation of foreign domination Sri Aurobindo objects. According to him, if national consciousness was not already present in the soul of the nation, it could not be roused or still less be fostered from without by physical force and circumstantial pressure. Over-impressed by the historical association and institutional factors responsible for the growth of nationalism, the objectivist misses the very soul factor of the nation idea. Sri Aurobindo concedes that this typical approach of the objectivist, of the empirical historian and sociologist, is quite natural and understandable, but he insists at the same time that it is not correct and defensible. We must not confuse the real ' cause ' or source of nationalism with its attending conditions and institutional factors.

Nation is *essentially* spiritual in its origin and character. Even when it is said that national unity is psychological in character, the term *psychological* is to be understood as a synonym of *spiritual*. We are often wrong in regarding political unity as national unity, in taking the idea of state as the idea of nation, and this is mainly due to our external or institutional approach to the activities, attitudes and assumptions associated with nationalism. In a metaphysical vein Sri Aurobindo affirms that the nations of the world are different manifestations of an indivisible spiritual principle, the *Virata Purusha*, the Great

Being. Unaware of this fundamental metaphysical-spiritual foundation of nations, we are prone to identify it with its institutional accessaries, adjuncts and associations. And as a result of that many of us assess or criticise nationalism in terms of the success or failure of those incidental institutional features. The misuse of the idea of nationalism by great powers, says Sri Aurobindo, is no argument against its right use. Referring to Germany's experiment with nationalism he observes that we must avoid it. ' We must look beyond the red mist of blood of the War and the dark fuliginous confusion and chaos which now oppress the world to see why and where was the failure.' We cannot get out of the confusion and chaos created by egoistic nationalism unless we succeed in identifying the spiritual origin and unity of nation. He writes:

> The soul of man or nation is something more and diviner than (Body and Force); it is greater than its instruments and cannot be shut up in a physical, a vital, a mental or a temperamental formula. So to confine it, even though the false social formation be embodied in the armour-plated social body of a huge collective human dinosaurus, can only stifle the growth of the inner Reality and end in decay or the extinction that overtakes all that is unplastic and unadaptable.[27]

Those who, like Laski and Kedourie, always speak of the dark aspect of nationalism and think that it is an essential nature of nationalism seem to have ignored the fact that there are many pro-nationalist thinkers who are quite alive to this danger of nationalism. Rabindranath Tagore, the great poet and a contemporary and an admirer of Sri Aurobindo, was also highly critical of the egoistic trend of nationalism. He was sorry to find that the liberal connotation of nationalism was almost forgotten and that its place was being taken by some form of chauvinism and parochialism. True national unity cannot be established on the basis of racial unity or economic uniformity or political power. 'The spiritual unity', on which it stands, Tagore observes, is to be realised and preached by ' men of thought and power '.[28] There is no inherent incompatibility between nationalism and internationalism. On the contrary, they are complementary. Internationalism without nationalism is an empty abstraction or a utopian dream, and nationalism without internationalism is blind or lacking in vision.

We have observed before that the empire is both the cradle and the grave of the nation. Most of the nations of the world owe their nationhood to some imperial or foreign domination. Sri Aurobindo points out that ' there is none of the modern nations in Europe which has not had to pass through a phase more or less prolonged, more or less complete, of foreign domination in order to realise its nationality '.[29] With reference to the role of British domination of India Marx himself observes that it has proved in a way ' regenerative '.[30] Whatever might be the unintended benefits which accrued to the colonies due to imperial domination and exploitation, the relation between the two cannot be cordial and permanent, for it is not based on freedom and choice. The empire is artificial and political, a creation of gun and sword, and having no spiritual basis of its own, is bound to perish. 'Empires are . . . perishable political units; the nation is immortal.'[31] The empire has no higher and other positive aims than exploitation and expropriation of the colonial people. If in the process of its economic exploitation, it sharpens the contradictions in its politics and economy or unifies the different sections of the people of the impoverished colony, that is certainly unintended and due to circumstances beyond its control.

Sri Aurobindo does not totally rule out the theoretical possibility of self-transformation of an imperial aggregate into a psychological unity. But, then, he points out, the basis of unity ceases to be domination and exploitation, and it must be mutual respect for freedom, independence and equality. In that case imperial unity turns out to be a voluntary federation of free nations. In this connection Sri Aurobindo refers to the history of England, Scotland and Wales. Federal unity may have an imperial past, but if it wants to survive and become permanent it has to discover a deeper and more abiding principle of unity. For an artificial aggregate is merely 'a transient device without any possible stable permanence' and only the true psychological unity lasts, grows, and contributes to the growth of the world-union.

# 8

# The State and the Individual

## Two Basic Tendencies of Human Nature and Society: Individualistic and Collectivistic

Two deep-rooted tendencies are observed in human society, one individualist and the other collectivist. From the academic controversy between the proponents of these two extremes one might think that these tendencies are antagonistic, opposed to each other. But a careful analysis reveals, as we have observed before, that an individual cannot be human without society and society is an empty abstraction without human beings. The true individual is unique notwithstanding his social identity and plural affiliations. It is, to quote Bosanquet, like ' a case of a law, or term of a connection ' and not like an atom of a material aggregate.[1] The individual could not be what he is and becomes but for the integral character of his relation to society. He grows or decays in society, depending on his ability or inability to utilise and subtilise the social forces and influences in and around him.

The individual, strictly speaking, cannot live alone. His apparent loneliness or solitude is silently animated and disturbed by invisible social influences. His life is intimately related to that of society. Not only factually but also purposively the individual and the collectivity are deeply related. Consequently when either of these two takes an egoistic view of itself and tries to enrich itself at the cost of the other, problems and conflicts start raising their heads.

At a pre-reflective level man seems to be a house divided against itself. His individualistic identity is always there, indefinite but unmistakable. He is like a growing god. He can grow indefinitely; but he needs, up to a point, a powerful external support to shape, guide and sustain his growth. The State answers that need. And it reflects the collectivist tendency which is perpetually working in human nature. Since the social relations in which man is obliged to live and grow are an essential part of his own being, man can ignore his relation with others only at his own peril. In other words, man is objectively required to maintain his relationship with his fellow human beings. He needs an institution, a machinery, to do this job for him. The State is the ultimate result. He needs the State but the individuality of his being must not be allowed to be destroyed by an irrational State. The State must not be vested with the power which, under the given circumstances, it would not be able to exercise rationally. The desired degree of harmony cannot be achieved in the field of inter-individual relationship without empowering an association, in this case the State, to look after it and regulate the conduct of individuals in question. The comprehensive character and power of the State entails some restraints upon individual action and choice. The freedom of the individual is not conceptually inconsistent with the power of the State. One cannot decide *a priori* the rational limit either to the freedom of the individual or to the power of the State.[2]

Broadly speaking, there are two different ways of defining the relation between *individual* freedom and *State* power. Positively speaking, individual freedom should be in principle unabridged and unrestricted. Since the potentiality of a human being is infinite, any restriction that we impose on him, however justifiable practically it might be, is inconsistent with the basic *principle* of man's essential being and the requirements of his endless development. Negatively speaking, one might say with Mill that ' the only purpose for which power can be rightfully exercised over any member of a civilised community, against his will, is to prevent harm to others '.[3] So long as the possibility of this harm is there, the role of power, however unwelcome it might be from the pure anarchical point of view, cannot be ruled out. Power in itself is not bad or unethical. The question is what sort of power we are thinking about. Even political power is not inherently unjustifiable or unethical. The liberal arguments in support of the minimal use of power and the maximal freedom of the individual are all based on an untenable assumption that every individual *qua* individual has the power to prevent the harm which may possibly be inflicted upon him by his fellow human beings. The negative utilitarian insists on *prevention of harm* both as the limiting condition and also as the defining character of State power. But there are others who think that the *promotion of collective welfare* should be accepted as the end of the rightful and rational exercise of State power. While *promotion* is a positive concept, *prevention* is a negative one. The preventionist is primarily interested in the uninterfered growth of the individual. The promotionist thinks that the State's primary responsibility is to provide the institutional conditions under which the individual would find adequate scope for the development of his personality. The preventionist is generally found to be an individualist and the promotionist a collectivist or socialist.

The movements of these two basic tendencies is dialectical in character. In the course of their cyclical progress these two tendencies exhibit a progressive mutual comprehension resulting in the establishment of larger human unities. Each of these two tendencies stands for certain institutional features and qualities. The collectivist tendency stands for authority, law, organisation, efficiency and the like, and the individualist one for freedom, perfection, variation, justice and so on. The interplay of these two basic human and historical forces may well account for all the past human aggregates, large and small, their formation, enlargement and gradual transformation. But it seems that human history has not yet succeeded in evolving a human aggregate in which these two tendencies could arrive at a permanent and ideal harmony which is absolutely necessary for perpetual peace and the sustained growth of human society.

## Man, Nation and State

The nation is said to be the latest historical product of the strife between the self-liberating individual (*vyaṣṭi*) and the all-engrossing collectivity (*samaṣṭi*). In the history of human aggregates it is observed that greater emphasis has always been laid in varying degrees, on the side of the collectivity and authority. The importance of variation and freedom has not been adequately recognised. The centrifugal tendency of collectivism has found its consummation in the idea of the all-engrossing state.[4]

Sri Aurobindo's critique of what he calls the cult of the State is to be understood in the context of his concept of man. Man is both individual and social at the same time. Individuality and social nature are two indivisible aspects of his being. Man is of course individual. And society is also individual. But there is a difference in the degree of the concreteness or abstractness of their individuality. Uniqueness, purposiveness or end-consciousness, and consciousness or, one might even rightfully insist, self-consciousness are intimately connected with the concept of individuality. All these characteristics of individuality are clearly found in man. It is claimed that all these characteristics are also present in society in a non-manifest form. Society, says Hegel, is an expression of the Objective Spirit. Sri Aurobindo claims that every society has its soul, working continuously underneath its different institutions and organisations holding them together and lending them a definite character. When man grows to full manhood and develops his highest potentiality, a sort of godhood, his society rewards him with bliss. Men seek in society a harmonious fulfilment of all their powers, now divided by instinct and passion in different possibilities, parts and groups of society. Unless they rise above passion and instinct and realise the spiritual unity or Self of society, they cannot experience ' the light of the integral self-existence '.

The purposiveness and self-consciousness of man are not adequately recognised by or in the State. According to Sri Aurobindo, the State is a ' soulless machine '. In this respect his view is significantly different from philosophical idealists like Hegel and Bosanquet. To Sri Aurobindo the idea of the nation is far more basic than the idea of the State. If the State is not based on nationality, it is bound to be artificial, mechanical and, therefore, perishable. Sri Aurobindo does not harp too much on the concept of the nation-state. He is quite conscious of its dangerous totalitarian past implications and possible ramifications. His idea is different. He thinks that the nation is immortal and bound to survive temporary political calamities. Given favourable conditions, he believes that every nation will be able to discover its own soul and establish its appropriate political structure, the state-apparatus. The State is a mere power-apparatus. He criticises the advocates of Statism who put the idea of the State above everything else and accuses them of a misplaced concreteness. There *is* a nation-soul, but nothing like a State-soul.

One may not accept Sri Aurobindo's view of the nation-soul or group-soul. Modern philosophers are out to discard what they call the Cartesian myth, the myth of the ghost, i.e., soul, in the machine, i.e., human body.[5] Psychological and logical behaviourists have gone to the extent of dispensing altogether with the idea of the disembodied soul. Sri Aurobindo's concept of nation-soul may not find favour with the professional philosophers, who believe and argue that the concepts of purpose, self-consciousness, and the like may well be explained without referring to our using the concept of soul.[6] When Sri Aurobindo speaks of the soul of a nation, there is no doubt that he really believes in its metaphysical existence. To me it is a metaphysical concept, serving a theoretical purpose, enabling us to organise or put together some institutional characters and functions in a definite and intelligible way. A metaphysical concept is empirically significant and not empty if its use could bring about some ascertainable difference in the organisation of our (in this case social) experience.

The main point of Sri Aurobindo's argument seems to me very important. And it is this. We cannot decide *a priori* the ideal type of the collective life, unless we are clear about the true character and purpose of the individual human life. Man is unique. He should be studied first as man, i.e., directly, and only thereafter can we profitably look into him through the changing features of his social, political and economic life. In other words, the institutional or objective approach must be of secondary importance in our study of man. Any value-judgement of the collective life must be based on the prior understanding of the basic demands and necessities of the human nature. Unless we know the basic necessities, both material and spiritual, of man, we cannot say in which type of collective life he would be happy. Nobody in his senses would deny the importance of authority, law, security, organisation and the other characteristics of collective life. But the question is what will be their impact on the individual human being, the dynamo of social dynamism. If these otherwise necessary institutional aspects of the collective life do not help him to be more perfect and happy but constrain or coerce him instead and do not promote free co-operation in the sphere of collective life, their existence turns out to be a positive hindrance to the growth of human personality.

True, man is essentially a mental being. But that does not describe the whole of his complex nature. Corresponding to the double motive of Nature's working in man we find two distinct aspects of his personality. On the one hand he creates, controls and constantly recreates himself in new, larger and, whenever possible, better forms. On the other hand, he also tries to conserve, modify and recreate himself in accordance with the demands and challenges of his natural and social environment. In other words, there is a movement in his being which is individual in character, and there is a larger movement which comprises not only the individual man but also other human beings and their multiple interactions between themselves, on the one hand, and society and Nature, on the other. The plain truth of life is this. Man cannot grow in isolation from the rest in a vacuum. Here lies the importance and necessity of his race, class, society and other group affiliations, through which he realises his higher potentialities. The interplay between the powers of man and the forces of society is to their mutual advantage. In the process man enriches himself and also the life of the large economic, social or political group to which he belongs. 'In modern times this society is the nation.'[7]

One may look at the broader implications of this point. When man enriches his national life, he also objectively improves the total life of humanity. His community or society being an integral part of humanity he cannot do any real good to his own society without bringing about some change in humanity at large. The subjection of man to his environment and group does not stand in his way to work for the good of the human race as a whole. Our care and concern for the suffering people of other countries and communities, whom we perhaps will never see in our life but with whom we are bound by an invisible bond of larger sympathies, unmistakably indicate our international or transcendental character.

Man is not immediately related to humanity. The community stands as an intermediary link and value between the individual and humanity. True, man's social relation or group affiliation is very basic. But that does not stand in the way of his quest for universal humanity. On the contrary, it shapes and helps him achieve that goal.

> Still the absolute claim of the community, the society or the nation to make its growth, perfection, greatness, the sole object of human life are to exist for itself alone as against the individual and the rest of humanity, to take arbitrary position of the one and make the hostile assertion of itself against the other, whether defensive or offensive, the law of its action in the world—and not, as it unfortunately is, a temporary necessity,—this attitude of societies, races, religions, communities, nations, empires is evidently an aberration of the human reason, quite as much as the claim of the individual to live for himself egoistically is an aberration and the deformation of a truth.[8]

Man is neither a hedgehog nor a Utopian cosmopolite. Belonging to and sustained by a community, he is always in secret touch with the humanity as a whole. But of this direct relation he may not be immediately conscious. Herein lies his need for social or community life.

For his self-enlargement or social growth man needs help from another quarter as well. He has to turn his mind not only on to his own deeper reaches, but also on other aspects of Life and Matter and material existence. The upward growth of man is preceded not only by his inward growth but also by his outward growth. Unless man wins his struggle against the forces of material existence, his outlook is bound to be distorted. A balanced growth of his being demands of him a victory against the lower forces of Nature. Unfulfilled and untransformed natural needs recoil upon man's rational and spiritual development. The double purpose of Nature in man keeps him in touch with Nature, on the one hand, and makes him aspire for the beyond, on the other.

We find in history that the individualist and collectivist tendencies have been always ascending through increasingly complex strife and fluctuations taking man forward and backward and not uniformly forward in the process of enlargement. This is how Nature works in history to give concrete shape to the ideal of human unity. Nature conserves the smaller aggregates even after they lose their apparent historical utility. That is why we find the simultaneous existence of different forms of social aggregates. Nature does it 'in order to serve her need or her passion for variety, richness, multiformity and only effaces the dividing lines or modifies the characteristics and relations sufficiently to allow of the larger unity she is creating'.[9]

This of course creates new problems. The conflicting demands of the immediate social aggregate, be it the nation or the State, on individual human nature and its inner urge for freedom are always raising some difficulties and complications. Now 'the need and interests of the small integralities and the growth of that larger whole which is to ensphere them all' raise a new set of difficulties and make the whole issue even more complicated.

The complexity and complication of the problem have a lesson to offer us, a clue to the correct understanding and solution of the problem itself. We have already observed that the social evolution of mankind is a simultaneous function of three factors—the individual, the community, and the human race. Theories have been offered and experiments undertaken in different countries emphasising exclusively the importance of the one or the other of the first two factors. But the total upshot of these theories and experiments does not seem to have justified any extreme position, individualist or collectivist. Sometimes the virtues of individualism are highlighted, sometimes those of collectivism given prominence. Sometimes people, tired of political instability and anarchy, willingly endorse or unwillingly become a partner of some form of collectivism. Sometimes people are terrified by the irrational exercise of the coercive powers of the State or Government and cry for individual liberty. History leans sometimes this way and sometimes that way. But the individual and the community, through their age-old strife and harmony, do not appear to have arrived as yet at an ideal and stable unity. The individual, however gifted he might be, cannot justifiably claim for himself an unrestricted liberty to realise his potentialities. For he has to bear in mind similar possible claims and counter-claims of other individuals and also the State's power to bring about a sort of balance and harmony between them. One might contend that both the ground and tenability of these conflicting claims are to be sought in the authority of the State. In other words, one has to concede that harmony cannot be brought about naturally, although it is claimed to be innate in human nature.

Within the framework of the relations between the individual and the community the much needed ideal of their harmony has not yet been realised. Its reason is not clear to the concerned. They do not know as yet why the individual and the community in spite of all their past efforts could not arrive at a stable and harmonious relation. To Sri Aurobindo's mind the reason seems to be their failure to realise their own deeper truth, i.e., the *essential* unity of the individual and the community with humanity as a whole. It is true that humanity as a whole has not yet been able to realise its inner consciousness at the level of organised political or even social life. Only very few of us are directly conscious of the secret operation of this ideal factor in the development of human society. The rest guess it on the ground of the repeated failures and transient character of all past human aggregates. They think that the gradual increase in the complexity and size of human aggregates is indicative of and bound to culminate in the establishment of a complete and concrete unity which may or may not be rich in diversity.

## The Clue to the Understanding of the Human Aggregates and Cultures

Sri Aurobindo thinks that most of us form our notion about the inner drift of our socio-political life on the basis of institutional and objective signs and symptoms that we come across on the surface of history. This derivative understanding of the inner drift of society, which manifests itself only very fragmentarily, is bound to be inadequate and confusing. From the opposite end, opposed to what Marx says, Sri Aurobindo proposes to turn history upside down. He insists that we must not try to understand the inner movement of history in terms of what we call objective necessities and institutional factors. For these are not really determining forces but a superficial by-product of the inner and more potent psychological and spiritual forces. The rationale of the history of human aggregates has to be gathered from these almost entirely submerged subjective forces. It is more by ' deciphering ' the symbolic mentality of a human aggregate than by analysing or scanning its conventional or typal mentality that we can get to the depth of its true character. It is on this ground that some thinkers are of the opinion that the true history of a society or nation is to be found mainly in its cultural heritage—in the arts, architecture, literature, music, painting and dance. But unfortunately most of us think uncritically that history *is* political history written on the basis of ' incontrovertible ' documents of the past. This is no doubt the most popular view but one wonders whether it is the most correct and tenable one.[10]

Thinkers also differ on the question as to whether the smaller or the larger aggregates contributed most to the growth of human culture and civilisation. According to the assessment of some, smaller aggregates proved culturally more creative and not only cradles but also rich centres of all sorts of intellectual activity. The larger socio-political aggregates like States and empires have no doubt proved very useful for the purpose of producing the material conditions of civilisation but their contribution in the field of culture is said to be a matter of opinion. ' Collective life diffusing itself in too vast spaces seems to lose intensity and productiveness.'[11] The best cultural aspects of European civilisation evolved mainly out of the smaller nations like England, France, the Netherlands, Spain and Italy, and the small states of Germany, and not from the huge mass of the Holy Roman or the Russian Empires. If we go back into the further past of the European history, we realise that modern Europe drew its inspiration at first from the religious life of the congeries of tribes of Israel and then from the Jewish nation, the Greek and Italian city-states, which were the centres and left behind the seeds of all subsequent intellectual and cultural achievements of the people of Europe.

Referring to the history of India Sri Aurobindo says that the most glorious and vigorous works of India belong to that heroic period of the country when it was divided into small kingdoms. Our civilisation and culture is said to have received its next best nourishment and contributions from the nations and kingdoms of the Pallavas, Chalukyas, Pandyas, Cholas, Cheras, etc., which were larger than their predecessors but still small in comparison with the great empires of the Mauryas, the Guptas, and the Mughals.

But the reason why, in spite of their superior cultural potentiality, these small kingdoms and nations did not survive is that they were more or less defenseless against the onslaught of larger organisations, sometimes settled civilisations and sometimes the nomadic hordes like those of Attila and Chengiz. The rise of larger socio-political aggregates is also partly due to their characteristic impermanence and internal disorder.

But it is interesting to note that permanence, orderliness and security are almost inversely related to creative activity and cultural efflorescence. The social mind, somewhat like the individual mind, has a tendency to burst forth or express itself creatively only when it is stirred and roused by some movement, revolution, or war. Otherwise, it may languish and pass through long periods of immobility and barrenness. Our objective choice appears to be very limited. The larger organisations, where we find considerable stability and security, do not provide much scope of initiative and enterprise to the individual, and the small aggregates, which otherwise encourage individual freedom, are very impermanent and weak. We have to choose between the two. Given freedom, the individual tries to exploit it to his exclusive self-interest and often to the detriment of society. He fails to see the equation between his own interest and that of society. This failure of the individual is inconsistent with the maintenance of the order and organisation of collective life. These defects of the smaller aggregates necessitated and explain the evolution of the larger aggregates—nations, kingdoms and empires.

Compared to the smaller aggregates of the past the present forms of polity are very much more organised, efficient, policed and secure. The modern State can provide considerable material amenities and prosperity to the citizen. But that can hardly be regarded as the sole criterion of a good or sane society. On the contrary, the excessive security of the outer life at the collective level often brings about a cultural decadence in the inner life of the individual. Russell remarks: 'Security is merely a refuge from fear; opportunity is the source of hope.'[12] Toynbee points out that without challenge a culture or a country does not respond and when it fails to respond its decadence or disintegration is inevitable. If the adoption of extensive security measures in economic and military affairs could save the human race from problems, crises, and disasters, perhaps the history of the revolutions and wars of the present century might have a different tale to tell us.

One is advised to remember that the general *tendency* that we come across in history in the relation between the smallness of the size of human aggregates and its creative character, on the one hand, and the bigness of the size of human aggregates and its relatively barren or decadent character, on the other, is *not* a necessary *law* of history. If the critic so desires, he may easily find exceptions to this general tendency.[13]

## Conflict and Harmony in Socio-Political Evolution

Society seems to progress through synthesis or harmony. Excesses in the movement either of individualism or collectivism are corrected by more or less successful adjustments and moderating compromises. Without this necessary correction through compromise and harmony of the excesses of either type human society cannot progress at all. This progress, though marked by harmony, is not linear in character. The elements of strife or contradiction are also there. But the forces of contradiction are subsidiary to and supervened by those of harmony and compromise.

England needed a strong monarchy during the period from Edward VI to Elizabeth I for the formation of the nation-unit. But when James I and Charles I made the unwise attempt to preserve the useless institution of absolutism, the people resisted and the country plunged into an internecine civil war. And that was followed by the rule of lawlessness. The failure of the Rump Parliament was misunderstood by Charles II and James II. They wanted to revive an absolutist monarchy and acted accordingly. This set the dialectic of events into motion leading to the Bloodless Revolution. The Restoration was not truly a restoration but the dissolution of the rule of the King and the beginning of the rule of the crown or law, i.e., constitutional monarchy.

A similar trend was present also in the history of France. The absolutism of the Bourbons, in spite of the concessions made by Louis XV and Louis XVI in the form of the extension of the right of franchise, could not save France from Jacobin terrorism and Napoleonic dictatorship or 'democratic despotism'. The French people fought and gave blood for liberty, equality and fraternity and they got in Napoleon the reward of the bloodshed—a democrat despot. He was indeed a democrat in the sense that he could claim the backing of the general will expressed through free plebiscites. His despotic character has been hardly a matter of dispute. Insofar as its immediate political objective was concerned, the French Revolution proved a failure. But its spirit came to stay to sustain and justify the popular claim to national unity and freedom as a safeguard of and a step as well to equality, liberty and fraternity. Perhaps it also marks the end of the era of absolutism.[14]

The alternation between *absolutism* and *populism*, the movement between the centralised power of the State and the highly decentralised power of the individual, may be characterised also as a *dialectic of organisation and freedom*. The power 'diffused' in individual human beings, unless it is properly organised, cannot generally produce any durable political good for all alike. When in the name of achieving the permanent and general welfare of the people the King or the dictator is allowed to concentrate and organise the diffused power of individual freedom in and through all the possible State agencies, absolutism starts taking an almost dreadful shape. When in the name of individual freedom a highly organised and power-packed State machinery is dismantled the individual does not get back the promised freedom; on the contrary, what generally appears is either the rule of lawlessness or a reign of terror. The dialectic operates somewhat in this way. Highly organised state power or absolutism abridges individual freedom. Absolutely free individuals not constrained in the least by any type of rules or organisations do not know how to define their mutual relations, especially in a situation marked by clash and conflict. One can well conceive of a state of society in which individuals are absolutely free and their mutual relation is not marked in the least by clash or conflict of interest. But this conception of anarchic society is hardly historical. The historical attempts to achieve even a near-anarchic state of society have resulted in dictatorship or despotism. And this explains the practical popularity (despite theoretical criticism) of absolutism of different forms, obvious and not so obvious. Absolutism is said to have been encouraged by all types of theories of the State, mechanical, biological, and divine. The mechanical absolutist thinks that only the whole, i.e., the State, is truly existent and active and that its parts, the citizens of the State, are more or less passive and therefore unimportant.[15]

In a somewhat similar vein the exponents of the biological theory of the State argue that the State-citizen relationship is to be understood in terms of the body-cell relationship. In other words, the citizen is nothing more than a cell of the body politic and his life must be entirely subservient to the requirements of the State. For practical success is the ultimate criterion of a man's or system's worth.

Absolutism has been defined in a slightly different way by the divine right theorists. The Hegelians, for instance, maintain that the individual in his personal capacity cannot have any right at all and that what is best in him is derived from his organic relationship to the personality of the State. As the ground of all our moral obligations the State itself is claimed to be above all moral questions and not answerable for the acts of its authorised agent. The individual citizen is not competent to pass moral judgements on the acts of the State. History is its only competent judge. The individual cannot possibly have any right against the State.[16]

The divine right absolutist has immensely glorified the role of 'the king who can do no wrong'. The king is wise and infallible almost by definition. He derives his authority from God and is not answerable for his actions to his own subjects. The citizen who does not submit to his will is wrong and capricious. When the moral agent chooses a wrong course of action, contrary to the will of the king, he loses his freedom. Freedom itself has been defined in terms of the submission of the individual to the will of the State as embodied in the king or somebody like him or authorised by him. The individual is spiritually elevated through his submission to the super-personality of the State.

The coalescence or convergence of monarchical authority and religious uniformity became a pressing necessity at a particular stage of history for the practical success of the cult of absolutism. The religious authority which had been enjoying an unquestioned position in both the intellectual and political spheres during the middle ages was not ready to give up its powers to the political authority which, by the beginning of the modern age, was strong enough to take away from the reluctant Church most of its powers and privileges. The issue was so important and deeply entrenched in society that it could not be settled in many cases without bloody religious wars. In France, Spain, and Russia, for instance, the issue was finally settled through war in favour of the monarchical state. In some cases religion became the handmaiden of a secular throne; and in other cases the king became both the head of the State and the representative of God on earth. Absolutism in its different forms undoubtedly shaped the process of the formation of the nation-unit. But, as we have seen before, the means resorted to in the formation of the nation-unit were in most cases political and mechanical and not subjective and psychological. The mechanical method of forming the nation-unit has left its strong impress on the nature of State authority and also on the modes of its exercise.

In the ancient world the relation between the State and the individual was rather direct and there was an element of personal touch in it. This was possible partly because of the smallness of the State's size and population and partly because of the absence of mechanical means and forms of communication and organisation. The modern systems of production and distribution and the gradual increase in the objective pressure on the life of man have made him very much self-centred. The world around him has become very much more impersonal and indifferent to him. Often he feels or finds that it is even hostile towards him. This grim struggle for existence throws him back on himself and fosters a sense of egoism and alienation in him.

But it would be wrong to infer from this that egoism and alienation were quite unknown to the citizen of the city-state. Even at that time the individual had to often sacrifice his freedom at the altar of common good, real or imaginary. And an element of coercion is perhaps there in the very nature of the State. The coercive aspect of State authority tends to alienate the individual from it and weakens the implicit moral bond between the two. When the main ground of State authority is consent and not coercion, the obligation of the individual to the State proves to be very deep and durable. But it seems that there cannot be a State which is exclusively based on *consent* and not armed in the least with the means and powers of *coercion* and *constraint*.

The question of individual egoism is implicitly linked up with that of State egoism. When the State can afford to let its citizens think and act in a very free manner, their egoism is generally found to be very inoffensive and not in any way inconsistent with the general aim of the State. If the individuals are very well organised and can effectively pressurise the State, a situation of confrontation quickly develops between the State and its citizens and which in turn feeds the egoism of the State. The egoism resulting from external causes and pressures does not generally prove to be wholesome and productive of the permanent common good. But the egoism resulting from some sort of genuine introspection, or earnest self-realisation, proves to be sane and non-aggressive.

The relation between State egoism and individual egoism may be better understood in terms of the cooperation or confrontation between the two. It is true that, other things being equal, the modern State is more authoritarian and egoist than its ancient and medieval counterparts. But that does not make us forget that the morally defiant Socrates was poisoned by the political authority of Athens. Referring to the State egoism of the medieval age Sri Aurobindo observes that it was ' brutal, rapacious, cunning, oppressive, and intolerant of free action, free speech and opinion, and even of freedom of conscience and religion '. This is because of the fact that by the medieval age individual citizens succeeded, at least partially, in organising themselves in order to protect their rights and interests against the possible onslaughts of State authority.

## The Modern State and the Moral Predicament of the Individual

The modern State, in spite of its egoism and deterioration in some directions, seeks its foundation in the general will and justification in the general welfare. It has arrogated to itself a new task—the task of presenting itself as an increasingly perfect, moral and intellectual being. The individual is being successfully persuaded and, if necessary, coerced to submit his will and activities to those of the State.

The cult of Statism received its finest formulation in the hands of Hegel. Marx and Bosanquet are often clubbed together with Hegel in this respect. But if we remember the humanistic origin and the anarchic, i.e., truly communistic, end of Marx's Theory of State, it would not be correct to club him with the other two absolutist thinkers. Absolutism or Statism in all its forms is more or less inconsistent with human freedom, dignity and progress. If the current trend of Statism, with or without its democratic facade, persists, Sri Aurobindo fears, it ' will surely end in a checked human progress, a comfortably organised stagnancy such as over-took the Graeco-Roman world after the establishment of the Roman Empire'.[17]

Theoretically speaking, the modern State is the expression of the general will or collective wisdom and its end is general good. The real will is identical with the general will *at bottom* and its best expression is said to be the personality of the State. But that bottom is hardly reached in real politics. Individual freedom is defined in terms of its conformity to that general will or submission to the State's personality. If one critically analyses the theoretical propositions regarding the foundation, composition and functions of the State machinery, one cannot but question their validity. On scrutiny one finds that the general will is not general and that its avowed aim and character are also very much partisan. The generality of the general will includes plurality of distinctly identifiable individual and group wills. Often what we call general will is dominated by group or class will. At times it is dominated by the will of the individual king or dictator. Sri Aurobindo thinks that in the contemporary world the concept of general will is being indiscriminately exploited to conceal the class will which is now in most cases controlling State machinery. The class character of the ruling groups is not necessarily of fundamental importance in practice. In spite of their origins, affiliations and declared aims, they subscribe uniformly to the main characteristic of the State idea which implies the subordination of the individual ' to a collective wisdom, political, military, economic, which seeks to justify certain collective aims and ambitions shaped and imposed on the great mass of the individuals by a smaller or larger number of ruling persons who are supposed in some way to represent the community'. Because of their deep-rooted egoism the individual and the collectivity do not know where and how to meet peacefully. The concept of general will is more a political fiction invented to justify State authority and its actions than a genuine expression of the psychological unity of free human beings. It is organic in character but cannot be called an organism. For in an organism the individual constituents are distinctly identifiable in structure and more or less autonomous in function. The free and creative individuality of the citizen is lost in the modern State. His identity is determined almost entirely in terms of his class or group affiliation. It makes little difference whether the origin of the individuals of the ruling group is bourgeois or proletarian. Their methods and aims are almost identical. 'In either case, there is no guarantee that this ruling class or ruling body represents the best mind of the nation or its noblest aims or its highest instincts.'[18]

Sri Aurobindo's method of studying the nature of the State is subjective and his approach evaluative. He rejects the objective or institutional method and the value-neutral positive approach on the ground that they do not take us to the heart of the problem.[19] He proposes to study the relation between the individual and the State primarily from the former's point of view and only secondarily through the institutions and organisations functioning under the State. The relation between the subjective method and the evaluative approach is quite clear. The ethical qualities or attributes of the State are reflective of the concerned human nature, particularly of the nature of the ruling group or class. In other words, the ethical aspects of political life cannot be fruitfully studied in an autonomous way, i.e., without reference to the character and composition of the ruling group.

If individuals are divided into different groups or classes and only one of these groups or classes enjoys the power and privilege to govern the rest, the existence of the State means only the maintenance and furtherance of the interest of the governing class. It also implies the widening of the difference between the party in power and the rest. And in that case the claim that the modern State is based on the general will turns out in practice to be hollow and indefensible. As the State power in its most effective form vests in the rich business community, the bourgeoisie, it is primarily to satisfy their interests and requirements that the State is found to act or abstain from acting.

The State idea has thus become very narrow. It reflects a very narrow sectional interest and its machinery is generally run by some narrow-minded sectarian persons. It has been argued that since the State in any case will be there and that its machinery has to be manned by some persons, our first duty would be to find out the right type of persons and to give them the reins of the State. Sometimes as an alternative to this argument and sometimes also as an extension of this argument, it has been claimed that once the right type of person gets the State powers, the narrowness of the State idea can be effectively combated and ultimately remedied and *that, given* favourable circumstances, the very idea of the State will disappear. The critique of the idea of the State generally takes two different forms—the subjective-psychological and the objective-institutional; but their goal is more or less the same, a Stateless society or anarchy.

The Marxist may be regarded as the most influential exponent of the objective-institutional approach to the State idea. Consistently with his notion of class he maintains that if we want to fight the narrowness of the State idea, we have to destroy or remove the narrow sectional ruling authority, the bourgeoisie. Once the broad-based proletarian class is in power and can exercise the State machinery, the character of the State would undergo a fundamental change. For, among its proclaimed aim is the promotion of the interests of the poor and establishment of an egalitarian society. The assumptions of the Marxist are not difficult to follow. Firstly, the difference between man and man is basically economic, and only incidentally political or religious. And, secondly, this difference can be removed by the proper exercise of State power. Some psychologists have given a psychological twist to the Marxist theory of class-state, suggesting that Marx tried to show that the irreconciliability of the economic *motivations* of different classes is the basis of the State. This interpretation is unfounded and entirely wrong. For it is nothing but an impermissible translation of the Marxist *sociology* of the State into a questionable *psychology* of the State. One may not agree with him but the Marxist is very clear on the point, viz., economic *motivation* is itself a derivative phenomenon. It is due to the place and position of the concerned individual within a system of production which is definable entirely in terms of some objective relations. Dissatisfied with the original Marxist theory of the State and/or its psychological version, a number of critics complain that the Marxist's view and its underlying assumptions do little or no justice to the human nature involved in the structure and function of the State.[20]

As we have seen, Sri Aurobindo is a critic of the very idea of the State. He is highly critical of the socialist cult of State. The State to him is a machine lacking in tact, taste and delicacy. The difference and distinction between man and man which can be done away with the help of the State machine is bound to be incidental or superficial and cannot be essential. By its very nature it is unable to go deep into human nature and get in touch with that reach of human consciousness where alone man knows himself and his fellow human beings as an expression of a common spiritual unity. Underlying the political unity is a social unity. And underlying that social unity is an invisible spiritual unity.

Unless modern man can realise that spiritual unity, the modern State cannot cease to be a huge exploiting machine. Most modern political leaders have no spiritual vision of human unity. They do not even have a philosophical insight into the social unity of different classes and sections of people belonging to a common culture. They represent, what Sri Aurobindo calls, the average pettiness, selfishness, egoism, and self-deception.

The sad state of affairs is due mainly to the fact that the common man of the modern world is indifferent to his own rights and unconscious of his duties. He hardly thinks of any values other than with what he is immediately and materially concerned. He is almost exclusively a creature of his material environment and does not try to change it in the light of some cherished ideal. Unless some of his own material and vital requirements are brutally denied, he takes no interest in politics, which, he has been told, is 'the last resort of the scoundrel'. His indifference and apathy are consistently exploited by the politician and the bureaucrat. He refuses to pay the price of liberty and is not ordinarily vigilant. He is mentally incompetent, morally conventional, timid, and pretentious. The politician, who is his constitutional or conventional representative, represents all his shortcomings punctuated and magnified by his own lust for and vested interest in power. 'Yet', Sri Aurobindo ruefully remarks, 'it is by such minds that the good of all has to be decided, to such hands that it has to be entrusted, to such an agency calling itself the State that the individual is being more and more called upon to give up the government of his activities.'[21]

The above statements of Sri Aurobindo on the nature of the average citizen, the politician and the State may appear somewhat sweeping but, generally speaking, they are true. Unless one is ready to accept this undoubtedly gloomy picture of the political world, one finds it difficult to explain the steady deterioration in the general character of the body politic of all countries. This view may be further confirmed by the competitive and acquisitive tendencies increasingly generated by industrial civilisation.

## Collectivism and Individualism: Their Different Forms

The State, refusing to let its people discover, realise and freely express what is best in them, defeats the very purpose of its own existence. It has no end in itself. Its end is not Divine. At least its historic functions and avowed goal do not indicate that. Its end is the development of the individual, or, to put it moderately, to help him in his effort for self-development.

The individual provides the dynamics of collective progress. 'The instinct of the collectivity is to stand still in its established order.' It is for the individual to break that inertia and immobility of the social mass, the collectivity. The State generally does not approve of the radical, i.e., unconventional, professions and actions of progressive individuals. Nor does it encourage the novel ideas and works of the creative minority. The individual who can discover his own true and inner individuality does not wait for the conventional approval of his thought and action and can therefore move much faster than the collectivity. From this general statement one should not infer either that every man is truly individual or that no collectivity can be truly individual. What can perhaps be safely affirmed is simply this—the organisation of the parts of a whole and its preservation, which are the necessary conditions for the development of individuality, are more difficult to be satisfied in the case of the collectivity than it is in the case of the ordinary human being. Only a few among us can sufficiently organise our mind and activities to attain a high degree of individuality. If it is difficult for an individual man, one may easily imagine how much more difficult it is for the collectivity. This highlights, among other things, the difficulty involved in the concept of general will. General will contains numerous individual wills within it. If the former does not express and recognise the latter adequately and yet is accepted as the basis of State functioning, a sort of totalitarianism is almost inevitable. On the contrary, if the former is totally sacrificed and reduced to the latter, individualism tends to degenerate into egoism, excite it within and expand it without. One is advised to avoid the extremes of egoism and totalitarianism. Sri Aurobindo observes:

> The non-recognition of the possibilities of human co-operation was the weakness of English individualism; the turning of a utility for co-operative action into an excuse for rigid control by the State is the weakness of the Teutonic idea of collectivism.[22]

English individualism failed to encourage and develop the cooperative instincts of man in the proper direction. Teutonic collectivism took advantage of this failure, but in a negative way. The cult of State or the appearance of the State as a huge machine is the historical result. And such a machine is unable to act freely, flexibly and harmoniously. 'For the State is not an organism; it is a machinery, and it works like a machine, without tact, taste, delicacy or intuition.'[23]

This mechanical character of the State organisation and the resulting dangers have been recognised by many contemporary thinkers. Of them perhaps Russell's view deserves special mention. The basis of the State is said to be the collective force of its people.[24] The modern States, whether democratic or totalitarian, 'leave little room for initiative, and fail to develop in most men any sense of ability to control their political destinies. The few men who achieve power in such States are men of abnormal ambition and thirst for domination combined with skill in cajolery and subtlety in negotiations.' People tend to follow them rather unquestioningly. This is mainly due to misunderstood tradition, a wrong notion of religion, fear of foreign powers and the desire to worship a hero. The result is that the State becomes more and more powerful. Russell is clearly against the cult of the State. This harmful nature of the State is attributed to the fact that power is its chief aim.

The nature of the State could be understood from two different, but related, points of view—from the point of view of the Government and from that of the governed. The State has no universal and intrinsic nature of its own. *What* it is like is to be gathered from *how* the concerned machinery of Government is constituted and how it functions. When the principles of Government are not reasonably open to the influence of the ideas and values of the governed, the State tends to degenerate into a lifeless machine and ceases to be a human institution. Both Russell and Sri Aurobindo explain the nature of the State primarily from the standpoint of the individual, the governed. Interestingly enough, both of them are pro-socialist in their political inclinations and against the monolithic trend of the modern State. They further agree on the point that despotism is unnecessary and under the present circumstances anarchism unattainable. Despotism has to be discarded and left behind, and anarchism is an ideal to cherish and follow. Living as we do in the transitional period, between a sort of despotism and anarchism, we must try to find out a compromise between the two.

The attitude we are talking about with reference to Sri Aurobindo and Russell is nothing new. Thinkers have always been talking of a free and stateless society and at the same time pointing out the necessity of having the State machinery to control and discipline some of the unruly instincts and actions of the individual. The tradition of authoritarianism is as old as that of anarchism.

Rightly understood, the State is not a machine. It is by acting under a wrong notion of the State that we transform it into a lifeless machine. The nature of the State depends upon the nature of government and that in turn on the character of the citizen in question. The government we get is the government we deserve. This may be interpreted as an attempt to legitimise the existence of any type of government, representative or illegitimate. But what I mean is this. The character of the governed can certainly influence the nature of the government and therefore of the State. The better and deeper we express ourselves in public life, the better and freer become the nature of the government and the State. But, understandably enough, we are more interested and involved in our private affairs and immediate environment, leaving the public or community life to the care of the politician and the administrator. As a result of that, other things being equal, the larger the human aggregate or institution, the feebler becomes the human touch in its functioning. Sri Aurobindo says: 'The man within the community is now at least a half civilised creature, but his international existence is still primitive.' Russell holds substantially the same view: 'The external activity of the State—with exception so rare as to be negligible—is selfish.'

The State is a necessary evil. Except for some full-blooded totalitarians like Hegel, nobody could totally deny the ' evil ' character of the State. Perhaps they will say the State is a spiritual entity and not mechanical . The individuals are said to be imperfect expressions of that spiritual whole. One may or may not agree with the pro-naturalist or the anti-naturalist justification of State power but it is very difficult to deny the *necessity* of the State. The denial is inconsistent with the actual course of history and also with our contemporary experience of the Marxist theory of the withering away of the State.

Sri Aurobindo is an anti-naturalist holist. To him it is not an ideal form of human unity. At the same time he does not deny its necessity for the human race in its present stage of development. Like many other contemporary thinkers he tries to strike a progressive balance between State power and individual liberty. His bias towards individual liberty is unmistakable. Individual liberty is curtailed not only for political reasons but also for economic reasons. Uncontrolled State power has the general tendency to move towards warfare. Formerly political domination was the main motive-force behind war. Now it is economic exploitation as well as political domination.

## Conflict, Harmony and Freedom

The spirit of conflict cannot be removed unless the spirit of freedom finds enough room for free play in our national and international political life. 'Unity would be the largest principle of life, but freedom would be its foundation-stone.'[25] We must accept *harmony* as the main organising principle of the State power.[26] The idea of harmony is to be taken in its wider human context, within and without. To realise his relation with the rest of mankind what he needs first is to enjoy freedom within his community or society. Otherwise his inherent freedom turns out to be meaningless in practice.

We all know that ideal freedom is actually unattainable. Ideal harmony is also actually elusive. There is thus a gap between the ideal and the actual. Different and conflicting class interests are put together and held in a balance by the State. This balance is sought to be maintained by the power sanctioned by popular consent. Often this consent turns out to be that of the dominant minority. The State justifies its power structure by coordinating and compromising different group interests and class antagonism.

In recent years, we have seen the development of a new class—the middle class—and an increasing cleavage in the labour class so that the Marxist theory of polarisation of classes is no longer really valid. This does not mean in the least that elements of conflict and antagonism have disappeared from society. All I want to say is that the influence of the process of decomposition of the capitalist class, the labour class, and also on the structural relation between the two has resulted in the further heterogeneity of both the classes. It has added to the complexity of the State apparatus. The State is *not* clearly divided into two homogeneous hostile camps. Despite its definite structural contours, every class is more or less amorphous and mobile. Mobility and conflict are the two essential features of industrial society. The elements of conflict are not necessarily economic in character or origin, unless, of course, we use the *economic principle* in the metaphysical sense and reduce everything to it.

The more interesting question perhaps is how to resolve the conflict between the different human groups. Human nature being what it is, some people argue, the ideal of complete resolution of group conflict is unrealisable. Indirectly they concede that the State has come to stay; its *rationale* is permanent. Others like Sri Aurobindo will reject this view. There is nothing like fixed human nature. They point out that it is evolving and developing. The developing human nature realises its higher potentiality and achieves more and more unity with fellow human beings. This inner unity is then reflected in social organisation. In this connection Sri Aurobindo says:

> If we may judge from the modern movement, the progress of the reason as a social renovator and creator, if not intercepted in its course, would be destined to pass through three successive stages which are the very logic of its growth, the first individualistic and increasingly democratic with liberty for its principle, the second socialistic, in the end perhaps a governmental commu-

nism with equality and the State for its principle, the third--if that ever gets beyond the stage of theory—anarchistic in the higher sense of that much-abused word, either a loose voluntary co-operation or a free communalism with brotherhood or comradeship and not governmnet for its principle.[27]

## Democratic Individualism as an Ideology for Resolving Social Conflict

Conventionalism and individualism are incompatible. For the all round development of the individual the *exercise* of freedom is an essential condition. Conventionalism requires the individual to be conformist. The individual who is required or forced to conform uncritically to the existing conventions, forms of thinking, and norms of conduct, cannot realise his higher potentialities. Fixed and worn-out institutions impede the growth of the human mind. The Age of Reason raises two very fundamental questions: Should the individual accept an institution simply because it serves some limited purposes of life? Cannot he have any higher and better purpose of life not yet realised by him? Nobody can remain impervious for ever to the appeal of reason. In the words of H.A.L. Fisher: ' Authority no longer went unchallenged. The past was no longer supreme. As the planet unfolded its meaning wonders, generations grew up for whom truth was not a complete thing already given in ancient books, but a secret yet to be retrieved from the womb of time.'[28]

It was the beginning of a new age. Lord Acton writes: ' A new type of man began with Petrarca, men accustomed to introspection, who selected their own ideals and moulded their minds to them. The medieval system could prepare them for both; but seeing the vicissitudes of fortune and the difficulties of life, they depended on the intellectual treasures of the ancient world, on the whole mass of accessible wisdom, to develop themselves all round.'[29] It was an age of cultural efflorescence. ' The long centuries of asceticism were forgotten in a riot of art, poetry and pleasure.'[30] The bright light of liberated reason, as Voltaire puts it, shone across the dark medieval sky of priestly tyranny and monarchical absolutism.

This reason could not but be the monopoly of the ruling class or clique. It was a useful instrument in the hands of the privileged few. If the members of the ruling class, taking advantage of the common man's ignorance, try to monopolise reason, they can do it, but only for a short time. Reason, which by its very nature is universal and meant for all, cannot be permanently kept in a prison house without degrading it into a sort of dogma. The best expression of reason is thought. And thought cannot be kept confined within the circle of a few chosen thinkers forever. Thought has a wider appeal of its own. Its light draws other people towards it. When thought is exposed or made open to the questions and experience only of the ignorant common man, it tends to become disfigured, ineffective and dogmatic.[31] Individualism without a rational basis degenerates into populism. But the experience and thoughts of the common man have also to be taken into account in shaping and running the government without of course disrupting the basis of civil society. However sophisticated its form might be, the thought of the political elite must be prepared to face the tribunal of all types of plebian experience. It is only in this way that the thought of the gifted individual, enriched by the experience of others not so gifted, may assume and defend its true universal nature.

The power of reason was intended to serve simultaneously two purposes—to provide a basis for a common life and to equip each and all to contribute to its build-up. Individualistic democracy owes its origin to this power of reason. The individual is to be given maximum possible freedom consistent with the rational uniformity of the State. And it is in this way that ' a liberal, a vigorous, a natural yet rationalised ' State based on common agreement could be formed. What mainly accounts for the failure of democratic individualism in practice is the individual's obdurate tendency to misuse his freedom. Instead of developing his individuality he misuses freedom to further his power and to consolidate it at the cost of curbing the freedom of his fellow human beings. Unfortunately he takes them to be his competitors who are indeed actual or potential cooperators. But as he has not gone deep into his being he does not know the true relation between himself and the rest.

Under the circumstances individualism tends to degenerate into egoism. And it has its institutional implications. Firstly, when the individual fails to realise his true relation with others, the philosophy of power takes its inevitable turn. Democracy degenerates into the rule of the dominant minority. Power (and *not* consent) becomes the only available sanction behind the ruler. Secondly, when the majority is not consulted by the minority even on issues which vitally concern it, the former refuses to extend its support to the latter.

Looking at the shortcomings of democratic individualism one must not think of it as a totally negative and useless ideal. It has its bright side too.[32] The main defects of the concept may be minimised in practice by the spread of education.

## Democratic Individualism to Democratic Socialism

The rational mind could not get from democratic individualism what it had expected of it.

> First natural result has been the transition of the rational mind from democratic individualism to democratic socialism . . . its real justification is the attempt of the human reason to carry on the rational ordering of society to its fulfilment, its will to get rid of these great parasitical excrescence of unbridled competition, this giant obstacle to any decent ideal or practice of human living.[33]

Democratic individualism and competitive industrialism can hardly afford to remain together indefinitely.

Marx's conception of the State is inseparable from his view of the class struggle. Firstly, classes exist in society only in some definite historical periods and as a result of some definite modes of production. Secondly, the dictatorship of the proletariat is the necessary outcome of the class struggle. And, thirdly, the dictatorship of the proletariat marks the transition of the class society to the classless one.

According to Lenin, the essence of Marx's teachings on the State consists in the extension of the idea of class struggle to the dictatorship of the proletariat. In the dialectical course of history some modes of production cleave the society into some classes and that accounts for the origin of the State. Engels lucidly states this view in *The Origin of the Family, Private Property and the State*. Engels' interpretation of the Marxist theory of the State has been further elaborated and modified by Lenin:

> The State is a product and the manifestation of the irreconcilability of class antagonism. The State arises when, where and to what extent that class antagonism objectively cannot be reconciled. And, conversely, the existence of the State proves that the class antagonisms are irreconcilable.... According to Marx the State could neither arise nor maintain itself if it were possible to reconcile classes....The State is an organ of class rule, an organ for the oppression of one class by another: It is the creation of 'order', which legalises and perpetuates this oppression by moderating the conflict between the classes.[34]

The Marxist claims that there is considerable difference between the proletarian State and the bourgeois State. While the latter is an instrument of exploitation, the former crushes the exploiter and leads the people to the work of organising a socialist economy. And this aim can be realised only through a violent revolution. Lenin points out that this revolution must primarily rely upon the 'revolutionary upsurge of the people' and not upon a conspiracy or upon a particular party. The time of the revolution has to be fixed when the activity of the advanced ranks of the people is at its height and when the vacillation in the ranks of the enemy and in the ranks of the weak half-hearted irresolute friends of the revolution are strongest. It is along these lines that Lenin distinguishes Marxism from Blanquism.

It is now admitted also in Marxist quarters that to overthrow the bourgeois State machinery, armed revolution is not an *essential* condition. In his report to the Twentieth Party Congress of the Soviet Communist Party, Khrushchev makes this point clearly. He argues that bourgeois rule under special circumstances may be overthrown by peaceful means as well. This was the beginning of the end of the cold war. Peaceful coexistence is now being followed up by meaningful cooperation between the super-powers, notwithstanding the local wars of tensions objectively encouraged by them with different ends in view in different parts of the world.

Lenin hoped that the dictatorship of the proletariat, which to his mind was the main plank of Marxism, would ultimately lead socialist society to its communist goal. Without the dictatorship of the proletariat the equal right of all men cannot be established. Equality is a sort of quantitative determination.

It means the application of an equal measure to different human beings who are not equal in capacity and alike in their attitudes and aptitudes. Equal right to start with, Marx himself admits somewhere, is a violation of equality and a concession to injustice. 'The first phase of Communism cannot produce... justice and equality.' In its initial phase Communism cannot be realistically expected to do away with all the bourgeois rights and privileges. For the effects of capitalism, gross and subtle, particularly the latter, go deep into the live veins of society and culture. And therefore they cannot be removed so easily. The institutional socialisation of the means of production can only put a *formal* end to the exploitation of a class by a class. If real content could be given to this formal institutional change-over, that would be a big step forward.

Even when that objective is realised, the aim of Stateless society, the withering away of the State, remains unfulfilled.

Socialism owes its origin largely to the defects of democratic individualism.[35] Its main characteristic, the spirit of competition, destroys or at any rate minimises considerably the importance of liberty in practice. Both Marx and Sri Aurobindo highlight this shortcoming of democratic individualism. Marx was deeply distressed by the terrible sufferings of the working class of Britain under the *laissez-faire* economy of his time. He would have refused to accept the argument that low wages, long work hours, and child labour are the characteristics of capitalism in its early stage and not in its developed one. His analysis convinced him that the labour-capital relation being intrinsically what it is the labour in its struggle with the capitalist is bound to be relatively exploited and weakened more and more. The proletariat does not have any liberty. And to him equality is an empty word.

The ideals of liberty and equality are individualistic in their origin. The individual demands liberty for him and free exercise of the powers of his body, mind and will. He claims equality with other individuals of the same society. But social reason, being somewhat archaic and uniform in its nature and functioning, fails to appreciate the demands of the individual for liberty and equality. Whatever might be the quality and excellence of individual reason in conventional society, it has to fall in line with the demands of social reason. The individualist is obliged to be a conformist sacrificing his dissenting judgement at the altar of the so-called common good. In the process of this rationalisation of social uniformity, the ideal of liberty is reduced to the liberty of a few privileged individuals to compete with the less privileged ones and thus to score an easy victory over the latter. The privileged few, because of their better organisation and competitive power and not necessarily because of the quality of their head or heart, dominate over the rest. Consequently, not only liberty is destroyed or curtailed but equality also turns out to be a very formal thing, viz., equality in the eye of law. Competitive liberty and legal equality are two distinct proofs of the failure of democratic individualism to establish justice and rationality in the state.

Sri Aurobindo is ready to recognise the merits of socialism but at the same time he proposes to point out the shortcomings of this revolutionary concept. His main point is that the socialist order fails to secure liberty and equality for the individual. The abolition of private property is all right. And the socialisation of the means of production and distribution is also welcome. These are undoubtedly bold steps in the direction of a socialist society. But the question remains: after the abolition of private property who will *own* it? The obvious answer is the community or society. The problem is the community *as a whole* cannot own. After all *community* is a concept and has no ontological status of its own. Naturally, the question arises: How can the community as a whole own or manage property?[36] In order to justify the possession of property of the community by the community the authority of the socialist state is required to take upon itself all that the individual possesses—his property, his labour, his education, his knowledge, his capacities and his family life. All this is done in the best interest of the individual himself. In the socialist society the individual surrenders all that he has to get in return for all that others have. Each is for all and all are for each. The community is supposed to exist and function on the basis of common interests. This is undoubtedly an ideal state of society. But again the question is raised: In whose interest is this community being planned? Another question is: Who is to determine the *best interest* of the individual? Obviously, the individual does not have the freedom to decide what is in the best interest of the community as a whole. It is the other way round. The community decides what is in the best interest of the individual. As the community itself cannot think or act, the dictatorship of the proletariat does it on its behalf. Once what is in the best interest of the individual and the community is decided by the dictatorship of the proletariat the next question arises: who is to execute this decision? Again we fall back upon the old answer: the dictatorship of the proletariat. According to Sri Aurobindo, ' the dictatorship of the proletariat amounts in fact to the dictatorship of the Communist Party in the name or on behalf of the proletariat '.[37]

This analysis and criticism of Marxism does not appear to have disturbed the orthodox Marxist very much.[38] He defends the view, as Lenin did, by stating that during the period of transition from capitalism to communism the proletariat must impose ' a series of restrictions on the freedom of the oppressors, the exploiters, the capitalists . . . in order to free humanity from wage slavery '. The sole task of achieving social good and paving the way to communism is assigned to the Communist Party as the representative of the proletariat. And individual liberty is allowed to the extent it does not clash with the egalitarian basis of the State. The liberty of the individual under the dictatorship of the proletariat is not very much different from the competitive liberty of the individual under bourgeois democracy. The little difference that there is, is more in form than in content. In bourgeois society all are equally free *in the eye of the law*, while in effect only the privileged minority enjoys all goods and material benefits in society. The dominant feature of the socialist society is *power discrimination* and *not class discrimination*. The group interests are also not compatible. And that mainly accounts for the survival of the State authority in a socialist society.

The same point may be mentioned also in the context of equality. So long as there remains a difference between man and man based on the difference in their physical and mental capacity it is bound to be reflected in the unequal and incompatible group interests operating in the society and necessitating the existence and exercise of State authority. The good communist will not deny outright the shortcomings of the Marxist ideal of equality in practice. But he will try to explain it in terms of the fact that socialism has not yet assumed a global character and the stranglehold of capitalism, though slightly relaxed, is still very much there. Further, he highlights the point that the political rights *formally* granted by the capitalist State are *practically* nullified by social and economic inequality.[39] The communist maintains that although it has not yet been possible for the socialist society to grant ideal liberty and true equality to all people, it is steadily moving towards the goal creating the economic and other necessary conditions. One points out that in the history of the half century of communism in practice there is no concrete evidence indicating that the State authority is withering away. On the contrary, even before it could assume a global character, the Marxist commitment to internationalism is being continuously violated by some of the socialist countries themselves. Socialist ideology is yielding place to *realpolitik.*

If from the philosophical trinity of God, Nature and Man the importance of the last two is minimised, the result is philosophical absolutism. Similarly, if from the democratic trinity of equality, liberty and fraternity the value of the first two is downgraded or distorted, fraternity by itself can hardly afford the social basis necessary for the fulfilment of the growing demands of evolving human nature. Fraternity which is not spontaneous, welling out of the inherent free nature of man, is not true fraternity. And it does not promote equality between man and man. Fraternity by implication is a matter of free realisation and should not be imposed from above or without. Sri Aurobindo is very much aware of the danger of fraternity without liberty and equality. For, in that case, it ' can be nothing more than like the associations of all—individuals, functional classes, guilds, syndicates, soviets or any other unit—in common service to the life of the nation under the absolute control of the collectivist State '.[40] This is distinctly a revival of what is known as the Spartan or Roman spirit of civic service. Sri Aurobindo clearly asserts that socialism is in the very nature of present-day history. He asserts this certainly not in order to justify it but only to point out its inevitability. In this connection he repeatedly refers to the pernicious excesses and failure of democratic individuals.

> Totalitarianism of some kind seems indeed to be the natural, almost *inevitable* destiny, at any rate, the extreme and the fullest outcome of Socialism or, more generally, of the collectivistic idea and impulse. For, the essence of Socialism, its justifying ideal, is the governance and strict organisation of the *total life* of the society *as a whole* and in detail by its own conscious reason and will for the best good and common interest of all, eliminating exploitation by individual or class, removing internal competition, haphazard confusion and waste, enforcing and perfecting co-ordination, assuring the best functioning and a sufficient life for all.[41]

Totalitarianism is a reaction against individualism. The ideal of *laissez-faire et laissez-passer* of the French free trade economists of the eighteenth century was given a fair trial. But its performance has not been very encouraging, certainly not for the toiling masses.[42] If proletarian totalitarianism discards democratic liberty, 'non-proletarian totalitarianism goes further and discards democratic equality no less than democratic liberty'. It is not easy to choose between the competing ideals. A harmonious combination of the two should not be ruled out *a priori*. One cannot prescribe a socio-political ideal without taking into account the social space, the historical time and the experience and aspirations of the people concerned.

This only indicates how difficult it is to shape an ideal society in response to the many-sided but indivisible aspects and urges of human nature which is an integral whole and which can attain its fullest satisfaction only in an ideal integral society. But in practice we find that society leans either towards State authority or towards the liberty of the individual. For, as I have said before, one does not know where exactly to strike a balance between the two. In his *Critique of Hegel's State Law* Marx observes:

> Hegel proceeds from the State and makes man the State subjectified; democracy proceeds from man and makes the State man objectified.... Man does not exist for law's sake, law exists for man's sake; it is *human existence*, whereas [for] the others man is *legal existence*. That is the fundamental difference of democracy.

Marx speaks of the whole man and Sri Aurobindo of the integral man. But the point is that the ideal man cannot grow except in an ideal community in which the ideals of liberty, equality and fraternity have found a harmonious combination.[43]

The Marxist is aware of the difficulties inherent in the functional envelopment of social life by State authority. In order to minimise these difficulties he has his own idea and plan of action. The origin of all these difficulties is stated to be the artificial division between the ruling class and the working class, between mental labour and physical labour. The Marxist is known for his clear view that the antithesis between intellectual labour and manual labour is basically economic, i.e., related to the economic mode of production. Once we succeed in evolving a political system *relegating* more and more power to the working class and their representatives, it will bring about a significant transformation in the power-structure of the State in a bourgeois society. The main purpose of the new system would be to relegate power to the working people who *delegated* it to the dictatorship of the proletariat only for the transitional period. Unless the political power is more and more decentralised and relegated to the social groups, the State cannot even start withering away. Power must circulate from top to bottom. And this can be possible in practice only when some power channels from bottom to top are kept open and functional. In other words, the process of power transmission from top to bottom must be taken up simultaneously with *free* circulation or delegation from the bottom to the top. In case the latter remains notional and the former alone is functional, an unwholesome totalitarianism, the unilateral control of socio-cultural life by the political authority, is unavoidable.

Sri Aurobindo thinks that it *is* unavoidable. But he explains it in a different way. According to him, our practical eagerness to bring about a sort of uniformity in our political and social life, ignoring the important difference between the two, lands us in great difficulty. The rationality or otherwise of a society cannot be decided in a one-sided manner, taking only the economic aspect of life into account, and excluding all other aspects or, alternatively, reducing the latter into the former. Besides, Sri Aurobindo does not believe that the economic division of labour is basic. He traces the evils of totalitarianism to the mechanical role of reason in shaping human life. He repeatedly asserts that reason has an inherent tendency towards uniformity—to freeze or mechanise the parts in a whole. 'The integral truth of things is truth not of the reason but of the spirit.'[44]

The Aurobindite draws a very important line of distinction between *totalitarianism* and *integralism*. In a totalitarian society the individuals are subjected to a rigid order in the formulation of which they have no say or hand. And as a result of that the said social order does not prove conducive to the growth of their individual personalities. In contrast to this the integral society provides sufficient freedom of thought and action to individuals enabling them to grow independently and yet harmoniously. The free individual can realise the deeper unity and potentiality of his personality—deeper than what is available at the rational level. 'The rational being is only a middle term of Nature's evolution.' So it will be unwise to choose the rational plane of our existence as the foundation of an ideal political order. Sri Aurobindo thinks that the basic identity of man is spiritual. If the mental being (*manomaya purusha*) is not allowed to grow freely, and if his basic identity is narrowly defined in terms of a particular mode of production, totalitarianism and stunted individuality become inevitable. The individual is something more than what productive relationships might indicate. The socio-economic identity of man, according to Sri Aurobindo, is clearly secondary and it has to be taken and treated accordingly. Otherwise we will be downgrading the role of the individual not only in the political sphere but also in the social sphere.

One cannot fail to take note of the dangerous consequences of extreme forms of democratic individualism. Even those who are quite persuaded of the central importance of individual liberty cannot but be struck as to how in practice it has been extravagantly used by a powerful ruling class, feudal or bourgeois, exploiting the toiling masses and enriching itself beyond the extent of moral permissibility. As we have already pointed out before, socialism is a natural reaction against morally impermissible and economically unjustifiable individualism. Highly institutionalised misuse of the ideal principle of individual liberty left the common man with no other alternative but to espouse the cause of socialism. Oswald Spengler was perfectly right in a sense when he asserted 'we are all socialist, willingly or unwillingly'.

It would be perhaps incorrect to suggest that socialism has no positive impulse underlying it. In fact it has. The socialist identity of the individual is indicative of a higher dimension of his own being. Sri Aurobindo's criticism of socialism is based not so much on the question of principle as on that of practice. According to him, the socialist ' ignores the complexity of man's being and all that that complexity means '. His unlimited zeal to standardise human life leads him to mechanise it unwittingly. Bewildered with its complexity he does not know how to tackle it satisfactorily at the institutional level. Consequently he starts working on the basis of an over-simplified blueprint of an ideal society and depending exclusively upon his mechanical reason and forgetting that ' life differs from the mechanical order of the physical universe with which reason has been able to deal victoriously just because it is mechanical and runs immutably in the groove of fixed cosmic habit '. The positive basis of a true socialist order is to be discovered within first. And only then can its institutional expressions be durable and flexible. Sri Aurobindo fears that the denial of freedom and the regulation of all aspects of the human life in a socialist society mark ' the end of the Age of Reason and of the ideal of rational society '.[45]

Sri Aurobindo's fear, though partially corroborated by some findings of the socialist society in its early phase, is perhaps a bit exaggerated. Without paying the price for socialism and granting unrestricted liberty to all individuals, irrespective of their socio-economic weakness or predatory habits, we cannot hope for a sane socialist society. We agree that merely by subordinating the life of the isolated ego to the life of the greater group-ego it is not possible to achieve socialism. But that is not an essential feature of the socialist *principle* itself. The practical distortion of socialism cannot be deemed to be an indictment of the ideal itself.

## From Socialism to Anarchism

The main question is how to ensure institutionally a rational transition from the ideal of socialism to its establishment in reality. I deliberately emphasise the *institutional* aspect of the problem of transition. At the *individual* level also the problem of transition is there. He has to control his impulses, the push-and-pull effects of his perceptions, his habits and desires, into an ordered whole, into an individuality. As every individual is continuously exposed to institutional influences and as individuals themselves determine the forms and history of the concerned institutions, it is not easy to achieve harmonious stability in the sphere of institutional life. The Marxist emphasises the *autonomy of sociology*, the dialectical independence of the *objective* social order, and thinks that unless this is properly organised and rationalised the aim or ideal of building up a rational social order is bound to remain unrealised or utopian. Sri Aurobindo, on the other hand, proclaims the *autonomy of the spirit* (or spiritual psychology) and affirms that unless reason, a subjective power, is allowed to shape social institutions we cannot escape uniformity and avoid an abridgement of liberty. He speaks of a deeper and spiritual principle of socialism. Socialism, which owes its origin to social reason, exhibits some definite mechanical characteristics. What we need is harmony and cohesion between the individual members of society. Mechanical reason cannot provide that principle and power of unity. It leads to a sort of collectivitism or totalitarianism.

> Collectivism may itself in the end realise this aim [of social living] if it can modify its own dominant principle far enough to allow for a free individual development on the basis of unity and a closely harmonised common existence. But to do that it must first spiritualise itself and transform the very soul of its inspiring principle: it cannot do it on the basis of the logical reason and a mechanically scientific ordering of life.[46]

The spiritualisation of the principle of socialism marks the beginning of anarchism. When the individual realises the unity of mankind in his own spiritual depth it is reflected in the community life. Spiritual unity knows no bounds. It transcends the bounds of community and assumes steadily but inevitably a global character. Sri Aurobindo believes in the innate or essential goodness of human nature. Its inspiration is not psychological, its character is not rational, and material gain is not its objective. It is this spiritual realisation of the super-rational good in human nature which alone can provide a firm and comprehensive base for stateless society. Unless individuals can realise and thus be assured of a deeper *unity of existence* between themselves, they cannot shed their dependence on some external authority, the State machinery. The individual needs the State not because it is good but simply because it serves a practical purpose which otherwise remains unachieved or unrealised.

Sri Aurobindo is a spiritual anarchist. Even in his early life when he was the spiritual leader of an anarchist movement in Bengal he was quite clear about the distinction between terroristic anarchism and spiritual anarchism. The outer forms of anarchism may at times assume a terroristic character but that has nothing to do with the essential nature of anarchism. Sri Aurobindo is clearly against what he calls 'the grosser vitalistic or violent anarchism'.[47] Although he is a consistent critic of the cult of State, he attaches great importance to collective social life.

He is also critical of the different intellectual forms of anarchism propounded, among others, by William Godwin, Proudhon and Kropotkin.[48] I do not know if Sri Aurobindo read the works of these famous anarchist thinkers, but it is clear that his criticism of intellectual anarchism is directed against their ideas. Intellectual anarchism is stated to have relied mainly on two natural endowments of the human mind—the enlightenment of reason and recognition of others' right to freedom. This reliance although not totally unfounded is not very well-founded either. The intellectual man, with whom reason is still an instrument or a technique and who is still very much under the influence of his own vital impulses, cannot be fair to the similar urges and aspirations of other fellow human beings. At this stage of evolution man finds himself placed indeed in an institutional predicament. If he allows free play to his vital impulses, they will destroy or distort his rational society. If he suppresses those impulses completely, the human society will be 'artificial, top-heavy, poor in the sap of vitality, mechanical, uncreative'. In a somewhat similar vein but from an altogether different philosophical premise Russell says the same thing.[49]

> Men are passionate, headstrong and rather mad. By their madness they inflict upon themselves, and upon others, disasters which may be of immense magnitude. But although the life of impulse is dangerous it must be preserved if human existence is not to lose its savour. Between the two poles of impulse and control (by reason), an ethics by which men can live happily must find a little point. It is through this conflict in the inmost nature of man that the need for ethics arises.

Sri Aurobindo is perfectly convinced that reason cannot save us from the endless conflict between the two poles of our nature, reason and impulse. Sometimes it mechanically stifles impulses, sometimes it becomes a slave to the impulses themselves. In either case our conduct or ethical achievement is questionable. Man knows no principle higher than that of reason to resolve this conflict. But reason being itself a party to the conflict cannot resolve it. It has to be clearly realised that man's nature is rather transitional. He must discover a higher principle within. And that is the principle of spirit.

The preservation and growth of both the poles of human nature, rational and impulsive, can be harmoniously integrated only at the spiritual level. We cannot possibly succeed in establishing an anarchist society without developing a spiritual motive-force within ourselves. We need 'a calmer and more durable motive-force' than what instinct and reason could provide.

> It is a spiritual, an inner freedom that can alone create a perfect human order. It is a spiritual, a greater than the rational enlightenment that can alone illumine the vital nature of man and impose harmony on its self-seekings, antagonisms and discords. A deeper brotherhood, a yet unfound law of love is the only sure foundation possible for a perfect social evolution, no other can replace it.[50]

Sri Aurobindo is aware of the difficulties involved in achieving this ideal brotherhood. But once we are persuaded that this is the right goal for us, there is no reason why we should not try to reach it. The spiritual man is the integral man. And it is in him that all the aspects, urges and aspirations of human nature find their highest fulfilment. Human fulfilment is not a purely private affair. It has to be sustained by a community, a social framework, some institutionalised form of brotherhood. When a brotherhood is reflective of the *realised* unity of mankind it never stifles the growth of individual nature. In the ideal anarchist society the individual is universal and the universal finds its perfect individuated expression.

Sri Aurobindo's concept of the *integral man* reminds one of the Marxist dream of the *whole man.* Marx thinks that it is primarily the institution of private property which stands *in the way of man's* (ideal) *becoming*. He conceives human *existence* as a sort of *social activity.* Man is both a producer and a product of society. His personality is the outcome and justification of society. 'Though man is a unique individual—and it is just his particularity which makes him an individual, a really *individual* communal being—he is equally the *whole*, the ideal whole, a subjective existence of society as thought and experienced. He exists in reality as the representation and the real mind of social existence, and as the son of human manifestations and life.'[51]

Man must have the freedom of creative labour, without it he cannot develop what is best in him. Marx is convinced that unless private property is abolished and the class struggle resolved, man cannot be free. The free man is the whole man, free from conflicts and constraints resulting from irreconciliable class-based private proprietory rights. It is only in a stateless society, in a true Communist society, that man can enjoy real freedom. This freedom is not to be confused with liberty. For liberty as a right of man is not founded upon the relations between man and man but rather upon the separation of man from man. A durable and ideal unity of mankind is founded upon freedom, free creative activity, and not liberty as a right granted to man by the State.

Marx is also aware that it is not easy to establish this Communist society, the realm of freedom. However, he believes that man will ultimately reach this Communist goal through ' a severe and protracted process '. But if he can organise revolution and bring about revolutionary transformations in the mode of production and inter-class relationships, the ideal process of becoming may certainly be expedited.

Marx's concept of anarchism and Sri Aurobindo's concept of anarchism provide an interesting political-sociological study in contrast. One highlights the institutional aspect or collectivistic pole of human nature and the other draws our attention to the inner and subjective aspect of the same. Neither denies the necessity of a harmonious combination of both. They differ on the method to be mainly followed in the matter of realising that ideal social harmony. Marx is never tired of emphasising the primacy of the role of social institutions—to be more specific, modes of production—in shaping human nature. He denies the autonomy of human mind or psychology. There is nothing in the mind which is not determined by the functioning of socio-economic institutions. Even human *existence* is described by Marx as a sort of *activity*. He tries to establish a close correlation between human nature and the mode of production. It is a dialectical correlation and not a unilateral causation. Marx never denies that human nature, determined by the attending social forces, can also influence the latter in its turn. In this dialectic of man-and-institution man is more influenced than influential in relation to society. From this dialectical formulation of the man-society relation one must not gather that man is always uniformly subjected to and influenced by the institutions of society. In fact the successive modes of production subsequent to the origin of private property are marked by a gradually increasing freedom of the human nature in its relation to the attending social institutions and cultural influences. Marx's point is that unless we can transform our productive relationship and accordingly revolutionise the objective character of the social institutions, the ideal of human freedom cannot be practically realised. In other words, human freedom needs some objective foundation and institutional guarantee.

It is perhaps on this point that the difference between Marx's approach and Sri Aurobindo's approach may be most clearly brought out. Sri Aurobindo very clearly asserts that freedom is primarily an inward adventure and achievement. It is primarily a subjective phenomenon, a self-possessed and tranquil *status* of consciousness. Freedom, which needs some objective foundation and institutional guarantee, is obviously derivative and unstable in nature. A truly free man is spiritual, lives in and by his soul-power. Without the aid or medium of social institutions he can realise the unity of his being with other fellow human beings. Sri Aurobindo emphasises the necessity of the spiritual transformation of man for the establishment of an ideal society, an anarchist society.

If my analyses of Marx's theory and Sri Aurobindo's view are correct, there is no reason why they could not be reconciled in a more comprehensive and concrete theory of society, State and individual. It is clear from Marx's writings that he is mainly concerned with the common man, the downtrodden, the proletariat of the capitalist society. His observation of the inhuman sufferings of the working class in an industrial society in its early stage impressed him very deeply. He is convinced that unless the working class through determined struggle can revolutionise the productive relationship and capture the State power, it will not be able to establish and defend its rights and freedom. For him it is a part of the general theory of the State. He, however, does not rule out the possibility that some exceptional individuals *qua* individuals can rise above their class affiliation and for almost all practical purposes achieve and enjoy freedom. But this is not an ideal form of freedom. Besides its limited individual connotation, it is without any secure foundation and therefore of little social consequence.

Sri Aurobindo contests the very underlying assumption of this view, viz., true freedom needs some basis or foundation. In fact, he argues, freedom means freedom from all dependents or determinations. Freedom is self-determination. Sri Aurobindo recognises the importance of the material, vital and intellectual satisfaction of our needs. At the same time he takes pains to point out that these satisfactions only pave the way for and do not provide the foundation for freedom. These are the necessary but not sufficient conditions for freedom. Freedom is essentially unconditional. Or, alternatively speaking, it is self-conditioned. In one sense the individual is free for ever. By the very *metaphysical* nature of his being he is free. It is only in the context of his *social* identity that the question of achieving freedom arises or makes sense. At the social level he is trying to achieve what is already achieved in his being. This is what has been often characterised as getting the got. Without resorting to metaphysical extravagance one can always plausibly maintain that when most of the people do need institutional help and guarantees to be free and to exercise that freedom, there are certainly some exceptional people who can enjoy freedom by the very power of their own nature. The question is whether we should develop our theory on the model of the exceptional few or on that of the ordinary many.

# 9

# Civilisation and Culture

## Conceptual Preliminaries

The twin concepts of civilisation and culture are often used but not easy to define. One way of understanding and explicating these two concepts is to trace their etymology. Civilisation is a state of civil society. And a civil society is marked by various institutions, means and mechanisms of life and living. Human institutions are of various kinds—social, political and economic. It is true that there is no hard and fast line of distinction between different kinds of institutions. A study in depth of the facts and fictions or beliefs interrelating different institutions and sustaining them as integral parts of a whole dynamic complex makes us aware of what culture really is. The metaphor of cultivation or agriculture is not quite irrelevant to a preliminary understanding of the nature of culture. Unless we scratch the surface of our institutions and dig deep into the sources and forces which support them, we do not know what really they are and cannot follow adequately their changing patterns of functioning, survival and modification.

Another way of explicating what civilisation is, is to contrast it with a state of society often critically characterised as barbarism. Civilisation and barbarism are relative terms. So the line of distinction drawn between the two changes from age to age. Peoples of settled civilisations generally develop a superior and supercilious attitude towards the nomadic peoples. For example, the Hellenic and Roman people had an unmitigated contempt for the Barbarians, Goths and Vandals. But it is a well-known fact that in running warfare the settled peoples of 'superior' civilisations are no match for the nomads. Attila the Hun, Chengis Khan and Taimur proved this truth repeatedly and very convincingly. In respect of war, an important institution of civilisation, the so-called barbaric peoples demonstrated time and again their superiority over the so-called more civilised peoples equipped with better technology. It is not necessarily the material means and mechanisms, including technology, of civilisation which impart strength to a group of people. The relatively less perceptible aspect of human living, art, science and other intellectual achievements collectively designated as culture, is also a factor to reckon with.

Different thinkers have used different principles for the identification and classification of culture. Some have tried to correlate culture with religious spirit. Religion is their classificatory principle. Some others have maintained that the character of culture is determined by that of class and the latter in turn by the economic mode of production. There were still others to defend the view that culture is to be classified following some psychological principles. Whether 'religious spirit' and 'psychological principles' are themselves autonomous or derivative is itself a matter of controversy between thinkers of different persuasions. Sri Aurobindo follows psychological principles in characterising and classifying cultures. The material forms of civilisation, modes of production, types of government and administration and the like, are, according to him, determined from within by the dominant psychological disposition of the age. In *The Human Cycle* he traces the development of the human mind in general and its changing character-traits, correlating them with appropriate institutional expressions. The means and mechanisms of civilisation and forms of culture are on ultimate analysis found to be cast in the moulds of human psychology. The inner history of the development of the human mind supporting and sustaining different types of civilisation and culture is more helpful than anything else in explaining external forms of our life and living.

Sri Aurobindo's concept of culture is essentially spiritual and comprehensive. It includes both the inner psychology and outer sociology of human life and its environment. There is also a teleological trend of perfection underlying every human culture. Some social anthropologists, especially the American ones, use the term *culture* in an all-comprehensive sense. Culture comprehends all aspects of social life, language and communication, modes of production and distribution, religion and morals and different forms of art, science and technology.

Culture has been conceived by some as a value-neutral and by others as a value-loaded concept. In sociology and anthropology culture is generally used as a value-neutral concept. It is true that ethics and religion figure prominently in the works of sociology and anthropology. But the approach there is positive and descriptive. The description of ethical or religious practices is not by itself significant from any evaluation point of view.

Of course this does not mean that culture has no value-connotation at all. When we say of a man 'he is perfectly *cultured*' or 'he is *urbane* and *sophisticated*' or 'he is *crude* and *rustic*', each of these concepts has, even if in an indefinite way, a value significance of its own. In this context culture is a body of norms and standards of perfection. In the scale of perfection human actions and dispositions are arranged in a graded manner. In the face of diverse usage of the concept of culture it would be wrong to suggest that there is only one correct view of it and the rest are indefensible.

## What Sustains and what Destroys Civilisation and Culture

Sri Aurobindo delineates the concepts of culture and civilisation both diachronically or dynamically and synchronically or in the still frame of time. He thinks that through the different phases of the human cycle we are moving towards a definite goal—the perfect end. Obviously all people of a particular phase of the human cycle cannot be of identical, or even similar, disposition. Diversity in unity is in the nature of all things and beings. Individuals being free as they are cannot be uniformly shaped or influenced by their contemporary civilisation and culture. It cannot be truly said of every modern man that he is more civilised and cultured than his primitive forefathers. Environed by modern civilisation and culture man is always free *not* to be influenced by his attending circumstances. So 'a primitive man in modern society' is not a contradiction in terms. What I am saying now is more a matter of exception than of general principle. All things being equal, the environment of modern civilisation is much more helpful than that of primitive society in shaping and developing the personality of man. One *can* live contrary to the spirit of one's time. But that does not negate the fact that mankind at large is very much influenced by the spirit of its times.

Because of his mind, mental will and symbolic power, man is not tied down to his own and Nature's physical part of the existence. He can turn his mind upon its own workings and also to their physical and vital conditions. It is the faculty of free and intelligent will which is said to have enabled man to be civilised, to disengage himself from his material and vital conditions of living and growing, and to explore some possibilities of wider and deeper organisation. Man alone is a symbolic and creative animal.

The deep secret of the mental being is yet unknown to man as a race. It is on the realisation of this deep secret that, Sri Aurobindo believes, a higher culture could be established. This higher culture is essentially an inner culture and spiritual in character. The man in the street is still predominantly vital. The instinct of possession is his dominant characteristic. If not otherwise regulated or controlled, the natural drift of his mind is towards possessive individualism. Of course this does not mean the reappearance of crude materialism and old barbarism. The materialist and the barbarian identify the self with the body and physical life. In the earliest period of the human cycle this complete identification was indeed a necessity. For it and it alone could afford the common ground of human unity. That period is long over.

Modern materialism or barbarism is considerably different from the old one. The new findings of natural and life sciences have discovered a new horizon before man. He has now good ground and strong reason to believe that the physical veil of nature more conceals than expresses the true and inner nature of reality. Physical nature separates man from man. It is only in the social space that man finds a common ground to meet and be united with fellow human beings. Underlying our social meeting ground or community there is a spiritual unity. Man must first know his true self and through the self the said unity. And that knowledge would be the basis of the richest and durable human unity.

Sri Aurobindo draws a line of distinction between the message of the sages, 'know thyself' and the message of the thinker, 'educate thyself'. Self-knowledge is a difficult and serious proposition. Self-education is an important proposition. Anything serious and difficult is generally avoided these days. The common man is generally interested to get something done either by machines or by others and not in doing it himself. A lack of self-knowledge is the main reason why modern man is becoming increasingly dependent on others and as a result of which the sphere and importance of State activities are steadily increasing.

Self-education is next best to self-knowledge. And man has opted for it. Education means ' recognition by the race that the mind and not the life and the body are the man and that without the development of the mind he does not possess his true manhood '. Quite in keeping with the demand of the time-spirit our aim of education has been defined rather superficially. It primarily *takes care of ' intellegience and mental capacity and knowledge of the* world and things ' and only secondarily and imperfectly gives some moral training and develops the aesthetic faculties. Modern education lays emphasis more on capacity and utility and less on duty and refinement. Unless and until the vitalistic overemphasis of the practical aspects of everything human is not regulated, tempered and refined by some superior forces of inner culture, the present drift is sure to persist.

Sri Aurobindo thinks that the modern industrial age is in a way returning to and developing in a different way the old Hellenic ideal. Our pragmatism is thinly quoted by conventional ethics and aesthetics. Moreover this culture has no deeper foundation to support it. It is an elitist culture confined to a very thin layer of the population and has no deep root in the life of the people. Rightly understood, culture is not a thing only of outer life, a mere elegance and ornament. Similarly, one might say, civilisation is not a mere state of civil society concerned only with the physical and vital aspects of man's living. An ornamental or a superficial culture dies a natural death, since it cannot draw its nourishment from the deeper reaches of the human mind and the life of the people at large. In support of his contention Sri Aurobindo refers to the ancient history of Greece and Rome.

> The old Hellenic or Graeco-Roman civilisation perished, among other reasons, because it only imperfectly generalised culture in its own society and was surrounded by huge masses of humanity who were still possessed by the barbarian habit of mind. Civilisation can never be safe so long as, confining the cultured mentality to a small minority, it nourishes in its bosom a tremendous mass of ignorance, a multitude, a proletariat. Either knowledge must enlarge itself from above or be always in danger of submergence by the ignorant night from below. Still more must it be unsafe, if it allows enormous numbers of men to exist outside its pale uninformed by its light, full of the natural vigour of the barbarian, who may at any moment seize upon the physical weapons of the civilised without undergoing an intellectual transformation by their culture. The Graeco-Roman culture perished from within and from without, from without by the floods of Teutonic barbarism, from within by the loss of its vitality.[1]

The decay and death of civilisation and culture may be prevented by science and technology. Yet it is very curious to note that what man produces at his technological best makes himself almost irrelevant in its practical use or application. Unless it is appropriately controlled by education, man's own creation will definitely overtake him. This is one of the inherent paradoxes of the modern industrial and technological civilisation.

A good system of education does not give man only that sort of power which has use-value but also that sort of power which enables him to regulate and control himself. Aggressiveness or militancy is no proof of the soundness of a culture. It is just the opposite.

## Two Cultures: Ethical and Aesthetic

The pursuit of the mental life for its own sake is what Sri Aurobindo calls culture. To reach the mental plane man has to pass through some other planes of existence in the course of evolution. The vital plane provides the base of barbarism which may be taken as the latest hour of the night before the bursting of the dawn of civilisation. The mental plane has two sides—the vital-mental and the active-mental. The former is predominantly expressive of the subjective direction of social evolution although with the objective as its occasion, and the latter of the objective direction of the social evolution although subjective as its occasion. If the subjective direction of the mental being loses its objective orientation, it degenerates into a sort of egoism. If, on the other hand, the objective direction is subjectively regulated by the intimacy and authenticity of knowledge, it tends to be a purposeless movement of an endless journey.

It is the tension and conflict between the subjective knowledge and intention and the objective needs and demands that kindle the ethical and the aesthetic being in man. The best possible balance between the two that man the rational animal can achieve by exercise of his dynamic power of intelligent will, the *buddhi*, is bound to be unsteady and imperfect.

To Sri Aurobindo's mind Hellenism is the paradigm of aesthetic culture and Hebraism of ethical culture. There is undoubtedly a lot of difference between different forms of ethical culture. But they are found to exhibit some common features like emphasis on will-power, importance of character, self-mastery and self-discipline. Sparta, Republican Rome before it was Hellenised, and Puritan England are some of the notable forms of ethical culture. The Puritan culture of England was more religious than ethical in its orientation. In spite of its emphasis on culture of conduct it gradually degenerated into a sort of ' bourgeois respectability ' and ' Philistinism pure and simple ' in the nineteenth century.

I do not know whether Sri Aurobindo had any acquaintance with Max Weber's *The Protestant Ethic and the Spirit of Capitalism*, the German original of which, *Die protestantische Ethik und der Geist des Kapitalismus* was published in the years 1904–5, more than a decade before Sri Aurobindo's own work on the subject, *The Human Cycle* (1916–18) published in *Arya*. Max Weber also traces the spirit of capitalism to the Protestant ethic.

The capitalist society, all said and done, makes man primarily money-minded and of acquisitive habit. The capitalist's typical moral attitudes are all coloured with utilitarianism. To him honesty is useful because it assures credit. Punctuality, industry and frugality are virtues because they pay. But these unpleasant and ugly aspects of capitalism obviously need some ethico-religious justifications. Calvinism on the continent and Puritanism in England provided this much-needed justification.

Weber points out that the most important opponent with which the spirit of capitalism has had to struggle is tradition. By the early twentieth century, when Weber was writing his book, the individualistic political, legal and economic institutions became so well-established that capitalism no longer needed the support of any religion or ethics.[2]

Weber observes:

> This worldly Protestant asceticism . . . acted powerfully against the spontaneous enjoyment of possessions; it restricted consumption, especially of luxuries. On the other hand, it had the psychological effect of freeing the acquisition of goods from the inhibitions of traditionalistic ethics. It broke the bonds of the impulse of acquisition in that it not only legalised it, but. . . .looked upon it as directly willed by God.[3]

Thinkers are not unanimous on the point whether culture is a unifying or a differentiating force. Rightly understood, religious culture, based on some or other forms of monotheism, should be or lead to a universal culture. But historical facts do not confirm this expectation or conjecture. Catholic culture, for instance, is not as tolerant as its name might suggest. Nor has the Protestant culture always lived up to its protestant profession. Often it has been found to be an ally of political conservatism and economic statusquoism. Further, one might point out, Hinduism has allowed a rigid and irrational stratification within its fold despite the fact that of all well-known religions it is the least institutionalised.

Any discipline that is imposed on man without being consented to by him may serve some dying cause but not without disturbing the natural development of his character. A one-sided emphasis on discipline of character cannot give man the abiding delight of living. The rigours of Spartan and disciplined Hebraic culture and Kantian morals take away the sweetness of life. Sri Aurobindo observes that the man of ethical culture ' tends to distrust art and the aesthetic sense as something lax and emollient, something in its nature undisciplined and by its attractive appeals to the passions and emotions destructive of a high and strict self-control '. In early Republican Rome every measure was taken to repel the Hellenic influence on the Roman people because of its alleged corrupting character. Similarly, Sparta did not allow an iota of aesthetic culture to grow within its realm except only in the form of martial music and poetry. A rigorous ethical culture entertains and encourages many customs and practices which, by every test, should be condemned as cruel or immoral and impede the development of the gentler and more delicate side of moral character and conduct. The delight of living demands freedom of living, growing and perfecting all human faculties, good and beautiful. ' The human mind needs to think, feel, enjoy, expand; expansion is its very nature and restriction is only useful to it in so far as it helps to study, guide and strengthen its expansion.'[4]

The main determining forces of aesthetic culture are beauty, enjoyment and freedom. The purest form of this culture was found in the Athens of Chidias and Sophocles. A refined aesthetic sense suffused the art, music, drama, poetry, sculpture and architecture of the time. The philosophical ideas of the contemporary thinkers have earned a proverbial importance for their aimlessness. They lacked in steadiness. Sophoclean Athens is known for its tepid, conventional and customary morality and superficial religion characterised by its pleasant rites and festivals, artistic creation and aesthetic enjoyment. It was an age of beauty but without any character and stability. It is this urge of the human mind to expand without being steady and without assuming a character which accounts for its rather quick decline within a century. The form of beauty overran its content and the art of rhetorical persuasion carried man away from his feeling for truth.[5] The structure of an aesthetical culture without an ethical foundation, without commitment to truth and justice, is bound to be unstable.

The reaction of the subsequent thinkers and artists against this brief and glorious period of ancient Greece is very interesting and instructive to note. Sri Aurobindo observes: ' Plato . . . felt himself obliged first to censure and then to banish the poets from his ideal polity '. One might controvert whether Plato really intended to exclude fine arts from his Republic. But his strictures against aimless aesthetic culture and his approval of a virile culture are unmistakable. Dunning emphasises this point when he writes:

> The *a priori* and idealising method of Plato's political philosophy does not conceal even from the casual reader the intimate relation between the doctrines enunciated and the currents of practical Greek politics. It does not require the explicit eulogy of Sparta which several times occurs to reveal that the Peloponnesian state and the system she represents constitute the model from which the philosopher draws his inspiration.[6]

The inadequacy and unsatisfactoriness of what follows in practice from an one-sided aesthetic culture deeply impressed contemporary thinkers and they were trying to find a way out. This view is clearly confirmed by Toynbee also.

> In adapting the Spartan system to their own ideas they (the Athenian postwar philosophers) sought to improve upon it in two ways: first by working it out to its logical extremes and, secondly, by the imposition of a sovereign intellectual caste (Plato's ' Guardians '), in the likeness of the Athenian philosophers [austere rationalists] themselves, upon the Spartiate military caste, which is to be taught to play a second fiddle in the Utopian orchestra.[7]

The aesthetic view of life needs a solid basis of well-formed character for its establishment and acceptance. Otherwise the cult of beauty which depends entirely on spontaneity and has no definite character of its own gradually loses its sense of direction and turns out to be blind or aimless. Similarly, religion without any spiritual foundation and of the superficial aesthetic type tends to degenerate into corruption. Sri Aurobindo refers to Italy of the Renaissance as a clear example of the insufficiency of the aesthetic view of life.[8] Acton, Hallam, Michelet, Voltaire and Burckhardt, among others, regard the Renaissance as pre-eminently a revival of classical rationalism. Sri Aurobindo rejects this view. According to him, this is not correct at least in the case of its birth-place, Italy. When Russell says, ' the long centuries of ascetism were forgotten in riot of art, poetry and pleasure ', we find a confirmation of Sri Aurobindo's view of the Renaissance. The riotous culture of beauty opened wide the door of the revival of learning, philosophical and scientific. But the aesthetic culture of the period was so completely devoid of the ethical impulse that it was deeply resented and strongly protested against. The voice of resentment and protest was raised first within Italy itself by Savonarola, a Florentian monk, but found more organised expression in the ethical minded Teutonic nations. This provided the background to the Reformation. Italy could not regain her own national character until Mazzini supplemented her aesthetic culture by the revival of a new impulse of will, self-discipline and self-mastery.

All human faculties have their own law and logic, but it is not possible for every man to discover them individually and clearly. Sri Aurobindo thinks that feeling or willing cannot coordinate the different functions of the human mind. The nature and result of mental activities make it abundantly clear that mind does act in a coordinated way. The task of coordination has been attributed to reason.

## Two Cultures: Transcendental and Hedonic

Sri Aurobindo is aware that spiritualism has often been mistaken and criticised as a sort of transcendentalism, a metaphysical denial of the sense-world. In the name of religion and spirituality, as we had occasion to refer before, poverty has been practically confirmed, austerity glorified and exploitation indirectly justified. Many pro-Marxist thinkers, who are otherwise very critical of philosophical empiricism and ethical emotivism, have particularly attacked this interpretation of spiritualism. Whether this interpretation is a correct interpretation or an intended one is of course a different question.

This sort of transcendental spiritualism gives rise to what Herbert Marcuse calls an ' affirmative culture '. The spiritual good is just opposed to the material good elevated somewhere beyond the reach of human senses. The epistemological dualism between sense and reason corresponds to the ethical dualism between material good and spiritual good. Spiritual good cannot be known by the sense-mind. We need a sort of rational insight, a third eye, to know what is spiritually good, good for ever and good for all.

By affirmative culture is meant that culture of the bourgeois epoch which led in the course of its own development to the segregation from civilisation of the mental and spiritual world as an independent realm of value that is also considered superior to civilisation. Its decisive characteristic is the assertion of a universally obligatory, eternally better and more valuable world that must be unconditionally affirmed: a world essentially different from the factual world of the daily struggle for existence, yet realisable by every individual for himself 'from within', without any transformation of the state of fact. It is only in this culture that value which elevates them above the everyday sphere. Their reception becomes an act of celebration and exaltation.[9]

The pro-Marxist thinks that the bourgeois culture suffers from an anxiety complex. This culture conceals the unpleasant and ugly conditions of social life. Defenders of this culture extol some abstract values, ethical and aesthetic, unrelated to the material conditions of life. In order to justify this rootless view of culture they have to develop an elaborate speculative system. Spiritual man, intuitive knowledge, self-evident theory of truth, permanence in change, beauty underlying the ugly and freedom within bondage are some of the main elements of the system. To beautify the soul man is asked to forget his bodily misery. To be good he is asked to cultivate and realise the virtues of poverty and austerity. The constraints of the mode of production and distribution of the capitalist system force a man to be lonely or atomic purely as a matter of fact. 'Factual loneliness is sub-limited to metaphysical loneliness and, as such, is accorded the entire aura and rapture of inner plenitude alongside external poverty.'

The pro-Marxist critique of bourgeois culture is understandable and to a certain extent acceptable to Sri Aurobindo. But the narrow connotation of spiritualism attacked by the Marxist is not what Sri Aurobindo proposed to defend. In fact, he in his own way scathingly criticises bourgeois civilisation and culture. In 'The Two Negations: The Materialist Denial and the Refusal of the Ascetic' of *The Life Divine* Sri Aurobindo argues that the materialist denial of the beyond and the spiritualist rejection of the transient are two untenable extremes. As a corrective to ascetism he recommends materialism, materialism with a difference. It brings us nearer to the intricate operation of the forces of physical nature and enables us to discover the laws underlying the chaotic multiplicity of the physical things. Materialism is self-corrective. Its own progress makes it conscious of its own inadequacy. The fallibilism of science is an indication of its limitations and also of the scientist's awareness of the same.

From the materialist's mistake one must not conclude that the transcendentalist is right in denying the importance of what is transient and worldly. The superficial or the positivistic affirmation of physical realities is a negation of supra-physical realities. The reason is very simple. Sri Aurobindo observes that the glimpses of supra-physical realities acquired by positivistic methods are 'still crude and defective'. This materialistic denial or positivistic affirmation is not the last word in man's quest for deeper truth and higher reality.

Sri Aurobindo speaks of subtle senses witnessing physical facts beyond the range of the corporeal organs.

While we must avoid the pitfall of the materialist denial of the spiritual range of reality, Sri Aurobindo warns us, we cannot afford to ally ourselves with the revolt of the spirit against the material world, the world of sense-perception.

> It is this revolt of Spirit against Matter that for two thousand years, since Buddhism disturbed the balance of the old Aryan world, has dominated increasingly the Indian mind . . . all have lived in the shadow of the great Refusal and the final end of life for all is the garb of the ascetic . . . renunciation the sole path of knowledge, acceptation of physical life the act of the ignorant, cessation from birth the right use of the human birth, the call of the Spirit, the recoil from Matter.[10]

Marcuse's criticism of the affirmative culture rests on a superficial appreciation of the spiritual culture. From Sri Aurobindo's point of view positivistic affirmation is not the only possible or even the right sort of affirmation. 'We seek indeed a larger and completer affirmation.'[11] This affirmation is essentially spiritual in character. Spirituality does not flourish in the void. It is based on the material conditions of life, on the power and joy of life. Stupendous vitality, prolific creativity and material abundance are the ranges which the spiritual mind conquers. The spiritual mentality is the foundation of Indian culture and civilisation. It rejects no part of human life, vital or intellectual. On the contrary, it affirms both the joy of life and the exploration of reason. 'It is a great error to suppose that spirituality flourishes best in an impoverished soil with the life half-killed and the intellect discouraged and intimidated.'[12] Sri Aurobindo is unmistakably for an integral spiritual culture which is opulent in vitality and opulent in intellectuality. He notes in the ancient Indian spirit a strong intellectuality which is 'at once austere and rich, robust and minute, powerful and delicate, massive in principle and curious in detail'. In *The Foundations of Indian Culture* Sri Aurobindo shows, with a plethora of examples drawn from the history of Indian art, literature and polity, that the Indian spirit has wonderfully harmonised vitality and intellectuality on its broad and sure foundation.

The broad and deeper interpretation of Indian culture offered by Sri Aurobindo should not lead one to believe that it has been accepted and practised in the correct way. The metaphysical bias dominated the Indian mind. That does not mean that we or our forefathers were quite oblivious of the importance of *kama*, sense-life, or *artha*, economic life. But since the transcendental attitude, a resultant of the metaphysical bias, got the better of other attitudes of life, the typical Indian mind started looking down upon the pursuits of pleasure and money. In the order of values, sacrifice, toleration and austerity have been rated higher over values like enjoyment and acquisition. It is not that the Hedonic tradition is unknown to the Indian culture or that sense-pleasure has always been dubbed as a natural quality of bodily sensation devoid of any ethical content. The basic point of Hedonism and utilitarianism has been conceded and this concession has been grudging, more factual and less evaluative in character. Necessity and utility are matters of fact and not of values. The metaphysical bias and transcendental logic succeeded in abstracting the order of value from that of fact, product from the process, extolling the former in isolation from the latter.

A degenerate form of a culture should not be singled out for the purpose of criticism. In the context of Indian culture it has been repeatedly argued that its practical aspect or behavioural exterior should not be taken too seriously. To understand it properly one is often advised to get into its soul, spiritual ingoings and depth. This advice is well taken by the sympathetic critic. But even then the question remains whether the identity of a culture is to be found only in its spiritual depth in total disregard of its material forms and behavioural manifestations.

In fairness to Sri Aurobindo it has to be clearly admitted that he has looked closely into this question. Notwithstanding his metaphysical bias he tries to discover and demonstrate a continuous thread between the spiritual ingoings and material outgoings of Indian culture. He is not one of those superficial philosophers of Indian culture who is easily vulnerable to Marxist criticism, as echoed by Marcuse, for instance, that the abstraction of the spiritual from the material and glorification of the former at the expense of the latter are the requirements of the feudal and bourgeois modes of production and exploitation. In fact, Sri Aurobindo does not resort to an abstractionist strategy. One might say his is an integrationist strategy. He proposes to integrate the two aspects of culture, the outer and the inner, and, what is more interesting to note, *in reality* they are integrated. The question of integration comes up in a big way before us only because the interest and attention of the sense-mind are almost exclusively confined to what is outer and easily perceptible. Once man develops his inlook, ceases to be satisfied with what is furnished by his senses and starts making use of his powerful intuitive capacity, he discovers a new world, a larger and richer world than he is ordinarily conscious of. Sri Aurobindo refuses to accept the dualism between fact and value. He rejects utilitarianism in its classical form, but is quite persuaded of its relevance in life.

> Utility is a fundamental principle of existence and all fundamental principles of existence are in the end one; therefore it is true that the highest good is also the highest utility .... Good, not utility, must be the principle and standard of good; otherwise we fall into the hands of that dangerous pretender expediency whose whole method is alien to the ethical .... There is only one safe rule for the ethical man, to stick to his principle of good, his instinct for good, his intuition of good and to govern by that his conduct.[13]

In terms of spiritual intuition Sri Aurobindo proposes to integrate the inner and the outer life of man. To ensure their integration and prevent a clash between them man has to free himself from his servile subjection to the sense-mind and disengage the intellect from its function of turning passions and instincts into ethical ideals. In other words, the intellect is not to be used to *rationalise* what is infra-rational. On the contrary, it has to discover the *rationale* underlying human passions, emotions and instincts. Man can do it only when he is guided by spiritual power and light. This power is not something alien to our own nature and this light is not to be borrowed from a different world. Social existence, daily life and the thousand other minor and major pre-occupations of man do not in any way stand in his way of realising the unity between his inner being and his outer environment. In fact, the reflective man does not quite know where his being ends and his environment starts. Being may be alienated from its root-reference and objectified by abstract reasoning, and environment incorporated and assimilated by intuitive consciousness within the being. The line of demarcation between the two cannot be clearly drawn and maintained. The dialectic of being and environment, man and nature, effects an increased integration between the two. This correct perspective is not clear before the sense-mind. The pull of instinct, the drive of emotion and the turmoil of passion provide him with a juxtaposed picture of man and environment. Unless man's intellect is calmed and illumined by spiritual power and light, he cannot quite see how natural stimulations and social connections could present him with a lavish and manifold opportunity to discover and express the deeper reaches and higher heights of his being. The spiritual standpoint enables him to realise that his so-called material environment and social situation are in different ways constitutive of his own being. This also opens up before him a new dimension of relationship between himself and otherselves. The relation between the subjective and the objective is rediscovered at a deeper level where the subjective is a doorway to the objective and the objective a field of freedom for the subjective. Without a creative and dynamic integration between the two an ethical society and an ethical culture cannot be established and maintained.

For, otherwise, moral values, unsustained by live and creative intentions, would tend to degenerate into dead conventions. Norms turn out to be mere forms. This is a typical symptom of the typal-conventional age. Strongly under the influence of this age human reason is unable to grasp the true meaning of Good. Good is an indefinable quality of the object of human desire. Intuitionists like Moore and Ross maintain that this quality is there in the very nature of the object and not attributed to it by the human mind. Sri Aurobindo thinks that basic values like Good and Beauty are not the creation of man. The sense-mind perceives them as pleasant and useful, the spiritual mind can apperceive them as Good, Right, Beauty and Just. But their existence or subsistence is said to be both eternal and historical, subjective and objective at the same time. Values are expressed but not exhausted in the time-process. Their time-forms may be eroded, distorted and worn out. But their locus is eternal. It is impossible for the ordinary human mind to follow the relation between the historical forms and expressions of the basic values and their eternal locus. It has been claimed that the spiritual mind is not subject to this limitation and disability.

Every culture has a career of its own and it can be studied for theoretical or analytical purposes independently of the life of the concerned people. But in fact the traits and qualities of individual human beings are ultimate constituents and determinants of the character of a particular culture. For classificatory purposes we differentiate ethical culture from aesthetic culture. Every culture has multiple value commitments reflective of the different aspects and intentions of basic human nature. Because of its dominant ethical bias a particular culture is characterised as ethical. That obviously does not mean that it lacks in aesthetic orientation. The same is true of an aesthetic culture as well. Man is the basic unit of society and therefore his intentions and actions cannot but somehow be reflected in his cultural environment.

The search for beauty and the search for good are native to human nature. The object of the search is real and independent of him and his intention is to realise it. The denial of this position results in committing the hedonistic fallacy, viz., to define good in terms of utility and beauty in terms of pleasure. It is well known that some virtues, love of knowledge, for example, have no apparent use-value. Similarly, one might point out, the tragic sense of life far from being pleasant is marked by a sort of drawing painfulness, a melancholic beauty, but its aesthetic value is undeniable. The morality and beauty of a society depend upon the development and strength of the ethical and aesthetic traits of the concerned individuals. I say 'development and strength' because the *origin* of these two sentiments are there in the very roots of our life. Aesthetic enjoyment and ethical satisfaction work almost as instincts of human nature. Both in our ethical and aesthetic pursuits the role of reason is intermediary or tertiary. It discerns, corrects, enlightens and points out the deficiencies and the crudities of our ethical and aesthetic instincts and impulses and tries to lay down certain criteria and norms to improve and purify our conduct and appreciation by superior taste and valid knowledge. 'A complete and universal appreciation of beauty and making entirely beautiful our whole life and being must surely be a necessary character of the perfect individual and the perfect society.'[14]

The common denominator of all basic values, good, beauty and truth, is *harmony*. Whether it is a work of art or right conduct or a true statement it must satisfy certain rules of harmony and must reject elements of incompatibility. Even when elements of apparent incompatibility are admitted, they are admitted deliberately to heighten a particular intended effect of unity or harmony. 'Beauty is the mutual adaptation of the several factors in an occasion of experience.'[15] It would be wrong to believe that the products of aesthetic imagination are not subject to any law or criterion. The very possibility of aesthetic judgement is indicative of the law-governed character of the aesthetic process and product. I speak of *process* in addition to *products* because I know that a little reflection would show that even aesthetic appreciation admits of gradation and valuation. It is in this context that one has to realise the importance of the Kantian concept of the *free lawfulness* of beauty. The artist's imagination is not licensed for flight from reality or truth. His freedom of imagination has its inner compulsion or regulation. Without trivialising the concept of truth one has to understand how the artist is faithful or true to his aesthetic experience and what prevents him to express something else within a time-frame.

'The work of art which on a given occasion a given artist creates is . . . created by him not merely because he can create it but because he must.'[16] The occasion and expression of aesthetic experience are bound to be harmonious. Similarly, it might be pointed out how harmony between (sentential) appearance and (referential) reality defines or accounts for truth.

The harmony which is capable of being apprehended and expressed by reason is said to be of the formal type and therefore superficial. The search for beauty and good which is native to and originates from instinct and impulse cannot be carried forward by reason beyond a certain extent. Since the involvement of reason prevents it from having a fuller picture of truth and a clearer vision of beauty, the richer harmony of the elements of the object of experience, desire and delight, are not revealed to the eye of reason. It is for this fact that Aurobindo assigns to the spirit the highest role of creation and disinterested enjoyment of beauty. The spirit is also the deepest fountain and the best knower of what is good. In *The Future Poetry* he argues that mental and vital interests, pleasure, pain of thought, life and action are not the source of aesthetic creation or delight. Reason provides only an insufficient perception and 'harmony that exist between our internal selves and our external experience'. It cannot sufficiently purify and tranquillise our emotions and feelings. Consequently, it cannot be the source of poetry or any other form of expression of aesthetic experience.

> That source, when we know better the secrets of our being, turns out to be the spiritual self with its diviner consciousness and knowledge, happier fountains of power, inalienable delight of existence. The cultures that were able directly or indirectly to feel the joy of this self and spirit, got into the very strain of their aesthesis the touch of its delight, its Ananda, and this touch was the secret of the generalised instinct for beauty which has been denied to a later mind limited by intellectual activity, practical utility and the externals of life: we have to go for it to exceptional individuals gifted with a finer strain, but the wide-spread aesthetic instinct has been lost and as yet to be recovered for the common mind and recognised once more as a part of human perfection as indispensable as intellectual knowledge and at least as necessary to happiness as vital well-being.[17]

Sri Aurobindo anticipates the objection against the spirit as the source of aesthetic creativity. For, it may be alleged, the spirit cannot possibly perform the role of reason. The main complaint against the spiritual mind is that it cannot perform some of the functions like criticism, discrimination and comparison which reason can. Sri Aurobindo rejects this complaint and thinks that the spiritual mind may well take up the functions of the rational mind and perform them 'with power, light and insight greater and surer than the power and light of the intellectual judgement in its widest scope'. The intellect excels in giving us faithful information about the form of beauty, the superficial or exterior truth of things. Its sense-aided penetration into the substance of the beautiful is never very significant and profound. It is only the spirit of beauty in us that may come in contact with both the form and the spirit, *svarūpa* and *svabhāva* of the beautiful and give expression to the form that is truly expressive of its spirit. Classical art because of spiritual inspiration highlighted what is universal and true in the spirit of the real. Romantic art, on the other hand, did much with the individual expression of what is striking. Both classical and romantic art are interested in portraying the universal in a subdued fashion, i.e., putting it into the background. While the former is more concerned with the spirit, the latter with its content. The primary concern of modern art is the form or rather the deformity of objects of experience and desire.

> In truth all great art has carried in it both a classical and a romantic as well as a realistic element,—understanding realism in the sense of the prominent bringing out of the external truth of things, not the perverse inverted romanticism of the 'real' which brings into exaggerated prominence the ugly, common or morbid and puts that forward as the whole truth of life.[18]

## Sociology and Psychology of Civilisation and Culture: Two Views

What Sri Aurobindo criticises as 'the perverse inverted romanticism of the real' has been vigorously defended by many modern anti-romantic thinkers, both Marxist and non-Marxist realists. Their main contention against the 'idealist-romantic' approach is that it ignores the real state of affairs simply because it does not conform to their value commitment or normative objective. Values and ideals are no doubt very important in shaping human life and destiny. But if material conditions of existence persist in their present ugly and unpleasant forms, the idealistic overtones of ethical culture and aesthetic culture would sound more as a mockery than a depiction of the truth of life. The world of the artist cannot be altogether different from the actual world he lives in. The 'autonomy of art' or 'art for the sake of art' is a utopian slogan, says the realist. This, if not something more, is confirmed by the Marxist when he says that art is not only the product of social life but in turn has a reverse effect on it. This effect may be progressive or reactionary, depending on the class character of the artist in question. The realist or the Marxist is not against such immortal characters as Shakespeare's Lady Macbeth or Gogol's Khlestakov. Their evil role does not diminish or take away their artistic significance. By depicting such characters the creative artist brings to the focus the importance of struggle against evil and social injustice. The Marxist's main allegation against bourgeois aesthetics is that it singles out the beautiful as the only object of art. This narrow view of aesthetics attempts to keep art away from the criticism of the bourgeois society, its ugliness, vulgarity and exploitation.

To the Marxist, 'the artist is only a special kind of man of action . . . art is not an end but a colour of an act'. The artist cannot afford to be indifferent to the social conditions of his time. Like the bourgeois artist he also tries to carve harmony or order out of conflicting social elements. But unlike his bourgeois counterpart he has always a social end in view while engaged in his artistic contemplation and action. The Marxist says: 'Our own position about beauty is this: whenever the effective elements in socially known things show social ordering, there we have beauty, there alone we have beauty.'[19] Here the important terms to be noted are 'effective elements' and 'socially known'. A man may know as an individual being; he may also know as a member of a class. In the second case of knowing, knowledge is said to be more authentic and representative. Knowledge may be taken as an end in itself as also a means to or a plan of action. When 'social knowledge' is of no 'effect', the order it discovers is of little aesthetic consequence. The Marxist speaks of socialist realism as distinguished from other types of realism. He is strongly in favour of using art as an instrument of social transformation. The real and objective situation of life and the aspirations of the people must find their expression in the works of the artist. It is admitted that the poetry of Goethe or Tagore, the music of Beethoven or Tchaikovsky or Bade Ghulam Ali, the paintings of Raphael or Ravi Verma, may satisfy the aesthetic taste of different generations at different times. This is explained in terms of the fact that the artist's depiction of reality has two aspects in it, objective truth and subjective vision. Because of his vision the artist can penetrate deep into the nature of reality and depict it in some artistic forms which do not lose their appeal and value in later epochs or to other societies. Every society, while retaining its individuality, shares many experiences, for instance, exploitation and struggle, with other people of other times and societies. Moreover, the Marxist claims that the great works of art of the past are somehow found to be directed against the powers of evil and injustice, against conservative and reactionary influences and are expressive of their national and popular character.[20] It is to be noted that the Marxist has definite value commitments. He is not interested in a mere description of the material and other conditions of social existence. Man's knowledge of his environment and of his own self must somehow be of some use-value in bringing about a progressive transformation of his social environment and for the betterment of the exploited class. Therefore, socialist realism is not to be confused with a sort of popular positivism. The Marxist is also conscious of his obligations to explain the universal appeal of the masterpieces of art transcending the place and time of their creation. Whether this explanation is acceptable or not is a different question. The socially conscious artist cannot indefinitely conceal his class identity and value preference.[21] And as a result of that his work is also subject to the demand for class partisanship. The appreciation and criticism of art and the artist cannot be uniform and universally acceptable.

Socialist realism is not inconsistent with value commitment. The socialist realist is certainly in favour of a scientific approach to the sociology of values, aesthetic and ethical. He rejects the claim of the non-socialist realist who thinks that *values* are *facts* of a different order. The controversy over the possibility of value-free sociology is an old one that has not yet lost its importance and relevance.[22] The Marxist is undoubtedly opposed to that form of aesthetic culture which highlights the beautiful in total disregard of what is not beautiful but tragically true and that form of ethical culture which talks only about the duty of the working class and precious little about its rights and privileges. But that does not mean that he is a pro-naturalist or positivist in the sense that he is free from any value-commitment or positive ideology.

The Marxist shares Fourier's critique of four false and deceptive sciences, 'moralism', 'politics', 'economism' and 'metaphysics'. By moralism Fourier and Marx mean the pre-scientific repressive or ascetic methods of controlling the passions and emotions of men. Suppression of passion cannot be in itself a duty or virtue. Passion is to be studied and properly utilised. In the name of suppression of passion people often resort to pretension, hypocrisy and falsehood. Kant has also been accused of rigourism and totally neglecting the importance of passions, emotions and self-interest in human life. The Marxist is in favour of the real and not the imaginary satisfaction of human passions. His accent on the necessity of coordinating one's passions and desires with those of the rest of his class puts restraints on the Hedonic impulses and excesses of man. But he is certainly against rigourism and ascetism. Man cannot certainly develop the full potentiality of his personality unless his body and its social needs are accorded due recognition by the economic and moral life of the society. The all-round development of human beings demands a socialist system of production and distribution entailing social justice.

In principle this position is unexceptionable. Sri Aurobindo points out the practical inadequacy of this 'objective view of life'. Our life, both individual and social, may be shaped from two different, but not necessarily conflicting, points of view, the subjective and the objective. Most thinkers, including Marx and Sri Aurobindo, agree that the freedom and perfection of man are twin objectives of culture and progress. They also more or less agree on the necessity of trying to realise this objective following two related methods, internal and external. Man cannot be ideally shaped exclusively relying on external techniques of planning and regulating his material conditions of existence. Nor can he possibly attain and develop his higher human potentialities only by removing his internal or psychological shortcoming and failings. The difference between thinkers regarding freedom and perfection is mainly a question of *primacy* of method and not of method itself.

While Marx attaches primacy to the objective method, Sri Aurobindo does so to the subjective one. The latter's main criticism against the objective view of life is that it prescribes a law for human development which lies outside the human being itself. Even if this law is discovered or determined by reason and accepted or enforced by individual will, it is unable to do justice to the endless intricacy, complexity and creativity of human nature. The law or even the analogy of true human freedom cannot be found or discovered in the outer world. Freedom is both a cognitive and conative capacity to master 'a mass of colliding results, a whirl of potential energy' and to bring about 'some supreme order and some yet unrealised harmony' out of them. Under the spell of objectivity human reason tries to conform to some external standards or criteria and therefore it excels more in systematising than in creating or innovating. Sri Aurobindo rejects the pragmatic or practical obligation of the artist as it is ordinarily understood. For it restricts his creative freedom. The artist must endeavour to see and depict human life and nature for their own sake and in their own characteristic truth and beauty. And then when spiritual insight takes him deep into the nature of things, he discovers the known things under a new and unknown light and ' sees in common things parable of deep things and analogies of divinity '. Sri Aurobindo reminds one of Carlyle and Ruskin. Carlyle speaks of the wonder discovered by the artist's eye in normal things. Ruskin says, aesthesis, a perceptive content of art, is in end a theoria, a spiritual beholding.[23] Sri Aurobindo sums up the position of the spiritual-subjectivist aesthetic when he says ' Genius, the true creator, is always supra-rational in its nature and in its instruments.'

Also in the field of ethics Sri Aurobindo is against objectivism and rationalism as specially defined by him. His main criticism against reason, as we had occasion to note before, is that it can systematise only those elements of our experience and life which have their ratios. Some philosophers say, unless our sense-manifold is ordered in space and time, understanding cannot transform them into objects of knowledge. Here knowledge means rational discursive knowledge. In other words, a sense content to be transformed into an object of knowledge needs some prior ordering or formation in space-time coordinate. The spirit is not subject to this limitation of the field of operation of reason. Even where the ratios are not there in the elements of sense-experience the spirit can work and harmonise them all. On ultimate analysis the character of our society and civilisation and the quality of human life in it depend on the instrument and means used in shaping them. What is shaped by human reason is subject to the limitations of human reason. Reason is said to be just incapable of correctly informing man of his destiny. Busy in striking a working balance between the conflicting and competitive forces unleashed by different human beings, different decision-units, human reason is unconscious of the aim of the whole dynamism. Only the objective half of the social life receives its attention. And in the inadequate light of it man makes a half-conscious attempt to solve the riddles of life. It would be incorrect to think that ' reason as the governor of life ' has not brought about a tremendous transformation in human history. Most of the things we are proud of today are the gifts of reason. The foundation of modern civilisation is ' practical reason or science '. One would again note here that Sri Aurobindo is using the term ' practical reason ' in his own way and not in its well-known ethical context. One could also perhaps point out that science should not be taken as a synonym for practical reason for there are several purely theoretical sciences. Besides, it has to be remembered that, scientific knowledge may quite plausibly be taken as a disinterested pursuit of knowledge. Simply because a particular mode of knowledge has or could possibly have some practical applications it should not be characterised as essentially practical. It may be pointed out that even the ' useless ' fine arts could be used or exploited for practical and commercial purposes.

However, the main point of Sri Aurobindo remains, namely, the practical use of reason rather than its power to discover truth is being almost exclusively highlighted these days. When human consciousness is sense-bound in most of its movements and workings, the practical orientation of reason is bound to produce and glorify a set of egoistic and vitalistic values. And that produces vitalistic and pragmatic civilisation and culture. Modern man has all the apparatus of civilisation around him which could not be even dreamt of by his forefathers. But he is not civilised within. He is obsessed by the means, mechanisms and techniques of civilisation, almost pressed under them. Modern man, in Sri Aurobindo's language, is an economic barbarian, ' who mistakes the vital being for the self and accepts its satisfaction as the first aim of life '. He has all the pretensions of culture, borrowed and conventional culture, but left to himself he is not cultured within. In the place of the old physical barbarian we have today the economic barbarian. He worships two gods—life and practical reason. His first motive of life is individualistic and that gives him an egocentric view of the world. Under this influence everything appears to him as a means for his satisfaction, possession, acquisition and reproduction. The total upshot is a narrow form of possessive individualism marked by an acquisitive tendency. Practical reason or science is known for its generalising tendency. But the life-forces are found to be more persistent than the rational ones. To counteract the resulting excesses of individualism, practical reason is being progressively used to develop a collectivistic or cooperative tendency. Attempts are being made to subordinate individual egos to this collectivistic tendency with a view to minimising clash and conflicts between them and maximising satisfaction of the primary impulses of life. This civilisation is a matter only for the vital part of the human being. Its size and superstructure are becoming too heavy and its paraphernalia too vast to be supported by the narrow and unedified vital foundation of our life. Therefore, one fears that it might collapse under its own mass, *mola ruet sua*. Its accompanying culture is also a mere intellectual pabulum, a matter of exterior life, means to beautify only its visible parts, but has no inner beauty and character of its own. This is a commercial civilisation and this is a commercial culture.

> The accumulation of wealth and more wealth, the adding of possessions to possessions, opulence, show, pleasure, a cumbersome inartistic luxury, a plethora of conveniences, life devoid of beauty and nobility, religion vulgarised or coldly formalised, politics and government turned into a trade and profession, enjoyment itself made a business, this is commercialism.[24]

Commercial civilisation on the basis of industrialisation had its origin in the West. It has been criticised from various points of view and by such widely different thinkers as Marx, Sri Aurobindo, Oswald Spengler, Arnold Toynbee and Pitirim Sorokin. The common denominator of their criticisms is the ' cash nexus ' which now dominates almost all types of human relationships. Everything, every work, every value, is being commercialised. It is no wonder that the ideas and ideals of utilitarianism, pragmatism and instrumentalism have found favour with a wide segment of thinkers. Some of their reactions, Spengler's for example, to this commercial civilisation have been tragic and pessimistic. Sorokin and Sri Aurobindo, though hopeful of the future of the mankind primarily because of their spiritual-metaphysical faith, are highly critical of the crudities and deformities of this 'sensate' or *vaishya* civilisation. Sorokin characterises modern culture as a sensate culture and finds it in the grip of a fearful crisis.

> Every important aspect of life, organisation, and culture of Western society is included in the crisis. Its body and mind are sick and there is hardly a spot on its body which is not sore, nor any nervous fibre which functions soundly.... We are seemingly between two epochs: the dying Sensate culture of our magnificient yesterday and the coming Ideational culture of the creative tomorrow. We are living, thinking and acting at the end of a brilliant six-hundred-year-old Sensate day. The oblique rays of the sun still illumine the glory of the passing epoch. But the light is fading, and in the deepening shadows it becomes more and more difficult to see clearly and to orient ourselves safely in the confusion of the twilight. The night of the transitory period begins to loom before us....with its nightmares, frightening shadows, and heart-rending horrors. Beyond it, however, the dawn of a new great Ideational culture is probably waiting to greet the men of the future.[25]

Sorokin's description of the dying sensate culture is undoubtedly very touching, but one wonders whether its dark side has not been rather exaggerated. Also the hope that the future will be better and brighter almost as a matter of course sounds a bit wishful. His hope, he claims, is based on the evolving and improving nature of man. He refers approvingly to Vivekananda and Sri Aurobindo in his book *Reconstruction of Man.* The reconstructed man, the spiritual man, will provide the foundation of what Sorokin calls ideational culture. Like Sorokin, Sri Aurobindo also speaks of the necessity of spiritual transformation. 'The secret of the transformation lies in the transference of our centre of living to a higher consciousness . . . upward transference of our will to be.' These conditions are primarily subjective and individual in character. Sri Aurobindo pointedly emphasises the concept of spiritual subjectivism, distinguishing it clearly from vital or intellectual subjectivism. The first essential condition for the coming of the spiritual age is the growth of the subjective idea of life, the idea of the soul, its powers and possibilities, its expression and the creation of a true, beautiful and helpful environment. The subjective age is only the first step towards a spiritual age. The individual will undoubtedly be the focal point of the subjective age. There must be at the same time a communal mind to receive and propagate its light and power. The task of spiritualising the communal mind is not at all easy. The method of short-circuit, ignoring the needs of our material and vital existence, must not be resorted to. Sri Aurobindo says: 'This was one principal reason of the failure of past attempts to spiritualise mankind.... They endeavoured to spiritualise at once the material man by a sort of rapid miracle.' A spiritualist society has to be first deserved and then gradually achieved. Sri Aurobindo has a fairly clear idea of what a spiritual society would be like. Its sociology would treat the individuals not as units of a social problem but as suffering souls willing to be free and to grow. The aim of its economics would be to give each man the highest possible freedom and joy of work according to his own nature and ability and not to create a huge machine of production. Its politics would discourage the cult of State forcing the individual to worship the State as his god and his larger self. All these conditions can be fulfilled only when a society like its spiritual individuals would live not in the ego but in its spirit. 'The spirit is unity, a conscious and diversified oneness.'

When a society can discover its spiritual foundation and power only then can a durable civilisation and a sound culture be developed on it. Whatever might be the ultimate nature of the foundation of civilisation and culture, there is hardly any disagreement between the materialist and the spiritualist regarding the contribution made by civilisation and the aim of culture. Broadly speaking, civilisation and culture are for making man more free and more perfect. Perfection and freedom have no limits. In other words, human progress, both ethically and aesthetically, is boundless. Optimistic and moral orientations are common to Marx's and Sri Aurobindo's thinking. Popper says, 'Marx's condemnation of capitalism is fundamentally a moral condemnation.'[26] Sri Aurobindo says, 'Our idealism is always the most rightly human thing in us.'

But one must remember that there is no law of progress or that this development does not take place as a matter of course. The progress and development made hitherto by human civilisations and cultures might exhibit some general tendencies on analysis and interpretation, but from that it would be wrong to think that our progress is *inevitable*. The doctrines of inevitability, religious and profane, belittle the role of the human agency in shaping the course of civilisation and in imparting a character to culture. The entire world of values is considerably impoverished by these indefensible doctrines.

Regarding the relative primacy of civilisation and culture the defenders of spiritualism and materialism Sri Aurobindo and Marx, for example, have expressed their fundamental difference. Marx says, that civilisation, the material conditions of life, provides the foundation stone or infrastructure of culture. Sri Aurobindo, on the other hand, thinks that culture, the consciousness-components of life, is the basis of choice and construction of the material aspects of civilisation. A somewhat similar view is expressed by MacIver when he says, 'culture is what we are and civilisation is what we use', and the former is 'the animating and creating spirit' of the latter.[27] In this context one feels tempted to recall Marx's criticism of Hegelian dialectics claiming that he has turned the matter-consciousness relation upside down. It is rather naive and trite to think that Hegel did not realise that matter influences consciousness or that he wanted to make history rest and walk on its head, i.e., consciousness. Similarly, it would be rather jejune to suggest, as it has been by Merleau-Ponty, for example, that Marx wanted to make history think by its feet, i.e., by matter.[28] In fact Marx repeatedly speaks of the interaction between matter and consciousness and the reverse effect of the superstructure, the products of consciousness, on the infrastructure, the material conditions of consciousness. Sri Aurobindo also speaks of the twin movements of ascent and descent between the material base of consciousness and the more evolved and higher levels of consciousness.

However, the similarity between them on some points should not make us blind to their fundamental differences. Their accounts of social dynamics are different. Their value-schedules are different. Also they differ on how to establish a just and beautiful society and on how to realise the ideal of human unity.

# 10

# Roads to World-Unity

## The Principle of Unity or the Principle of Uniformity

Man is never satisfied with what he has achieved. He always wants to exceed himself, both personally and socially. His journey, both inward and outward, knows no end-point. His knowledge is growing and this growth knows no limit. He is discovering, inventing, innovating and creating new things, new techniques and new values. All his actions and thoughts are converging on the end of his self-perfection, taking *self* in a wider sense.

Human perfection is being carried on on different lines—aesthetic, ethical, religious, scientific and technological, and philosophic. These lines are not parallel or divergent. Man is a multi-faceted and a multi-dimensional being. There is something essential in him and which is common to all these aspects and dimensions of his personality. And that provides the clue to the possible integration of all these functionally distinct aspects of the human life into a rational whole. About the desirable nature of that rational whole thinkers are not unanimous. Is man essentially spiritual on his own account? Is his spirituality an excerpt or an internally related fragment of an impersonal absolute or a personal spiritual whole? Can't we take man as a rational and semiotic being, dispensing altogether with the metaphysical presuppositions regarding his ' essence ' or ' inner being '? These questions are indicative of different views on the true identity of man.

The average man is exclusively interested in immediate actualities. His concern for others is negligible. The intellectual or the ideologue whose guidance is generally accepted by the average man is himself deeply confused. His own reading of the crisis situation is negatively motivated. Often he speaks of replacing the individualistic basis of society by a scheme of collective life as a possible solution to recurrent economic crisis and wars. Though this prescription has been well received generally, it is not being followed appropriately in practice. The intellectual's motivation being negative and theoretical, it carries little conviction with the common man. Even the politician follows only half-heartedly the lead given by him. His scheme of socialism is being used by the politician mainly to manipulate the existing state and relations of things in furtherance of his own interests on the basis of a superficial understanding of the situation and drift of the timespirit. If for the time being we forget the halo of his power, the politician represents the mentality and all the shortcomings of the average man. Consequently, his understanding and actions produce ' usually something much nearer the minimum than the maximum of what is possible'.

Sri Aurobindo is interested in discovering the positive basis of the internal unity of all nations. And he thinks that it remains still undiscovered. The mechanical and loose uniformity that is of late taking a vague shape is moving on the negative lines—to prevent a possible global war and worldwide economic dislocation. However, he does not reject this negative line of approach suggested by the present state of affairs and formulated by the intellectual and the pacifist. He thinks that it should be supported and supplemented by some positive human initiatives. Effective measures have to be taken for the limitation of armaments, for the satisfactory solution of dangerous territorial disputes, commercial conflicts and intra and inter-ideological rivalries.

The experience of the last three decades has made certain things very clear. The profession and practice of the principles of peaceful coexistence and meaningful cooperation have not been uniform and consistent. Most of the major international issues have to be sorted out through negotiations between or by the intervention of the superpowers and that too not formally on the floor of the UNO.[1]

Detente is far from what we badly need today—stable peace. The international means of control over national communities and interests are indeed very weak. At the approach of a cataclysm they are likely to crumble or become defunct. The weakness of the international community results mainly from national egoism.

Those who think that the shortcomings flowing out of national egoism may be remedied by codified international laws are mistaken. The motive-force which vitiates the character of municipal law will also affect the practice of international law. The norms, criteria and even concepts of municipal law are influenced mainly by two factors—first, the strong desire of a class to conserve its interest and, secondly, the possession of an armed force to make that interest effective. These forces are kept aloof as far as possible from the cross-currents of national politics and are controlled by a person or a body of persons in whom the sovereign authority of the nation vests. The main sanction behind municipal law is the *notional consent* of the people. Notional consent on analysis turns out to be a sort of *loose consensus*. And that too is formed in and through different kinds of organised and propagated views of political parties and pressure groups. Consequently, the foundations of municipal law continues to remain weak and its violation, though it attracts penal measures from the lawful authority, is not infrequent in practice. In other words, law has so far failed to remove the economic and psychological causes of crime. The crimes committed by the criminal and the penalty imposed upon him by the State authority in the name of the vindication of justice embody 'a kind of mutual violence'. Because of its partisan character and superficial motive-force a municipal or national legal system fails to go deep into the causes of civil strife and criminal offence or to command the respect and obedience of the involved classes or persons. A class or a point of view which is oppressed and denied justice gradually develops a definite hostility to the ruling class and its method of administration of justice. This unresolved civil strife ultimately refers itself back to the ancient arbitration of might.

The causes underlying the weakness of municipal law are very relevant to the understanding of the ineffective character of international law. The source of international law—custom, usage, treaties, general principles of law, the decisions of tribunals of law and the writings of jurists—are all more or less subject to the limitations referred to in the context of national law. What ultimately counts as a sanction behind international law is force. Consent, consensus or some such normative concept constitutes only the unimportant part of the sanction behind international law. What matters most in the enforcement of international law is, as in the case of municipal law, a sole and central armed force. But that does not exist. Even if a ' peace army ' is raised by the UNO for, say, a particular peace-keeping job, its constituents are drawn from different nations and owe their primary and practical allegiance to their own nations. If there should ever arise a point of conflict between the so-called international army and a national armed force, the latter will act and the former is likely to wait and watch, if not disintegrate. This is somewhat like the chaotic organisation of the feudal ages when the nobles had their own armies and jurisdiction and could defy the sovereign at will. Unless the citizens of the world and the members of the international armed forces develop an international consciousness and unless that consciousness is a dominant one, the centripetal force of national egoism will continue to weaken the sanction necessary for a just and effective administration of international law.

The limitations and failings of international laws and agreements and the like have been understandably attributed to the invidious position of the UNO. The lack of adequate institutional sanction explains much of the present-day conflicts. The ideal solution to these problems lies in the evolution of a higher consciousness of the human race as a whole which alone could give real content to the international bodies like the UNO and their decisions. Sri Aurobindo is realistic enough to have realised the impossibility of this condition being satisfied under the present circumstances. Therefore, many people are thinking along the alternative lines and trying to initiate ' a movement towards greater rigidity, constriction of national liberties and the erection of the unique central authority with a uniform control over the earth's people '.[2]

The ideal of human unity could be approached, broadly speaking, in two different ways—from within and from without, by developing the social consciousness of the human race or by building up a representative and sufficiently strong international organisation. Rightly understood, these two alternatives are complementary and not divergent. In fact, the main question underlying this controversy is how to define a rational and workable relationship between the principles of *liberty* and *order*. In every human aggregate, liberty and order have been reconciled in practice. The principle underlying this practice might not be quite clear to the people concerned. If we want to develop a living international unity, the question of a workable and rational relation between liberty and order has to be decided. This decision may not be arrived at quickly and it may take time. The international consensus underlying this decision may have to be evolved through discussion and experience over a period of time. But a decision on this basic question has to be taken after all. Frankly speaking, under the present circumstances it is almost impossible to arrive at a unanimous decision regarding the ideal relation between national liberty and international order. We may differ in our assessment of the 'present circumstances'. But, given realism and judgement, we are likely to agree that the state of national egoism being what it is and the role of the super-powers being what it is, the smaller or weaker nations cannot be very hopeful about the actual outcome of ideal human unity. The conditions necessary for establishing an ideal unity being absent we are perhaps well advised to take the help of the available forces of unity. Sri Aurobindo thinks that the intermediate powers of nationalism and imperialism and their corporate egoism would do their most before the evolution of a global unity becomes a distinct possibility. Though the ideal agencies of human unity are silently at work in the very nature of things and beings, yet as they remain substantially unrecognised by most of us, their efficacy is subordinated to the unideal necessities of life. Consequently, the institutions corresponding to those necessities are the only available means of unification at our disposal. These means are undoubtedly secondary in character.

The idea of a just internationalism is still a mere possibility. It may perhaps be safely asserted, without fear of contradiction from impartial quarters, that the big and powerful nations have little respect for the freedom of the smaller nations. Before the Second World War no empire thought of liberating its dependencies without being compelled to do so in some way or the other. The best relationship that the imperialist powers and their theoreticians could conceive of was in terms of autonomy under imperial protection or parental affection. 'There is a sign perhaps of the obscure growth of the idea of federated empires' which Sri Aurobindo considers as one of the possibilities of the future. Apparently, this possibility, which Sri Aurobindo referred to in the second decade of the century and which he reviewed after the Second World War, has not taken any perceptible shape. It is true that some imperial powers did try to convert and treat their dependencies as 'integral parts or provinces' but this experiment has not been generally accepted at its professed face value or as a model to emulate.

The possibility of a temporary drift towards a supra-national political evolution is always present and might arrest or dissolve the tendency towards larger imperial aggregates. In that case policies may be based on continental rather than on national considerations. There may, for instance, come about an Asian or an American confederacy along the lines of the concept of a Federal Europe which made a brief appearance in the mediaeval ages. Often we hear the slogans of 'an Arab Union', the 'Muslim world' and the 'Socialist Bloc'. The present shape and drift of the European Economic Community (EEC) gives some credence to the idea of a United States of Europe. Other regional groupings are gradually being formed. The forms of coercion that would probably be resorted to, to make the idea of continental confederacy a reality, are likely to be dominantly commercial in character and somewhat different from the forms hitherto known to us. But the result would not be much different from what the lesser unformed aggregates have experienced in the past, namely, partial realisation of the objective and partial failure. Nevertheless, it would be a step forward. Even if it does not turn out to be a complete success, the idea of a continental confederacy would certainly ease some international problems by promoting the growth of peace and mutual understanding.[3]

Sri Aurobindo speaks of another possible solution of the problem of international unity. And that is in terms of a worldwide confederated empire under one king-nation or two or three big imperial powers. Undoubtedly, it would involve much moral and economic coercion. But it may succeed in establishing at least half-order out of total disorder, some tolerable form of legality and justice. Thus, it may prove to be a starting point for more concrete international movement for higher unity.

Looking at the present drift of events it seems that none of the above three possibilities of supra-national unity has any chance of practical success. The idea of a continental concert is hardly better than an ideal. There are of course some military alliances on different continents, but they are purely military in character and embody no true principle of unity. If the countries belonging to this or that alliance profess an ideological unity, it is more a strategic move than a genuine feeling. Secondly, the possibility of the establishment of a worldwide confederated empire seems to be very remote at present. One might refer in this context to the Commonwealth or the Socialist Bloc of Eastern Europe headed by Russia. The idea of the Commonwealth as it stands today is essentially cooperative and not imperial. If the UK occupies the most important position in the Commonwealth that is because of her superior military power and economic resources; and that has little to do with her imperial past. The same may be said of Russia to explain her leadership in the East European Socialist Bloc. If the leading socialist country is more successful in practice than its democratic counterpart in establishing and maintaining a common political and economic order that is because of its firm adherence to the principles of socialism. But that is something quite different from imperial domination or what is termed *social imperialism* these days. Besides, it is not quite clear how, at this stage of national unity, a struggle for national liberation and the decline of classical imperialism, a class-struggle can split national and empirical aggregates into two clear-cut halves and pave the way for world unity.

The above three possibilities, conceptually different but practically overlapping, may not attain immediate success, yet in different ways they are said to be influencing the process of world unity. The military alliances of the NATO, SEATO, CENTO and Warsaw Pact countries may not provide an ideal unity, but military compulsions certainly bring the 'allied' countries close to each other at least to some extent. Admittedly, the Commonwealth does not have a common political bond or aim today, yet some commercial considerations, and what may be loosely called English language and culture, provide a sort of supra-national unity of different countries spread over different continents. Perhaps it would not be entirely correct to suggest that there is a psychological unity among the Socialist countries. Even then, as they follow some common principles of Marxism and Leninism in the spheres of production, education and administration, they have succeeded in developing a sort of unity. The conflict between Russia and China, both professing principles of Marxism and Leninism, is a pointer to the unfortunate fact that national egoism does get precedence over internationalism even in the case of Socialist countries. The doctrine of Communist Internationalism by itself may not destroy national egoism but certainly creates a worldwide political climate favouring international unity.[4]

Sri Aurobindo draws an important line of distinction between the concept of uniformity and the concept of unity. The trends and the possibilities we are encountering today are all more or less beset with one common difficulty, the difficulty attending the concept of uniformity. As it was embodied in the German gospel of imperial, national and racial domination or in some sort of imperial federalism or ideological internationalism, the idea of uniformity does not stand in any right relation to the ideal of liberty. In each of the above three movements for uniformity the initiative came from a dominant country and followed a path strictly or leniently regulated by some strong sense of the economic or military or ideological interests of the initiator. That being so, the freedom of the junior partner means little more than the freedom to be a pliant tool in the hand of the dominant partner. The demand for equal freedom of all partners is generally met with one of the two arguments: either they are unfit for it or that the demand was ill-timed. An unheeded demand is normally followed by strong resistance which invariably brings into play the forces of suppression and restriction against the defiant and agitating partner. But in all fairness to the dominant country it has to be admitted that with the advancement of civilisation and culture and except in the cases of a hot war, the manner of bringing pressure to bear upon the weaker countries has taken more and more subtle, civil and ideological guises. The dominant power's zeal for uniformity takes away the zest for the same of the dominated; for the weal of the former turns out to be the cause of woe for the latter. Unity is recognised as the true motive-force of human development, but what is being practised is unmistakably the principle of uniformity. Hence the problem and the difficulty.

The ideal of liberty is being eclipsed also under the shadow of the State cult. In order to achieve uniformity rapidly at the administrative level more and more powers and functions are being assigned to the State. This tendency has found its most manifest expression in the rapid march of socialism, and which, according to Sri Aurobindo, entails, among other things, rigid regimentation under a central authority, tremendous organisation for uniformity, and suppression of the principle of free variation. This portrait of socialism need not be taken at its face value. But Sri Aurobindo, like many other honest critics of socialism, tends to underrate the noble motivations underlying the transitional regimentation. The choice before the poor nations, for example, is very limited. Either they have to wait for a long time to see how the law of Nature slowly works up its way through the concerned human agents and smaller aggregates to an ideal unity based on minimum centralisation and maximum free variation, or they adopt a political system based on a judicious combination of regimentation and free variation, preserving the inbuilt safety valves to undo the possible mis-effects of the excess of regimentation, and ensuring rapid development of the economic standard and the quality of life of the millions of people living below the poverty line. The question of the poor millions is not merely a quantitative question; it has its other side as well. If the very metaphysical *rationale* of the law of Nature is questioned, as it has been, the ideal of a socialist transformation assumes added importance and urgency.

Sri Aurobindo's opposition to the principle of uniformity and hope in the ideal of human unity is based on another concept and consideration. The contemporary international situation is being influenced by the important force of the idea *sans-patrie*, the citizen of the world. Though the unity of mankind is said to be our ultimate destiny, yet it is not coming about through enforced uniformity nor through the disembodied force of freedom. In the structure of the social group Sri Aurobindo finds something which, he thinks, would liberate the force of unification-through-free-variation from all-embracing State uniformity and give an organic body to the idea of the *sans-patrie*. He anticipates that the ideal of liberty would be eclipsed and defeated by the ideal of uniformity and regimentation, and that socialism would establish itself on the earth; the socialist period of mankind would be of brief duration like that of monarchical absolutism in Europe. This idea of Sri Aurobindo has often been presented as prophetic. I for one do not believe in political or any other sort of prophecy in human affairs. I take his view as being the outcome of a serious study of world affairs marked by a deep historical insight. I am not quite sure of the correctness of the historical parallelism drawn between the monarchical absolutism of Europe and the contemporary experiment with socialism. Much depends upon the character, content and forms of the socialist experiments now being undertaken and executed in different parts of the world. The adherents of the so-called principles of uniformity are not themselves speaking of interpreting the principles of socialism in the same manner. The ideas of polycentricism and different roads to socialism and the like are being seriously talked of and even practised in different parts of the world. In other words, contrary to Sri Aurobindo's apprehension and that of some other serious critics of the principle of uniformity, we note today that socialists themselves are encouraging, allowing or at least tolerating free variation in the practice of the basic principles of socialism. The idea of free variation is no longer peculiar to the principle of unity. Extending this argument one might say that the idea of *sans-patrie* could be very consistently related to the principle of socialist internationalism. Internationalism is not an outgrowth only of nationalism or liberalism based on the principles of unity but also of patriotism based on the principle of uniformity. Sri Aurobindo does not deny the inevitability of the stage of uniformity in the human cycle but he persistently questions its proclaimed virtues. According to him the ideal principle of world-unity, and for that matter any unity, provide due room for diversity or free variation.

> Group-units there must always be in any human unity, even the most entire intolerant and uniform, for that is the very principle not only of human nature but of life and of every aggregation; we strike here on a fundamental law of universal existence, on the fundamental mathematics and physics of creation.[5]

Sri Aurobindo thinks that the establishment of a perfect harmony between unity and diversity is now only a remote possibility. And unless we can realise that possibility our interim ideal is uniformity; but this method should be applied carefully and flexibly according to the logic of the situation. Otherwise, the growing social life may dry up at its very roots. Sri Aurobindo concedes that the ideal solution of the problem regarding the relation between unity and diversity and also between law and liberty cannot be obtained under the present circumstances, and at the same time asserts that this difficulty should not be used as an argument against the advisability of following the principle of unity. Clearly, this raises a basic question: if in the course of inevitable history we come across the stage of uniformity and its political correlate, socialism, is there any reason why it should not be accepted as rational and ideal? If the remote possibility of unity is welcome, why not the immediate possibility of uniformity? After all, unity and uniformity are two stages of the same historical process. If historicism or the inevitable character of history is inconsistent with human freedom and the ascription of the values to the human thought and action, then this is true of all human aggregates and all stages of the human cycle. It is not without justification that the exponents of the idea of inevitable history have often been accused of moral positivism and moral futurism. To say 'whatever is has sufficient reason behind it and, therefore, it is God-ordained, rational and moral', is to give a *post-hoc* stamp of legitimacy to whatever happens in or is thrown up by the course of history. Attempts may be made to meet this criticism in terms of the traditional definition of freedom as recognition of necessity. But that too is questionable.

A system of free and natural groupings is favoured by Sri Aurobindo. For, he thinks, this is quite in accordance with the law of Nature. Natural groupings make possible an all round and smooth growth of unity, leaving no room for the preservation of moral centres of revolt. An enforced or imposed system, national or international, may easily be given an appearance of justice. But it cannot last long as it goes against the principle of psychological unity. Racial and national unities are basically pscyhological in character, whereas administrative unity imposed upon a nation results in evolving a superficial uniformity. Natural unity is very complex in its constitution and organic in its structure. The life-power favours this form of unity as it is the expression of its very nature. The power of reason, on the other hand, prefers a comparatively clear-cut or graphic model of unity to a complex, organic one. But graphic unity is not in the nature of things. It is an ascription of the rational mind cast in the mechanical mould. It is to this mechanical bent of the human mind that Sri Aurobindo traces the drive towards centralisation and uniformity. The defender of the principle of uniformity apprehends that, if the nation-units are conceded real independence, then it would lead to disruption and disorganisation. Some form of coercion has to be resorted to, to preserve the envisaged world-union. Natural affinities, economic and other common interests, are not sufficient to afford a final basis to a stable world-union. Under the present circumstances, stability without uniformity is impossible in the international sphere. Stability demands that the units should not be allowed to possess more than nominal separateness or minimal independence. Without centralised Government and uniform administration the life of the world-union cannot be ensured. While Sri Aurobindo is forthright in his analysis of the international situation and trends, he does not conceal his apprehension about the practical outcome of the socialist principle of uniformity. It reminds him of the unitarian Jacobins of the French Revolution. To establish his case and to emphasise the importance of a centralised Government and administration, the Marxist might refer to the miserable weakness displayed by the feudal unity of France and Germany in mediaeval Europe and the loose national unity of China in the closing decades of the last century. These historical references are quite in order. But their lesson is to be taken with circumspection. From one error we need not move to another error. Besides, it would not be entirely correct to suggest that the principle of uniformity owes its origin to the failure of the French, German and Chinese experiments in the past. A drive towards centralisation and uniformity is a logical development of the idea of the State.

The modern idea of the national State favours the growth of centralisation on two grounds—the necessity of single-mindedness and the necessity of defence and war. The international organisation that is likely to appear on the basis of a centralised Government and administration could aptly be termed a *world-state* rather than a *world-union*. The world-state would be somewhat like an enlarged leviathan conceding little or no liberty to its constituent units. Sri Aurobindo fears that the tragedy experienced by the Bourbons and the Young Turks will be repeated in the life of the world-state. But in the same breath he asserts in his characteristic way that this political centrifugal tendency is natural and inevitable. In other words, one might infer, the tragedy of the world-state is inevitable. Today or tomorrow, directly or indirectly, the drive towards centralisation is definitely going to gain more and more momentum both in the national and in the international spheres.

In order to explain the tragedy of the possible world-state Sri Aurobindo refers to its divergence from the subjective necessity of evolving mankind. It is true that the human society does not evolve in the same way as the self-conscious human mind does, for its first course is determined by the pressure of circumstances, and, later on, it tends to be self-conscious. The human society is characterised by two movements—one emanating from the *subjective* side, ideas and ideals, and influencing its administrative, economic and other social structures; and the other originating from the *objective* social environment which influences the more flexible and self-conscious side of life. Society strives to organise its whole life—military, economic and political—by means of the State apparatus. Both the democrat and the socialist claim to have developed a theory in terms of which they want to show that the State and society are synonymous at the successful end of the socio-political evolution. Democracy proceeds to that goal following the principle of freedom, and, says Sri Aurobindo, socialism does the same through violent regimentation. It is clear from the context of his discussion that by democracy he means classical democracy or, what the Marxists call, bourgeois democracy. And when he speaks of socialism he has the Marxist model in his mind.

The main point which Sri Aurobindo tries to make is this. If the objective structure of society does not adequately reflect, or is altogether different from, the structure of the mind of the people in question, it will prove very oppressive and mechanical and will gradually lead to a sociological gap between the objective and the subjective aspects of social life. On this general point the democrat and the creative Marxist need not quarrel but on its interpretation and on the relative importance of the subjective and the objective they are sure to fall apart. Sri Aurobindo proposes to draw the *ideal* of social transformation from the *actual* course of social evolution itself. He wants to derive the *ought* from the *is*. The justification he offers is this. The *is* conceals the *ought* or, to put it from the other end, the *ought* is an implication of the *is*. Under the pressure of the necessities of his environment the human beings at first develop some flexible habits, *nomoi mores* and *acara*. These flexible forms of human response to the symbolic age degenerate into rigid *instituta* in the conventional age. Manu, Moses and Lycurgus are law-makers in a special sense. They lay down only the general and flexible principles of law-making. But they themselves do not enact laws in the sense we have and use them today. The changing needs and permanent necessities of social life demand codified laws enacted by a fixed legislative authority. When the head of a society assumes the power of law-making and also the supreme military command he becomes the executive ruler. And then the drive towards centralisation both in foreign and in internal affairs becomes almost irresistible. Executive supremacy is coupled with diplomatic secrecy. The policy of secret diplomacy ordinarily keeps the people in darkness. And they are consulted by the executive only at the last moment when they cannot withhold their sanction to peace or war without endangering national interests. The lack of balance of power between the executive and the legislature often results in the former being forced to give its approval to an already determined course of action. This explains the insistent demand for real Parliamentary control of foreign policy and for open diplomacy.[6]

The centrifugal tendency is resisted by different groups and classes having their own age-old habits, rights and privileges. The unification of the executive and legislative powers in a person or a group of persons aims to establish control of the central authority over all official matters, especially financial ones. The control over the national exchequer enables the central authority to exercise real sovereign power in a most effective manner. In England it was only after defeating the Stuarts in the seventeenth century that Parliament could establish not only its control over the throne but could also lay its hand, for the first time, on the purse of the nation. Thus, the real sovereign power shifted its locus from the throne to the aristocracy. Then, after the Industrial Revolution, this power was captured by the bourgeoisie. Now, in this age of socialism and democracy, the necessary preliminaries are under way, to shift financial control, and therewith real sovereign power, to the whole people or at least to the proletariat. Financial control is necessary but not sufficient for the effective exercise of central authority. Without uniformity of judicial administration, especially of the criminal side, the drive towards legislative and social centralisation cannot be complete. In order to tackle the law-breakers and the disruptive elements the sovereign authority wants to wield all judicial powers. Once the ruler succeeds in getting the criminal judicial authority in his grip he finds it rather easy to control the civil side. The control over the civil side is not terribly important from the point of the unitary objective. What the sovereign basically needs is the power to crush all rebellion against him and stifle all criticism of his administration as high treason.

This drive towards centralisation of the judicial administration is associated by Sri Aurobindo with the cult of State. He points out that the case was quite different in early human society. He refers to the Indian *panchayat*, the Athenian *deme* and the Roman *comitia*. All these smaller and flexible human aggregates of ancient times used to manage their affairs more or less independently and without interference from a central authority. The advent of the State idea began to destroy these autonomous administrative and judicial units. The religious sentiment of the community tried to resist this strong centrifugal tendency. The *Shastra*, the Church and the Ulemas wanted the kings and the rulers to be just Christian or upholders of *dharma*. This opposition from religious quarters led the State authority to accept some Pundits, Ulemas or Bishops in the judiciary to help the professional judges or to allow the oppositionists to have their separate ecclesiastical authority and jurisdiction. But the centralising tendency of the State was always anxious and eager to hold back the autonomy reluctantly conceded to the religious order. The first two Henrys started the process in England which found its aim realised in the Church policy of the Tudors. With the evolution of society the conflicts of group relationship became more and more complex. To remove these conflicts and also to prevent their recurrence the necessity of codified laws makes itself deeply felt. From the fluid customary laws what evolved first were *decreta*, partly written and partly unwritten, partly fixed and partly flexible. The process of the gradual ossification of organic customs at its rational stage produces cadres which are fully rigid and admit changes only under the impact of external necessities.

The law that is enacted only in response to some external necessities and not as an expression of the social milieu's own psychological urge for freedom does not serve its best possible purpose. What concerns everybody should be consented to by everybody. And that cannot be left to the coercion of one single person or class. The mode of the regulation of the entire life of society has to be agreed upon by the representatives of the whole society. By implication Sri Aurobindo rejects the idea of the philosopher-king and also the idea of class rule.[7] Whatever might be his philosophical wisdom or rational insight, the king is not above human failings. The same is true of every class—the bourgeois, the petty bourgeois, or the proletariat. Sri Aurobindo's point about the limitation of a particular human being or class is understandable. But when he says in a rather blanket way that the very Western notion of administration is restrictive and confined only to the external life of society, he might be accused of fallacious generalisation. His alternative model of legislation is based on the concept of the *dharma* of the Indian polity, which he finds very comprehensive, covering all the aspects of life—social, economic, legislative, cultural and religious. If law is not reflective of other, especially the subjective, aspects of life, it fails to achieve its end—conscious and willing acceptance and obedience from the people. Both democracy and socialism are two different approximations of the same idea—the regulation of the entire external life of society on the consent of the highest possible number of people. But it is not easy to define ' the highest possible '. Nor are the spokesmen of the different schools of thought unanimous on this point. Sri Aurobindo fears that the ruler or the ruling class is destined to fail to lay its hands on the inner part of the social life, for that lies beyond the sphere of external administration.

To get rid of this difficulty the method often resorted to by the ruling class is opposed by him. First, authority makes an attempt to change and interfere with the most sacred relations and liberties of the individual and society. This negative method casts the mind of society into a controlled mould and objectively encourages absolutism. The other method, though positive, is dangerous in a straightforward manner. This is the control of social life by imposing and propagating a State religion and a State culture. In other words, what is most adversely affected is the realm of values—values which the people should be left to decide for themselves, individually or collectively, without hindrance or coercion from the political and bureaucratic authority. Both these methods, as evident from history, strengthen the trend of authoritarianism and lead to stagnation, decay and weakness of the social life. It is to these two methods that Sri Aurobindo attributes the decline of the Indian and the Chinese civilisation in the East, of the Muslim nations in the Middle-East, and the Graeco-Roman civilisation of Europe.

In spite of their failure, absolutist monarchy and the aristocracy are believed to have rendered an important service to the cause of socio-political progress by demonstrating the ways and means to organise and unify the whole social life by centralised administration. The idea of organised unity was taken up by democracy from the king or aristocracy. But the democrat adds a new dimension to this ideal by trying to bring about a self-conscious unity, and not an unconscious one, in the social life. Socialism is declared to be the complete expression of the idea of a highly centralised and administered socio-political unity. While the democrat relies heavily on administration for developing a self-conscious unity of the people, he does not deny, at least not in principle, the possibility of its evolution from within. So, in spite of his institutional approach, he frequently speaks of freedom, non-interference, and spontaneity. The anatomy of the democratic society has convinced the socialist that, under the present circumstances, freedom means freedom of the privileged and powerful few at the expense of the exploited millions. He is therefore strongly in favour of promoting socio-political unity through centralised administration. However, he points out that unless adequate material conditions are created for the poor people they cannot successfully fight for and earn their due freedom. Freedom has to be earned; it is not given.

## The World-Union or the World-State

The ambivalence of Sri Aurobindo's political sociology is evident from the fact that while he recognises the inevitability of the centralising tendency leading to a world-state, he consistently emphasises the desirability of world-union. He rejects the rigidity or uniformity inherent in the very concept of the world-state. And what the existing nature of the international state of affairs demands is a world-union marked by freedom and flexibility. The development of science and technology, industry and commerce and above all the rapid growth of an extensive and intensive communication network has now made it impossible for us to live as disparate masses of humanity. Points of contact are developing so fast that the vital relation which we already have between us is transforming itself into 'a common mental existence'. Sri Aurobindo affirms that the idea of one World is natural and organic and not an adopted child of the speculative and the forecasting mind of the thinker. Its immediate causes might be institutional, but its real cause is psychological. I have already pointed out that this psychological-institutional dualism is untenable. Our psychological make-up and drive are not as autonomous as they are made out to be. Certainly, they have an autonomy, but it is defined by institutional influences, visible and invisible. For our immediate purposes, we may ignore the genetic and other factors shaping the 'social mind'. It is also possible to argue that if we care to follow the spiritual implications of Sri Aurobindo's law of Nature, the question of dualism does not arise at all. For, he has repeatedly said that the objective and the subjective in history are sociologically interlocked, and, metaphysically speaking, two aspects of the same truth. This idea, though interesting and insightful, is not new. The main difficulty with it is that its reasonableness or otherwise cannot be questioned on the basis of historical and other empirical findings. What is still worse is that, given this idea, alternative and equally plausible interpretations of the same fact or trend of history could be easily offered.

The idea of one world generally assumes two forms—either the form of the State founded upon the principle of centralisation and uniformity or the form of a union based upon the principle of liberty and variation. In spite of its attending difficulties the idea of world-state is gaining ground and can no longer be regarded as utopian. But that is not a good enough reason for taking it as a sound principle of world unity. Sri Aurobindo prefers the idea of world-union to the idea of world-state as the basis of human unity. The nations and not the States should be recognised as our *natural* starting point. A loose union of nations, under the pressure of problems and difficulties associated with a closer inter-working of their interests, is likely to convert itself into a relatively rigid form of world-state.

Sri Aurobindo's preference for world-union is unmistakable. Even then his interest in a detailed analysis of the idea of world-state, which is perhaps now more than an idea, makes at least one thing very clear. Notwithstanding his normative and metaphysical bent of mind, he takes a lot of trouble in sorting and sifting the cross-currents of international political sociology. In his objective and institutional analysis of contemporary international affairs one might even find the partial answer to the dualism of the actual and the ideal. The trend of actual world politics can undoubtedly be characterised primarily in terms of uniformity. But that need not detract us from finding out the possible relation between this trend and what Sri Aurobindo considers the ideal trend of the subjective forces which are also believed to have started functioning deep beneath the institutional or visible surface of history.

To clarify his point, Sri Aurobindo takes the help of the well-known body-mind analogy.[8] In the course of evolution the mental existence is preceded and prepared by some non-mental (not anti-mental) existence. The transition from the possible to the actual necessitates and is facilitated by some objective circumstances. The mind needs a body. The nation has a soul. But, according to Sri Aurobindo, the State is a machine. I have already explicated these concepts of Sri Aurobindo. Almost all the conditions for the formation of the nation-unit were there, Sri Aurobindo argues with reference to Indian history, but it did not come into existence until and unless some sort of external or mechanical uniformity was enforced by British domination. The uniformity created by the governmental power, though mechanical, prepares the necessary ground for the development of psychological unity within that mechanical framework. Without body there cannot be a soul within it.

What happens in the case of a nation-unit would be repeated, of course in a different form, in the case of the prospective world-union. If we accept Sri Aurobindo's reading of the international trend, the world-state would precede the ideal world-union to prepare the practical conditions for the emergence of the latter. But the starting idea would be a looser type of union of nations. Somewhat like the history of the nation-unit, the process of the establishment of ideal global unit would possibly pass through three different stages—the stage of loose union, the stage of stringent organisation or the world-state, and the stage of free groupings of mankind or the world-union.

When one closely looks into the idea of the world-state what first draws one's attention is the question of the character and composition of its governing body. Sri Aurobindo's approach is *via negativa*. The monarch will not do.[9] The monarchical idea is not even worth experimenting with, for 'the seal of the night upon it' is clear. It has already ceased to exist and very soon it will cease even to survive. The practical needs and the mental make-up of modern man provide no room for its living or survival. The monarchical idea might be retained now only as an innocuous but useful symbol for heterogeneous empires or nations. The European form of monarchy is destined to die its final death. But, Sri Aurobindo believes, the old forms of Asiatic monarchy and theocracy may reappear with some modifications in the future. Sri Aurobindo does not explain why he is convinced of the inevitable death of monarchical idea in the West and its reappearance in the Asiatic world. But one could guess at the reason on the basis of his general position. The history of monarchy as an institution has perhaps run its full course, exhausted itself and become completely alien to the consciousness and life-style of the people. The case is somewhat different in Asia. Here the idea of monarchy under the impact of Western rule might have temporarily lost its relevance, but it may stage a comeback in a different form. For, the social milieu and the national character have not suffered that massive distortion under the pressure of State administration as to render it quite unfit to re-establish or regain a governing apparatus which is consistent with its native requirements. This hypothesis to my mind appears coherent in principle. But I do not know how far it is in accordance with contemporary circumstances and trends.

In this connection, two important facts are to be taken into account, namely, in the proposed world-state nations would take the place of individuals and all these nations are more or less self-conscious. The nationalistic sentiment is marked by a separative tendency. Even then the growth of a cosmopolitan internationalism cannot be gainsaid. And this force may lead to the emergence of a worldwide republic with the various nations as more or less autonomous provinces of it. This world-republic might be governed by a council or parliament responsible to the united democracies. Or it might have a disguised oligarchy of the semi-passive democratic character as its ruling organ. Somewhat like an international council this body might be constituted through election and its ability to rule would depend on the assent of the nations concerned.

The outer characteristics of modern democracy must not be given undue importance.[10] Their inner functional content has to be closely looked into. Most of the modern democracies, according to Sri Aurobindo, are dominated by the bourgeoisie incorporating in its fold some rising stars of the working class. Through trade unions and political mass action the working class has now assumed a definite class identity of its own. Bourgeois domination need not be confused with bourgeois rule. The bourgeoisie might dominate without ruling. To ensure its domination and, at the same time, to make it look rather non-partisan, the bourgeoisie strategically tolerates the participation of the working class in its ruling organ to a limited extent. Just as at the national level this class makes its impact felt, so too in the international sphere it plays a dominant role. If the constituent nations are in most cases bourgeois in their orientation, the world-state itself can hardly have a different character.

At the national level the bourgeois State is opposed both by the intelligentsia on the one hand, and the working class and the peasantry on the other; the former feels frustrated when its ideals of power and culture are distorted and destroyed by the obstinate and vulgar commercialism of the bourgeoisie, and the latter finds in this class its blood-sucker. These two classes are common in their opposition to the bourgeoisie and find a ground of alliance between themselves. The result of the alliance depends again upon which of the two partners dominates it. If the intellectuals dominate the alliance the result is a sort of intellectual bureaucracy or official aristocracy, drawing its cadres mostly from the people of 'merit' irrespective of their class of origin. Experience shows that since the opportunities for higher education and an enlightened environment are readily available only to the privileged few of the upper class, the bureaucracy tends to assume a pro-aristocratic character. Even then it has to be admitted that the rise of what is called the meritocracy has somewhat diluted the erstwhile purely bourgeois composition of the ruling elite. If, on the other hand, the working class and the peasantry prevail over the intellectuals, the outcome is a sort of socialism. Whatever might be the form of the State which arises in opposition to the bourgeoisie, it is bound to be oligarchic at the top and democratic at bottom.

In the context of the world-state the problem involved in the above two possibilities gets further complicated by another very potent factor, nationalism. Weighing the pros and cons of conflicting interests and tendencies Sri Aurobindo concludes that some form of parliamentarianism would perhaps be the most suitable form of Government for world democracies.[11] The principle of parliamentarianism is immaculate and unexceptionable in principle, but in practice often it turns out to be the rule, if not the tyranny, of the majority. Even this majority in most cases is purely formal and sometimes worse than that—manipulated and machinated by money-power.

Sri Aurobindo visualises also another and, according to him, a more feasible form of Government for the world-state. And it might be somewhat like a Supreme Council of the free and imperial nations of the existing world system. But he fears that this form of Government is also likely to be haunted by the spectre of oligarchy, the oligarchy of a few strong imperial nations. He finds it difficult to believe that the strong nations, given their present psychological make-up, would wilfully give up their separative existence and dominant position, and thus pave the way for a unified mankind.

It is evident from the preceding discussion that every road leading to world-unity has its own problems, and they cannot be settled *a priori*. The main problem concerns the method of reconciling national diversity with international unity. The part played by *military necessity* in the process of nation-formation perhaps provides a partial answer to this problem.[12] The central authority of the State is armed with military measures and equipment in order to defend itself from external aggression, internal disruption or disorder and also to override the moral rights of its subordinate units. When moral force and psychological suggestion fail the nation resorts to the naked force of arms ostensibly to preserve its own unity. Military necessity has begun to play the very same vital role in the making of the world-state. International trade, commerce, communications, cooperation and some other forces and agencies have already made us conscious of a loose international unity. But for the two global wars and several regional conflicts this new born unity could have taken a more concrete shape.

Three different conditions are necessary for stable international peace.[13] Once it was seriously contended that German militarism was the sole cause of international conflict and tension and the resulting insecurity, and that its destruction would secure the future peace of the world. Sri Aurobindo rejects this crude and foolish contention. The true cause of German militarism is national egoism and it is not the monopoly of that country alone. Because of its instinctive and natural egoism every nation feels proud of its own cultural and material possession and wants other nations to accept the same. The egoist is not satisfied with his pride. He insists that it must be appreciated and endorsed by others. Sometimes the strong nations force the weaker ones to accept their culture. In the wake of political imperialism comes cultural imperialism and domination. Secondly, it has been suggested that a league of free and democratic nations might possibly preserve peace by force. This suggestion reminds Sri Aurobindo of the system practised by Metternich, and he thinks that its end would be no better than the end of that old rigorous idea. No voluntary league consisting of members of different and conflicting interests can preserve its unity in the face of a challenge or a trying situation. There was a time when war between the young titan, Socialism, and the Olympian gods of the bourgeois-democratic world appeared inevitable; and that might destroy this voluntary unity. It is true that international circumstances have undergone significant changes in the last three decades, especially after the discovery of the operational possibility of nuclear war. The doctrine of the balance of power has been replaced by the idea of detente. But the weakness of the voluntary league is inherent in the very nature of the idea itself. Unless human nature undergoes a profound change, the possibility of realising the idea of a league of free and democratic nations is rather remote. Thirdly, it has also been pointed out that the success of democracy and liberalism would objectively encourage every nation to determine its own affairs and, in the process, encourage a limited national outlook. Democracy demands individual liberty as its basis. There can be no two opinions about it. But the world we are living in is still full of conflict and tension; local wars frequently flare up and one cannot be sure that the danger of a global war has been totally eliminated. Under the circumstances, the champions of democracy can hardly be permitted to pursue the nationalist-chauvinist lines regardless of other's legitimate interests and aspirations. Classical democracy never realised the obvious incompatibility between its basic principle of liberty and colonialism. Many democratic countries like England, France and the Netherlands had vast colonial empires. By contrast, Sri Aurobindo fears, future democracies would lean heavily towards concentration in matters of administration and evolve some form or other of socialism. The fact that socialism has so far proved passive in practice, if not in profession, is no argument for the view that like capitalism it does not require war for its expansion. The socialist of the Marxian variety does not claim to be a pacifist. He has no hesitation in making use of force for the purpose of overthrowing an oppressive bourgeois regime. On the contrary, he finds enough justification for the use of force in his ideology of class conflict. Sri Aurobindo points out that the socialist's ideology enables him to organise his party apparatus, State machinery and military force in a very efficient manner. And, therefore, when the necessity arises the Marxist socialist parties and countries are generally found to be in a state of better preparedness for defending and promoting their cause. Perhaps it was in the light of post-war developments in East Europe and Far East that Sri Aurobindo changed his earlier view regarding the pacific orientation of socialism.[14]

National egoism has established itself as a very strong force—stronger than democracy and even socialism. I say ' even ' because socialism is known for its professed internationalism. Given the present trend of national egoism and/or expansionism, the working agreement between the nations, the foundation of the world-state, is bound to prove very hopeless in the event of a global or regional war. A system of enforced arbitration or a peace guarded by arms affords no secure basis for the world-state. This does not of course mean that we should not try to make use of these less promising forms of achieving world-unity. To rely only on the psychological assent of mankind for the maintenance of the world-state is unwise and unsafe. Some added institutional guarantees, however inadequate, are also necessary. At least in its beginning the world-state must back its moral authority by military force. And *then* it should try to unify the nation-units psychologically. Sri Aurobindo's incurable idealistic disposition does not make him blind to the insistent demands of recalcitrant political reality. This is clear when he says: ' While man remains what he is, force, in spite of all idealism and generous pacific hopes, must remain the ultimate arbiter and governor of his life, and its possessor the real ruler.'

Military necessity is only one of the forces that are visibly or invisibly active to make the establishment of the world-state possible. The economic and commercial necessity is undoubtedly a more potent force. Sri Aurobindo admits that the economic part of our life is always important and even fundamental. In the past it was only primary but perhaps not fundamental. The dominating consciousness and motive of the time was political. He rightly disputes the universal impotence of politics. Under better circumstances, the political motivation may get the better of the economic one but Sri Aurobindo is painfully aware of the reverse order of the day. Economic matters are the prime mover of our life in all its aspects, from politics to aesthetics. Science and education are not encouraged on their own account; their value is only instrumental. The creative power of man is decaying. The authenticity of his existence and action is being compromised and questioned. Religion is moribund. And literature is ' teeming and spawning ' under the yoke of commercial and political motives.

It is clear that Sri Aurobindo does not like the cult of State and the dominant role of the economic and commercial aspects of life. He wants to carve out an autonomy for artistic pursuits. At the same time he quite sees the point that the contemporary historical trend is in favour of socialism, i.e., concentration of power in the State and the expansion of State activities. He takes pains to point out that the cult of State is neither essential nor peculiar to socialism. It goes well with the egalitarian ideal, the revolt of the proletariat, or even with democracy as ordinarily understood. He cites the example of Fascism in support of his contention that there is an inherent tendency of degeneration and tyranny in the cult of State. One might argue that it would be incorrect to ignore the difference between the saner forms of socialism and its degenerate ones of the same and club them together. Sri Aurobindo is prepared to accept socialism, in spite of all its shortcomings, on the simple but questionable ground of historical inevitability. This materialist and objective form of socialism is said to be a necessary step towards a spiritual and subjective form of socialism. He is quite sceptical about the alleged golden age which is often referred to both by Marxist and Conservative thinkers. 'The sign of the extreme conservative mind for the golden age of the past, which was not so golden as it appears to an imaginative eye in the distance, is a vain breath blown to the winds by the rush of the car of the Time-Spirit in the extreme velocity of its progress.' The reflective historian assures us that the past world, contrary to the uncritical belief of the utopian and the ideologue, was not at all free from the contradiction of war and peace. The necessity of peace for the purpose of development was no less keenly realised by the people of the past than it is being realised by us today. Despite its hated character, war as an institution continues to survive. For, in the past it was the only effective measure for a nation to counteract the pauperising moves—for example, a barrier of tariffs, closure of markets and fields of exploitation—adopted by rival nations or groups of nations. The political separativeness of the nations did not allow them to enjoy a conscient unity. In the modern world the war-and-peace contradiction has changed its character. The highly organised nations are very self-conscious. The increasing interdependence of nations for economic and commercial reasons has developed a more or less conscient unity. The impact and implications of science and technology have further enabled us to realise the functional shrinkage of the physical world. The discovery of deadly nuclear weapons has negatively drawn us towards the goal of peace. Most nations have started realising that unless they control the competitive character of commercial life, war is inevitable. The idea of the world-state is drawing its negative sustenance from the commonly shared fear of nuclear war.

Strict regulation of international relations and a system of enforced arbitration, conciliation, negotiation, good offices and mediation can at best only prevent the overt state of war.[15] But, given the conditions of economic and commercial rivalry between the nations, the covert state of war can hardly be removed. The nerve warfare is the first result. And that may be followed, if necessary, by more severe methods like retortion, reprisals, intervention and blockade. The commercial pressure in the form of blockades was tremendously effective in the last two World Wars and Germany witnessed its efficacy in a measure analogous to what Napoleon had experienced under the continental system. To take recourse to the blockade in self-defence is legally permissible under Article 51 of the UN Charter. The member States of the UNO can refuse to sell certain goods to other States who are equally members of the same world organisation. Certainly this is not a desirable state of affairs. And to remove this much more power has to be given to the world-state. Military unification is not the answer. Economic unification is also an absolute necessity for global unity.

If the authority of the proposed international unity is not to be a mere ' concert for palaver ', the uncritically accepted concept of national sovereignty has to be somewhat modified. This modification will entail the self-subordination of the national units to international unity. The nation should voluntarily surrender the power of the management of most of their affairs to the world-state and retain their authority only over some exceptional ones, which cannot be satisfactorily tackled from its relatively ill-informed central organisation. From the other end it may be pointed out that the world-state cannot afford to remain satisfied only by nominally extending its jurisdiction over nations and settling occasional disputes. If the covert state of war is to be brought to a permanent end and if peace is to be established for good, the world-state itself must have a permanent legislative body and an executive organ. One is afraid that in course of time a well-equipped world-state could usurp the functions of the national government and try to coordinate and unite the life, culture, science, organisation, education and efficiency of mankind as a whole.

## Forces for and Against the Process of Unification

Sri Aurobindo recognises, among others, three great forces of unity—science, thought and religion. While these forces are strengthening the idea of the world-state, chauvinistic nationalism is proving to be a very powerful obstacle in the way of further unification of the world. The present state of international relations is like that of an unstable equilibrium, an intersecting point of the working of two opposite forces and ideas. One is centripetal and the other is centrifugal. On the one side there is an underlying unity partly because of economic and commercial reasons and partly because of military reasons; and, on the other, there is a national egoism, ideological aggressiveness and equally blind opposition to the idea of unity. The opposite forces are under the pressure of circumstances patching up their differences in an *ad hoc* manner, just tolerating each other and managing to go their own chosen ways without voluntarily disturbing the delicate balance of the situation. Undoubtedly this is neither a tolerable nor a durable state of affairs. In order to stabilise the international situation and to prevent any possible catastrophe and the recurrence of minor clashes and conflicts the world-state would be compelled to control the free and flexible relations between nations. It is Sri Aurobindo's apprehension that a day is bound to come when the world-state, somewhat in the fashion of the modern Socialist State, would control the industrial production and distribution of the world. Even if under some compelling circumstances some variations in local or regional matters are admitted, the apprehension persists that the world-state would try to remain very uniform and rigid in its principles of administration.

Another unwelcome feature of the envisaged world-state is likely to surface in the sphere of judicial administration. In order to effectively combat the criminal propensity of the corrupt human material the titanic policy of the future would perhaps have to resort to a greater centralisation and uniformity. The world legislature could certainly lay down juridical and judicial principles and methods. There is no denying the fact that they would prove beneficial in some respects, for instance, the tendency of national separativeness would be somewhat checked. But its interference in the internal affairs of the nation would not be perhaps beneficial. It is evident from history that the policy of non-interference is absent or operates in a low profile only in the event of some war or at its beginning. But what we witness today is something different and new, i.e., the policy of interference as a deliberate rule of international life.

Another aspect of this titanic policy should also be borne in mind. The idea of the all-powerful Socialist State would throw a great challenge to the future world. Capitalism would not be tolerated a minute more than is absolutely necessary and there is no valid reason why it should be. The full-fledged Socialist world-state would control everything human—birth and marriage, labour and leisure, education and culture, training of body and mind. Sri Aurobindo's persistent fear is that a uniform and highly centralised internationalism would destroy nationalism, weaken race and group-culture. The world-state can tolerate only an emasculated national life. The independent and creative forces of national identity and autonomy would be forced to give way before the all-powerful socialist internationalism. The increasing points of contact between different group-cultures may be used and interpreted in two different ways—to remove individual distinctiveness or to promote it. The world-state is likely to move along the former path. We have already observed that ' the differences between the European nations are simply minor variations of a common accidental culture '. The United States of Europe is in the making. The formation of the European Economic Community marks its unmistakable first phase. The idea of peaceful coexistence between the East European countries and the West European ones is no longer in the air but settling firmly on the ground and sending its roots deep into the European mind. The case of Oriental culture is not quite comparable now to its Occidental counterpart; but under the impact of the changing world forces it is sure to follow suit. Sri Aurobindo perceives that a common world culture is silently taking shape. However, it would not be an easy process. The process of establishing the world-state will be obdurately resisted by the racial sense of the nations. This sense is less rational and more instinctive than that of a nation and culture and therefore could preserve itself longer than the other unyielding forces. But the ultimate victory of the Titan, the idea of the world-state, is inevitable. Sri Aurobindo goes even to the extent of believing that a common world-language could finally evolve out of the existing languages. Even if this belief of Sri Aurobindo does not historically materialise, his central thesis about the evolving world-state remain unaffected. He observes that ' the dream of the cosmopolitan socialist thinker may therefore be realised after all. And given the powerful continuance of the present trend of world-forces it is in a way inevitable.'

The logic of inevitability, as I had occasion to observe before, is common to the Marxists and Sri Aurobindo. Treading a different path the former also come to the conclusion that the larger human aggregates, empires and nations, ultimately give way to the largest possible human unity, the world-state. The dynamics which makes this final transition possible is said to be objective-economic and not subjective-spiritual. The inherent contradictions of capitalism explain the emergence of imperialism. In the imperialist stage of the world economy several advanced capitalist countries enter into a dangerous or even an internecine competition, either individually or collectively, to capture the world market for purchasing raw-materials at cheap prices and selling industrial products at high prices. The accumulated capital of these countries assumes such a proportion that it is definitely to be exported to the less developed or developing countries. Some times the forms of export are so subtle and sophisticated that one might take it to be an interest free outright grant or aid. The process of capital export determines the pattern of the relationship between the countries concerned. Finally, imperialism lets its inevitable contradictions loose into wars of redivision of the world.

The First World War brought an end to German and Austro-Hungarian imperialism. The former was of course only temporarily liquidated. How it re-established itself in a different form is now well-known and a matter of record. Japan and Italy, though in league with the victorious side, had their own imperialist designs which they could not realise. The United States of America emerged out of that war as the strongest economic nation in the world. The victory of the world's first socialist revolution, due to a concatenation of circumstances, forced Russia to withdraw from the arena of imperialist rivalry.

The character and consequences of the Second World War are rather complex in comparison with the first one. Like the First World War it was not merely an inter-imperialist war confined between England and America, on the one side, and Germany, Italy and Japan on the other. Russia's participation in the war added an anti-imperialist dimension to it. China's anti-imperialist war of resistance is indicative of another growing world-force, viz., the force of national independence.

Imperialism has to face and fight two opposition forces. The first opposition against imperialism is put up by the working class of the imperialist countries. The working class is said to have no common interest with the capitalist class of the country in the matter of exploiting internal resources to sustain war tension and expand the arena of imperialism. But the opposition of the working class, however well-motivated it might be, generally fails to make itself sufficiently effective against the highly organised capitalist society with its dominant bias towards imperial expansion unless its power is considerably weakened under the crushing economic pressure of a long-drawn war. This is exactly what happened in Russia in 1917 and in China in the late forties. The second opposition to imperialism owes its origin to the inequitable relation between the imperialist country and its colonies. The capitalist mode of production introduced by the imperialist country in its colonies destroys its pre-capitalist social structure. As a result of the destruction of village industries in competition with the superior productive system of the metropolis the number of people depending upon agriculture increases alarmingly. In its own interest and also in the interest of the landlords and the producers of the colonies the imperialist country does not like to reform the land-tenure system or provide the colonies with any tariff-protection. As industrialism is not encouraged and in the absence of a rational system of laws of inheritance and succession, the pressure on the cultivable land steadily increases. Added to these difficulties are the characteristic vices of private ownership of land. The little industrialism that is allowed by the imperialist country draws an increasing number of landlords towards the towns. The colonial system of education is introduced to strengthen and protect the imperialist rule and economic exploitation. This is how the national bourgeoisie comes into the picture. This class plays an ambivalent role. Its education and orientation are pro-imperialist but its persistent experience of the misery of fellow people draws it into the whirlpool of the struggle for national independence. And with all its limitations the bourgeoisie provides the leadership to it. The working class of the imperialist country is stated to have a silent, and at times even active, sympathy for the struggle of the colonial people. And thus two major forces working against imperialism find a common footing for an alliance between themselves.

The triumph of the colonial bourgeoisie over the imperialist is no doubt a very important step towards the world revolution. But it is not the most important step. The bourgeoisie has before it a very limited objective. It does not want the establishment of a socialist society. For it is afraid that it may not be able to control and rule it. Over the tomb of international capitalism it only wants to establish a national capitalism which is contrary to the interests of the working class. The growing antagonism between the national bourgeoisie on the one hand, and the working class and the peasantry on the other, develops a new situation marked by tension and conflict. While the former want a sort of bourgeoisie democracy sharing a part of its power with a newly emerging middle-class, the latter tries to move towards the socialist goal smashing the opposition of the ruling class.

The above cluster of Marxist concepts of capitalism, imperialism, colonial rule and its historical consequences, the emergence of the national bourgeoisie and the antagonism between it and the toiling masses, might appear rather simplistic and highly general.[16] Counter-examples to the implicit theories are abundant and well-known. Firstly, one could easily point out that there are capitalist countries without any colonies in the traditional sense. And what is worse one can also refer to a socialist hegemony or covert imperialism resorted to by some socialist countries themselves. Secondly, contrary to the Marxist contention, it has been observed that the post-independence history of the former colonies is not marked by the polarisation of power and the antagonism between the bourgeoisie and the toiling masses. The shifting strategy of the capitalist mode of production and distribution has successfully, maybe temporarily, arrested in many cases what are called the polarisation of forces and the gradual pauperisation of the working class. On the contrary, the advanced capitalist class could be correctly characterised by synchronic stratification and diachronic mobility. Thirdly, the Marxist contention that the working class of the capitalist countries has a community of interest with and a sympathy for its counterpart in the colonies has been falsified in numerous cases. One can think of several former imperialist countries where the socialist governments refused and the conservative governments granted freedom to their colonies in the last quarter of this century. Finally, of course, scholars can always differ in the definition and interpretation of such crucial terms as ' democracy ', ' socialism ', ' the bourgeoisie ' and ' the working class '. Even Marxist scholars themselves are not unanimous in their explication of these crucial concepts. I do not propose to enter here into a lengthy discussion on the tenability or otherwise of the Marxist theories of imperialism, structure of colonial economy and the precise sociological character of the post-independence political struggle in the former colonies I am aiming at a limited objective, namely, to give a brief, perhaps too brief and thereby running the risk of being misunderstood, classical Marxist account of these matters.

## The Marxist Theory of International Unity: Two Views

The controversy and confusion of the socialist group are not confined only to semantics but also extend to the method and timing of internationalising this ideology. In the twenties Stalin argued that the socialist experiment must be made successful first in one country and then its revolutionary good effects would spill over to the rest of the world. This view was strongly opposed by Trotsky in the name of Marx. And his view, as we all know, was that there is no holiday from revolutionary life. The true socialist revolution must be permanent and international. Its effect cannot automatically spill over or spread to other countries without a deliberate plan and programme. Socialism established in one country cannot be assured of its permanence unless it is followed up by the planned victory of the same ideal in some other countries giving it a broad-base and an international character. It is not that Stalin could not see the point in Trotsky's argument. In fact he could. But his sense of responsibility and realism advised him caution and therefore he highlighted the point that once the socialist ideal could be given a concrete shape in one country, its experience, achievements and support would awaken the revolutionary spirit in all countries.

> Most probably, in the course of development of the world revolution, side by side with the centres of imperialism in individual capitalist countries and with the system of these countries throughout the world, centres of socialism would be created in individual Soviet countries and the system of these countries throughout the world, and the struggle between these two systems will fill the history of the unfolding of the world revolution.[17]

This theory replaces the old one. According to the old theory, world socialism would come through the gradual decay and disintegration of the forces of capitalism due to its inherent contradiction and through the regular maturing of the forces of Socialism. And it was also predicted that more advanced and industrialised countries would lead the rest in this process. The new theory speaks of the different methods of establishing the worldwide socialist system. It would be preceded by a series of revolutions in separate countries and not by a single international revolution. But immediately before its establishment the final struggle between the two rival systems would take place. The forecast was that the movements generated by the revolution in different countries would objectively create a worldwide vortex drawing more and more countries into itself. A somewhat similar idea has been propounded by Che Guevara in the limited context of international guerilla warfare.

Marx has consistently spoken of the unity of theory and practice and staked the fate of all his major theories before the tribunal of historical practice. It would, therefore, be quite in order to see how the career of these kindred theories has taken shape in the contemporary world. Naturally, the first question to be raised in this connection is whether the success of socialism in one or other country has in effect laid bare the contradictions of the capitalist society, strengthening and unifying the socialist forces within the capitalist system and thereby enabling them to destroy the system from within. I do not propose to bring up that old and boring question as to whether the fact that the socialist revolutions have taken place first in the agrarian countries and not in the industrialised ones indicates a partial falsification of Marx's prediction on the matter. But it is evident that the conflict and tension of the capitalist society, contrary to the Marxist line of thinking, have not yet reached a bursting point at the instance of the international socialist movement. The changing face of the contemporary world is very complex indeed. The lack of homogeneity is clear not only in the capitalist but also in the socialist world.

The United States of America, the United Kingdom, the Federal Republic of Germany and France, notwithstanding the fact that they have introduced various social services and control over production and distribution, are known to be the main capitalist countries and, as we all know, have many policy differences between themselves. But they are united in respect of at least one issue, i.e., to resist the possible expansion of the socialist camp of East Europe. This single negative motivation explains their membership of the NATO. Those who have been persistently failing to see eye to eye on the major positive issues for the welfare of the human race are united curiously enough on a slender negative plank. The relative irrelevance of ideology in the matter of promoting the cause of unity may be illustrated also by reference to the history of the socialist camp. No objective person could deny the multifarious economic and scientific achievements of the Socialist countries. It is a matter of record that the distortions and aberrations of the capitalist economic system could not significantly affect the economies of the Socialist countries. Positively speaking, one might further add, their rate of economic growth, the equitability of distribution and the stability of prices are very striking indeed. But the point remains that the two leading Socialist countries, Russia and China, who claim to have been following the correct Marxist-Leninist path, are openly involved in an ideological warfare and accuse each other of subverting and betraying the cause of the socialist revolution. What is still worse is that both China and Russia are being criticised by third countries for their allegedly unprincipled cooperation with the main 'capitalist-imperialist' of the world, the USA. Not only that, but some characteristics of bourgeois politics, economics and culture have made inroads into the socialist camp providing a little more incentive to the private farmer and the producer and imposing a little less restriction on the intellectual and the creative artist. Another thing to be noted in this connection is that, in spite of the impressive performance of the Socialist countries in different spheres of life, contrary again to Marx's prediction, they have not yet been able to win over the socialist and progressive forces of the capitalist countries to their side to the degree that was expected. If the common man is not adequately conscious today of the grave defects of the capitalist system, a satisfactory explanation of the matter cannot be found within the system itself. Part of the answer lies elsewhere—in the endless confusion and controversy within the socialist camp itself. Even the most uncompromising critic of Marx cannot lightly dismiss his incisive critique of the capitalist system and its contemporary relevance. Marx's severe indictment of the capitalist system has been amply borne out by the history and economic developments of the last hundred years or so. Even those who are opposed to socialism as a political ideology cannot deny the essential truth of Marx's criticism of the classical theory of economic growth. It is true that modern theorists of economic growth have done away with some of the defects of the classical theories and incorporated, with or without acknowledgement, some of the basic ideas of Marx in their works enabling them thereby to provide a theoretical foundation for the plans and programmes of the welfare state. The strong point of socialism is that it is not based on exploitation and, rightly understood and correctly followed, does not need to wage war to realise its objective. Positively speaking, if a Socialist country concentrates more on improving the quality of life of its people in a peaceful manner rather than on competing with its rival system, it might in all probability win over one day the moral and the active sympathy of the common man in capitalist countries who is on the border line between traditional capitalism and emerging socialism. And it is in this peaceful way that the Socialist countries could launch their counter-offensive and take the ideological war into the 'enemy' camp.

## Socialism, Democracy and the World-State

The world has become a very small place. Because of modern science and technology space has been effectively annihilated. And therefore time has assumed an unprecedented importance. Partly because of its capacity to bring about rapid developments in the standard of living and partly because of the unbearable poverty of the people in developing countries, the influence of socialist ideas has been growing fast. It is believed that socialism could reach its main goal sooner or later—a worldwide socialist system. But it is difficult to predict whether the transitional age will pass off peacefully or be marked by some devastating war. There are two clear possibilities—democratisation of socialism and incorporation of some fundamental socialist features in democracy. The latter possibility is being tried and perhaps has been more or less a success. Of the former nothing could be asserted definitely. Or, one might cautiously observe, it is too early to assert anything definitely about it. For discipline is the central plank of socialism and without it the socialist system cannot work or survive. It has been often argued by the critic of socialism that the relation between socialism and democracy can never be cordial for the simple reason that the concept of discipline as understood and practised by the socialist undercuts the very basis of democracy, i.e., individual liberty. The democratic society is open and entertains socialist ideas and even anarchist ones which encourage violence and are basically against the ideal of individual liberty. In other words, the democratic society is open even to enemies of democracy. Quite in contrast to this, the democrat points out, the socialist system is closed and does not tolerate any pro-democratic and anti-socialist idea. Morally speaking, the two systems are said to be placed not on an equal footing. While one is rational and tolerant, the other is emotional and impatient.

Whatever might be the merit or otherwise of these arguments and counter-arguments for and against democracy and socialism, one can hardly deny that they are almost entirely academic in character and with little or no practical significance. Except for the privileged minority of the democratic society, very few people are really interested in the highly publicised virtues like the openness of the democratic society. The oppressed masses are mainly interested in their problems of food, clothing and housing. This does not of course mean that the issue of individual liberty is unimportant. These problems have no fixed and quantified character of their own. Their magnitude and seriousness should be assessed and expressed by those who are themselves directly involved. The wearer knows where the shoe pinches and it is very difficult for others to appreciate and share this experience. There is no substitute for experience in human affairs. The irrevocable subjectivity of social experience is a very important factor in the matter of the formulation and choice of political ideology. Even those who are theoretically committed to democracy with all its well-known virtues find it very difficult to prescribe it honestly for the developing countries haunted by the spectre of poverty. Here theory and practice work at cross-purposes. The survival of democracy in the world today, especially in the developing world, depends mainly upon its ability to fight expeditiously and effectively the basic problems of poverty and suffering. But that demands an imaginative integration of some essential socialist features with a democratic way of life.

It is very difficult to say whether the socialist system would respond equally to the demands of democracy. It is widely believed today, and Sri Aurobindo shares the belief, that socialism as the culmination of the State idea is sure to assume an international character, if possible by the democratic way or, if not, otherwise. The prospect of the worldwide socialist system *ex hypothesi* may be delayed but not destroyed for ever. If another world war breaks out, one can rationally assume that it would stop before the whole human race is exterminated. And in that event the present pattern of conflicts between different ideologies and the related actions and responses would in all probability survive in the character and disposition of the fortunate survivors. When the effect of the physical shock of war and the social disorganisation are over, the inherent socio-political dialectics would come out of their temporary suspense and assert themselves functionally once again. Sri Aurobindo and the Marxist differ in their premises but agree on the inevitability of the world-state. It is said that there is nothing contingent about the evolution of the world-state. Sri Aurobindo is very clear on this point.

> The State principle leads necessarily to uniformity, regulation, mechanisation; its inevitable end in socialism. There is nothing fortuitous, no room for chance in political and social development, and the emergence of socialism was no accident or a thing that might or might not have been, but the inevitable result contained in the very seed of the State idea .... Strict unification, a vast uniformity, a regulated socialism of united mankind will be the predestined fruit of our labour.

It is anticipated that the world-state, at least immediately after its formation, would inaugurate a great age of culture and intellectual efflorescence. A well-regulated and administered socio-political order is expected to provide its people with all means of material and vital satisfaction. The mutual understanding between the nation-units would largely increase and the interfusion of their cultures would take place to pour down their individual gains into the common fund of human knowledge and experience.

It is interesting to note that, in spite of these good things that are likely to emerge out of the world-state, Sri Aurobindo does not welcome it for a different reason and from a higher point of view. By ' a higher point of view ' I mean a normative point of view. There are two different but related levels in Sri Aurobindo's study of the human cycle leading to the formation of the world-state. From an external and a positive point of view it is quite clear that the evolution of the world-state is inevitable. His arguments against it are based on an inner perception of the possibility of a higher ideal of human unity. Sri Aurobindo fears that quite in consonance with its aim and achievements the world-state is bound to be very vigorous, highly centralised and therefore would not be in a position to tolerate any variation and differentiation in the patterns of society and culture of its units belonging to different parts of the world with their peculiar historical, psychological and commercial moulds. Classical democracy would be no cure for this malady, even if it is tried. For under the socialist idea of the State and the tyranny of the majority, democracy is no longer a sure preservative of liberty. The success of democracy, as we learn from its classic example of ancient Greece, requires the fulfillment of two conditions—first, the personal and effective participation of each citizen in all possible governmental affairs, and, second, freedom of individual thought and action. But these two difficult conditions can hardly be fulfilled by the impersonal group-being that would be saddled with the responsibility of regulating the destiny of mankind. And consequently it is feared that the people would be denied freedom of thought, speech and action and even perhaps the right to profess and practise their religion. The individual man with his variable disposition and action is the pivot of all progress. He is the unrecognised vanguard of all human advancement. If he is sacrificed for the sake of a vast and artificial uniformity, the result would be reminiscent of the decline and fall of the Roman Empire. Sri Aurobindo predicts: 'After a time, there would be a dying down of force, a static condition of the human mind and human life, then stagnation, decay and disintegration.'

While the emergence of the world-state is admitted by him as an inevitable *fact*, he continues to oppose it in *principle*.

One might perhaps justifiably assert that Sri Aurobindo's theory of the human cycle is systematically bedevilled by a dualism of fact and principle. I don't deny this possibility. But I am persuaded that a careful study of Sri Aurobindo's works provides a plausible answer to this criticism, which may not be accepted by all.

## In Defence of the World-Union

Sri Aurobindo's alternative to the world-state is what he calls the world-union. In this connection too he claims to have drawn his guiding principle, unity in diversity, from Nature. The evolving Spirit in Nature always maintains its oneness at the foundation of all things and that foundational unity is said to have been realising itself progressively in and through diversity. The higher the stages of social evolution the more and more complex are the forms of oneness. This evolution is marked by an interplay of two opposite but necessary forces, the forces of unity and those of diversity. Unity in diversity is the law of Nature. This law holds good even in respect of the evolution of the human society.

The idea of the world-state is an abstract idea of intellectual man and is entirely unrelated to the natural law of unity in diversity. Consequently, one apprehends, the idea in practice will lay emphasis only on the side of order and uniformity and neglect liberty and variation. Order without liberty succeeds at first, but then stagnates, and finally disintegrates. If order is not based on the genuine consent of the people concerned, it does not work. Sri Aurobindo is quite aware that under the present circumstances the principle of liberty and variation cannot be given an absolutely free play. For freedom is to be deserved first before it can be given or granted.

To make his point of diversity in oneness Sri Aurobindo stresses the necessity of what he calls natural groupings and specifically refers to the role and importance of language. Language is an 'intellectual, aesthetic and expressive bond which tempers division where division exists and strengthens unity where unity has been achieved'. Thus it serves two related purposes, of unification and of variation.[18] If a group loses its own tongue or has none to call its own, it cannot produce something very distinctive and rich and suffers from a sort of cultural identity crisis. The former English-speaking colonies of the UK in general and America in particular are not certainly mere replicas of the UK, yet culturally they perhaps may be safely regarded as provinces of the UK. The same is the case with Central and Southern America and that is again because they have no distinct tongue of their own and depend on Spanish. Ireland had a rich and distinct culture so long as she had her own independent language; but soon after a foreign language was imposed upon her that culture began to die. The history of modern Indian culture illustrates the same truth. The English language has no doubt united an otherwise diffused Indian culture, but the body, to extend the analogy, is somewhat alien to the soul because of its Anglicised exterior. Bengal was the first province to receive the shock of foreign domination, and perhaps therefore did look back into her cultural past and began to develop her own tongue. This helped her greatly to Indianise her culture and pave the way for a rich cultural efflorescence. This shows that the unity of Indian culture has been preserved and enriched by diverse languages. The same happened also in Maharashtra and Tamil Nadu later on. This is not peculiar to the modern age. What we find true today was also so in the past. So long as the Latin language was insistent on maintaining its prominence, it failed, except for a brief period, to prove its worth as a vehicle of a rich culture. But the old languages evolved out of the dying Latin gave to Europe its richest cultures. Even Sanskrit, only in its derivative forms, and not in its unitarian stage, had been very creative and expressive of group-culture.

The rationale of the history of languages is very interesting and instructive. A careful analysis of the relation between group-language and group-culture clearly establishes the desirability of preserving the *autonomy* of the *real* units within a bigger whole. When the world-state becomes a blind unitarian whole and destroys the live character of the real units, which are so necessary for its self-formation, growth and enrichment, Sri Aurobindo warns, the outraged necessity of Nature will have its revenge. And the possible consequence would be destruction of the unitarian and mechanical world-state and the emergence of some sort of anarchism, intellectual or spiritual.

Sri Aurobindo develops his argument on the matter in a rather metaphysical way. He relied too heavily on a highly interpreted law of Nature or what at best could be taken as an analogy of the organic world.[19] I for one do not dispute the undesirability of too much of order and too little of liberty. But I do not see why an organisation primarily built on the foundation of order and discipline and not on that of liberty and variation would necessarily crack and crumble. It is of no use to draw on history in a scissor-and-paste way. For, historically speaking, one could easily show how many states and organisations decayed and disintegrated because of their excessive reliance on the reverse principle of liberty. The decline of Athens, the cradle of European democracy, was certainly not due to the denial of freedom to its citizens. And the ascendency of Sparta cannot be ascribed to its love for liberty. The

Fourth Republic of France certainly did not collapse because its attitude towards individual rights and liberties was more severe and conservative than that of the Fifth Republic. The principle of liberty or that of an order in itself takes us neither here nor there. Other related principles and considerations have also to be taken into consideration. Further, I would like to add that the emergence of anarchism is not likely to follow immediately the disintegration of the world-state. Intellectual anarchism is too abstract to be easily perused and practised, while spiritual anarchism is a lofty ideal, too lofty to be reached by the common run of mankind.

Sri Aurobindo himself admits that the followers of intellectual anarchism are only few in number and that spiritual anarchism is nothing more than a utopian creed. Nature's intention might be to evolve a free society conforming to the anarchist's vision in the distant future, but Sri Aurobindo is doubtful of its real outcome as a remedy of the ills of an over-centralised world-state. Having an eye on the realities of the present-day world he is now primarily interested in a rather flexible form of union which would preserve the group-characters of the units, rationally regulate their obstinate separatist tendencies and try to make them gradually more and more conscious of their foundational oneness. Sri Aurobindo believes that Russia with her characteristic idealism started experimenting with the principle of free confederation. Under this ideal form of unity the cultural and linguistic autonomies of the units are preserved but not at the cost of confederal unity. In this connection Sri Aurobindo refers to the idea of a League of Nations as advanced by President Wilson and also to the changing patterns of the Commonwealth. But unfortunately when the League of Nations was actually formed, America remained isolationist and the US Senate did not endorse Wilson's ideas. As a result, its short existence was characterised by ineffectualness. Moreover, the later development of the Russian experiment does not confirm Sri Aurobindo's early expectation and disappoints him deeply. But his incurable optimism, based on the logic of inevitability, is unmistakable in his writings. He believes that the Russian experiment with all its ups and downs would yield a 'moral principle' which will act as a corrective to aggressive nationalism, an unintended result of the French Revolution; and he assures us: 'It has a better meaning for the future'.[20] It is also evident that Sri Aurobindo could not but feel sad at the eventual burial of Wilson's 'magnificent nebulous idealism'. Its sad end was certainly due to its nebulous character, but its inherent magnificence can hardly be denied. The immediate prospect of the Commonwealth is also not bright; for it embodies a psychological unity of the peoples concerned. But even then, one has to admit, it is an important experiment. Its importance, like the importance of the other two ideals, consists in making the world silently ready for positively responding to the necessity of the ideal human unity at an appropriate time in the future.

Any ideal unity of mankind should be psychological both in its inception and execution. Otherwise it would be purely temporary and superficial. But before unity can attain an ideal character it might preserve and stabilise itself to a certain extent by following the principle of the Commonwealth or Free

Confederation. To create the right environment for the emergence of a free world-union certain conditions have to be fulfilled, namely, the removal of war, the recognition of the right of self-determination of the people and the arrangement for the peaceful settlement of economic and commercial disputes between them.[21] In the face of the present-day conditions of the world, even the most optimistic among us is bound to feel a bit sceptical about the immediate emergence of a world-union. Perhaps the time is not yet ripe to make that ideal unity possible. What we need, besides the three conditions referred to before, is a psychological realisation of the basic unity of mankind.

Favourable sociological conditions are undoubtedly necessary but not sufficient. Sri Aurobindo's emphasis on the psychological argument rather than on the sociological one is perfectly understandable against the background of his philosophical persuasion. But one hardly finds a sufficiently strong and organised motive-force in the world which could bring about this fundamental modification in human nature. Interestingly enough, Sri Aurobindo does not share this reading of the world situation. His spiritual mind could perceive some movements deep in world history indicating the vague beginning of what he calls the subjective age. Man is looking within instead of looking around for the golden principle of human unity. The subjective age found its first expression in the fields of literature, art and philosophy. The philosophy of Nietzsche is of crucial importance to Sri Aurobindo.[22] His concepts of will-to-be and will-to-power are indicative of a determined effort to resolve the antithesis between voluntarism and intellectualism, between Schopenhauer's Will and Hegel's Idea. In him Sri Aurobindo finds a distinct departure from the period of rationalism and utilitarianism, a happy beginning of the vitalistic period of human development. Bergson's concepts of *élan vital* and intuitive knowledge confirm this new trend. The abstract character of rationalism is evident from the increasing outwardness of the mind of man and as a result of which he fails to strike the right balance between the demands of his self and those of his environment. Sri Aurobindo is persuaded that the brave new world cannot be found without. Man has to look within for that. Art and literature embody the primary modes of human experience. In different forms of art, especially in literature, one observes a new, introverted orientation. The novelist concentrates more on inward journeys and on the conflicts of characters than on the course of outward events. And the poet is a singer of feeling, of subterranean knowledge, where emotions may be studied in a crystallised form, in the intermediary stage between the subconscious and the conscious. The new psychologies of Freud, Adler and Jung were engaged in an epoch-making study of the unconscious.[23] Thereafter, a new form of psychologism, depth psychology, began to take the place of vitalism and knock at the sealed doors of the spirit, the discovery of which is a supreme desideratum of the age of subjectivism. Nietzsche's was not the only protest against Hegel. Others came from Brentano, Husserl and Heidegger. Their broad thesis is: the reality of everyone's existence is to be found within one's own inwardness. Truth is subjectivity. Existentialism and humanism and their different forms owe much to the spirit of the subjective, the primary mode of experience.

'There is no other universe', says Sartre, 'except the human universe, the universe of human subjectivity.'[24]

While nobody would deny the importance of modern literature, arts and philosophy as a motive-force behind world unity, their operational role amidst numerous constraints should not be overrated. The ideal of internationalism is still lying dormant deep beneath the abstract ideas and symbolism of philosophy and poetry and its emerging power can be perceived only by a few inward-looking men. The majority of us trace the ideal of internationalism in its first recognisable form to the French Enlightenment and the French Revolution. This institutional history of internationalism gives us a very surface view. This ideal had and still has its limitation but undeniably it is the single most powerful factor favouring international unity.

The intellectual sentiment of internationalism was present only in the early idealistic stage of the French Revolution. What followed the revolutionary spirit was self-conscious nationalism and not internationalism. Prior to its coming in alliance with socialism and anarchism, internationalism was a pure idealism of the subjective mind. The utopia of internationalism became a forceful ideology under the influence of anarchism and socialism. Owen, Saint-Simon, Fourier, Cabet, Lamennais, Christian Socialists and others started and developed what has been characterised as Utopian Socialism by Marx and Engels. They gave the name Scientific Socialism to their own ideology. Elements of anarchism are unmistakable in Scientific Socialism, especially in its envisaged final form. Proudhon and Godwin were perhaps the pioneers of anarchism and they were followed by distinguished thinkers like Spencer, Tolstoy and Bakunin. The imposing idea of internationalism attracted the attention and imagination of the intellectuals of the nineteenth century. The Christian dream of universal brotherhood reappeared in the shape of internationalism. All these were hardly anything more than ideal. For mankind was not yet prepared and equipped to accept it as a practical guiding principle. But meanwhile, actual conditions developed fast to change this abstract ideal force into a very concrete and real one.

The internationalist of the nineteenth century realised that the solo performance of its ideal, i.e., internationalism, could not carry the world very far forward.[25] As a result of that internationalism aligned itself with two very powerful movements of the century—Socialism and Anarchism. Their career was different. By the end of the last century Anarchism diffused itself in Syndicalism, Guild-Socialism, distributivism and some other intellectual-idealistic reactions against the cult of the State. Internationalism found its surest ally in growing socialism and with it internationalism identified itself. Finally, of course, this ideal was overshadowed by Socialism. Socialist internationalism was nearer to the idea of national community rather than to the true ideal of the internationalist. And that was because, says Sri Aurobindo, socialism has no essential relation with internationalism. It is an outgrowth of the nation-State. The working collaboration between socialism and internationalism is said to be just an accident. In other words, Sri Aurobindo does not believe that the socialist profession of internationalism is integral to his ideology. Socialism may be the precursor of an international concert but that would not prove that the latter is the necessary object of the former. One might pointedly refer to many developments in contemporary history wherein professed socialist countries have let down at crucial times fellow socialist countries and pro-socialist Governments in non-socialist countries.

## INTERNATIONALISM: NATURAL AND ARTIFICIAL

Sri Aurobindo's main criticism against internationalism is that it is still at the abstract level. While nationalism is a *living* ideal, internationalism is not. It is ' not yet a thing near to our vital feelings or otherwise a part of our psychology'. It is the intellectual's idea of unity of all proletarians of all countries. It is a noble idea indeed. But the point is that if we look into the mind of the socialist and forget for the time being his intellectual profession and jargon, we might easily recognise in him living nationalist sentiments. Internationalism is bound to remain ineffective so long as it remains merely an idea and cannot develop into a true psychological unity. One can hardly forget the distinction between the living-moving force of nationalism and the intellectual's clear-cut but dead blue-print of internationalism. One cannot expect to be an internationalist merely because one *thinks* of internationalism or considers it to be an indispensable ally either of Socialism or Anarchism. To be truly internationalist a profound modification has to be brought about in our inner being. This is undoubtedly a difficult demand to fulfil but at the same time an inescapable necessity. Unless we are psychologically moulded by the living and moving ideal of internationalism, our actions are not likely to further the cause of internationalism in an appreciable manner.

It is through two negations that Sri Aurobindo explicates his psychological theory of internationalism. First, he negates the institutional-objective approach to nationalism, simultaneously taking care of the Marxist approach. Secondly, he negates the intellectualist approach to internationalism. By its very nature the intellect is static in form and one-dimensional in operation and consequently its products are not rooted in the true being of man. One might further recall in this connection Sri Aurobindo's notion of depth psychology or integral psychology, as distinguished from ordinary empirical psychology. We must not commit the mistake of defining mind in terms of images, ideas and emotions generated by sense-contacts with the external world. This inadequate definition of mind provides no clue to the real community of minds and no foundation for a durable socio-political structure.[26]

Whatever forms a human aggregate takes, it springs from our vital necessity and attains, under suitable conditions, psychological unity. The vital and the mental are the two related levels of the being. The family, the clan and the tribe are truly psychological aggregates both in character and in composition. The notional idea, though originally it was merely geographical and historical, has, under the pressure of circumstances, assumed a psychological character. Without this psychological unity no human aggregate can successfully stand the trials and tests of history. The unity that is created by circumstances but not held together by some vital and psychological forces from within is again destroyed by circumstances. Unless the force of subjectivity asserts itself effectively, it is likely to be distorted and destroyed by the pull and push of the objective world. The existing economic, political and mechanical forces can create, and have perhaps already created, a preliminary framework of human unity. It seems, however, that there is no sufficiently living psychological force within it to sustain it. The present international organisation, the UNO, exists more in body and words than in mind and spirit. Its functions and scope are preventive and curative but not creative, certainly not consciously so. If we really want to transform this organisation into a living and growing reality, we have to bring it closer to the foundational oneness of the human nature. It must fulfil and express the basic and positive urges of the human mind.

In this connection Sri Aurobindo refers to an unconscious or sub-conscious process continuously working in Nature in order to create favourable circumstances in which some intended events and human aggregates may evolve. Because of our empirical bias and rigid intellectual cast of mind we often fail to understand the significance of evolving nature. An average and alert student of international relations is not likely to be very enthusiastic about the future performance of the UNO. He might very well pointedly refer to many major problems which could not be solved at all by this world body. But Sri Aurobindo does not share this pessimistic assessment of the situation. With his characteristic insight he reads something deep into it.

Here we could again profitably recall Sri Aurobindo's characterisation of the modern age as the Subjective Age. This might sound paradoxical. The common man thinks that this is the age of science and socialism. Contrary to the common run of thinking, Sri Aurobindo associates these ideas with the Age of Individualism and Reason. Science is said to be groping in relativity and probability, while socialism reduces the individual to an insignificant part of the social body. While Sri Aurobindo does not deny the importance of science as an objectively verifiable form of knowledge of the surface objects of nature and their various movements, he is not prepared to accept it as a paradigm of the human knowledge. He concedes that whatever he might have to say about the inner subjectivity of the modern age, its outer characteristics are undoubtedly materialist and utilitarian. It would perhaps take several centuries before the main forces of the age of individualism, science and technology, materialism and socialism, can unfold all their potential forms and are ultimately exhausted. Sri Aurobindo cautions us not to be misled by the surface movements of history and consistently maintains that some new forces of the subjective age are silently developing simultaneously with those of the closing rhythms of the human psychology.

Politically speaking, the Age of Individualism and Reason fails to produce a just type of society in which the individual could preserve and develop his true individuality. Democratic individualism was the dominant political ideal of the time. Of its three principles, equality, liberty and fraternity, the first two were destroyed under the influence of competition, 'a very vital tendency of the infra-rational in man'. The third principle of democratic individualism, fraternity, has been taken over from it by democratic socialism, an omnibus name of the new socio-political world ideology. Socialism has discarded the ideas of individualistic liberty and equality and stressed the necessity of preserving them in a manner which may not jeopardise social fraternity. The emphasis of the ideal socio-political order has been shifted from competing individualism to organised collectivism. There was nothing very harmful in this shift in emphasis; for it really became necessary. But, one fears, the crusade of collectivism has been carried too far and to the detriment of individual liberty. The democratic elements of socialism have now become almost completely eclipsed in practice. And what was intended to be a transitional arrangement for upholding human dignity and ensuring human freedom has now assumed the unintended character of a negative institution. The reason is not far to seek. The original idea was to motivate and mould the structure by the individual man, by his free initiative, creative thought and action. Unfortunately, the initiative passed over to the impersonal group-being, the custodian of the State apparatus, lacking in taste, delicacy and perception of the individual. The result is well-known: socialism can hardly be associated with democracy. In fact, Sri Aurobindo says, its ally is now totalitarianism.[27]

Some thinkers anticipated this unfortunate development long ago in the nineteenth century. The growing scope of the functions of the State first disturbed them. The voice of their criticism was raised against the socialist idea, the theoretical justification of the cult of the State. Their panacea was anarchism, a plea for decentralisation and against totalitarianism. It was rightly apprehended by them that once the enormous State powers are used to ensure human freedom from poverty and inequality, these powers would remain there objectively operative curtailing freedom itself.

They developed their positive doctrine, anarchism, in different forms, vitalistic or violent, intellectual and spiritual.[28] Vitalistic anarchism is merely a crude reaction against the cult of State or the socialist principle. It takes man to be a mere vital being and interested mainly in his own welfare, and wrongly supposes that the only method capable of bringing in the new society is violence. Sri Aurobindo does not pay much attention to this crude idea. He closely examines the idea of intellectual anarchism, as a revolt against the opposite exaggeration of the socialist principles. The intellectual anarchist declares that 'all government of man by man by the power of compulsion is an evil, a violation, a suppression or deformation of a natural principle of good which would otherwise grow and prevail for the perfection of the human race'.[29] The State in any of its forms is said to be an unnecessary evil. By giving protection to the unjust monopoly of power of the few and thus depriving the bulk of people of what they naturally and rightly deserve, it is objectively responsible for continuance of an unethical order. On the basis of this argument the anarchist not only objects to further expansion of State power and activities but also pleads for their substantial reduction. Since true power could be morally exercised and retained only by the individual man, it must be our endeavour to see that all powers ultimately vest in the free man and he is made the only locus of power. Authority in any form stultifies the individual. Secondly, the State cannot be an ideal human aggregate for the simple reason that it is not free from the fallacy of representative government. No citizen, and still less a party politician, can truly represent another man. His ability and moral right to represent a group of men are bound to be much less. Every man is unique with all his qualities, good, bad and indifferent. Given this fact, the best form of government should consist of people who have the ability to understand other minds, and not of mere professionals or amateurs. The anarchist concludes that the modern representative system is either unnecessary or unrepresentative. Thirdly, power has in it an inevitable corrupting effect. The State idea being based as it is on power exerts its corrupting influence on the citizens. Goodness in man and political power are inversely related. Given power, even a good man is likely to turn egoistical, oppressive and thus alien to others. Power weakens the bond of sympathy between man and man and promotes alienation and anomie. Somewhere Kropotkin has ruefully observed, ' this or that despicable Minister might have been an excellent man, if power had not been given to him '. Sri Aurobindo's criticism of intellectual anarchism rests on two planks. One, he turns the table upside down against the anarchist and argues that it is not because of the introduction of Statism or Socialism that man has fallen from his paradise of the natural state of society but just the contrary is the case, i.e., some form of collectivism has to be introduced because of the degeneration of human nature. Two, the anarchist view of human nature is unhistorical and asocial. One must realise that human freedom and development cannot possibly be achieved in a void or vacuum. Society is a system or field of relations and it provides man the opportunity to develop and realise himself progressively. Anarchism is right in asserting the importance of cooperation between man and man and sympathy in our social life. Sri Aurobindo shares the anarchist denunciation of the collectivist zeal. But he dismisses the latter's ideal of a free society as entirely Utopian and unworkable. If reason could be regarded as the highest faculty of man and law of the universe, the ideal of the intellectual anarchist might be more feasible and as well as acceptable as a theory of what human life might be in its reasonable perfection. But in Sri Aurobindo's scale of evolution the rational man stands midway between the vital being and the spiritual one. He is in a transitional phase constantly pulled by the lower vital tendencies and simultaneously inspired by the spiritual motive-force to exceed himself. If he is to perfect himself, he must aim higher and go further.

Hence the necessity of a spiritual or spiritualised analysis. An ideal human order must be based upon ' the spiritual comradeship ', ' a yet-unfounded law of love '. It is only in this type of social order that the individual can enjoy real freedom and discover a sure and durable motive-force sustaining the order. In a spiritual anarchist society the spirit in man would realise his spiritual oneness with all other individuals and also understand that the perfection of life and nature is one with universal life and nature. An ideal human unity must regard man as a growing godhead and not merely as a mind, a life and a body. Spiritual anarchism is a higher approximation than any other hitherto made to this end.

Sri Aurobindo attaches profound importance to this view of an ideal society. If it is not considered as an adequate solution of the socio-political problem of this age, he frankly admits, then there is no better solution to which the individual with his present capacities and tendencies is capable of. One wonders whether this lofty ideal has any operational significance at all. Even if we assume with Sri Aurobindo that man is a growing godhead, the question remains whether he has grown enough to accept this ideal as a practical proposition. Otherwise, we can hardly draw a line of distinction between practical idealism, which we are for, and utopianism, which is of no consequence in solving the problems of mankind and shaping its destiny. We must not forget that one might even question the very basic assumption of Sri Aurobindo, viz., man is a growing godhead and something more than a body, a life and a mind. The tenability or otherwise of his view hinges on it. Of course he personally believes that spiritual anarchism, based on the spiritual nature of man and his foundational oneness with the rest of mankind, is not only the ideal solution but the inevitable one also.

Socialism and internationalism are no doubt very powerful ideas and have significantly influenced the course of human history in the last one hundred years or so. But these ideas are what Sri Aurobindo calls vitalistic and intellectual. As we know, these terms have definite connotations in Sri Aurobindo's system of thought. The vitalistic tendencies because of their body-based character cannot awaken the spirit in man. They are powerful but blind, not conscious of their end. In this respect the intellectual tendencies are definitely at an advantage. Intellection is end-conscious mental action. But its limitation consists in its rigidity, relative simplicity and superficiality. Because of these limitations the intellect cannot grasp the complexity of the human situation and see through the distant rhythms of the human cycle. The socialist and the internationalist are intellectually quite persuaded of the necessity of a world order. They are also conscious of its practical conditions and requirements. But, unlike the spiritual anarchist, they could not discover *the* sure foundation of an ideal world unity, i.e., the spirit in man. In vain we are searching for without what is already within.

With his characteristic spiritual insight and vision when Sri Aurobindo looks at the UNO and studies its organisation and functions he discovers something in it which we do not quite see. He considers it to be a grand achievement of the internationalist and the socialist and an institutional expression of their quest for a world order. But he recognises that it is still only a framework. If it is to be vivified, a soul must grow within it. The mere ideas and desires of the socialist and the internationalist cannot ensure the growth of that soul. For, most of the statesmen of the world are almost exclusively concerned with the promotion of the interests of their own nation-States. It makes little or no difference whether the concerned national interests are consistent with the aims and objects of the UNO. Even then Sri Aurobindo does not feel disheartened. Deeply convinced of the logic of inevitability he believes that the subjective age is giving birth to some forces which would make mankind conscious of its spiritual unity and that is the sure guarantee of the possible survival and success of the UNO as the beginning of a new world order.

## Sri Aurobindo's Religion of Humanity and the Marxist Humanism

The religion of humanity is such a force that it is more powerful than the subjective forces working behind the new types of art, literature and philosophy. Sri Aurobindo hopes that the religion of humanity would stabilise the outward uniformity of the world order and gradually develop a collective soul within this Olympian framework. The rationalists of the eighteenth century developed the ideal of the religion of humanity as an alternative to Christianity. The fundamental idea of this intellectual religion is that humanity is to be respected and human values are to be preserved for positive social benefits and not for any metaphysical reasons.

This view of life and society received a comprehensive formulation at the hands of Comte.[30] He learnt from Saint-Simon that the end of philosophy must be social and its work betterment of human society.

Humanism demands the removal of institutional impediments and barriers between man and man. The capitalist mode of production has alienated man not only from other men but also from the process and product of his own labour and ultimately from his own self. In other words, capitalism puts up barriers not only between man and man but also between the inner man and the outer man. To enable man to get back to his own true self he has to be freed from the alienating, atomic and negative forces of the capitalist mode of production and distribution. Marx claims that it is on the basis of socialism alone that man can discover his true identity which freely unites him with other human beings on an equal objective footing. The true identity of man is social and not mediated by any class or distorted by its constraints, elation or depression. The free social identity of man knows no national barrier. He is related to and united with the rest of mankind. Marx claims that socialism is not merely consistent with but is an absolutely necessary condition for the development of humanism. Unless the objective conditions for the humanist society are secured, it would be idle to think of establishing a world-union on the basis of religion or humanity. This approach, though well-meaning, is obviously metaphysical, sentimental and utopian. Unless we are prepared to face the reality and ascertain the institutional causes responsible for the alienation of man and the de-humanisation of human relations, our well-meaning spiritualism will take us nowhere. Man's return to his own fullness demands of him the ability to appropriate the living legacy of history and reject its dead hangover. He has to conquer not only history but also Nature, appropriate it by knowing it and acting on it by means of his developing science and technology. Marx says:

> Communism is the positive abolition of private property and thus of human self-alienation and therefore the real re-appropriation of the human essence by and for man. This is the communism as the complete and conscious return of man conserving all the riches of previous development for man himself as a social, i.e., human being. Communism as completed naturalism is humanism and as completed humanism is naturalism. It is the genuine solution of the antagonism between man and nature and between man and man. It is the true solution of the struggle between existence and essence, between objectification and self-affirmation, between freedom and necessity, between individual and species. It is the solution of the riddle of history and knows itself to be this solution.[31]

Though expressed in careful and cautious language, Marx's vision of the future society, like Sri Aurobindo's, is highly idealistic, definitely anarchist and, one might even say, utopian. The abolition of private property has not proved to be an easy proposition. What Sri Aurobindo calls the possessive instinct of the vital man is getting the better of his public or self-effacing spirit. The institution of private property not only alienates man from man, successfully preventing him from getting to the *essence* of mankind, but also motivates him to make use of his knowledge of Nature in a selfish way and even to the other's disadvantage. Unless the ideas or the techniques of man's mastery over nature are themselves socialised and shared by all alike, the results of man's struggle against Nature are bound to be less than maximal or unsatisfactory. Man's domination over man depends upon the uneven ownership of the productive and distributive forces. Nature and society can abridge human freedom and alienate the individual from his species simply because of the overwhelmingly odd and negative forces of the situation and he is obliged to be at the receiving end. With the abolition of private property and the State this dichotomy between 'him' and 'them' is removed and 'he' becomes one of them. Its possibility was already there. For they all are essentially the same. But this has to be historically realised. Looking at the history of Socialism from 1917 one does not dare say that this is going to be an easy process.

According to Marx the abolition of private property and all its institutional ramifications, especially the State, would enable man to negate his negation or undo his alienation and to be freely and fully united with the rest of the human race. This return of man to his own true nature is not an inward spiritual journey culminating in a God-realisation. It is essentially a historical journey with a definite social end, i.e., anarchist society, in view. To Sri Aurobindo's mind the communist society is intellectualist-anarchist and subject to all the limitations of its type referred to before. If Marx is right in asserting that it is through violent revolution that the class institutions have to be overthrown and that it is the only way to establish the true humanist society and a conflictless world-order, then Sri Aurobindo's critique of objective-institutionalism and his thesis of spiritual anarchism based on the religion of humanity turn out to be untenable. The ideal society must have its own institutional supports, a new mode of intellectual and economic production and distribution, a new method of cooperative struggle against the forces of nature. It cannot be based on what is called a spiritual foundation or turned upside down. For Marx, as we all know, ' spiritual ' is super-structural and *not* foundational.

It is not that Sri Aurobindo has not thought of this possible criticism of the subjective approach to human unity on the basis of the religion of humanity. He clearly asserts that it must be a more explicit, insisted and categorical imperative for self-effectuation and combating human egoism in all its forms—individual, class and national. Human egoism is the enemy of all true religions or ideologies. If any religion of humanity wants to get itself successfully established in the world, it must develop 'a living sense of human oneness and practice of human oneness in thought, feeling and life '. The question is how to bring about this transformation in practice. Should it start from within, or has it to be given initially a shape and direction from without by appropriate institutions? Sri Aurobindo's answer is categorical. Only a spiritual religion of humanity can do it, can bring about a real transformation in human consciousness. He is not referring to any institutionalised religion. The principle of this transformation is to transfer our will-to-be and power of life from the vital and the intellectual being to the spiritual plane of being. At first this change is to be accomplished in the individual and then in a large number of individuals. Only then can a higher spiritual consciousness dawn in the social mind. Before our socio-political institutions and economic organisations reflect this profound change, it is reflected in philosophy, in psychological thinking, in the arts, poetry, painting, sculpture, music, in ethical thought and other finer pursuits of life. The spiritual religion of humanity is the aim of mankind in the subjective age. The reason that religion has so far failed to unify mankind is that it has always lost itself in credal dogmas and forms. For the first time in human history this new religion would show the spiritual unity of all religion without ignoring, but rather making intelligible, their credal differences.[32] The essential unity of different religions does not require the people concerned to give up their vital difference which is necessary to preserve some lesser and yet very important characteristics of every religious community. Sri Aurobindo hopes that the religion of humanity would play for the first time in human history a social role, very truly social. It woul touch and transform every aspect of human life and cease to be merely a Sunday affair or transcendental pursuit. Once this spiritual religion of humanity gets its deep and sure seat in mankind, the human cycle of social development with its incomplete repetitions would come to an end and the spiritual age would start. And the believer would regard it as the beginning of the Kingdom of God on earth.

What the Kingdom of God on earth would be like is very difficult to indicate. The idea perhaps is that both individually and collectively man has been trying forever to perfect himself and his social order. Since his self-perfection entails and is entailed by the perfection of his fellow human beings, his quest for the perfect society has to be a collective enterprise and not a solo venture. Sri Aurobindo himself admits that the spiritual transformation necessary for creating the ideal human unity must comprise and spread to a large number of individuals. It cannot be left to the spiritual enlightenment of this or that individual human being only, however extraordinary he might be. The idea of human perfection and what it means is so fundamental and general that it cannot be peculiar to any system of thought, religious or political. Scrutiny reveals that freedom is a central concept in almost every perfectionist strategy. It is no wonder, therefore, that some form of anarchism, providing the maximum possible freedom to the individual, is advocated by so widely different thinkers as Marx and Sri Aurobindo. Whether it is in the Kingdom of God or in the communist society, the freedom of the individual occupies the focus of attention and interest of the idealist.

## A Possible Reconstruction of the Two Views

The common point of interest of the spiritualist and the materialist must not make one blind to their fundamental difference referred to before, viz., the means and method to be followed to ensure the freedom of the individual. Briefly speaking, the difference could be put this way. While the Aurobindite maintains that we must first try to realise freedom in the life of the individual and then only can we successfully move to the objective order of freedom, Marx is clear in his mind that social freedom must precede individual freedom. Unless the conditions of social freedom are obtained, the ideal of individual freedom, however laudable it might be otherwise in itself, cannot be realised in practice.

Sri Aurobindo's point of objection is that the character and the process of creating these institutional conditions for securing individual freedom are found to have an inbuilt constraint insofar as they thwart or negate the attempts to liberalise or relax the conditions in question, even when they outlive their necessity and the individuals themselves demand it. The rigidity of the socialist institutions are ascribed to some inherent limitations of the socialist system and the practical inability of the people to infuse liberalism in them even when it is badly needed. It is on this alleged ground that the institutional approach to freedom has been criticised by the subjectivist. The institutionalisation of human relations is said to be basically antithetical to the freedom of the individual.

I am not quite sure how far this criticism is valid. I can see its validity as a principle. But a close analysis of the history of the socialist experiments since 1917 makes it abundantly clear that the doctrinaire zeal and the inflexibility of determination which marked the understandable approach of the founding fathers of the first socialist country in the world are no longer to be found in their faithful, critical or creative followers in other countries. One can always learn from one's own and other's mistakes and, given the desire, avoid them at least to some extent and remedy their unintended ill-effects. Man can never evolve a foolproof strategy to plan and determine his social situation exclusively to his own advantage. Nor is he an absolutely helpless prisoner of his own decisions. Certainly he can partially undo what he himself and others have done. If this is true, and I think it is, the subjectivist's criticism against the institutional approach to the freedom of the individual loses its main thrust. A somewhat similar defence for the subjectivist's argument for individual freedom against Marxist criticism could be offered and sustained. While the subjectivist makes no secret of his basic contention that the main dynamics of social development is provided by the individual and that his freedom is the first thing to be taken into account while creating an ideal society, never for a moment does he underestimate the importance of the objective conditions of preserving and promoting the inner potentiality of the individual.

On ultimate analysis the difference between the two approaches turns out to be one of degree only. I don't deny that that too is very important. For, so many things depend upon a difference in emphasis. After all any careful student of social philosophy could easily see that the difference between Marx and Sri Aurobindo, and for that matter between any two great thinkers, is not as wide as their overzealous and less criticical followers try to make out.

One cannot but be impressed by the immense fertility of Marx's dialectical method and Sri Aurobindo's integral method. Unless we are very careful and critical these methods are liable to be, and in fact have already been, extravagantly misused. The law of the unity and struggle of opposites seems to be the most vulnerable point of Marxian dialectics. It seeks to explain not only the presence and operation of opposite forces within a part or half of the whole truth but also the possibility of unity of itself or its opposite with any part or the whole of the other half. The implication, though not easily understood without further analysis, could be shown to be very uncritical and therefore pernicious. It can permit and prohibit any sort of unity or combination within and between the parts of the dialectical thesis and antithesis, and, consequently, the synthesis is likely to be spurious and of doubtful significance. Besides, the question of initiating motion in the elements of unity and opposition is difficult to explain without postulating some sort of prime mover. The only way out consists in taking motion as a primitive concept, as primitive as the concept of matter itself. This difficulty of Marx has been avoided by Sri Aurobindo in his integral system by postulating that *force* (not *motion* in the physical sense) is inherent in the very nature of consciousness. Reality is consciousness and a spiritual whole and the spirit of the whole permeates the parts, internally relating and integrating them notwithstanding their apparent opposition or contradiction. This metaphysical doctrine-cum-method has been used by Sri Aurobindo also at the level of social reality to explain as well as to eliminate the elements of conflict and contradiction. The methods followed by the *dialectical* materialist and the *integral* spiritualist to tackle the problem of the unity of opposites and to achieve harmony overriding contradictions objectively encourages uncritical systems of thought and society. I will return later to this point in the concluding chapter. In this limited context of world unity, I would only like to state that their methods do not take adequate notice of the complex problems and tasks and tend, instead, to treat them in a rather uncritical manner.

That is why even today in the face of so many disturbing trends and cross-currents of world history the followers of Marx and Sri Aurobindo are quite hopeful that the ultimate emergence of world unity is inevitable. Optimism is undoubtedly indicative of a healthy attitude towards life. So when Sri Aurobindo ascribes profound significance to the role of the UNO and interprets it as a very important factor promoting the ideal human unity or when the committed communist claims that the establishment of the worldwide socialist system on the basis of Marxist internationalism is inevitable, one does not question his idealistic motivation. The question is whether his messianic zeal is in accord with the logic of the contemporary world situation. We all know that in the last thirty years or so none of the major international issues, especially those in which the superpowers are involved, could be resolved on the floor of the UNO itself. Some of the conflicts of interest have been deliberately kept alive without of course allowing them to flare up in a big way. The superpowers themselves or through their subsidiary allies are dominating the world scene, keeping the UN flag fluttering over their heads but allowing the world body to do precious little. The Third World did not get even its minimum due from the industrially developed and politically powerful countries and the objectives of the first and second development decades remain still unrealised. In other words the world body is yet to have its own soul and exercise its own judgement and will. Sri Aurobindo himself admits that there is an element of oligarchy in the international organisation. The problem lies not so much within the UNO itself as outside it. The peoples of the world are clearly divided into two ill-defined camps, ' the free world ' and the ' socialist world ', with superpowers holding the uneasy balance under the new name of detente. The emergence of the third world or the non-aligned group from the days of Bandung has added a welcome complexity to the situation. None of these camps or groups has a homogeneous ideology or a clear political objective.[33] But, very broadly speaking, they all agree, at least in their public professions, on two major points, viz., the necessity of peace and the urgency for the economic development of the developing countries. Yet one feels disturbed by the unpleasant truth that the total money spent on armament, euphemistically called *defence* equipment, meant for killing human beings, runs into astronomical figures and that, in quiet disregard to the repeated UN resolutions urging the developed countries to spend at least 1 per cent of their GNP as aid or grant for the improvement of the quality of life of their less fortunate brethren in the developing countries, nothing very significant has yet been done in this respect. The anatomy of the hungry world is yet to receive the serious attention of the affluent West. The line of demarcation in the human geography of today has been drawn in effect between the affluent nations and the poor ones and not in terms of any ideology. This of course does not mean that material and intellectual commerce is not taking place across the line of demarcation or that all nations are equally indifferent to the miseries of others. Sri Aurobindo hopes that in the future this commerce will increase not only quantitatively but also qualitatively. In this utopia of the future the third world does not figure in a big way. Apparently he believes that it will disappear and merge with either of the two power groups—' congeries of socialistic States ' and ' the States following some modified form of capitalism '. He sees no reason why these States, despite their ideological differences, cannot coexist peacefully. If the UNO is allowed to play its envisaged role it can definitely strengthen the forces of peace and unity and as a result of which the transition from the era of peaceful coexistence to that of meaningful cooperation would be achieved at an accelerated pace. One is advised to remember that the realisation of this welcome prospect is very much dependent on a fundamental transformation of the character, power-structure and objectives of the nation-States. Unless economically and/or militarily powerful nation-States evolve sincere national consensus and act accordingly to share their weals and woes, materials, ideas and technological know-how with the less developed nations of the world, I don't quite see how the un-utopian utopias of Sri Aurobindo and Marx could be given concrete shape by the conceptually magnificent but functionally poor UNO.

The other side of the picture is not very encouraging either. The proletarians of all countries in the world are in no mood to be united on a common political forum for the same social objective. Even the talk of transition from socialism to communism, from each according to his ability to each according to his necessity, is not being heard any more except in uninfluential closed-door academic meetings. There is no sign of structural fatigue in the overall State machine of the socialist countries. The abolition of private property and the withering away of the State are no longer on the official agenda. Any objective student of the history of socialism would admit that several predictions of the original socialist thinkers have been falsified by subsequent developments. And he who is mainly interested in critically assessing this development, and not to merely justifying by using *ad hoc* and auxiliary hypotheses, cannot honestly disown the social and intellectual obligation to review the theory and practice of socialism in the light of instructive details of world history. To my mind this is the counsel of realistic idealism and not of pessimism.

# II

# Methodological and Ideological Reflections

## Philosophical Sociology: Its Strength and Weakness

At the risk of being repetitious I would like to explicate certain points which occurred to me as a sympathetic critic of Sri Aurobindo's integral sociology. Its strength and weakness both consist mainly in its philosophical foundation or dominant theoretical bias. The sociologists having no professional acquaintance with philosophy would regard Sri Aurobindo's sociology as very abstract and highly theoretical. Undoubtedly, it *is* abstract and theoretical. But that as such cannot be a matter of criticism. On the contrary, the philosophical type of sociology, though abstract, has its strength or advantage. Because of its well-defined concepts, classificatory schema and explanatory hypotheses, all things being equal, it is likely to be rich in subject-matter and fuller in its implications. The *ceteris paribus* clause, ' all things being equal ', has to be taken rather seriously. Otherwise, even conceptual richness may well go with empirical poverty. The concepts which are purely *a priori* in their origin *and* not testable by experience might bring about remarkable orderliness in apparently unrelated historical facts or empirical data, but as one cannot delimit the scope of their application one is hardly able to demarcate between their right and wrong use.

The *natural* and the *spiritual*, for example, are two key concepts of integral sociology which have been rather lavishly used from the beginning to the end. The tenability or otherwise of the main thesis of integral sociology, namely, the end of the human cycle is the establishment of a spiritual anarchist society on the basis of what is called the religion of humanity, hinges on the soundness of these basic concepts. But it is not easy to determine what precisely Sri Aurobindo means by the concept of Nature. Various expressions, ' conscious force ', ' executrix power ', and ' force-nature ', have been used to denote, or have been employed as synonyms of, Nature. But analysis reveals that these expressions, strictly speaking, are not synonymous. That apart, the main point is whether the processes and workings of Nature are really conscious. In other words, whether there is an intelligent principle determining the course of history and the shape of human affairs. Assuming that there is such an intelligent principle, one might even pertinently question whether Nature is that principle.

In his criticism of materialism Sri Aurobindo reiterates the traditional argument against it, namely, the intelligibility of the natural and the social phenomena and their orderliness are essentially due to an all-comprehensive intelligent principle. This argument has two aspects, theological and secular. Both these aspects have received different formulations. One may think that all things have been conceived by an all perfect God and executed accordingly by its ' executrix power ', Nature. Another may think that the intelligibility of all things is exclusively due to the intrinsic laws of Nature which have nothing to do with God. These concepts of intelligibility are descriptive and objective. What makes social phenomena and the historical process intelligible and explainable is said to exist in the very nature of the phenomena and the process.

Another view is that the intelligibility of social and historical phenomena is derivative and is to be found in the structure of human understanding or in terms of the concepts formed by the human beings. There is nothing intrinsically rational in the nature and process of history and society. If that is so, intelligibility may be said to be subjective in origin and attributive in character.

Whether we examine objective-descriptive or attributive-subjective theories of sociological and historical explanation one disturbing feature is common to them. Some irrational and baffling phenomena inconsistent with the explanatory laws and concepts often turn up in history and society. What to do with these ' awkward ' objects? How to explain them?

These questions provide the theoretical motive-force for the construction of the grand sociological theories, which derive to a great extent their apparent plausibility from the methods of *dialectical* materialism and *integral* spiritualism.

## Abstract Theories and the 'Awkward' Facts
## The Dialectician and the Integralist

Respect for fact is a very important desideratum of sociology. The sociologist with a dominant theoretical bias in his eagerness to construct neat and comprehensive theory often ignores or at any rate minimises the importance of the ' awkward ' facts, facts which do not conform to his conceptual and explanatory schema. It is true that for scientific theory-construction bold and creative imagination is extremely important. An exclusive reliance on facts, or what I have called a fact-fetish, is inconsistent with the very aim of science and other forms of rational inquiry.

The theoretician always faces a dilemma. Since he is faithful to all the facts he comes across, he cannot go beyond the facts and construct a theory. If, on the other hand, he is indifferent to the facts and relies only on imagination or speculation, his theory is of little empirical significance. In other words, its factual content is bound to be poor.

Both Marx and Sri Aurobindo have addressed themselves to this dilemma and tried to tackle it in terms of their own methodology. Both of them have been accused of grand theory-construction and not of fact-fetish. One might even go a step further and say against Sri Aurobindo, in particular, that he refers to facts only in order to illustrate his theories and laws and not to establish them. One cannot fail to note that he is not a sterile inductivist. Certainly he cannot be accused of excessive reliance on empirical data. He himself has observed somewhere that one should not care too much for the 'froth and foam' of history and must try to discover the underlying rational thread.

Marx's major works, unlike Sri Aurobindo's, contain extensive data collected by patient research. Even then when it comes to the question of generalisation or drawing conclusions Marx is often found to be highly selective, selecting and quoting facts and figures which justify and do not really test his theories. This criticism may be levelled against both Marx and Sri Aurobindo, especially with reference to their theories of historical rhythm or the human cycle.

This uncritical method of theory-construction has been used by them not only vertically or historically but also horizontally or sociologically. What I mean is this. Social reality may be conceived as something given at a particular period of time and spread over a geographical area. Although social reality is subject to historical wear and tear, for theoretical purposes one could easily conceive it as a simultaneous whole, a sort of static framework. The other mode of conceiving social reality, i.e., the historical or the dynamic mode, is very well-known and extensively used. Consciously or unconsciously what most of the theoreticians follow is an interesting blend of these two methods. Either a static segment is shown moving along the time dimension according to some historical laws, or a moving segment is cut loose and analytically abstracted from its natural place and projected against a static canvas. Perhaps the human mind has a limited ability to see things in what we call their natural place.

When historical reality is conceived in a very big way, in terms of very comprehensive concepts, grand theories or highly general laws, the theoretician is always at an advantage. For then he is not called upon to relate his concepts to all and sundry facts. He refuses to be bothered by the latter. But when the critic says that his theory is purely speculative and not fair to facts, he *is* under a rational obligation to show the connection between his abstract theories and concrete facts. This exercise of relating the former to the latter at times turns out to be very difficult and delicate. For facts may refuse to confirm the theories and conform to the concepts used in those theories. In other words, some facts may really prove very 'awkward' and 'uncompromising'. One might of course argue that facts are after all theoretical constructs and there is nothing sacrosanct in them. This is an extreme object-attributive position.

The dialectician, however tackles this sort of problem mainly in terms of his novel interpretation of the law of contradiction and the sub-law of internal contradiction. He draws an interesting distinction between 'popular evolutionism' defined in terms of mere 'decrease and increase' and 'constant repetition' of what was already present right from the beginning, and dialectical evolution, a 'unity of opposites'. While the popular evolutionist thinks that the first cause or mover of the evolutionary movement lies external to what evolves, the dialectician locates the source of evolutionary motion within evolving matter itself. The concept of matter-in-motion is postulated and not proved in order to avoid the fallacy of infinite regress and dispense with the Aristotelian concept of God as the prime mover. The dialectician rejects the traditional law of contradiction—'A cannot be both A and not-A at the same time'—as metaphysical. Contradiction is not merely a law of thought but also a law of what is thought about, including natural and social reality. The metaphysician is said to be mistaken in his belief that a thing cannot maintain its identity as a unity of opposites. In fact Nature develops itself in accordance with its own laws from lower forms to higher forms. It is because of an internal contradiction or self-propelling motion that inanimate Nature has given rise to its other, its opposite, organic Nature. In inanimate Nature social development is also explained in the same way. The inherent contradictions of capitalism bring about its opposite, socialism. Contradictions pass through different stages and various degrees, viz., difference, opposition, conflict and resolution. Resolution means temporary unity. What is permanent is opposition or conflict.

The implications of the dialectical law of contradiction are far-reaching. First, it denounces what is called the metaphysical view of the nature of things. Secondly, it tries to establish the point that the laws of thought and things are identical at bottom. And this reminds one of Hegelianism from the reverse end. Finally, and what is most important in this context, it takes away the awkwardness of awkward facts by legitimising the presence of the contradictory characters in the same thing and at the same time.

The integralist's contention is that it is only in the light of spiritual intuition that one can rightly grasp the complex relation of the 'opposite' characteristics of matter and spirit. The course of evolution is marked by more or less bondage of evolving matter to its form, by more and more subtlety and flexibility of its substance and force. According to him, material and spiritual objects are essentially integrated and their relation is to be understood in terms of interfusion, interpenetration, power of assimilation, power of interchange, power of variation, transmutation and unification. Material objects are marked, among others, by persistent separation, physical resistance and mutual exclusion. They are also subject to the relatively longer durability of their forms. In contrast, social objects are more open to change, interfusion and interpenetration. Consequently, the laws of social dynamics are immensely complex in nature.

Sri Aurobindo says, all cosmic existence is a complex harmony. In Nature and society what appears to be involved in conflict and struggle is not violative of the spirit of harmony. The surface movements are often deceptive and do not reflect the character and ingoings of the human cycle. The difference, the opposition and conflict between the natural and the social, are entirely mental and 'conceptual' in origin. In other words, Sri Aurobindo holds 'normal reason' responsible for its failure to grasp the harmony and integral character of the objects of knowledge, natural and social. Here one must note the very important difference between the dialectician and the integralist. While the former finds elements of contradiction both in nature and mind, the latter speaks of them only in the context of 'normal reason' and sense-mind, and affirms that spiritual mind being itself an integral part of cosmic existence and its complex harmony is free from all these defects and deformities.[1]

The liberal use of the concepts of contradictions, interpenetration, mutual inclusion and the like enables both the dialectician and the intergralist not only to smoothen the rough edges of awkward facts and remove them but also to transform—transformation by interpretation—disconfirming facts, giving them, though deceptive, a confirming character. In the face of disconfirming facts the integralist can always argue that its surface character should not be accepted as its real character and that *essentially* it is an integral part of cosmic existence and its complex harmony. Similarly, the dialectician can always take refuge behind the law of contradiction and interpret a counter-example as a pro-example to save a pet theory. The methodological liberalism of the dialectician and the integralist tends to take away the rigour and precision of the concerned views and encourages a certain degree of looseness of thought. Comprehensive theory-construction is of course welcome in principle but it must not be done on the basis of too wide definitions and by rolling all disparate facts together within the spacious fold of holistic theories.

## Integralism and Holism

The more one can forget the parts of a whole and concentrate on the whole itself, the more easy it becomes for one to construct a neat and comprehensive theory. The temptation of neat theory construction is very difficult to resist.

Integral sociology has been worked out on the basis of an evolutionary interaction between Man, Community and Mankind. One might say these constitute Sri Aurobindo's sociological triune. Like his ontological triune, God, Man and Nature, it has also been *conceived* in a rather holistic fashion. I say *conceived* rather than *defined* because, strictly speaking, Sri Aurobindo rarely defines the concepts he uses. For every key concept he has several synonyms. It is from the context of its use that one has to gather the intended meaning of his concepts.

Because of the metaphysical primacy of Sri Aurobindo's system of thought, one feels naturally inclined first to follow the significance of his ontological triune, God, Man and Nature. It is on the plausibility of his views on these concepts that the main structure of integral sociology hinges. After all, his views on man, community and mankind are essentially metaphysical. It has been repeatedly said that the rationale of the social life and its evolution is to be found only in its deeper psychological or spiritual basis.

I for one do not find any compelling reason to accept this position of Sri Aurobindo. I think that it is quite possible to defend a substantial part of integral sociology without postulating a metaphysical foundation.

I have already mentioned the central position of the concept of Nature in Aurobindo's sociology: Nature is in God and God is in Nature. Phenomenal Nature is said to be a movement of God. The object of the movement is to create forms of different types—material, vital, mental and social. All forms are in motion and God is the soul or the conscious principle of unity of all these forms and directs their movement and relations.

These ideas, though interesting, raise certain basic difficulties. Why does the all-present reality, God, articulate Himself in different social forms? Why cannot this force of consciousness inherent in existence be held at rest? Or, in other words, why does this social evolution take place at all? In his characteristic metaphysical vein Sri Aurobindo would perhaps say: the object of the movement is to create forms of God's own consciousness in motion and in which He, as the One soul in many bodies, can take up His habitation and enjoy the multiplicity and the movement of their relations.

It is on the basis of this metaphysical foundation that one has to understand the significance of concepts like nation-soul, group-soul, and also how their integrated movement is directed towards the unity of mankind.

Whoever is acquainted with Sri Aurobindo's works would readily concede that he does not have a theoretical bent of mind. But he is perhaps a theoretician in the literal sense of the term, i.e., one who has the vision to see things as a whole. One is bound to be impressed by the breadth of his vision and wonderful ability to weave together widely different strands of thought into an integral whole. But if we propose to correctly appreciate and critically assess his thought we should not be overimpressed by this vision and must have a close look at the facts which are said to have been organised in the light of the vision. Vision without verification is a blind ally of grand theory construction and objectively encourages holism. The invocation of the metaphysical foundation of a sociological theory rather than trying to relate it to ascertainable facts exposes the weakness of the theory.

The main thesis of holism is rather simple and attractive: society is a whole which is more than the sum of its parts. One could use such other terms as *family*, *clan*, *community* and *nation* and defend holism in each case. The other thesis of holism is also interesting and extensively used, although uncritically. It is insisted that social wholes like nation and class have their *own* distinct aims and interests. It is in the light of the first thesis that one has to understand Sri Aurobindo's view that the true identity and unity of a nation is to be found in its inner soul and not in its territory and political institutions. Sri Aurobindo does not deny the necessity of outward means and conditions for the realisation of the nation-soul in the life of a nation. Nation is said to be something more than what its territorial and institutional aspects ordinarily denote. The second thesis of holism is illustrated in some such expressions as that ' the Indian nation has a spiritual message to offer to the world afflicted by materialism ' and ' the aim of Nature is the perfection of the individual in a perfected society.' It is not that one cannot make plain and coherent meaning out of these expressions, but the point is whether the meaning thus made out is the intended meaning of the author in question. Most of us know that India has produced a number of great religious personalities and that their teachings have been well-received by the people of the Western industrialised countries where economic considerations and material comforts are generally rated above other values of life. Let us then take up the second expression. An unbiased perusal of the known history of human civilisation and culture shows that the quality of human life has been gradually improving. This improvement could be indicated in terms of man's increasing ability to control and utilise his environment, devising and using means to regulate conflict between different human groups and interests and in various other ways. It is certainly not surprising if some of us, encouraged by what we have achieved, think of further improving the quality of our individual and social life. Now this common-sense 'translation' of holistic expressions may or may not be accepted, depending on one's theoretical commitment. If the theorist himself happens to be a holist and believes that there is really something like the soul of the Indian nation, he is not likely to accept the 'superficial' common-sense translation of what he thinks is a deep metaphysical truth. Similarly, he may also reject the historical development of the human society in ethics and politics and insist on retaining his original thesis that Nature is the all-powerful agency of God realising His idea of the human cycle leading to an ideal world order.[2]

We may of course translate the holist's language into our own; but even then, consistently with his own ideas, he can always reserve the right to reject our language. It is not merely a question of a language difference, it is a case of a substantive difference. His contention and ours are substantively different. Sri Aurobindo firmly maintains that the metaphysical foundation of his sociology is integral to it and not a mere delinkable adjunct which could be taken out without breaking up or jeopardising the system itself. He is equally firm in maintaining that historical events and social phenomena present only a confusing kaleidoscope of changing external situations and that unless they are viewed against their appropriate metaphysical backgrounds they do not convey any coherent meaning or disclose their inner truth or rationale.

Facts without theories are indeed incoherent and meaningless. But the question is whether fact-organising theories must be necessarily metaphysical, especially when the facts in question are sociological in character. Besides, we are well-advised to remember the distinction between bad metaphysics and good metaphysics. While the former used with care and circumspection enables us to get rid of fact-fetishism, the latter encourages unbridled speculation, hypostatisation of ideas and ideals, and ignores the important line of demarcation between what is testable and what is not.

Materialism is also a metaphysical system and because of the dialectical method its Marxist version assumes an apparently irrefutable character. But one good point about the system is that the critic may at least point out where it has gone wrong. It is very difficult to remove its metaphysical wrapper, i.e., dialectical materialism, but the critic can certainly indicate where the specific assertions and predictions of the historical materialist have turned out to be false or inaccurate. This shows at least one thing—it has an empirical character. Moreover, his respect for scientific laws and readiness to stand by their validity are of considerable help to the critic. Unfortunately, bad metaphysics has no stake in the fortune of science: it 'survives' whatever happens to the laws and theories of the latter. In other words, it has no necessary relation with the facts of life. It is very interesting to note that some distinguished scientists have propounded metaphysical systems, both of the materialist and the spiritualist varieties, which are not at all central to their scientific theories and consequently the latter could be corrected or refuted without even touching the former. If integral sociology, I mean its empirical part, could be defended without its philosophical 'foundation', integral monism, I do not see why we should insist on defending the whole. Whether the proposed defence could stand the scrutiny of an impartial critic is of course a different question. I think it could.

The rejection of holism does not leave us completely defenceless. Other and perhaps better methods of understanding and shaping history and society are available. We have already said before that society is not a mere aggregate of individuals and that history cannot be satisfactorily explained exclusively in terms of individuals, and their dispositions and actions. In other words, one cannot deny that in social life and the historical process there are some systems or structures which cannot be reduced to the life of the concerned individuals without remainder. Metaphysics is not called for to explain this remainder. We need not postulate the existence of a social system or structure which could be said to have a life of its own and which could be explained without reference to concerned individuals. The point which even the diehard individualist has to realise is the limitation of the programme of reduction or translation. All social entities cannot be translated into or reduced to 'their' individual components. Social systems may be understood as a field of human action and interaction. They may be understood also as a complex set of relationships between different individuals, or groups, or both. In whatever way we understand such notoriously indefinite objects like social structure and social system, at least about one thing we all must be clear and that it is the life of these entities is more stable than that of the concerned individual human beings. This is of course another way of admitting the partial irreducibility of the institutional factor and its indispensability to the understanding of social phenomena. The alternative to holism is institutionalistic individualism or individualistic institutionalism and not psychological individualism. The whole thing may be summed up in this way: sociology cannot be reduced to psychology without remainder.

It will be interesting to note the integralist's response to this criticism. Unlike the Marxist, he will appreciate the accent on the individuals and their dispositions and actions. But he will reject our argument in favour of the institutional approach. His rejection is based on the metaphysical commitment to integral psychology. And that again brings him into a clash with our individualistic psychology. For we do not speak of the psyche or soul except in the context of identifiable human beings. We prefer the term mind and not psyche or soul. Here our approach is somewhat close to the Marxist's. He also rejects the programme of psychological reduction and speaks of sociological primacy. True, the Marxist's theory of mind also has a metaphysical commitment. But it has to be admitted that the commitment of his psychology is open at least in principle to such scientific inquiries as physiology and neurology. And that lends an empirical credibility to his view. In contrast, the integralist's view of mind is an inseparable part of his spiritualist metaphysics and does not lend itself to empirical scrutiny beyond a point. The empirical mind is said to be quite unable to discover its true identity and unless it can realise its fathomless spiritual depth whatever it knows is fragmentary and doubtful. It is mainly for this reason that the integralist rejects psychologism which is not founded in metaphysical spiritualism. But analysis reveals that this method of rebutting psychological scepticism leads one back to holism. For the spirit is said to be something more than the individual souls or psyches. And the character of this ' more ' is inexplicable or elusive forever.

## Integralism and Historicism

Another difficulty which seems to have adversely influenced integral sociology is historicism. The main thesis of historicism is very simple: the course of history is governed by certain definite *laws* and is therefore *inevitable*. Working historians, however, maintain that historical events are unique and that any attempt to connect them in terms of a law or a set of laws is unfortunate and rests on a misconception regarding their character. Historical events should not be taken as examples of any general law. Consequently, it has been argued that historical explanations framed in terms of general laws are bound to be uninteresting and will fail to highlight the uniqueness of the events in question.

We have noted Sri Aurobindo's view that history teaches us nothing. The historian has been criticised for his alleged preoccupation with external data, laws, institutions, rites, customs and economic factors and also for not paying due attention to the deeper psychological facts. Sri Aurobindo speaks of the fundamental necessity of studying the mental, emotional and ideative activities of man; for the perceptive historian can find in them ' profound psychological, even perhaps soul factors ' of the economic motives and causes of social and historical development. He does not deny that the psychological theory of history may be bad or even disastrous. But that depends how psychology is conceived—superficially or profoundly.

If psychology is conceived superficially, i.e., empirically, then the doctrine of historical autonomy or an amended version of it could somehow be defended. If the mind and its activities are taken as somewhat independent of what happens in Nature of things that are subject to the laws of Nature, then certainly a privileged and autonomous position could be carved out for them. In that case a line of distinction could be drawn between the historical and the natural. But this doctrine is inconsistent with integral metaphysics. For we have already noted Sri Aurobindo's views that mind is only a self-conscious part of Nature and that Nature is itself consciousness, even if only in an inert form. Natural phenomena and historical events are integrally related. The soul factors of history are not unrelated to the life process of Nature. The deeper laws of Nature which make their presence and operation adequately felt at the level of matter and life are also half-consciously influencing the events of history through human beings. Strictly speaking, the guiding spirit of history is Nature and we are all said to be her agents. Laws are the form of Nature's action-process. The law-governed character of history entails inevitability. Sri

Aurobindo's belief in historicism, the inevitability of history, is unmistakable when he maintains that ' the unity of mankind is evidently a part of Nature's eventual scheme and must come about '.

The process of history can be followed at different levels—local, national, regional and global. The number of these levels could be increased or decreased, depending on the historian's preferences and standpoint. It is true that Sri Aurobindo thinks that the units of history, though evolving, are objective, i.e., not mental, constructs. A nation, for example, is a natural and an objective historical unit but not a State. The true units of history are to be understood in terms of the inward and upward development of the human mind. The ordinary sense-mind cannot get into the heart of history. ' Normal reason ' gets bogged down in the froth and foam, the surface events of history and their apparently aimless movements. It is only by enlarging the area of its sympathy, cultivating its native powers of intuition and identifying its own workings with those of Nature that the human mind can get into the heart of history and discover its ' soul-factors.'

Sri Aurobindo has spoken of the superman gifted with extraordinary powers of directly apprehending the past, the present and the future, ' not as a logical series of separate segments ' but as a totality of the evolving powers of consciousness which interpenetrate and are interfused and thus modify each other. The superman is not subject to the limitations of normal reason, for he does not use this instrument at all. The native capacity of a supermind is intuitive in character. It is said to have a fourfold power—a power of revelatory truth-seeing, a power of truth-hearing, a power of truth-touching or immediate apprehension of significance, and a power of true and automatic discrimination of the orderly and right relation of things and also the right relation of idea with idea. A superman's intuition does not fail or falter. Directly in touch with the past and having assimilated the present, the superman is credited with the infallible power of prophesying the future. The idea of infallible prophecy makes sense only if it is assumed that the course of history is *necessary* and that there is nothing contingent in it. To put it in a different way, we must assume that the metaphysical structure of the world as a whole, comprising space and time, is absolutely rational and therefore orderly and foreseeable. Besides, one has to assume the power of directly and rightly foreseeing the future. Both these assumptions, the metaphysical one and the epistemological one, have been seriously questioned. Foreseeing can be of two types—prophetic and predictive. Prophecy is generally regarded as infallible. Prediction is of course corrigible and questionable. Sri Aurobindo is careful enough to say that the intuition of the supermind does not view history as a series of separate segments but as a totality of ascending and evolving powers. According to him, the superman is a ' swallower of formulae ' and he is not guided or governed by conventional rules and regulations. The Buddha, Christ and Mohammed are referred to as genii of that rare type. They are to be taken more as the architects of history than as its products. Strictly speaking, they are the best ' expressions and instruments ' of the spirit of time.

This way of looking at history and distinguished historical personalities has its obvious limits. First, it is very difficult to rationally convince an open-minded man of the infallibility of the views of these great human personalities. In some cases the views of the great religious teachers and thinkers are not themselves mutually consistent and compatible with facts. Perhaps we should bear in mind that a man may be great without being infallible. Secondly, without being identified with the course of history itself, it is very difficult for a man to prove that it is rational, necessary and free from all types of contingency. Certainly the mind of the ordinary man is not free from the defects and deformities of the normal reason, and as a result of that it cannot be actually identified with the necessary and the inevitable course of history. The supermind which can directly apprehend the totality of all integral steps and powers of Nature cannot be said to have grasped history as it is ordinarily understood. History, given as a simultaneous totality, may be reality from the standpoint of the superman; but the ordinary man or the working historian is very unlikely to take it as history. For we often find to our disappointment that our forecasts turn out to be inaccurate, if not false. Many of our predictions are contradicted by facts. In other words, we are not blessed with the powers to apprehend the necessary relation between possible and actual. We must not confuse hopes and ambition with ability and achievement.

Historicism is not necessarily spiritual in its origin and orientation. It could be of other types as well. Of the secular types of historicism one can readily recall Comte's law of three stages and Marx's historical materialism. The first is positivist and the second metaphysical. Without committing oneself to spiritualist metaphysics and intuitional epistemology one could well defend the central thesis of historicism—that the course of history is inexorable and inevitable. Comte speaks of three stages, the theological, the metaphysical, which is said to be a mere modification of the first, and the positive. The human mind and the human race are bound to go through these three stages. In the positive stage, according to Comte, while dealing with human nature and social phenomena, however complex they might be, we must follow the method of the basic sciences like physics and chemistry. The aim of all positive philosophy should be to record all phenomena subject to the invariable laws of Nature. The positivist's concept of Nature is different from the spiritualist's. He finds no purpose concealed in the process of Nature. Yet he agrees with the spiritualist that the process is inevitable and the stages are invariable. One naturally feels inclined to raise the question: what precisely did historicists like Comte, Marx and Sri Aurobindo mean by the *invariable laws of history*? Sometimes their writings give the impression that they are merely describing the process of history or the sequence of its distinctly identifiable stages. Sometimes their claim appears to be much larger. They believe that they have succeeded in discovering certain basic and general laws of history which hold good in respect of all social aggregates, small and big.

These views and claims are not new. My uneasiness with these views and claims is mainly due to the fact that historicists persistently tend to ignore the complex character of social phenomena. They do not ask themselves whether their so-called laws of history are derived from the facts of history or they themselves read laws into facts in order to give a facile factual justification of the laws. One could understand the eagerness of the positivist and the materialist to give history the dignity of science in terms of 'factually justifiable' laws. But one feels intrigued that the spiritualist also endorses this approach. It is true that his assumptions and aim are both different from others. But that is no proof of the correctness of his view.

My opposition to historicism is not merely because of the theoretical considerations and inadequacies that I have indicated already; it is partly because of its pernicious practical consequences. A particular theory may be associated with some other theories without entailing them or being entailed by them. We have already noted that all historicists are not of same philosophical persuasion. Some are spiritualist like Sri Aurobindo, some are materialist like Marx, and some others, like Comte, are agnostic. It shows that philosophical theories associated with historicism have no necessary connection with it. Similarly, it may be argued, the practical and ideological implications of it are also not identical. This is just to anticipate.[3]

Let me clarify my point. The main criticism of historicism is that it negates or at any rate curtails individual freedom. A theory by itself obviously does not affect human thought or action. When historicism is criticised what primarily the critic has in his mind is its pernicious practical consequences. They who believe in the theory of inevitable history, given opportunity, are normally expected to act accordingly. For example, if some persons, kings, dictators and religious prophets, whoever they might be, do believe, as the historicist does, that human beings are mere instruments and expressions of the universal Spirit, or, alternatively speaking, their thought and action are all determined by the necessary laws of history, then, given the opportunity, they will act and think accordingly and prescribe similar codes of conduct for others as well. Of course, there is an implicit assumption underlying this position —they will try to be consistent in their profession and practice, which, I concede, may not be necessarily correct.

Of the many unfortunate consequences of historicism what strikes one first is determinism. If our thoughts and actions are determined by the necessary laws of history or by some conditions and circumstances governed by those laws, we cannot be deemed to be free. Lack of freedom takes away the basis of our ethical life. If we are not free to act or think in a particular way, good, bad or indifferent, we should not be praised or blamed for that. Responsibility without freedom makes no sense. If our option is unique, it is no option at all. Determinism destroys the foundation of moral life and objectively encourages fatalism.

I agree that the determinist's position could be formulated in a better way. The dialectical materialist, for example, might rightly point out that he is not speaking of any naive form of determinism. Admittedly, the thoughts and actions of individuals are not directly determined by social circumstances. Ways of determination are much more subtle, complex and indirect. Determination has to be understood and explained primarily in terms of certain forms of society or some modes of production which themselves are historical in character; and then the relation between those changing forms has to be established in terms of so-called laws of history. Each of the law-connected forms is a parallelogram of forces, actions and interactions. In the medieval age, freedom was a sort of privilege. Now in the capitalist society freedom is a law-guaranteed right, notionally so at any rate. Because of the dominant class bias of the bourgeoisie this notional freedom is not real for the proletariat. In the socialist society the dictatorship of the proletariat is said to be engaged in the task of broadening the institutional base of freedom for the proletariat. Even there the continued existence of class structure and the resulting State order and bounded freedom are admitted by implication. Once the institutional basis of bounded freedom, i.e., private property, is *completely* abolished, the Marxist sincerely hopes, man would become truly free, and that would put an end to the self-alienating process of production. All these forms of freedom of the past, present and future are necessary and related by laws of history. Even without spiritual teleological assumptions, the Marxist observes, the process of history is marked by the gradual freedom of man—freedom from *alien* institutional constraints. History is the path of man's homecoming.

It may appear a little surprising that without committing himself to any type of spiritual teleology the Marxist arrives at a theory of history, which in many respects is similar to a Hegelian or an Aurobindite position, especially in its definition of the relation between history and freedom. The 'surprising' element becomes understandable provided we remember that Marx, like Hegel and Sri Aurobindo, is a full-blooded *metaphysician*, that Marx is *historically* rather heavily indebted to Hegel, despite the former's well-known claim that he has put the latter's dialectic upside down, and that their *conceptual* affinity is, to a great extent, independent of their metaphysical commitments, spiritualism and materialism. The conceptual affinity between Hegel and Sri Aurobindo is much closer than that between Marx and any one of them. Since I do not propose to undertake a comparative study of their metaphysical systems I am not going to discuss the details of their points of agreement and difference. The point of interest to me is how these two theories of history, one teleological and the other anti-teleological, come to the same conclusion regarding the relation between history and freedom, despite their quite antithetical metaphysical positions.

First, let us look at the historical materialist's response to the point. Historical events, in spite of their leaps and breaks, are continuous. What holds them together and sustains their continuity are laws. Laws are neither purely conceptual nor instrumental. The Marxist rejects the conceptualist account of law, according to which law is an *a priori* ascription or construction of the human mind. There is a slightly modified version of this view. Laws are forms of reality itself and the highest of them, the Form of forms, is God himself. The instrumentalist and the conventionalist characterise law as a mere instrument or a mutually agreed upon convention for serving some explanatory purpose. The Marxist, being an uncompromising realist as he is, rejects both these views of law. Law to his mind is an attempted general description. Its factual content is absolutely undeniable. It has to be admitted at the same time that law is not just a generalisation based on facts. There is something *more* in it. It has some suggestive and anticipatory implications which may or may not be confirmed in terms of actual and possible facts. But once we claim as the Marxist does, that historical laws are necessary, the possibility of laws being disconfirmed by facts is ruled out. This curious counter-intuitive claims of the Marxist is to be understood in terms of his highly *interpreted* characterisation of law. Besides, his dialectical method proves immensely helpful in this context. The law of contradiction and the sub-law of internal contradiction taken together highlight different and even contradictory facets of facts, and that facilitates the process of confirming contradictory laws by identical facts.

The matter and method of history are essentially isomorphic. The facts of history and the forms of their interrelation are basically dialectical in character. This is a Hegelian view taken over by Marx, rejecting Hegel's spiritual metaphysics in the process. Denial of the universal Spirit, says the Marxist, does not in the least affect the main points of his theory of history —namely, that history is continuous and the continuity is due to some inherent laws. True, this inherent dynamics of history is not a mysterious metaphysical power or God's will. But for all practical purpose the all-powerful Marxist laws of history are found to have performed the theoretical purposes ordinarily assigned to or associated with the concepts of God's will, Nature, or Spiritual teleology. Irrespective of the physical, psychological and social characteristics of what is basically matter, the inherent motion of matter mould them, broadly speaking, in the same general ways. Consequently, the laws of physics, psychology and sociology do possess some broad structural similarity. I say ' broad ' bearing in mind the Marxist's repeated emphasis on the quantitative and qualitative distinction between different stages of change and his categorical assertion that his view must not be confused with the *mechanical* materialist's. Here again the validity of his assertion largely rests on the efficacy of the *dialectical* method and its derivative laws. Whatever allowance one might be prepared to make for dialectical and qualitative distinctions one has also to bear in mind the Marxist's monistic metaphysical assumption, i.e., all is matter. In spite of all variations and complexity the laws of matter must have some bearing or determining influence on other types of laws including psychological and sociological ones.

It is true that neither the materialist nor the spiritualist is prepared to retreat from his own metaphysical commitment. It is not enough barely to reiterate this commitment. It has to be factual and critically justified. No theory of history can be saved merely by retreating to its parent metaphysical theory.

I agree that on this point there is scope for differences. The materialist might argue that his metaphysical theory, materialism, unlike spiritualism, could be defended in terms of the progressive achievements of science. By implication he claims that materialism is inseparably wedded to the scientific method. If the ultimate composition and function of matter are still a controversial subject, that does not mean that the concerned theories are uncritical commitments or assertions of faith. The very fact that these controversial views are testable in principle shows their empirical or non-mysterious character.

Now this defence of materialism and the satisfaction of ' normal reason ' with it are precisely the point of dissatisfaction for the spiritualist metaphysician. In the name of science he is not prepared to deny 'the profound mystery of the cosmic existence'. The limits of normal reason should not be allowed to define the boundary of reality. Disability should be confessed but one should not make a virtue out of necessity.

I find it very difficult to express myself clearly on this point. It is not easy to refute the argument of the materialist. The spiritualist's consideration has also a point in it. It will be too simplistic to argue that scientific method is a good enough instrument to unravel all the mysteries of the world. The true scientist does not perhaps claim it either. In fact he wants to explain facts of experience in terms of assumptions and hypotheses the truth of which is partly unknown or unfamiliar. To avoid the fallacy of positivism we must not insist on trying to understand and explain the known in terms of the known. In that case the horizon of our knowledge does not expand. The gradual expansion of that horizon is evidently a trend of history. What I want to say is this. We *are* expanding our horizon of knowledge relying partly on the unknown. But that ' unknown ' is relatable and answerable to the known and there is nothing mysterious about it. If one's response to ' the unknown ' is one of mystery, it is emotional and personal and may be explained psychologically and perhaps even interestingly. But this psychology must not be taken as a good enough foundation for a general theory of sociology and history or sociological history. If the spiritualist claims, and it seems he does, that his metaphysical theory of spiritualism and integral methodology is also fully consistent with *this* requirement of science, I do not propose to enter into a verbal dispute with him. I have a persistent fear that the dispute is more than verbal. And in this respect my sympathy lies with the materialist.

In his revolt against metaphysics and all forms of metaphysics, the positivist tries to show that historicism need not be metaphysically committed. To illustrate the point he refers to his own theory. The laws of history as conceived by him are neither theological nor metaphysical but purely positivistic. Elsewhere he says that these laws of ' social physics ' are as good as the laws of physics itself. He does not quite see why sociology, following the method of science, could not assume the dignity of science. The wrong lies with the sociologist's untenable commitment to theology or metaphysics, God or Matter.

Admittedly it is possible in principle to formulate historicism without any metaphysical commitment. The attempts made in this respect, both classical and modern, are found on scrutiny to not be strictly true to their positivist professions. I wonder whether the positivist theory of history can be *coherently* formulated at all. Laws of history are claimed to be valid not only in respect of the past and present facts but also in respect of the facts of future. ' Future facts ' are objects of imagination and *not* of experience. The positivist's sense of certitude about their character and behaviour is apparently based on the laws of history. Logical analysis reveals that laws themselves are not ' solidly based on facts'. Their total extension or the whole field of their application cannot be an object or a set of objects for any human experience. To avoid metaphysical commitment the positivist is obliged to fall back on his *own* experience and that experience being limited by physical, psychological and other objective constraints, his attempt to understand the world turns out to be totally abortive unless he commits himself to certain laws which he cannot immediately justify in terms of his own experience. The unity of personal experience, rightly understood, is grounded in a community of human experience. If my experience is not supported and sustained by others' experience, and that too not necessarily *actual*, it is blind and cannot possibly help me in carrying out my own programmes of thought and action. The moment we start believing in a community of experience, we go beyond the narrow circle of 'personal experience' disowning at least partially both positivism and solipsism and thereby commit ourselves, may be unconsciously, to a sort of metaphysics, grand or modest. Laws are invariably grounded in metaphysics—the world not immediately given to our experience. And these laws are *general descriptions of the structure of the world and*, in the case of sociology, *of society*. The generalisations are of course *provisional* in the sense that in the face of newly found facts their character and scope might undergo *change*. Once we accept this possibility of change we cease to be full-blooded historicists. If the historicist becomes modest and concedes that his attempts to foresee the future are uncertain, more or less *predictive* in character and there is nothing *prophetic* or sacrosanct in them, I for one am not going to quarrel with him. But when Sri Aurobindo, for example, speaks in a firm voice that the true and inner history of the human race knows no contingency in it, I do not know how to accept it in good faith, being subject as I am to the conditions of mortal life and changing society.

## Freedom, Society and Culture

The doctrine of freedom as the recognition of necessity has been attributed not only to spiritualists like Spinoza, Hegel and Sri Aurobindo but also to materialists like Marx. To my mind Marx is in a relatively better position to deny this charge. As he does not believe in teleology and axiological ontology, he can always say that it is for man to create his history through *action*. The role of *thought* is rather secondary. Thought enables man to act appropriately and appropriateness is to be defined in terms of Natural and social laws which are more or less independent of the thinker. Thought has no end in itself; it is only a necessary condition to be successful in action. Thought is more influenced by action than it can possibly influence the latter. Accordingly the Marxist is not in favour of defining history in terms of the secondary human characteristic, i.e., thought. History is essentially history of human actions and interactions and to which thought has been playing second fiddle. Since thought is not an independent phenomenon and its forms are subject to the laws of society and Nature, freedom of thought has to be understood in a realistic and somewhat restricted context.

Engels endorses Hegel's notion of freedom as the recognition of necessity and says: 'Freedom does not consist in the dream of independence of Natural laws, but in the knowledge of these laws, and in the possibility this gives of systematically making them work towards definite ends.' It is very interesting to note that Hegel and Sri Aurobindo on the one hand, and Engels and Plekhanov on the other, define freedom as 'the willing of nothing except itself'. Freedom is the consciousness of necessity, the ability to decide and act according to that consciousness. In other words, free actions are the conscious and free expression of necessity. One is of course strongly advised to bear in mind that crucial terms like consciousness, freedom, action and necessity are not used in *an* identical sense by the spiritualist and the materialist. When the spiritualist, for example, says that freedom is 'the willing of nothing except itself', he has a metaphysical presupposition at the back of his mind which says that there is an infinite Being which knows no limitations imposed by any alien object. The same metaphysical presupposition may be *in a way* attributed also to the Marxist. But the Marxist's notion of Being is fundamentally different from Hegel's. For it is matter-in-motion and not consciousness, and therefore in his case willing cannot have itself as its sole and unlimited object. Consciousness being a derivative phenomenon of matter-in-motion its character and function on ultimate analysis must be subject to certain laws which are seemingly external to it. Consciousness as consciousness cannot be conscious of the whole Being, matter-in-motion. Similarly, will as will cannot effectively will the whole of Being as its object. This impossibility is intrinsic. The Being of the Materialist is not consciousness or spirit in which parts are supposed to be internally related. The parts contain the whole and the whole is in the parts. In the materialist's scheme of things man with all his ability of thought and action cannot in any mysterious way be in touch with the past and future men forming a sort of spiritual community with them. He cannot possibly recapture the lost thought of the dead. He cannot be a spokesman of those who are no longer in the world or a foreknower of the minds of the men yet to be born. Somehow his being is historical, historically limited—limited from without by other times, places and persons. This limitation does not mean discontinuity and it has to be explored and established by acts of will and consciousness in the material conditions of life. The more we can control and plan the latter, the more advantageously placed we are in the matter of predicting the future and for that retrodicting the past as well.

Here one comes across the question of true consciousness and false consciousness. Consciousness is true or false in relation and proportion to its proximity to and distance from the material conditions of production. The truth or falsity of human relationships are not something static or mere objects of cognition. Our relations with fellow human beings are determined by the system of production to which we all belong in different ways, the difference being a function of class or status affiliation. Marx thinks that the close and continuous acquaintance of the working class with the system of production enables it to have a deeper understanding of the structure and function of the system. Its experience, understanding and organisation equips the working class to bring about a change in the conditions of work and thus to put an end to the process of exploitation. The experience *and* action of the working class give them a clearer consciousness of not only their comtemporary situation but also the perspective of action. By its very nature the proletarian consciousness is likely to be authentic and creative. The possible cause of its distortion and confusion is the alien influence or the lure of the bourgeois life-style. Because of its distance from the actual process of production and the resulting lack of experience this class is positionally parasitical, less interested in bringing about any change in the existing system, and historically their consciousness turns out to be false and static. According to this analysis of Marx, the bourgeois class develops vested interests in the *status quo*, becomes prisoner in the situation of their own making and, what is worse, tries to justify its own fear of freedom by referring to imaginary threats to law and order. Lack of freedom is the result of the institution of class. Unless this institution is abolished freedom cannot be achieved and man will not be able to return to himself. It is only in a classless society that man will be able to rise above his class loyalty, regain his true identity and dignity and enter into free relationships with fellow human beings. In short, the establishment of a communist society is the *sine qua non* of freedom.

This account of why human freedom is bounded and how the bounds can be removed has not been universally accepted. Freedom is an indefinable *power* of consciousness. Some say it is an indefinable *state* of consciousness. Lack of freedom is attributed to the intrusion of an alien power or object into the realm of consciousness. According to the spiritualist, institutional determination as such does not mean negation of freedom or an obstacle to the nature of consciousness. It depends upon the character of the institution. If an institution could truly reflect the structure or the urge, whatever that might be, of consciousness, it would not then be regarded as a negative determinant of freedom. With slight variations this argument could be adapted also to the Marxist blueprint of the ideal communist society. When social institutions reflect the true consciousness of the proletariat class most of the elements of *human* contradiction disappear. Although this disappearance is a gradual process, it is strikingly facilitated by the removal of class antagonism and the consequential withering away of the State. The much sought after harmony between human urges and social institutions, if established, does not mean the end of the basic dynamics of history. In fact the end of social conflict and the establishment of harmony between man and man opens new vistas before man and his encounter with Nature assumes an added significance. For free man is better equipped in terms of knowledge and technology to understand and control Nature and thereby to remove gradually the elements of contradiction between him and Nature. If one rightly understands the materialist's scheme of things, one finds no *necessary* contradiction even between man and Nature. Strictly speaking, one cannot be perfectly free without recognising the necessity of natural laws. Freedom should not be abstractly conceived independently of Nature. But then it is very difficult to think of a level of knowledge and technology which would enable man to master Nature completely, to remove man-Nature antagonism altogether and to grow into a *total man*. Also, the Marxist notion of freedom thus turns out to be an ideal—to be approximated and never completely realised.[4]

The spiritualist arrives at a somewhat similar conclusion, from the reverse end. His positive thesis runs like this. False consciousness is unnatural and results from the subjection of consciousness to the bodily senses and physical matter. Consciousness is said to be self-expressing by nature. Its power of expression is impeded when it is embodied. For even the human body, including the senses, are material, gross or attenuated. Consciousness can return to its own nature and express itself fully when it is not associated with external senses and not constrained by material conditions. Mind too is a sense; it is inner sense and therefore material in its structure and function, although in a very subtle form. The freest state of consciousness is not mental. When consciousness as subject can freely encounter itself as object without any alien determination and inner dualism we can take it as true freedom. This again is an ideal state and it is very difficult for us actually to experience it. We do not know what consciousness without objective determination and internal dualism is like. We can perhaps think of this ideal form of freedom or consciousness or freedom of consciousness. But one wonders whether we, being what we are, can as a matter of fact act accordingly. The linkage between ideal freedom and practical action is missing. My institutional environment seems to be an intrinsic part of my personality mediating myself not only with my fellow human beings but also with my natural environment. Completely free man, *superman* or *total man*, whatever he is called, is undoubtedly an inspiring ideal but hardly a practical possibility. I do not deny that even an ideal could be justifiably regarded as real provided it is followed or approximated in practice.

The idea of institutionally determined freedom has been questioned and rejected on several grounds.

First, it has been pointed out that conditional freedom is no freedom. Freedom is not to be understood negatively in terms of lack of constraint. It is positive and spontaneous. Strictly speaking, it is indefinable and has to be postulated or intuited. Only what it is negated by is object of sense experience. The best way to *represent* the idea of freedom is to indicate the formal properties of its paradigm product, moral law. '*All* human beings *must* do what is just' is a moral law. It is *universal* in form and *necessary* in content.

Secondly, it implies *cultural relativity*. The products of institutionally determined consciousness, forms of thought and norms of action, for example, are always open to question. The forms of one society may appear alogical or even patently fallacious to other societies. The norms prescribed and followed in one society might be questioned or rejected straightaway by other societies. The difficulties of cultural relativity, which could certainly be indicated in a static time-frame, become even more clear in larger historical perspectives. If the products of social consciousness are subjects of so serious questioning and criticism, one could well understand why the formalist insists on excluding the material world or Nature from the realm of values like good and right. The question of beauty is somewhat different. Facts are facts and values are values and they are quite separate things. Formalists like Kant maintain that Nature is mechanical, and consciousness, being essentially free, is not a part of it. Even our body is material, a part of Nature; and to the extent that consciousness is influenced by it it fails to grasp and prescribe the right type of moral laws characterised by *all* (universality of form) and *must* (necessity of content). Kant says that morality is imperative and not merely suggestive; it is categorical and not conditional. Nature negates freedom and society constrains it. True freedom is conditioned by neither. It is free from both natural compulsion and social influence. And therefore whatever originates from it is free from the blemishes of cultural relativity.

The formalist's way out of cultural relativity has its own difficulties. He can indicate only the formal properties of the paradigm product of freedom or free will but cannot concretely identify it as an object. Whenever he does so one could easily point out its social affiliations and in that case it turns out to be criticisable on the relativistic count and loses its claims of *universality* and *must* character. Consequently it has been argued in a rather paradoxical manner that either free will wills nothing or whatever it wills is subject to historical wear and tear and cannot escape criticism and question.

There are two possible ways out of the difficulties created by the notions of relative freedom. One is represented by formalists like Kant and the other by spiritualists like Sri Aurobindo. To take the latter's view first: God's freedom is absolute and knows no bound—material, mental or social. This point has at times been represented in a highly metaphysical manner by saying, for example, God *is* Consciousness and Consciousness *is* Freedom. Whatever lacks in Consciousness and Freedom is more or less undivine, depending upon its degree of deficiency. Only God is completely self-determined; there is nothing other than Him to determine His being and the process of His becoming. The spiritualist assumes God as a very embodiment, and not merely as a locus, of freedom. To him human freedom is an imperfect analogy of divine freedom. And this imperfection is attributed to material, mental and social circumstances. In fairness to the formalist it has to be admitted that he does not at least *identify* freedom with God. To him God's freedom has no moral significance. Like man He is not subject, at least not *in principle*, to the constraints of Nature. It is man's openness to the conditions of life and society which *practically* oblige him to think, adjust, choose and act. Adjustment and choice obviously presuppose limitation and determination. In the context of God's supposed perfection and all-knowing capacity it makes little sense to speak of God's choice. If we believe that unique choice based on perfect knowledge is also genuine choice, only then can the notion of God's choice make sense; but in that case this choice is nothing but recognition of necessity, necessity flowing out of His own nature. However, it is argued, unique choice does not mean limited choice or no choice. It means *perfect rationality* of choice, leaving no room either for ignorance or contingency. Similarly, when man rightly knows *the logic* of his situation, all that is possible and all that is not, his choice turns out to be unique and the question of preference does not arise in his case, unless of course it is assumed that his knowledge of the situation is not really right. *Rationally* chosen ends and means are uniquely and necessarily related. A man who can grasp this system of ends and means is said to be a partaker in the life and power of God and competent enough to prescribe *the form* of action which would be acceptable to all *rational* men.

This ' formal ' presentation of the whole fact of the matter could be perhaps represented in the spiritual manner by saying that man, being an integral part of God, has in him all the powers of the latter and when he realises it his life and community became universal in form and necessary in content. God is said to be fulfilling Himself in infinite ways, but each of the ways is uniquely related to the rest. One might point out that the logical structure of both the solutions of the problem of relativistic freedom is basically same. Their motive-force is also perhaps similar. Although man is told that he is born free, he finds it impossible to believe in the face of his persistent contrary experience, and then follow the elaborate theories of contrary experience, explaining why it should not be trusted and, further, why 'reason' and 'intuition' should be trusted as the infallible guides of life.

Sri Aurobindo is likely to reject this analogy between the spiritualist's position and the formalist's as simplistic. Spiritualism itself is liable to different interpretations. Spiritualists like Aristotle, for example, are known for their accent on the formal aspect of spiritual unity. In the course of physical, biological and mental evolution the diverse forms of different objects gradually get reduced in number and converge ultimately on a unique form, the Form of all forms, God. Opposed to this interpretation of spiritualism is Sri Aurobindo's integral spiritualism which accepts the notion of evolution, relating unity and diversity but, unlike the other view, he firmly maintains that, even in ultimate reality, the Spirit, objects and individuals are preserved with all their richness of diversity.

Sri Aurobindo's attempt to avoid the formal rigidity of spiritualism and to justify cultural relativism up to a point without giving up the universal claim of the spiritual culture is essentially philosophical in its inspiration. To develop a comprehensive philosophical theory of Reality and Society highlighting the integral character of the parts and the whole—individuals and society—and of everything with the rest of the world does not by itself establish the practical credibility of the theory. I am aware of the position taken by some followers of Sri Aurobindo claiming that Sri Aurobindo's views on related matters are truths of fact and should not be regarded as theories. Personally speaking I do not see how a particular view can claim immunity against rational criticism on the ground that it is based on the truth of facts. After all *human* knowledge is subject to the conditions of human life which, I agree, might be transformed by reason and action over a period of time and not overnight. Sri Aurobindo is apparently very keen to keep human values free from the effects of body and sense-mind. For he fears that the normal body-mind complex inclines man to a materialistic and hedonic life-style. Although he does not fail to mention the danger of ignoring the importance of body and mind, or what he calls ascetic denial, his preference for spiritual culture is unmistakable from his criticism of ' the office and limitations of the reason'. Culture is disinterested pursuit of knowledge and delight of existence. Spiritual culture enables man to arrive at a ' harmonised inner and outer perfection', to ' discover . . . the divine Reality behind our existence and the complete and ideal Person within us ' and also to ' shape human life in that image'.

What happens, for instance, if one questions the reality of harmony between inner and outer perfection? Pointing to the conflict between the actual and the ideal if one expresses oneself in favouring of facing it rather than running away from it, what should be our response to this attitude? Is it no more rational and moral than trying to ' discover ' an ideal solution based on a metaphysical assumption that the divine Reality behind our existence and the ideal Person within us are inherently harmonised? Unless we are determined to ignore our own persistent experience and ask others to do the same in the name of a ' transcendent spiritual ideal ' I do not see how we could possibly defend ' the suprarational ultimate of life'. Perhaps I would be asked at this point to move towards a deeper and larger and non-sensuous experience. Although at the level of argument the spiritualist says that the integral unity of the spirit preserves and respects the elements of ' lower life,' material and sensuous, the ultimate picture turns out to be quite different; the identity of every element changes almost beyond recognition. The alchemy of spiritual experience lends an altogether new identity to the world of sense and science. One does not know at that level whether we all are talking about the same world, the same set of objects, or whether our communication has broken down at some crucial point.

It is *normal* reason and experience which provide the surest basis of communication between man and man. Supra-normal reason might open up strange vistas before the spiritualist, but that hardly bring him closer to the common man. Even to understand the artistic, behavioural and other achivements of supra-normal reason, man is required to rise above the normalcy of reason and experience; otherwise, he is sure to miss their deeper implications. I know Sri Aurobindo's strong objection to what I call *normal* reason and experience. According to him, man is an abnormal phenomenon in the normalcy of Nature and he is a growing God. In the name of normal experience it would be wrong on our part to ignore the importance of artistic, innovative and creative types of experience. When experience only confirms experience and does not transform or exceed it, we do not move and cannot make progress. In the name of normal reason we do not propose to endorse formal rigidity either in the sphere of ethics or of politics. Normal reason is criticised by Sri Aurobindo on the ground of its alleged association with sense-perception and emotion. It is also said to be coloured by the passions of practice and seized of by the desire to govern life and action by a single sovereign idea or law. Unless our reason becomes dispassionate and disinterested in its pursuit of truth, its findings turn out to be half-truths, lending support to contradictory ideals like optimism and pessimism, and offering equally good arguments for materialism and spiritualism, for individualism and socialism.

My preference for normal reason and experience is mainly intended to provide a sound and functional basis for communication between common men and not to create any conditions which might even remotely affect the growth of knowledge and progress of society. On the contrary, I fear, too much emphasis on supra-normal reason or spiritual vision demands of man to believe in something for which he has neither good reason nor necessary experience at his disposal. Consequently he feels obliged to fall back on faith, unsupportable belief, or some sort of authority. If I believe in something for which I have neither good reason nor the necessary experience which could be shared with others, my fellow human beings in all probability would refuse to accept it, and I would not know how to blame them for that. Sri Aurobindo's main criticism against the organised State is that it unduly depresses or suppresses the working force and thinking mind of important minorities and represents the selfishness of the average man, and that it makes a determined bid to bring about a semblance of orderliness in the conflicting popular claims and demands by using certain abstract and rigid rules and laws. The State machinery and its mechanical function are expressive of the formal and conventional character of human reason. In the eye of the spiritualist, normal reason stands for order and authority and not liberty and creativity. It is the spiritual mind which, according to him, is marked by openness, spontaneity, harmony and creativity. The antithesis between the spiritual and the rational is, to my mind, a purely theoretical supposition and is not borne out by the records of what the man of normal reason and experience has achieved so far. The man of extraordinary ability is not a regular visitor to our daily life. Revolution of thought or action does not take place every where and all the time. And it would be wrong to believe that the progress of human ideas and institutions is mainly due to the revolutionary ideas of the heroes or *avtaras*. The rejection of normal experience and reason gives rise to an elitist interpretation of history and an equally elitist theory of society and culture which systematically underestimate the importance of communication between the common men themselves. Within the bounds of normal reason and experience the sympathetic mind finds extraordinary gifts, techniques and scientific discoveries which are often attributed in a biased manner only to supra-normal reason and experience. The prejudice against the mental equipment and behavioural forms of the common man puts up a barrier between man and man, between the tribal man and the modern man, between the urban gentry and the rural folk.

It is also perhaps pertinent in this connection to remember that many scientific discoverers, artistic creators and social reformers were confirmed materialists and they rejected spiritualism as an unsupportable creed. They have nothing against spiritualism as such; their main point is that it may be sociologically understandable and psychologically soothing, but there is no good reason to accept it except that it is acceptable to and valued by some others. If we are not moral positivists, there is no reason why should we not contest and question the types and conventions which are simply dead and not rational. Sri Aurobindo's own admiration of the subjective age contains an implicit rejection of typalism and conventionalism. I say *implicit*, for his moral positivism makes it logically difficult for him to pass an open stricture against any age from within it. At this stage one might intervene and say that the so-called great gifts, artistic, scientific or otherwise, of the common man or the materialist mind are essentially spiritual in their inspiration: but of that we or even they themselves may not be aware. From this someone with a spiritual bias might even conclude that the materialist is also a spiritualist, of course unknowingly so.

To assert one's spiritualism without taking note of one's own denial of it seems to me rather perverse and puzzling. If I am told that I am a spiritualist, although I may not be aware of it, I would not know how to respond to this sort of curious characterisation of my beliefs. This argument, interestingly enough, cuts both ways. The materialist can also then plausibly tell the spiritualist that his spiritualism is nothing but a rarefied version of materialism itself. In fact, the materialist is interested in and experimentally studying many parapsychological or supernormal mental phenomena which hitherto had been regarded as occult, esoteric, mysterious and in some cases spiritual. Fortunately for the materialist he does not credit the spiritualist with a view, in this case materialism, without caring to look into the latter's denial and its rationale. His criticism and rejection of spiritualism is mainly based on the view that so-called spiritual phenomena are derivative in character and explainable at least in principle, in terms of certain physical and physiological concepts and laws. If the materialist does not insist on a reductive method, I don't find anything wrong with his *basic* aim. No rationalist, whether he is a materialist or a spiritualist, could possibly insist on using only those explanatory or interpretive concepts and laws which are well-founded and well-known. In the quest for knowledge and in the search for truth we are often obliged to go beyond our experience and knowledge. The adventures of ideas are rewarding and productive notwithstanding the element of risk involved. In this respect the spiritualist's readiness to explain the known in terms of the yet unknown is of course welcome. The other positive feature of spiritualists like Sri Aurobindo is that they make use of the concept of evolution to supply the missing link between the known and the yet unknown. But the question is whether the unknown is a matter of faith or assumption, and whether the supposed linkage is purely speculative. Questionable assumption is rationally preferable to unquestionable faith. While the latter tends to encourage dogmatism or at any rate imperviousness to the critic's queries and questions, the former always puts us under the rational obligation to ' defend ' our case or cause when contrary arguments or facts are offered. There is a different and to my mind more plausible way of defending spiritualism. And that is quite consistent with our anti-reductive attitude.

## SPIRITUALISM, RATIONALISM AND THE IDEAL HUMAN UNITY

The spiritualism that I have in mind could be rationally defended but it is of course of a different sort and very modest in its claim and scope. In this connection the first point to be borne in mind is that there is no necessary connection, neither historical nor logical, between spiritualism and theism or absolutism. One may or may not believe in a personal God or an impersonal Absolute; it has little or nothing to do with one's belief in spiritualism. Historically speaking we know of many philosophical systems, for example, Buddhism, Jainism and the Sāmkhya, in which the concept of God finds no place. Yet anyone who is acquainted with these systems could hardly deny their spiritual character. Naturally the question that arises here is what *is* meant by spiritualism. This question is different from the question what *should* be meant by spiritualism. Sri Aurobindo says, ' The Brahman, the Absolute is the Spirit, the timeless Self, the Self possessing Time, Lord of Nature, creator and continent of the cosmos and immanent in all existences, the Soul from whom all souls derive and to whom they are drawn' (*The Life Divine*, Ch. XVII). The intention of this view of the spirit is very transparent; everything is spiritual and even its denial presupposes its truth. I do not propose to go once again into the flaw of this logic. For I anticipate the standard objection: the logic of the finite is the magic in the infinite. Let me address myself to a rather modest task: whether the concept of the spirit could be given a tolerably clear meaning within the limits of the finite, the confines of our life and experience.

First, we do use in our ordinary life such expressions as ' the spirit of the age ', ' the spirit of the poem ' and also utter or write sentences like ' Please don't bother so much with the grammar of the music, try to get into its spirit; otherwise you will miss the most important and interesting thing.' In these and similar other contexts the use of the word *spirit* certainly does mean something more or less definite, and yet it is not a howler. I say 'more or less' because the very purpose for which this word is used is not clearly and uniformly definable. It means, depending of course upon the context, something immaterial or incorporeal, some animating principle, a non-intellectual character not perceptible merely by sense-organs. It may also mean, among other things, a tendency, a disposition, an inclination, a power, or a frame of mind. It would be futile to try to discover a universal metaphysical foundation of all these meanings of *spirit*; for, I fear, that would again oblige us to fall back on *the spirit* without enabling us to defend it except on that well-known weak ground of faith. From this one should not rashly conclude that there is not even a sort of family resemblance between the different meanings of *spirit*.

Sri Aurobindo himself admits that the spirit is active in the body. We have now abundant evidence at our disposal to prove that by resorting to regular yogic practices like meditation, contemplation and breathing control one can achieve psychosomatic excellence, peace and power of mind, and good health. Psychosomatic excellence may as well be called spiritual excellence. And one need not postulate a God or an Absolute to explain the supernormal features of the transformation of this normal body-mind complex. Somewhere Sri Aurobindo himself has said that yoga is nothing but practical psychology.

Secondly, many of us differ from the positivist view that whatever can be *said* can be *said clearly*. Many things can be said but *cannot be said clearly*. This is true even in the sphere of sciences where everybody seems to be interested, and rightly so, only in well-defined concepts and well-formed formulae. There are at least certain things or expeiences which *cannot be said* but *communicated.* Aesthetic experience, experience of love and sympathy, of ecstatic joy and acute pain, and of yogic experiences, for instance, belong to this class. In the process of communication some original qualities of experience, their richness or intensity, are bound to be lost or reduced. There are strong reasons for characterising specially aesthetic experiences as spiritual. It is blissful, exceedingly pleasant (*ānandadaikaghana*), and as a result of which one forgets oneself in this sort of ecstatic experience. Aesthetic experience (*rasānubhava*) is supernormal (*alaukika*) and has at times been described as a state of ' total immersion ' or even analogous to god-experience (*brahmāsvāda*). Besides, the success or otherwise of communication, linguistic and non-linguistic, depends upon individual ability and willingness and commonly shared (or at least understood) societal presuppositions, both factual and valuational. Art communication presupposes the presence of art connoisseur.

This brings me to my third and last point in support of a modest concept of spiritualism. We do have certain basic concepts in common with other human beings which enables us to organise, communicate and share our experiences with them. As I have already said, the process of communication and the methods of sharing experience are subject to certain conditions, to some wear and tear. When the conceptual apparatus and the societal presuppositions used in the organisation and communication of experience are very widely known, our experiences are found to form a sort of community marked by greater complexity. I draw a distinction between *community of experience* and *commonly shared experience.* The silting process of the normal experience of a particular cultural milieu over the years results in what is called *community of experience*, an objective situation, which provides the necessary background for the understanding of supernormal experiences. The people who speak the same language, have more or less the same historical and traditional background, are subject to more or less similar political and economic conditions of life and also share more or less similar objectives, are naturaly placed in a very good position to form a community of experience. At a higher and more abstract level this community of experience is found also among the professional groups of academicians spread over different countries of the world. But their historical background and their cultural milieu being different the range and subjects of their communication, though intellectually subtle and sophisticated, are somewhat limited in character. In other words, common language, culture and interests facilitate communication and widen its scope. It is for this reason that non-intellectual communication, though lacking in precision, is ordinarily found to be more effective and moving than the intellectual one. Our relative failure to formulate clearly and communicate successfully some of our supernormal experiences does not mean that they are devoid of significance. Given time, patience, care and sympathy perhaps we can communicate and understand many things which might appear confusing, bizarre, meaningless or even illogical at first.

Intra-group communication and understanding are always more easy and successful than inter-group communication and understanding. Without much fuss we could all accept the well-known distinction between *intellection* and *intuition.* All that we are intuitively aware of cannot be intellectually formulated and represented. Even logically we are obliged to admit that our ability to conceptualise what we are given in experience is somewhat limited and the limitation is due to necessary abstraction, leaving the empirically given at least partially out of the subject (or proposition) or referring expression. The relative lack of intellection in grasping a poetic or an artistic theme does not take away its life or spirit and that becomes evident when it is expressed or represented in language or colour. In fact, intuition or direct experience of object (almost automatically organised by unsaturated concepts) is the fountain of cognition and creation. It is this intuitive component of experience, rich in quality and very live in character, which is often characterised as spiritual. It is the subjective surplus attending the objects of experience (*ānandasamplava*) which can never be completely formulated and fully communicated. However, one is advised to remember that this incompleteness of formulation and the sense of lack in communication is neither permanent nor fixed. It varies, and the variation depends on different factors like the quality and richness of the *original* experience, keeping it live and fresh in mind by frequent remembrance, the pains that the person in question undertakes to articulate it and his own ability in this respect, and also the sympathy, understanding and perceptiveness of the people to whom the experience in question is sought to be communicated.

The spiritualist's stricture against rationalism is perhaps wrong on two main scores. First, it is just not correct to think that rationalism is antithetic to spiritualism and that the two are necessarily incompatible. Secondly, this supposed antithesis is based on a narrow and somewhat arrogant notion of reason. To criticise rationalism one should not take its caricature as one's target. An interesting criticism of the opponent's position demands of us to try to appreciate it first with sympathy. It is true that there was a time, during the period of the French Enlightenment, for instance, when some people, especially intellectuals, had *boundless faith in the power of reason.* And it is quite possible that a few people still exist to defend this indefensible tradition of uncritical rationalism. Faith in reason is a contradiction in terms. Reason and faith—faith as ordinarily understood—do not go together. If one speaks of rational faith, faith based on reasoning and experience and not on authority, personal or scriptural, that is a different proposition. In that case we could better use the term rational belief rather than rational faith. The connotation and association of faith are different from those of belief. One need not be unnecessarily romantic or sentimental in one's espousal of reason. The factor which damaged the cause of rationalism most was perhaps the romantic attitude shown by some of its more ardent champions. Less of romance and more of articulate spirit is called for to make the best possible use of reason.

The history of rationalism makes it abundantly clear that the immodest claims of some of its more optimist defenders has not been born out by facts, even their own views and prophecies are found to be conflicting at times. If we take up any romantic theory of reason, whether it is in the form of Hegel's teleological law of human progress or Comte's secular or natural one, we are led to the same sad conclusion. They apply their preconceived notions to well-known facts in order to justify their theories and their favourite views about an ideal social order. At least on two points their similarity is indeed very striking and interesting. First, they hate ' awkward ' facts which do not fit into their schemes of thought and ignore them scrupulously. Secondly, they are equally confident about the correctness of their views on the course of human history, on what has happened and what will happen. It is perhaps of interest to note in this connection that the pro-naturalism of Comte and the anti-naturalism of Hegel did not affect in the least their boundless faith in reason. One should also recall Sri Aurobindo's position in this connection. We have already referred to his unfortunate aversion to 'awkward' facts which do not lend support to his thoery of history and society. One point which emerges out of this comparison and contrast between naturalism, rationalism, materialism and spiritualism is that unless reason is *critically* used we cannot evolve any criterion in terms of which the conflicting claims of different metaphysical systems could be rationally settled. It is perhaps even not possible to show whether the different metaphysical systems are really conflicting. When different systems claim to have absorbed and interpreted all facts and rejected none, one does not know whether their factual claim is really sound or based on mere speculation.

The compatibility or otherwise of empiricism and rationalism, materialism and spiritualism depends to a great extent upon how we understand these concepts. For example, the phenomenologist is also an ' empiricist ' but he does not share the scepticism of the naturalist. Some materialists like Marx and Lenin, reject empiricism, while many others defend it strongly. Rationalism could also be of different types—theological and secular, metaphysical and romantic and anti-metaphysical. What is necessary is a careful analysis of the different aspects of each position. The emotive and unstudied reaction or wholesale rejection or acceptance will not do. Metaphysical systems often contain and conceal sound components of empirical theories. The same is true of spiritualism. *Per contra*, romanticism and optimism may pass for rationalism because of sophisticated verbiage. Called upon to judge comprehensive and complex systems we must make critical use of reason sorting and sifting arguments and facts without being unfavourably disposed even to the speculative elements. For speculation also contains, conceals and is prompted by perception.

Personally I believe in what I call anthropological rationalism which I have argued at length elsewhere. Spiritualism has also been conceived in different ways. I have already indicated what I mean by the modest concept of spiritualism. It is quite consistent with, in fact a part of, anthropological rationalism. Rationalism as I understand is not at all incompatible with empiricism or spiritualism. Our reason, because of its inherent *human* character, must not be used in an arrogant or intolerant manner. It is not a moral suggestion that I am making. If we critically examine what human reason does we have no good ground to think that it is always perfect and right. The achievements and possibilities of reason are influenced by the conditions of human life itself. I have deliberately raised the issue of ' what reason does ' and *not* ' what human reason is '. Reason is a power and not a substance as some metaphysicians are inclined to think. It is the hypostatisation of reason that leads one to think that it is sovereign or autonomous. Human reason in fact is neither sovereign as Hegel thinks nor autonomous as Kant believes. It is influenced by our body and the environment, both natural and social. But because of its power of abstraction it is not a slave to the passions of the body nor to the immediate influences, of the environment. Biologically seated and psychologically influenced this ability of man can be strengthened and put to diverse uses. When we bear in mind the essentially human character of reason we are obliged to feel modest about its achievements and prospects. The main characteristic of human reason is its openness—openness to all problems irrespective of the fact whether it can tackle them or not; open to all experiences—predictable, baffling or inexplicable. There are many phenomena and problems which might ordinarily be characterised as spiritual, mystic or mysterious, and which our reason might not be able to explain at first and yet it does not shy away from them. The modesty and beauty of human reason is that it admits and recognises even those ' things ' which cannot be understood or explained by it and therefore might easily be cited as a proof of its poverty or inadequacy.

It is not easy to make a choice between the competing claims of spiritualism and materialism as theories of reality. As I have said before, this difficulty of choice is mainly due to their metaphysical character which does not easily lend itself to empirical tests. So far as their theoretical aspects are concerned these two views to my mind are comparably consistent. Obviously this adds to one's difficulty in making one's ground of choice publicly ascertainable. The choice in this respect is left purely to private considerations and this does not show either the rationality of the chooser or that of the chosen. Besides, one must also remember that both spiritualism and materialism could be, and in fact have been, formulated in different, sophisticated and anti-reductive ways; and, as a result, some forms of materialism can well take care of and explain a large number of hitherto unknown spiritual phenomena and problems. This claim has been put forward even more robustly by some spiritualists. It has been said by the latter that they can explain all that the materialist possibly can and something more. These larger and anti-reductive claims and counter claims of spiritualism and materialism make the choice situation extremely complex and consequently also render the formulation of logic of choice very difficult.

What is true of the competing claims of materialism and spiritualism as theories of reality is also substantially true of the competing claims of rationalism and empiricism as theories of knowledge. Both the doctrines could be consistently formulated and theoretically defended. When one comes down from the theoretical level to the practical one, one encounters difficulty. The exclusive claim of reason that it *is* the origin of and therefore can explain human knowledge, when put to test, turns out to be much less solid than what it appears initially. With no materials of experience to òrganise the forms of reason, or with no fields of experience to apply them the principles of reason are not only useless but also run the risk of being proved incoherent in their mutual relationship. As without light eye cannot see, so without experience reason cannot work. The extravagant claim of the empiricist that experience *is* the origin of and can therefore explain human knowledge also appears to be equally indefensible. The exclusive identity of experience does not contain within itself any organising power or connecting link. The pure empiricist cannot satisfactorily explain how one experience is related to other experiences. The metaphors of stream and thread are not of much consequence in this context and can hardly solve the empiricist's riddle of *related* experience(s). Conscious of the difficulty of his position, the critical empiricist postulates or 'sees' the inherent connection—a connection in terms of principles or categories between different experiences. Again it is this cautious, critical and anti-reductive formulations of rationsalism and empiricism which makes it difficult for one to choose between the partly competing and partly conciliating claims of these two theories.

The human choice seems mainly to be a matter of practice and not of theory. When alternative theories are offered and found to be equally good in terms of explanatory power, internal or external consistency, simplicity and other well-known criteria for choice, we may temporarily hesitate, contemplate or calculate, and then examine them on the basis of available facts and figures, maybe under the influence of personal predilections; but in any case we cannot indefinitely postpone our decision-making, putting a dead stop to the concerned mental process which in fact is a practical engagement. What I mean to say is this: *what cannot be theoretically clinched is practically decided.* It is perhaps for this reason that I often find it more rewarding to follow the practical rather than the theoretical history of materialism and spiritualism, of empiricism and rationalism; for, while theory can only indicate, practice shows. Exclusive and even conflicting at the theoretical level, these theories or at any rate their sober versions do influence and are influenced by each other in practice. Views and opinions are generally shaped more by practical experience than by abstract theoretical considerations. The precision and clarity of theories are achieved at a high price; their suggestions and implications are deliberately ignored and, even then, when put to the test of practice, their 'deceptive' character is easily exposed. One must realise that this deceptive precision and clarity of theories are deliberately aimed at, interestingly enough, again for a practical purpose —*practical* of course in an abstract sense and at another level.

Two or three clarificatory remarks are in order. The practical inclusiveness of different and even conflicting theoretical views should not be taken in a rather facile and uncritical manner as a justification of the integral or dialectical method. The truth of the matter lies perhaps in the other way round. The attractiveness and reasonableness of these two methods are to be found mainly in their practical inspiration, in their concern for what is being practised rather than theorised or professed by different people from different points of view. This positive aspect is evident both in integral sociology and dialectical sociology, but only up to a point. Thereafter it seems that, despite their professions to the contrary, the proponents of these views were overtaken by a theoretical zeal and a love for uniformity and generality.

There seems to be no rational escape from the practical demands for bringing about a sort of functional relationship between different ways of life, social philosophies, or what may perhaps more pompously be called world-views. In fact the process of history exhibits an almost continuous practical effort to bring about a synthesis or an integration of different views. It is true that this normal process is occasionally interrupted by abstract theoretical enterprises. From what I say one must not think that I am an anti-theorist. Far from that. We *do* need theory not only to meaningfully organise our experiences but also to act purposefully in life. The question is *not* whether we are for or against theorisation. The relevant question in this sociological context, marked by an ideological or a practical orientation, is at what point of the abstract-concrete scale should we formulate our theory. The strength and relevance of a theory is mainly a function of practical demand and has to be decided according to the logic of the situation.

In every real social situation human ideas and ideals interact continuously. This process of interaction is continuous and spontaneous. One has to take note of, but should not uncritically welcome, the spontaneous part of interaction. We must not accept as right whatever happens as a matter of fact. Reactive and imitative habits have to be replaced by innovative and creative ones. While we must try to understand and respond to others' views even if they are not acceptable to us, we must not stand neutral in the struggle between reason and unreason, between right and wrong. While we must not interrupt communication between different or even conflicting ideas and ideals, for that might backfire on or adversely affect our own cherished values, we can hardly afford to be passive spectators or merely theoretical interpreters of what is fallaciously believed to be the inevitable course of history. History has to be understood so that a better social order can be created. This does not mean the introduction of an external motive-force into history. In fact history itself is an action-process, a dynamic system of actions and responses, and has its own internal praxis. The preservation of the conditions necessary for successful communication between man and man, and also those necessary for the creation of a just social order is absolutely essential. I can well imagine that the conditions of human communication might, under certain circumstances, prove somewhat incompatible with the conditions of building up a just social order. It is quite possible that those who have a vested interest in an unjust society would insist on the perpetuation and legitimisation of the conditions which suit them only. But I see no compelling reason why the ideal human society should be conceived on that negative assumption. Rather, we must address ourselves both theoretically and practically, giving primacy to practice, to the problems and causes of social injustice and increasingly recognise the importance of those conditions which could ensure justice to the weaker sections of society and institutionalise them. Of all normally accepted social values I attach the greatest importance to justice.

It is not easy to clarify the concept of justice. In the context of social life justice seems to have two aspects—regulative and prescriptive. It regulates and equilibrates the virtuous aspects of human conduct and removes the vices. What justice proposes to establish could perhaps more appropriately be expressed from a seemingly negative point of view. If the vices which tend to corrupt human intentions, actions and relations with fellow human beings have to be taken care of, it can be done by framing and enforcing correct rules of conduct. The correctness or otherwise of a set of rules of conduct cannot be decided *a priori* and for ever. It is in this connection that one has to perceive the subtle but important relation between substantive justice and procedural justice. In the quest of the 'essence' or 'substance' of justice one must not lose sight of its more important aspect, that is, the procedural one which is basically historical and an active process. Primarily because of the elusive character of substantive justice some thinkers are understandably more concerned with the concept of law; and, according to them, rationally conceived and employed law can take care of the requirements of justice, ensuring universality and objectivity. It is also partly because of the non-perceptible and 'mysterious' character of substantive justice that much importance has been attached to the concept of distributive justice which is reflective of the positive aspects of justice.

The administration of justice necessitates not only the formulation of correct rules but also a critical review and, whenever necessary, a correction of the rules. Distributive justice by itself cannot automatically take care of the injustices meted out to the people and therefore society also needs what we call corrective or remedial justice. A just social order cannot be established merely in terms of distributive and remedial justice which can be enforced, at least up to a point, by a lawful authority. There is another area of justice, which lies in the area of human psychology, where the lawful authority of the State or even the sanction of society has only limited relevance and yet it is widely believed that if this area is not properly attended to and cultivated by reason and sympathy, it becomes increasingly difficult for the approved authorities to administer justice by exclusively relying on enforceable laws and rules. It is in this area that morality gets engagingly close to law. It is difficult to persuade a man, who is not morally disposed to do so, to be effectively law-abiding. The authority of law is derived from reason and man's concern for other human beings. It is this inner authority which has often been described as the foundation of all laws, both moral and legal, primarily moral and perhaps derivatively legal. The persuasive character of this authority seems to contain a structural presupposition about human nature itself in general. Unless man is deemed to be dispositionally rational and concerned about his fellow human beings, it is not quite clear why man, without being coerced by the approved authorities of the State and society, willingly goes out of his way to help others in difficulty and distress and tries to protect and promote their interests.

This view is certainly inconsistent with the utilitarian position which says that pleasure-augmentation or pain-reduction is the sole criterion for deciding whether a particular course of action is just. There is undoubtedly an element of pleasure or, perhaps the better expression would be, happiness attending the process of doing or even understanding what is just. The body is a necessary condition of human action. And the hedonic undertone of the latter is quite understandable. But what the hedonist cannot satisfactorily explain is the self-exceeding and self-effacing dispositions of human nature. I for one do not deny the subjection of human nature to value-predilections, biases and prejudices. This aspect of human nature must not make us blind to its underlying praxiological implications. Our biases and prejudices are obliquely indicative of suppressed value-judgements and not of irrationality. True, our reason is not a slave to our passions. But it is certainly open to their influence. If in our quest for an absolutely rational state of mind as a pre-condition for conceiving and doing what is just we propose to ignore or suppress all that is somatic and hedonic, we will be doing a wrong thing, repeating in ethics and politics the blunder of the rationalist in epistemology. One might also recall in this connection Sri Aurobindo's criticism of the ascetic denial.

The quest for justice has been lightly dismissed by Marx as a frivolous exercise in capitalist society ridden by class distinction and marked by inequality. We seek justice precisely because it is not there. Social justice does not accept the existing society for granted and demands of us that we change it in favour of the weaker sections of society to whom justice has been denied and, therefore, all things being equal, who deserve justice more than others. I have already said that justice is a regulative and equilibrative force, regulating the causes and courses of injustice, and endeavouring to establish a just and dynamic equilibrium of inter-human and inter-group relationships. Justice means the active process of preventing or remedying what would cause or strengthen the forces of injustice. It is not a mere static quality of human will; it is an active process or what I call praxiological engagement.

Of course, we need freedom and the ability to exercise that freedom to know and to do what is just. Whatever form of society we want to establish or in whatever manner we want to change the established society, some measure of freedom we need to initiate the necessary steps. The significance of freedom can be understood from different points of view—for example, freedom as an end-value or value-in-itself, as a means to the pursuit of other values, freedom as a mental phenomenon and freedom as a requisite of intentional action, action to which some value is attached by the agent. It is not surprising that, because of its pre-eminence in the sphere of values, freedom is sometimes described as the basic value, the value of values. To highlight the significance of freedom as a basic value I don't think it is necessary to regard other values as secondary or derivative in character and origin. The underlying assumption of the slogan 'Freedom for the sake of freedom' is not as impressive as some people, mostly of the intellectual milieu, are inclined to believe. Generally we do not take the necessary critical care to look into the hidden assumptions and sociological factors underlying our own value-scales and preference-schedules. Often we forget that the placement of different values in our value-scale is influenced by certain considerations which are peculiar to *our* milieu and could not be regarded as universal. Therefore, one very interesting way of determining the relative significance of freedom, among other values, is to ascertain empirically how people of different groups, given the existing freedom and constraints, draw up their different or similar value-scales and preference-schedules. In this respect the peasant and the worker, on the one hand, and the professor and the journalist on the other, for instance, are likely to differ to a considerable extent. A closer look is likely to reveal a difference even between the needs and demands of the worker and the peasant, although they are ordinarily supposed to be the members of a homogeneous group. Similar differences could be traced between the professor's value-scale and the journalist's.

Unless it is very abstractly defined, the issue of freedom proves interesting only in reference to concrete social situations, the intentions and actions of concerned groups of individuals. Insofar as primary needs and demands—food and shelter, for example—are concerned, all groups are more or less similarly disposed. Consequently, the operational area of the demand for freedom is widest at the economic level. The worker and the peasant are primarily interested in and almost exclusively preoccupied with the basic needs of life. Freedom of thought and freedom of expression hardly appear very important to them, unless of course they are persuaded to think along that line under the strong influence of the well-organised social or political leadership. Whether one needs food and shelter or demands equality and fraternity one has to encounter *operational* issues of freedom, leaving behind the *conceptual* ones for the time being at least. Intellectuals are more preoccupied with conceptual freedom and the working class and the peasantry with an operational one. Certainly, there may be exceptions to this general rule. Since the conceptual and the operational aspects of freedom cannot be completely separated from one another, all groups of people have to face at some stage or other the *practical problems of freedom*. Even the alienated intellectuals, who are often rightly blamed for their well-known indifference to social issues, are found to be very much interested in their own economic welfare.

Another way of understanding the practical importance of freedom as a social value is to look at it from the standpoints of the normal man and, in the absence of a better term, I would say supernormal man. While the normal man is mostly guided by tradition, convention and conventional authority, the supernormal man follows his own light. Of course this does not mean either that the former cannot break tradition and convention or that the latter is impervious to the social and historical forces. Even when he is oppressed by social conditions the normal man does not clearly know what is to be done, how to combat those forces, and he thinks that his capacity being limited as it is he has no option but the accept rather tamely the given situation. His assessment of the situation is marked, among other things, by a traditional and an unencouraging opinion about his own capacity to bring about a change in society. Generally speaking, he is a conservative and a conformist. Being traditionally disposed as he is, he wants almost habitually to conserve the values handed over and communicated to him by others, and lacking somewhat in the spirit of enterprise he tends to conform to the existing forms of conduct. The normal man's assessment of his society and of himself seems to be highly subjective, and it does not reveal his true capacity to change the society in the intended direction intended by himself and others of his own group. His intention itself is coloured by a subjective assessment which, though incorrect, in practice is almost entirely valid. I say ' almost ' and thus qualify the validity of intention because I think that there is an element in intention which is in touch, as it were, with reality and thereby at least partially remedying the incorrectness of his assessment. To put it in plain language, because of social conditions the normal man, though wrong in his subjective assessment, is objectively powerful from the standpoint of social change. But one must bear in mind that this objective power unless properly organised is in the nature of potentiality only. Since he represents numerically the bulk of the people, when this power is organised and used in war and revolution, for instance, we perceive its true (but ordinarily non-manifest) character.

A word of caution. In my discussion of the case of the normal man I have repeatedly used words like ' generally ', ' often ', ' ordinarily ' and also I did not try to define ' the normal man '. This qualification and omission is deliberate and the result of my feeling that this concept is very complex and the related issues vary from society to society. The normal man cannot be pictured in a universally accepted manner and therefore the propositions about him should be formulated in a careful and qualified way.

Freedom for the normal man has to be objectively, i.e., institutionally, organised and thus given a manifest character. Otherwise his own fellow beings are not likely to understand and believe it. The case of the supernormal man is quite different. He is a much better organised and equipped personality which enables him to live a life considerably free from the socially conditioning influences. There are two aspects of this character of the supernormal man; while, on the one hand, he certainly enjoys some subjective freedom, rising at least partially over social influences, he invariably faces, on the other, problems of communication in relation to the normal man and his group. The mental make-up and conduct of the former are not ordinarily intelligible, and still less acceptable, to the latter. This creates a communication gap between the two. Given the gap, the supernormal man, at least to start with, is an object of adoration and awe for the normal man. But when the latter does realise his objective power and can organise it appropriately together with his fellow beings, his attitude undergoes a significant change and with that the situation in question too. Again, all this partly depends upon the character and orientation of the supernormal man.

Obviously all supernormal men are not of the same category. They can belong to the religious, intellectual, political, military and even other categories. The supernormal man is passionately attached to his own understanding and conviction and is firmly determined to follow his own chosen path. His seriousness, devotion, courage and sacrifice distinguish him from the rest of society; and his own qualities do not allow him to be a commoner, one among many, and to identify himself with his fellow beings. It is quite possible that some of them, especially of the religious category, are subjectively and sincerely disposed to identify themselves with their own people; but in the eyes of the latter they are fundamentally different from them and this difference is objectively persistent and functionally valid. Here develops, though unintended, an interesting situation. The supernormal man wants to 'come down' and 'freely mix' not only with the normal man but also with the depressed and the downtrodden; but the latter in their turn by intensifying the process and evolving numerous forms of admiration, adoration and worship, in that order, put him at a distance and start simultaneously suffering and enjoying the distance between him and themselves. The communication process suffers, gets distorted and gradually impersonalised; the cognitive relation is replaced by the emotive one and personality by institution (legitimised by supernormal authority). The institutionalisation of the supernormal personality tends to take away its charismatic authority and degrade it to the routine life. Honestly, though mistakenly, the normal man attributes certain extraordinary qualities to the supernormal man which do not truly describe his character. In his subjective exuberance he sees extremes of intense action or of willed passivity in his chosen supernormal man. In spite of his psychological attachment to his 'hero' he becomes sociologically distant and also perhaps separated from him. The other aspect of this paradoxical situation is also marked by an incompatibility between the supernormal man's subjective disposition and attitude to the normal man and what the latter in themselves really are. Partly due to his extraordinary and intensely subjective character and partly because of a communication lag he forms a mental picture of the people which may be conceptually coherent and emotionally inspiring but hardly reflective of the true objective situation. It is for this reason that the supernormal man is, or at any rate appears to be, very individualistic. In his eagerness to change society and improve the lot of others he often forgets the deficiency of the latter and expects them all to be like himself without quite realising the practical difficulties involved in the matter. If all normal people could be like the supernormal man, the former could do as well without the latter.

What is true of the religious type of the supernormal man is not true of the intellectual or the military type, for instance. The intellectual leader theoretically realises the problems and difficulties of the normal man and, given sympathy, can also perhaps indicate in principle the means for the possible solution of the dilemma. Admittedly, he takes immense pains to analyse a situation and the relative merits of the alternative proposals to tackle it. But if he is himself called upon to take an active part in tackling and solving the problems, he either abstains or fails. The case of the military leader is somewhat different. The extraordinariness of a Napoleon or of a Tito consists partly in his personal courage, imagination and skill and partly in his ability to promote and sustain a team-spirit. His achievement is always a group achievement and in this respect his difference from the intellectual or the spiritual leader is very clear and consistent. For him communication with the rank and file is not a problem. But this communication is mainly (*not* exclusively) one-sided, from his end to their end, and of a relatively limited nature pertaining only to their warlike activities. For the time being I am ignoring the myths and legends which grow around the lives of the ' heroes '. Communication is perfect when the end, means and substance of communication concern totally and in depth all the persons involved. The conditions of ideal communication change from time to time and place to place and are never fully satisfied, certainly not when some persons in question belong to the supernormal category. One special thing must be said about the religious supernormal man and that is his loving nature, sympathetic disposition, kindness and compassion which considerably narrow the communciation gap between himself and others.

All supernormal men are not practice-oriented and forward-looking. And many of them do not have any conscious intention to uplift the poor and the normal man and bring about any change in the existing society; indeed, some of them may well be very conservative or merely theoretically disposed. In the total field of the relation between the supernormal on the one hand, and the normal, the poor and the weak on the other, one thing comes out very clearly and that is the communication gap. Even where there is a genuine intention to remove the gap, it cannot be removed so easily. This problem is grounded in some objective conditions and cannot be easily understood in terms of the intention of this or that individual human being. Successful communication is a necessary condition of human freedom and we must see to it that the constraints of communication are removed first and only then can freedom be safeguarded and institutionalised.

The institutionalisation of freedom is necessary particularly from the point of view of the normal, the weak and the poor. The supernormal man can reasonably secure his freedom by his own individual effort, intention and excellence and which do have and leave behind a significant social impact.

One very important thing about freedom is that it is always open to ' external ' influence and the possibility of its resulting abridgement or expansion as the case might be. This is true both of individual freedom and institutional freedom of belief, thought and action. Even what is called ' private ' dispositions also undergo change, almost against the will of the concerned individual himself, due to new experiences, and intentions which prove inconsistent with existing dispositions and therefore either create mental disturbance and tension or, depending upon the nature of the case, enlarge the area of freedom. The possibility of a clash or cooperation between the freedom of one institution and that of another or others is more pronounced and easily understandable. Like an institution personality has its own structure. And there is an interesting similarity between the two, particularly in respect of their claim for freedom and capacity to retain it. A better organised personality, organised in terms of experience, reasoning power, love and sympathy, courage, integrity and the like, is always at an advantage not only to acquire and enjoy freedom but also to expand, deepen and retain it with suitable modifications and the analogy of the personality structure could be usefully applied to the institutional structure. When an institution can organise its internal affairs and define its own relation with other institutions competently and correctly, bearing in mind the genuine and changing needs of other institutions, it can better enjoy the fruits of freedom and preserve the same against external claims and pressures. It is relatively easy to indicate the conditions necessary for securing and preserving freedom but, I agree, it is extremely difficult to do so in practice. This difficulty is felt more acutely within the personality structure and that again is mainly due to the competing claims of different mental phenomena, desires and values and we should also bear in mind that one cannot run away from one's own self without being schizophrenic or at least suffering from serious psychological tension. Unlike a personality, an institution exists more in its outer relations with other institutions and lives less within itself and consequently its psychological depth and suffering or enjoyment are somewhat less than those of a person. The State and the society under which both an institution and personality are obliged to work, have always a clear bearing on their life, but because of his subjectivity person *qua* person is ordinarily less pervious to the overall and external socio-political influences. It is mainly in and through its association and identification with an institution that a personality structure is exposed to what the State and the society decide and do. In this respect perhaps the institution is less favourably placed; because of its dominant outward looking structure and character it is always open to the push and pull effects of other institutions with different objectives. It is here that the role of the society, and especially the role of the State, become very relevant in order to define the relation between different institutions, to ensure that the different objectives of the institutions do not turn out to be conflicting, and to establish finally a functional rapport between the personality structure and the institutional structure. Different forms of government and ideals of human unity express our efforts to define the best possible relationships between the ends and means of individual human beings and those of institutions. The other side of the picture also deserves our attention. While the institutional structure and its functions are directly rule-governed and relatively impersonal, the personality structure, because of its inwardness and indirect openness to social influences, is susceptible even to the subtle and unorganised impulses of change. Persistent ambivalence of the latter is an interesting subject of study for the social psychologist.[5]

It is indeed very difficult to think of a general principle governing the ideal relationship between personality structure and the institutional structure and between the needs and capacities of the two. Freedom is not a unique need or preservative of the individual; institutions need it too. In fact without appropriate power and freedom to exercise their authority institutions cannot provide individuals with the conditions necessary for preserving and enlarging their freedom. Individual freedom and institutional freedom, rightly understood, are basically complementary. The lack of an in-depth analysis of their basic and dialectical relations is responsible for overestimating the importance of one at the expense of the other. Of course, it has to be admitted that the individual has primary need of freedom and that an institution's demand for it is intelligible partly in terms of necessity of maintaining the objective conditions for individual freedom and partly on the assumption that the demands for freedom of different individuals and groups are not always rational or consistent and therefore some ' external ' help and mediation are called for. If and when this assumption turns out to be irrelevant, the question of providing the objective conditions of individual freedom also becomes somewhat of a secondary concern. If and when individuals *qua* individuals can freely decide themselves the actual form of what may be called the commonwealth of ends and means, the *raison d'être* of institutional freedom and State authority becomes questionable. The self-improvement or perfection of the individual reduces the authority of the State and renders many of its agencies and functions useless.

## Freedom and Human Unity: Ideal and Actual

Nobody, at least no serious thinker, questions the basic ideals of freedom and human unity and their fundamental importance. I find that Marx is no less interested than Sri Aurobindo in the defence of freedom and, similarly, I find that Sri Aurobindo is as clear as Marx about the inevitability and the necessity of providing the conditions for the establishment of a just society. It would certainly be wrong to think that perceptive thinkers like Marx and Sri Aurobindo are not quite aware of the implications of what they say. For example, when Marx says that our ideal society would be free and classless communist society, he is certainly aware of the struggle which has to be launched to establish it and also of the necessity of denying freedom to those against whom the struggle would be primarily directed. According to Sri Aurobindo, the ideal human unity will be preceded by a sort of world-state marked by the preponderance of State authority over the legitimate demands for individual freedom and group freedom. The great thinkers differ primarily in their assessment and evaluation of the different factors—individual, community and mankind—involved in the quest of the establishment of an ideal human order. In an unjust and irrational or even in a classridden society all people do not deserve and cannot be given equal freedom at the same time. In fact, institutional endeavours to enlarge and equalise the freedom of all citizens are admittedly an objective of every democratic society. But the question is how to achieve this otherwise laudable objective. First, the people responsible for manning the institutions under consideration are themselves not subjectively and equally free and, besides, the institutions which environ and influence them are not mutually coherent and convergent in terms of their purpose. This is seemingly a paradoxical situation. People need free institutions for their own freedom and the institutions need free people to man them so that they can freely exist and act.

Freedom is conditional and dialectical; conditional, because it is difficult to conceive of unconditional and absolute freedom in the human context, and dialectical, because the institutions and individuals which influence us are themselves in turn influenced by us. Influence and counter-influence, action and reaction in the human situation, are creative and not repetitive. Neither planning nor the execution of our actions, individual or collective, correspond exactly to our 'original' conception. Nearly always some unpredictable and unintended factors intervene. This brings to our notice two very important points. First, there is a limit to what is called human spontaneity, spontaneous coherence and convergence between different human and institutional objectives. Secondly, there is a need for initiating deliberate steps to coordinate different decision-making units, individual and collective. I would like to mention one important implication of these two points. Human unity cannot be a function of and does not flow out of spontaneous human consciousness. The idea that spontaneity is the essential characteristic of freedom appears to be mistaken.

Unless it is assumed that the source of spontaneous consciousness is one or that the sources, though diverse, have a pre-established harmony between themselves, it is difficult to believe in the face of contrary empirical evidence that the human cycle would inevitably lead to the establishment of an ideal society marked by boundless unity and freedom. In fact, this assumption implies that the human cycle is only an intermediate stage between an implicit spiritual unity and an explicit one. Further, the dynamics of the cycle is believed to be contained within the origin and the character of the cycle itself, and, consequently, the whole process is stated to be governed by an inherent necessity. As I have said before, this gigantic metaphysical assumption is the basis of the view that freedom is the recognition of necessity.

Human unity is given to man only as an ideal to be realised through action and not as a metaphysical fact to be passively accepted. Nor is it an analogy of God's nature to be rediscovered in our own social life. The ideal human unity need not be deemed as God's home-coming, a return to the city of God, according to his own design carefully concealed from the human view. Besides the objective imponderables, elements of human intention, action and organisation are always present in the formation and transformation of the ideals of society. It would be wrong to think that human history is an obscure analogy of God's own self-evolution, a transition from the inward and involved state to the manifest state. For this idea is basically inconsistent with the reality or genuineness of human freedom. Freedom is neither entirely an objective-institutional imposition nor a purely psychological spontaneity. It is an achievement marked by two aspects, psychological and institutional or sociological, and one *cannot* be completely separated from the other in practice. This is a very difficult and interesting area where individual and institution are obliged to interact and even clash; and they often do it even knowing fully well that they need each other. This has to be understood in terms of the objective dialectics of the situation. The reflective individual is simultaneously persuaded of two things—the necessity of preserving the right of psychological spontaneity and whatever follows from it like initiative and productive or creative imagination, and also the necessity of the institutional framework on which the individual in need, i.e., lacking in sufficient initiative and enterprise, might fall back upon and enjoy what may be called a minimal-normal measure of freedom. If all its inner frontiers are undefined, freedom could be deemed to be a function and confluence of practical initiative and institutional safeguards. When the personality structure of the individual acquires sufficient strength and stability and retains at the same time spontaneous and creative powers, its dependence on institutional safeguards is reduced, but it never disappears completely. If institutions could develop an inherent resilience and flexibility, then its negative aspects, as indicated by its manifest safeguarding character, become secondary and its dependence on this or that individual supernormal man or charisma goes down. In short, it is only by enabling the individual to develop a stable and yet open personality structure and imparting a responsive and resilient character to the institution that we can create a durable atmosphere of freedom.

Man needs freedom for thought, action and communication. The paradigm or the prime locus of freedom is man and *not* God. As we understand Him God does not think; He embodies thought; He does not act out of any sense of need, for He is full and perfect; He has *really* none to communicate with, for all individuals are His mortal analogies or determinate forms. Even then we are used of course in an anthropomorphic way to characterise God in terms of thought, action and communication. To the extent human thought, action and communication are taken seriously, and not taken as mere dim duplications of God's own identical attributes or abilities, the concept of God loses its position of real eminence and independence. In fact the notion of God's freedom is an extrapolation of human freedom and not the other way round. It is in this context that one must realise the hollowness of the 'freedom for the sake of freedom' view. We need freedom for determinate and related purposes, viz., thought, action and communication. Of all the human purposes perhaps the most theoretical one is thought. Even then it is related to and tries to fulfil itself in some action or communication and has no end in itself. The practical character of action and communication is too obvious to be analysed in detail.

In the course of expounding his view about the value of philosophy Russell says something which is of interest for us here.[6]

> The free intellect will see as God might see, without *here* and *now*, without hopes and fears, without the trammels of the customary beliefs and traditional prejudices, calmly, dispassionately in the sole and exclusive desire of knowledge—knowledge as impersonal as purely contemplative, as it is possible for man to attain. The mind which has become accustomed to the freedom and impartiality of philosophic contemplation will preserve something of the same freedom and impartiality in the world of action and emotion .... The impartiality which, in contemplation, is the unalloyed desire for truth, is the very same quality of mind which, in action, is justice, and in emotion is that universal love which can be given to all, and not only to those who are just useful or admirable.

If Russell is right, universal and impersonal knowledge and love are distinct possibilities within human reach. One should bear in mind that when he said all these things he was very much under the influence of Platonism. In this context it is interesting to compare his view with Sri Aurobindo's, whose basic premises were altogether different. To quote Sri Aurobindo:[7]

> Man needs freedom of thought, life and action in order that he may grow, otherwise, he will remain fixed where he was, a stunted and static being ....Given a full development and free play of the individual mind, the need of freedom will grow with an immense variation which this development must bring with it, and if only a free play in thought and reason is allowed, but the free play of the intelligent will in life is inhibited by the excessive regulation of the life, then an intolerable contradiction and falsity will be created ....This is the central defect to which a socialist State is bound to be convicted of insufficiency and condemned to pass away before the growth of a new ideal....It is a spiritual, and inner freedom that can alone create a perfect human order and a deeper brotherhood, a yet unfounded law of love is the only sure foundation possible for a perfect social evolution, no other can replace it.

Both Russell and Sri Aurobindo admit the importance of the practical or action aspect of freedom. While for Sri Aurobindo the foundation and true nature of freedom is spirituality, Russell highlights the relevance of reason, calm and dispassionate reason, in enabling man to be really freed. The free mind not only enables man to acquire impersonal and universal knowledge but also equips him better to act for what is just. The unbiased and unprejudiced mind is credited with the power to enlarge ' not only the objects of our thoughts, but also the objects of our actions and our affections '. Man's true freedom consists in the citizenship of the universe and liberation from the thraldom of narrow hopes and fears. Russell is very clear that philosophical contemplation helps us in a very big way to acquire that unique quality of mind given which thought becomes truth-seeking and action just. Sri Aurobindo does not question the importance of reason in man's quest for truth and justice but, as we have noted before, reminds us that ' the business of the reason is intermediate ' and that ' the integral truth of things is truth not of the reason but of the spirit'. The quality and excellence of mind which Sri Aurobindo attributes to the spirit in man are often ascribed to reason by rationalists like Plato and Spinoza. The supposed antithesis between rationalism and spiritualism is ill-founded. The spiritualist apparently concedes this point and then hastens to add that the spirit can perform in a much better way all that reason performs and can perform some other things which reason cannot. From his end the rationalist claims that all the extraordinary powers and excellence of the spirit, like intuition, foresight, larger sympathies and vision, are native to reason itself. If, in terms of ability, propensity and performance, reason and the spirit are found to have produced almost identical results, there is no point in quarrelling over terms or words to describe those results. The only interesting point for me is whether to believe in these powers and characteristics of ' reason ' and ' the spirit ' one has to postulate some metaphysical substances and processes which are not only unquestionable and incorrigible but also inconsistent with the law of parsimony. To my understanding, metaphysics is necessary only in this limited sense that it provides certain heuristic guidelines and some postulates whose empirical bona fides could be progressively (not immediately) established.

Marx is well-known for his rejection of the particular metaphysical Hegelian concept of freedom in which the actual man as a member of civil or bourgeois society is left to his own wills and objectives within his own limited sphere as defined by the State. Granting freedom to individual citizens the State itself is left only with an abstract freedom; and consequently its sovereignty turns out to be more notional than real. While Marx himself is a strong protagonist of the unity of thought and action he finds to his utter dismay that there is no unity between man and man, within man, and between man and the community in bourgeois society. Because of the capitalist mode of production man's thought is alienated from the process and product of his own action. Each man is split into real man and the abstractly ideal 'Sunday' *citoyen*. This class-divided society cannot ensure true harmony; their limited communities of interests are a direct consequence (of course in different manners and degreess) of their common subjection to the process and constraints of production. There is no unity either between the real man, who is free, aliennated and fragmented, and the bourgeois society which is the ground of all freedom but is itself abstract. The political organisation of bourgeois society is entrusted with the difficult responsibility of holding together the individuals, communities and classes characterised by disunity and conflict and in order that it can discharge its responsibilities more and more power is 'given' to it. Alienated and anomic individuals in a class-divided society are not in any way, subjectively or objectively, equipped to communicate successfully between themselves. Besides the regulative supervision of the State their own immediate conditions of living and dispositions of mind persistently discourge and interrupt the process of communication. Man needs 'freedom' not merely to know that he is not free and the reasons thereof; for him the need for freedom is deeper and larger. He needs freedom to act—and his actions are intended to bring about change in the positive as well as negative conditions of his freedom. In other words, freedom has to be objectively and institutionally guaranteed, making it lawfully available to all deserving individuals of society. Freedom is practice- and goal-oriented, even its theoretical aspects carry within them a practical orientation. From this it would be rash to conclude that the intended unity between theory and practice could be easily and spontaneously achieved; the mediation and intervention of some authority is always more or less necessary. In some extraordinary or supernormal cases this authority may be found within man himself, within his own personality structure. For the normal human beings, especially the weak and the poor, the helping hand of the institutional authority becomes necessary and at times even imperative.

The main issue to be decided is how to simultaneously ensure adequate powers to the political authority and enough of freedom to the individual without disrupting the unity of the society as a whole. If we want to avoid the possibility of a stunted growth of the individual, the stagnation of society and the resulting discontent and anarchy, we have to have a *practical* solution of this issue. The root of the issue is to be sought in the fact that the political authority never feels it has adequate power to deliver the goods and therefore goes on asking for more and more power without quite realising the problems of retaining and administering it in a just manner. And the authority also tends to forget that its assumption of more and more power is primarily intended to help the people to establish, maintain and improve an orderly society, and that it is the people who delegate *their* power and thus constitute the ultimate ground of authority. The assumption and delegation of power are implicitly approved of on the understanding that those who delegate the power will be 'ultimately' benefited by those who assume the power on behalf of the authority. When this understanding is in jeopardy due to a communication gap, or for some other reasons like functional inefficiency and deliberate exploitation, the unity of society is threatened by tension and conflict and revolution. In so far as the authority is concerned the orderly inflow and outflow of its power have to be ensured, and insofar as the individual is concerned he must have the benefit of delegation of power to authority. The give-and-take dialectic operative between authority and the individual must be institutionally guaranteed without allowing any one to disrupt the process unilaterally. The dialectic ceases to operate in advancing and growing ellipses or, as it happens in some cases, breaks down altogether for either of two reasons: (*a*) authority's belief, self-induced or due to the inefficiency of the people, that it can retain and exercise its assumed power without caring to answer questions regarding its rationale; or (*b*) the people's refusal to delegate power to authority and to obey the laws already authorised. Neither the exercise of authority nor obedience to the authority could be left to the momentary and *ad hoc* impulses or decisions of the micro-units, officers and citizens, and, therefore, creates the necessity for the institutionalisation of this authority-individual dialectic.

Like most other social issues it is relatively easy to pose the question at the theoretical level, but it is extremely difficult to find a practical solution. Let me reformulate the difficulty of the issue and primarily from the individual pscyhological point of view. If, because of institutional considerations and constraints, an individual has to refrain from taking a decision or executing it, which to the best of his understanding and belief is correct and just, then he is bound to suffer some mental tension and conflict and that in turn is likely to impair his personality structure. Even if the question of conscience or authenticity is set aside for the time being, the implication of psychological wear and tear is enormous and negative. The bounds of individual freedom are restrictively defined by decisions which are due to be taken but are not taken and which, if taken, are not implemented. Restrictive freedom implies crippled responsibility and crippled responsibility implies maimed morality and the seriousness of these deformities should not be underestimated, for, though not immediately, they are bound to affect social groups and institutions in course of time. One may extend the argument against restrictive freedom even further to the psychosomatic level and point out that if man is continuously denied the right to move freely and his movement is seriously restricted, he feels unhappy, sad, angry and frustrated and that these mental reactions in turn create psychological tensions in him and create an attitude of revulsion against the source of the restriction on his freedom. It is one thing to identify the source or ' enemy ' of freedom and it is quite another to eliminate it or even to reduce its power and efficiency. For, ultimately,the underlying issue turns out to be an unquantifiable input-output analysis: whether by reducing the power of authority and restricting the freedom of institutions, i.e., by putting curbs on institutional freedom, we could in fact enlarge the area and the quality of freedom of the individual; or, given the present failings of different individuals and the lack of harmony and convergence in their objectives, whether reduction in the power of authority will not objectively encourage instability and confusion, benefiting the organised and the strong and adding to the misery and exploitation of the weak and the poor in the process. I know my formulation of the issue is very general, but I do believe that, given time and opportunity, it could be presented in a clear and concrete manner. Further, I know, what is worse, that my formulation might be used as an argument in support of authoritarianism.

I am very much for the freedom of the individual and against the idea of giving more power to the State than what is absolutely essential and that too must be for the good and welfare of the individual. On this specific issue there may be difference of emphasis, but in principle I think that it will be agreed to by all concerned. Where we do really differ is not easy to indicate. It is a question of assessment, assessment based on quite a number of variables, dependent and independent, subjective and objective; and the assessing individuals in their different capacities, public and private, attribute different values to the variables, depending on their own different and changing value-scales and preference-schedules. Even if I make, as I do, due allowance for sociological determination, at least in the short run, we must bear in mind that the people who are committed to bringing about social change, though they might recognise the sociological determinants of their ideals and objectives, would in all probability try to reject them in practice. Irrespective of their formal education and ability, individuals must be allowed to choose their ideals and the courses of action to realise those ideals. On behalf of authority one might intervene here and raise the question whether any and every individual *should* be allowed to choose his ideal and the course of action he thinks necessary for realising it; for it is likely to entail conflict with the ideals and the proposed courses of action of other individuals who are also notionally entitled to arrogate to themselves the authority of free decision-making. Even if we agree in principle that individuals should be allowed to decide for themselves not only their own objectives but also their social goals, we have also to agree on the necessity of following certain general forms and norms both in the matter of taking the decision and more so in the matter of executing them. In other words, a workable methodology has to be found by which the innumerable and incompatible decisions of individuals and groups functioning in the same social field could be reconciled without disrupting altogether the existing social order and destroying the very means and mechanisms necessary for free decision-making and decision execution. The fact that even the pro-changer wants to capture the State machinery is a proof that, in spite of its repressive and partisan character, he does need it to realise his objectives.

Whatever is established in the political sphere by power has to be defended and kept going by power. If a social order or a State machinery is established mainly by power and not on the basis of willing obedience or the consent of the people, it will be obliged ultimately to fall back upon that power when challenged. Among the most power-dependent organisations, one counts the police, the army and the State, especially the last. Not that these organisations do not have, besides power, other elements, like willing obedience, free consent and even fraternity, in their structure and function. But what sustains their structural strength and functional efficiency most is well-organised power, power notionally derived from the people and actually exercised by a dominant minority. When the power structure of the State or society loses its functional intimacy and relation with the people, the main power reservoir, it starts suffering from a sense of insecurity, partly real and partly imaginary, and tries to assume more power than what is necessary for realising its declared objectives. At any particular point of time the total power available in a society is bound to be operationally limited; and, that being so, if the State machinery assumes, retains and exercises more power than what is justifiable for the welfare of the people and other commonly accepted objectives, then the people's freedom and power are bound to be adversely affected. In this situation the State machinery alienates itself more and more from its power base, the people, who, institutionally speaking, become increasingly powerless and, psychologically speaking, unhappy and restive. This is a paradoxical situation. The political organisation of power notionally encourages people's power but actually regulates and at times suppresses it. Since political power has no end in itself and it is only one of the means of enabling people (maybe through some organisation) to better their conditions in every sphere of life, a functional and dialectical relation between the political authority and its power base, the people, must be maintained. The paradox of power is structurally similar to the paradox of violence and I have argued this point elsewhere. Many thinkers, as widely different as Marx and Gandhi, find in the very existence of the State an undue concentration of power rationalised in terms of people's welfare and needs. When people's needs are persistently disregarded or narrowly defined and welfare forgotten,the gulf between the people and State authority widens. The powerless people start questioning the authority of the State and the supportless State authority starts suspecting and policing the people and gradually develops an objective situation of unrest, struggle and revolution. To tackle this grave situation the steps called for are restoration of effective communication between the people and the authority, the power base and the power structure and functional inflow and outflow of power between the two, enabling them to fulfil the generally agreed objectives.

Two remarks are in order. First, if the 'generally agreed objectives' are commonly shared by authority and the people, then we have a near ideal situation and do not face any insoluble problem. But what actually happens is this. The objectives which are notionally agreed upon are not acted upon with equal earnestness by all concerned. Authority picks and chooses the objectives which primarily strengthens its power base and only incidentally highlights the secondary objectives which are economically attractive (and not necessarily productive) or have some welfare content. It is true that all people are not deceived by the camouflaged and wrong priorities of authority. But their continuous projection and publicity through the mass media substantially satisfies the underlying motivation. The dissenting minority who can see through this power game of authority often moves to the other extreme in the vehemence of its dissent and loudly speaks of the necessity of crushing authority first before anything which is for the good of the people can really be achieved. One can well appreciate the difficulties put up by the State machinery in the way of people's welfare, but one is not clear how people could be benefited without a well-organised power authority. Whatever might be the character and orientation of the power authority, it cannot fail to see to it that its ability to defend itself against possible opposition is not impaired or eroded. Even the pro-people authority thus willy-nilly develops a *status-quo*ist tendency in it and this becomes gradually manifest in various acts of commission and omission, despite the care and caution that it takes to conceal this tendency. Briefly speaking, there are some difficulties almost inherent in the practical implementation of what we call generally accepted objectives. This brings me to my second remark.

The difficulties are *almost* inherent but not necessarily so. I concede that this distinction is fine, but I must add that it is very important. Had these difficulties been really inherent, the paradox of the power structure could never be solved. The human aspects of this power paradox ordinarily receive much less attention than they really deserve and the structural aspects, which are undoubtedly important, are almost exclusively highlighted. Exclusive attention to one or the other aspect of the paradox makes one often forget that it is the *totality* of the situation which reveals the paradox while the piecemeal approach conceals it. The ambivalence (in the good sense of the term) of the human aspect is of interest for us in this context. The persons who are called upon to represent authority and hold the power structure should develop a principled ambivalence, a sort of rational flexibility of character, in playing their role. To what extent the intended dialectic or functional relationship between authority and the people can work smoothly depends to a great extent on the role played by the chief representatives of authority, their professions and practice and the unity between the two. While they are required to hold their status as defined by the laws of the land they must not put a narrow construction on it justifying their lack of initiative and routinised work and absolving themselves from the responsibility of serving the people appropriately. Responsibility may not be freedom in itself but it is certainly an important aspect of it. If the custodians of the power structure do not behave responsibly and exercise their freedom, they not only cause suffering to the people and alienate them from authority but also confirm their own subjection, the lack of freedom, in a static power structure. What is true of the custodians or representatives of the power structure is also true of the people in general from the other end. Unable to communicate with and influence authority, if the people develop an angry and individualistic attitude and do not cooperate and associate between themselves, as extensively and as intensively as possible, they *qua* individuals cannot change (at least not in any significant manner) the power structure. In other words, the people also must feel responsible to organise a power structure at their own base level so that the more organised power structure at the top responds to their needs or faces the consequences. The responsible man, whether he represents the authority or the people, has always some freedom to bring about change for better and in the intended direction. He himself is the best possible premium to ensure effective communication between the people and the authority and to keep their functional dialectic going.

The arguments based on the assumption of 'generally agreed objectives' lose their main thrust because the assumption itself is unrealistic. The normal man of our society is so deeply involved in his personal and family problems, most of which are economic in origin, that he has little or no enthusiasm left to question the rationale of his restricted freedom. The case of the poor man is even more tragic. He has so deeply reconciled himself to the lack of freedom and the denial of justice that he has almost forgotten the matter of reconciliation itself and taken it, i.e., a sub-normal life, as the norm. If under political or moral inspiration the normal and the poor assert that their objectives could not be downgraded or distorted under the pressure of theoretically constructed 'general objectives' and insist on pursuing their own 'sectarian' or 'partisan' objectives on the ground of economic priority and urgency, I would not know how to dispute it honestly and rationally. This sad situation is liable to two different interpretations.

First, one might argue that since it is a stark reality that most of the normal men and almost all poor men, because of their crushing poverty, lack of education, organisation and freedom, and other factors, are unable to choose and follow their *own* goal, others more favourably placed should be asked and authorised to define their objectives on their behalf. This argument encourages the formation of an aristocratic form of authority and justifies an elitist power structure and all the ancillary agencies and institutions that sustain the latter. Plato's concept of the guardian class is based on this type of argument. Secondly, quite a different, almost contradictory, interpretation, could be given to this situation. Since the proletarian does not have the minimum necessary freedom and power to determine and realise his own objectives and since the privileged and the powerful persistently deny him the cooperation necessary to evolve 'generally agreed objectives', he is left with no other alternative than to try to decide his objectives according to his own understanding and interests. Naturally, this decision, when taken, turns out to be inconsistent with, maybe contradictory to, the objectives of the privileged people and authority. If authority with all its power supports the privileged (and the rich, the perpetuation and promotion of whose interest would further impoverish the proletarian) the proletarian is pushed to an intolerable position, and in that case if the proletarian revolts against authority and if under certain unavoidable circumstances the revolt turns out to be violent, it can hardly be condemned.

If these two interpretations are proved to be equally valid, then there is no common ground of rationally determining and deciding the ' generally agreed objectives ' which would be *almost* equally acceptable to all concerned in a given society. But a human situation in fact need not be so desperate and hopeless; at every point of time human problems are liable to be tackled in more than one ways. Those who speak of ' one and only one ' method of solving the paradox of power and everything that flows out of it, e.g., vulgar affluence, conspicuous consumption, inhuman oppression and unbearable poverty, they may be honest in their convictions, but because of their subjectivity they forget one major implication of human response and freedom, namely, the end-means relationship is never *unique* to a *free* man, no matter whether he represents authority and the privileged class or the proletariat. Free man can always think of and, given conviction and the ability to endure suffering and struggle hard, can find out and follow the alternative means of tackling a situation and solving a problem. It is undoubtedly true that because of his acute economic poverty the proletarian is placed at a very disadvantageous position in relation to others and, moreover, he is subject to severe constraints; therefore, in practice his freedom to explore and establish new means are very restricted. Because of these objective constraints and a subjective sense of despair he at times follows the path of violence and bloodshed. His impatience is understandable and when one recalls his preparedness to die for a cause, one cannot but admire him, despite his being wedded to violence. The problem from the end of authority is somewhat less pressing and serious; for it is already armed with sufficient power to justify its violence, provided it is resorted to under certain permissible circumstances, and one should remember that *permissibility*, given State power, can always be liberally defined. The distinction between killing and capital punishment is drawn in terms of the power of the authority and its ' permissible ' modes of exercise.

Whether we intend to promote or suppress the freedom of the people or of authority or of any other class or group, the intention in question has to be given an institutional form and organisational power. The psychology of intention by itself is far less than what is necessary to give it an effective or influential shape, and when an attempt is made to give it necessary shape it is likely to be resisted because of its incompatibility, real or imaginary, with the ' generally agreed objectives '. When the poor people decide to overthrow authority and the ruling classes or groups by violent means the decision is not of much practical consequence unless the decision to use violent means is given institutional teeth and a durable character. The decision of the poor and oppressed to assert their freedom is often taken under compelling impoverished circumstances and emotional pressures and, consequently, it has been argued that the decision is not really free from an ' objective ' and a ' rational ' point of view. Even if this academic and rationalist argument against the poor man's free decision to use violence for asserting and enlarging his freedom is discounted or rejected for the sake of argument, one important question still remains unanswered. How can an unfree man establish and enjoy the freedom which he deserves by virtue of his being a rational and social being and in the teeth of stiff opposition from the powerful authority and the ruling classes or groups? A realistic answer to this embarrassing and persistent question has to be found; otherwise, our commitment to the noble ideals of freedom and justice will be regarded as purely academic and hollow.

The strength of this criticism has been conceded readily or grudgingly by different thinkers like Marx and Sri Aurobindo for different reasons. Marx's defence of the institutionalisation of violence is rather straightforward and consistent with his social philosophy of revolution. In a class-divided society it is through sustained class struggle that the proletarian has to defend and enlarge his rights and liberties and it is only by finally overthrowing the ruling authority and capturing the State machinery and power that he can get back his historically lost freedom to enable him to grow as a full man. Of course, this argument has been reformulated later on in a watered-down form: the proletariat need not necessarily undertake a violent revolution to be truly free, for, under certain circumstances, a peaceful transition from capitalism to socialism is a distinct possibility. It is true that, all said and done, Sri Aurobindo also recognises the necessity of using 'external method and mechanical means' for helping the proletarian to put an end to his misery and poverty. With his characteristic bias towards spiritual anarchism Sri Aurobindo observes that, pending the emergence of ideal conditions of establishing ideal human unity, we have to make the best possible use of the State machinery and its mechanical arms of power to remove the patent inequities and the irrationalities of the social order. In the very idea of the State he finds the growing totalitarian power of socialism. Totalitaranism and regimentation are said to be the unfortunate aspects of socialism negating human freedom. From his point of view even the capitalist State by immensely expanding its sphere of activities is steadily but inevitably moving towards the socialist goal—socio-political uniformity. To this movement his attitude is somewhat ambivalent; one might say that he appreciates it but does not approve of it. Here the intellectual predicament of the moral positivist becomes evident in its worst form. The spiritual anarchist can at best recognise and put up with the inevitability of the socialist revolution and the establishment of socialist society, but he always longingly looks beyond it.

This reminds one of Hegel's attitude towards the French Revolution. Certainly Hegel was not a revolutionary and his political ideas hardly betray any special sympathy for the downtrodden and the cause of revolution. His philosophical anxiety to let every man grow as a *person* was carefully balanced by his nonethical concern for the absolute character of the State. But, interestingly enough, this does not prevent him from extending his support to the French Revolution. In the scheme of God and, therefore, in the course of history there is nothing accidental and whatever happens has an underlying reason. The distorted surface of some actual phenomenon may conceal its underlying rational character, but ultimately the rationality of history is vindicated and the 'cunning' features of reason are erased. In the face of it the French Revolution might appear, as it did to Hegel, irrational, bloody and violent. Since it did take place, Hegel is convinced that in God's scheme of things it has its necessity, and this necessity, because of its divine affiliations and perspective, is obviously rational. This a speculative argument or way of proving the rationality of the French Revolution on the basis of the well-known metaphysical thesis that 'the real is rational and the rational is real.' I have already tried to show that, given this type of assumption and this type of argument, everything empirical could be shown to be essentially rational without offending the logical law of contradiction. Under the circumstances any anti-revolutionary and pro-establishment man can project himself as a genuine revolutionary 'at heart' despite his profession and practice to the contrary.

In contrast to this one could instructively reflect on Edmund Burke's indictment of the French Revolution. True to his empiricism and conservatism Burke thought of the French Revolution as a sharp and irrational departure from the traditional mode of settlement of political disputes between authority and the people. The fact that the revolution took place is no argument for him to accept it as something rational and welcome. The actual and the ideal, the *is* and the *ought*, need not be taken as identical at bottom, and the pre-reflective propensity of the moral positivist to justify the actual as necessary, though imperfect, embodiment of the ideal must be questioned and resisted. Burke's attitude (and not Hegel's) to the French Revolution appears to me to be consistent. If the distinction between right and wrong, good and bad, and other pairs of moral attributes is virtually denied on the ground that whatever happens is expressive of a necessity, that basic necessity being grounded in the nature of God or in a process leading to Good, then what is primarily encouraged is submissiveness and conformism, which at times become practically indistinguishable from moral opportunism and intellectual eclecticism. In the battle between right and wrong one who is intellectually honest and morally just is obliged to take a 'partisan' stand (of course without being dogmatic about one's rightness and other's wrongness).

In whatever way we grapple with the problem of human unity we encounter two things again and again: one, the gap between the ideal and the actual; and, two, to close the gap we need an institution commanding more power and authority than what we ourselves individually or in groups can actually and lawfully command. In our quest for an ideal human unity we have been always working peacefully or violently or using both the means to narrow down and, if possible, remove the gap between the accepted ideal of unity and the actual state of affairs. Both the ideal and the actual on scrutiny turn out to be historical, changing and growing, and cannot be defined or determined once for all. The ideal of today is different from the ideal of yesterday and the actual of tomorrow will be different from the actual of today; and, all things being equal, what is likely to happen is this: the actual of today modifies *and* reflects the ideal of yesterday; the ideal of today partially reflects the actual of yesterday and the actual of today will be partially reflected in the ideal of tomorrow. The ideal influences the actual and modifies its course; and the actual in its turn adds to the practical content of the ideal and brings it down and makes it relevant to social life from its natural height and abstraction. In the endless dialectic of the ideal and the actual one always observes a *trend of problem-shift and solution-shift*. The nature of our social, economic and political problems are continuously changing and so also our comprehension and acceptable solutions of those problems. In a sense whatever we have and whatever we are is in a flux; and in a sense this is *not* quite so, for in that case the identity of the ' flux ' itself would have remained an incomprehensible enigma forever. What gives stability and identifiable continuity to the social flux is, very generally speaking, structure.

Experience becomes intelligible and meaningful when it is unified and organised by structurally appropriate concepts; otherwise in itself experience is rather vague and does not clearly disclose its objective preference. Extending this epistemological analogy to sociology one might say that social structure lends unity and organisation to what we call historical ' flux ' and makes it articulate and intelligible. It would be incorrect to believe that the social process or historical flux has no structural unity and organisation whatsoever in it and everything is attributed or ascribed to it by the human mind in the form of types, concepts, laws and theories. These categories of thought have a dual role: they are derived from society and applied to society. The acts of derivation and application are performed by the human mind which, influenced by society and its different forms (*not* flux), in its turn influence the latter.

Social change is a continuous process. For theoretical purposes we are obliged to view this process under certain concepts which are taken to be fixed or static in the short run. If we take a ' series ' of ' static ' concepts or pictures of the process in question and carefully compare them under an appropriate generic type, we will find that in the long run even these ' static ' concepts exhibit their historical character and continuity. The histority of the social process itself is almost directly perceptible; but that of the concepts used for the purpose of understanding the process is derivative and becomes clear only within a larger and a longer perspective. It is quite possible to think of the social process and related concepts in a de-historised manner, i.e., in a static and synchronic frame; but this possibility is very theoretical and can hardly provide us with any practical guidance for successful action. Only in exceptional cases and at abstract levels does theory prove to be the terminal point of understanding. Generally speaking, theories and concepts facilitating our understanding of the social process, being influenced as they are by the process itself, are steadily drawn to the practical level. The argument of theoretical necessity cannot entirely lift the concepts, types and theories from the process of social change to which they are being continuously drawn and by which they are being influenced and modified.

The historical character of the intellectual apparatus can be shown in another way, i.e., through the sociology of knowledge. Notwithstanding its theoretical use, the immense corpus of knowledge, because of its public character, is open to social influences, appreciation and criticism, perceptual scrutiny and correction by application. When it is said that concepts and theories are unilaterally applicable to, but not corrigible, by social reality, the implicit assumptions are (*a*) the intellectual means of knowing social reality are not themselves social (a denial of the *sociology* of knowledge); and (*b*) social phenomena are solid states (a denial of the *psychological* or the ' subjective ' aspect of social phenomena). Both these assumptions are highly questionable. The strongest argument against the denial of sociology of knowledge is the changing career of knowledge itself, its own growing or dying character. By questioning the solid or uni-dimensional character of social phenomena one brings to one's notice what is intuitively obvious, i.e., their ' subjective ' aspects, and does not commit oneself to a type of subjective idealism. Once we realise the untenability of these two assumptions, we can well see how concepts and theories prove their appropriateness or lack thereof in relation to social reality and that there is a continuous and critical interaction between the two.

The issue underlying the relation between social concepts and social reality can be formulated in different ways, general and specific. The very general philosophical problem of the relation between form and flux or form and matter has been differently answered, among others, by Pythagoras, Heraclitus, Buddha, Sankara, Russell and Wittgenstein. One extreme view is that pure form is ultimate reality and whatever is in flux is unreal; and the other extreme view is that ultimate reality is flux and form an unreal intellectual abstraction from it. In between the extremes there are other mixed views. When one speaks of the dialectical interaction between social concept and social reality what one has in mind is somewhat like this. Social concepts are partly *a priori* and partly factual or empirical: *a priori*, because these are not inductively derived from social facts; factual, because their validity is dependent on facts. By implication what is conceded is this. Facts have an independent identity of their own and therefore have a say in the determination of the correctness of the concepts which are, at least in respect of ' origin ', *a priori*. This view has a further implication and, that is, the mind is free to conceive reality in ways not hitherto known. I do not readily rule out the possibility that there may be some metaphysical relation between the possible ways of conceiving reality and actual ones.

The self-exceeding character of man is evident in all spheres of his activities. The epistemological dialectic of form and flux has its structurally close analogy present also in the sphere of sociology. This can be shown by analysing the relations between the individual and the group, between the groups themselves and between the group and the society. Group dynamics could be represented as a unitary whole ignoring individual dynamics altogether for theoretical purposes. Similarly, individual dynamics could be phenomenologically studied deliberately disassociating it from group dynamics. Whatever we might do for the sake of theory construction and precision, individual dynamics and group dynamics for all practical purposes are constantly overlapping and interacting. A close phenomenological analysis of the personality structure and the traits of the individual clearly indicates their group orientation or institutional affiliation. A structural analysis of the group and its different components unmistakably reveal their human origin, what they owe to individual human beings. Of course, it is true that individuals *qua* individuals, i.e., as monadic entities, cannot meaningfully communicate and interact between themselves. The individuals we are talking about are all human beings, that is, institutionalised individuals. This is a true description of the human situation and not a new definition of human beings. The most basic trait of the individual is his symbolic ability, the ability to symbolise and the ability to understand the meanings of symbols. Theoretical or logical symbols could be established by definition and thereafter used for the purpose of communication in between those who can follow the definitions. Most of the symbols used by us in practical life are learnt from society and given currency by tradition and convention. And there is a family resemblance between ' following definition ' and ' following tradition and convention '. It also should be mentioned here that theory serves a practical purpose, and from that end one should not interpret the difference between theory and practice as something absolute.

The human element of social structure becomes very clear when we look into the generic functions of the society as a whole and the specific functions of its different institutions or organs. Social structures are not like steel frames, fixed and permanent. Structure in society is what concept is in experience. It brings about unity and organisation in innumerable, complex and changing inter-human and inter-group relations. Like the rules of a game, structures are man-made and yet in the short run relatively independent of the will and action of those who make and use those rules. The role and status of the individual and group of individuals in relation to the society as a whole are directly or indirectly—directly in the case of the group and indirectly in the case of the individual—determined by the structure(s) in question.

The functional aspects of different social units and their changing character very clearly reveal their essential human base. When it is said that man is a self-exceeding being it refers not only to individual human beings but also simultaneously to the concerned social structures and their multitude of generic and specific functions. No society is self-propellant. Its propulsion and stimulus for change, like its function, is due to human thought and action, their grounds, consequences and feedback. No society is self-expansive. Its expansion or lack thereof, i.e., stagnation, like its function, is again due to human thought and action—their grounds, consequences and feedback. My emphasis on the human aspect of social structure and function might be criticised on two scores. First, I might be accused of labouring an obvious point, that is, the intimate and inseparable relation between the individual and society. Secondly, I may be accused of ignoring the importance of the autonomy of group dynamics. If for the time being one decides to ignore the obvious truth about the human base of social structure and function, and concentrates on the study of autonomous workings of group dynamics, one evidently gets a clearer perspective of social development. For example, to understand the development of a language we need not go into how the individual speakers of the language make use of it. Similarly, the results of a macro study of an economy as a whole cannot be derived from the behaviour of its constituent microeconomic units unless some general principles are assumed or taken for granted.

Group dynamics itself may be studied in different ways and from different points of view. I have already indicated that how, from the psychological point of view, the formation and transformation of different social units—family, community and so on—could be understood and explained. The whole process of change can be studied from an ' external ' or sociological point of view as well. What is characterised as a psychological point of view or a sociological one is very broad, at times even vague, and open to further refinement. The psychological approach may be preferred on the simple ground that all social phenomena are not only subjective but also, on ultimate analysis, found to be psychological. The psychological approach may be presented in a simple empirical form and again against a metaphysical background, assuming the whole reality as psychological or spiritual. Of late an influential theory has been offered which not only rejects the metaphysical (background of) psychology but also goes a step further and points out the categorical mistake involved in postulating the mind or a mind-like entity in order to explain psychological concepts. According to this view, the distinction drawn between the ' external ' or sociological point of view and the ' internal ' or psychological one has been drawn on the basis of insufficient logic and inadequate scrutiny of the language of psychology. Personally I do not believe in the autonomy of psychology in the sense that psychological occurrences and dispositions constitute an exclusive category by themselves, existing independently of physical, physiological and social facts and processes. On the contrary, I have good reasons to believe that the latter, with which sociology is concerned, in spite of their human base, could be well understood and explained in terms of certain objective concepts and theories. This view, which at times is called the autonomy of sociology, takes care, on the one hand, of the ' subjective ' aspect of social phenomena, and, on the other, rejects the metaphysical psychological view that the internal-external distinction is drawn within the psychological whole, reality itself.

To understand social development and the historical evolution of larger human aggregates out of smaller ones I think we must look into both individual dynamics and group dynamics and that too both from the psychological point of view and the sociological one, carefully sorting and sifting the means and magnitude of their interaction. An insight into the working of the individual minds provides an important key to the understanding of the workings of society at large, although there is *no* one-to-one or even causal correspondence between the two. Every man has certain ends in his mind and tries to realise them to the extent he *can*. Within each personality structure different ends are almost continuously interacting, converging and diverging but not in identical manners. These ends are not strangers or intruders in the theatre of mind; rather, they are more or less conscious and active products of the mind itself—mind as environed by society and other minds. It has to be finally admitted that ' because ' of my freedom I am responsible for my value-scale, preference-schedule and ends (chosen). Even then looking within and honestly speaking I cannot deny that my ends together with their values and priorities undergo change, at times very significantly and to my own reflective surprise. This means, among other things, that I cannot satisfactorily and permanently organise even the ends of my own choice. Under the ' burden ' of freedom and due to the continuous, but not consistent, influence of society and others on me I am obliged to review and reorganise my ends and redefine their mutual relations, trying all the time to eliminate the causes and elements of divergence from them. Conscious of the unesay gap that exists between the ideal and the actual, I try, primarily in my own interest, to narrow it down to the minimum. What is true of me is more or less true of other people as well. And as a result of all this the scope both of the actual and the ideal steadily grow, bringing in more and more subjects and objects within their growing scope.

This divergence and the convergence of ends are found to have another dimension of added importance at the level of inter-individual relationships. Without a considerable measure of convergence of the individuals' ends our collective or social life itself would be impossible. Ends themselves are primarily a matter of individuals' choice, but when they come across the question of the means necessary for realising those ends they have to depend on institutional means, including technological ones. The peculiarities of individuals are clearly evident in the wide divergence of their ends, but, interestingly enough, their subjection to more or less similar social constraints and conditions oblige them to make use of the existing set of technological means and social institutions. Because of the inherent ambivalence of social institutions, individuals with the same ends, and certainly those with different ends, are inclined to and do use and mould them in diverse ways. Technological means are relatively fixed, but when they fail to answer the changing and growing human needs new innovations are called for and which, once established, function for some length of time at least, in the process generating new needs and issues which partially diverge from the existing ones. Consequently, social structures of all types of human aggregates, small and large, are continuously exposed to functional tension or conflict. A proper understanding of the end-means relationship, even at the individual level, brings to our notice the overlapping character of individual dynamics and group dynamics. Individual ends, however individual they might appear at the point of conception, are necessarily interlinked with institutional questions. In brief, individual dynamics and group dynamics are continuously interacting, injecting elements of divergence in group life and providing it with stimulus or propulsion for growth and expansion.

The identity of the group lies in its structure and generally agreed objectives. The unity of the group does not rule out either the possibility of structural dislocation or that of difference and divergence in generally agreed objectives. In fact, group dynamics are partly sustained by the convergence and unity of individual ends and partly by their difference and divergence. In spite of their inability to agree on all points between themselves, individuals ordinarily do not propose to destroy the structural basis of the group identity, for by allowing the group to function as a group (and, if necessary, in partial disregard of their own ends) they gain more than otherwise. Naturally they think of the difficulties they are likely to face if the group itself disintegrates because of their persistent animosity resulting from conflicting ends. The individual's calculation is generally based on these types of considerations. Left to himself he cannot regulate and use those institutional and technological means which are absolutely necessary for realising *his* basic ends. As he gets the group's assistance in matters which are basic to him, he is prepared to compromise with others and especially with the group itself insofar as the inessential issues are concerned. The functional survival of the group is essential to his own interests. Even in respect of the basic issues he is prepared to put up with certain difficulties rather than destroy the functional equilibrium of the group itself. This of course does not prevent him from asserting his own ends and from questioning and disturbing the divergent ends of the group and others. This he normally does up to a point and not beyond that. It is only in a revolutionary situation that the divergence of the ends within a group becomes sharp and irreconcilable and, therefore, its *functional* unity and identity are seriously threatened. Unless the group can set up within itself some institutional safety valves and shock absorbers, its endogenous divergence and conflicts slow down its forward movement without necessarily destroying its structural forms. To what extent the group can contain the elements of divergence and conflicts within its institutional folds without structurally breaking down depends to a great extent on the quantitative and qualitative nature of its interaction with other groups functioning within the same society. In rare cases the fate and functioning of a group in one society may be influenced by its specially established interaction with a group belonging to a foreign society or within that society itself. I am speaking especially of the different power groups of political society.

One of the best methods to understand the process of social development and the gradual transformation of the smaller human aggregates into larger ones is to analyse the causes, effects and patterns of inter-group dynamics, that is, how different groups with similar and conflicting ends in view interact between themselves. When this method is followed in conjunction with other methods—namely, the methods of analysing intra-individual dynamics, inter-individual dynamics and in-group dynamics—one can not only avoid holistic fallacies and superficialities but also identify various factors, large and small, determining the forms and direction of social development. The relation and interaction between the groups are influenced more by sociological factors and less by psychological ones. It is well known that the functional constituents of the group are not dispositionally and behaviourally homogeneous and therefore group decision and action are not uniform and predictable over a long period of time. This makes inter-group dynamics all the more interesting and complex. And the fruitful study of complex phenomena cannot be carried on by *a* fixed and primitive methodology. The simultaneous and discerning use of several refined methods is called for. Since the group structure itself is the result more or less of the permanent convergence of individual ends in a society, the role of imponderables and accidents should not be exaggerated in human affairs. Fleeting sensations and changing ideas may reveal endless aspects and levels of human personality but do not destroy its structure beyond recognition. Similarly, for instance, different types of individuals may add to or take away the homogeneity of the group but do not destroy its minimum functional unity and identity. The macro-level events and processes of society may not for theoretical reasons disclose their human base and other micro-level social aggregates, but for all practical purposes the latter sustain, enrich and enlarge the former. The unstable patterns of growth and occasional regress of inter-group dynamics cannot be adequately explained unless their more variable individual constituents are borne in mind. It is also because of this fact that the ends of different groups do not necessarily converge. The mere co-existence of and interaction between the groups do not ensure their uniform and continuous coordination with the generally agreed objectives of the society as a whole. The lack of homogeneity and convergence in the ends of different individuals and groups in a society necessitates the subordination of all of them to the authority of the State, although one knows that this authority cannot deliver the goods expected of it unless the individuals and the smaller aggregates generally agree to obey its rules. One cannot think of conducting the high affairs of the State relying all the time on the uncertain support of free individuals constituting and manning different groups with partly convergent and partly divergent ends in view. Consequently, there arises the institutional necessity of putting inter-group relationships on some firm, durable and objective footing. The result is the State—the price of divergence of individual ends and group ends.

The image of the State as an upshot of human discord has not been universally agreed upon. Positive content and objectives have also been found in it or ascribed to it. Some holists are of the view that the State combines in it the highest political authority with the best moral power and that it is the inherent duty of all individuals and groups to obey its command for their own good; and that good has been defined in terms of the accordance of their ends with those of the State. I have already referred to the weakness of the view ascribing unquestionable rationality and morality to State authority. No useful purpose is served at all by a *general* discussion of the rationality or otherwise and the moral content of the State. Perfection and rationality are not intrinsic elements of the concept of the State. Any worthwhile and interesting discussion of the State is bound to be historical, analysing the various aspects of its group dynamics and, at least to some extent, individual dynamics, indicating the ideas and actions of those who are wielding and exercising the authority of the State. If this aspect of the State is relegated to the background because of its obvious empirical character, then what one is left with instead is merely the conceptual aspect of the problem. For the sake of argument, even if one refrains from questioning the supreme moral and legal authority of the State, the question regarding the adequacy of the ground or sanction of the authority remains open. If my analysis of the ground of individual dynamics and group dynamics and of the interaction between the two is correct then one cannot escape the conclusion that the more comprehensive the group the lesser the area of convergence of the concerned ends. As the State happens to be the coordinator and the super-ordinator of all groups, it represents and expresses only the minimal area of convergence of group ends. Is it not rather curious that the minimal area of end-convergence, the minimum common denominator, is chosen as the best ground of and the highest sanction for exercising maximum power? One might interpret it as another facet of the paradox of power structure. Because of the inability of individuals and groups to manage their own affairs they are obliged to delegate power to an authority which, without adequately reflecting the ends and aspirations of individuals, is objectively placed in a position by themselves to rule and regulate them. Perhaps this criticism may be partly met if the legitimate ends and aspirations of individuals and groups are defined in such a manner that their correspondence with those of the State is assured *a priori*, and whatever falls outside the approved and the defined domain of the State is automatically ignored. But in that case the ground of State authority will be determined by the State itself; and the people who are said to be the real base of power would be ignored and will lie outside the functional sphere of the power structure. Given this analysis, I admit, the paradox of the power structure 'disappears'. But then, by implication, the State becomes supreme irrespective of the quality of its performance and, what is worse, the people are de-based to the position of its mere pawns.

The national supremacy of the State becomes real and rational when its power base, consisting of a wide area of convergent ends of different groups and individuals, is fairly and continuously reflected in the decisions taken by the top authority of the State. Often the means of delegation of power from the bottom to the top are distorted because of structural dysfunction or dislocation. And in that case the superstructural authority becomes more an object of fear and criticism than a symbol of collective self-expression. This makes the task of the State authority very difficult. Saddled with the responsibility of co-ordinating, super-ordinating and serving all law-abiding individuals and groups, the authority does not have enough strength and support from its base to discharge duly that responsibility. To make good the deficiency of the structural alienation of authority from its own power base additional 'legal' powers are given to the administrative arms and organs of State authority. Broadly speaking, there are two different methods of using these arms and organs, with two different ends in view. Conscious of its structural alienation and sincerely desirous of making good the resulting deficiency, authority, by a judicious use of its powers, might try to bring about an *integration* in the ends of different individuals and groups, and promoting thereby their compatibility with the most general aims and objectives of the State itself. Another method is based on the assumption that, left to themselves, the ends of individuals and groups cannot converge on any common objective or set of objectives; and to achieve the necessary convergence—necessary for establishing a minimum functional compatibility between the ends of groups and individuals on the one hand, and those of the State on the other—the State authority must exercise its power effectively. If the first method is called *the method of intergration* the second one might be called *the method of regimentation.*

The integrationist's objective is twofold—to minimise ingroup and inter-group divergence of ends, and to promote the maximum possible convergence of ends in both cases. And the strategy is also twofold, namely, to create and promote conditions of vertical integration and to rely more on the durable effects of horizontal integration. The method of integration is based on the recognition of the value of in-group cohesion and is marked by a studied reluctance to use *force* for the purpose of bringing about a horizontal unity of different groups and their ends. Once the integrationist leans too heavily on the strategy of vertical integration he is obliged, because of the various factors involved in the paradox of the power structure, to underrate the importance of individual dynamics and the power base and to overrate the importance of the power-packed superstructure of the apex authority. The continuous downflow of power from above, even if it is legitimatised by laws and rules, cannot be sustained for ever unless it is somewhat suitably compensated by the delegation or up-flow of power from the base. Besides, the other functional dimension of power structure has also to be borne in mind—that is, various intermediary groups not only interact between themselves but also affect and influence the modes and contents of the delegation of power by the people and exercise of it by authority. The integrationist wants to give some real importance to the people's power and thereby tries to preserve the autonomy of intermediary groups so that the State authority cannot unilaterally exercise its power reducing the process of integration into that of regimentation. Integration is not an imposition from above, imposition of authority on the people without their *real* (as distinguished from legal or legalised) consent. Nor is it a process of suppression, suppressing all divergence of ends as if to bring about a convergence of ends by any possible means as a necessary method to achieve the ideal human unity.

The method of regimentation often results from the failure or distortion of the method of integration and, at times, interestingly enough, its origin and efficacy are due to an impatient type and temper of idealism. The guilt of delayed justice forces the idealist to resort to the method of regimentation. The idealist claims that he is a realist and according to him the reality of the situation is such that the compatibility and convergence of ends of different groups, however, laudable they might be in principle, cannot be brought about in practice merely by means of persuasion. Almost all groups, except the groups of the very poor and exploited people, develop vested interests in the perpetuation, if not in the hegemonistic expansion, of their group interests. The method of integration is found inadequate to divest these powerful groups, often aligned to and backed by the State authority, of their propensity to gain and profit, expand and exploit. It would be wrong to think that these groups in their eagerness to gain and profit are disposed to submerge their mutual differences and form largely homogeneous groups. Because of these and other related considerations the regimentationist firmly believes in the necessity of bringing them together by means of force, by setting up and maintaining objective conditions and institutional mechanisms formulating and propagating *uniform* theories and practices, value-scales and preference-schedules. All these are intended to standardise, first, the sociological environment and, then, the psychological and ideological aspects of individual and group life. Standardisation is a part of the method of regimentation. The underlying idea of regimentation is not as negative as it is often made out to be. As I have said, some regimentationists are undoubtedly prompted by very positive and idealistic considerations based on a careful perusal of the workings of some very powerful, hegemonistic and conflicting group dynamics.

Unless the State authority effectively intervenes in containing their activities and redefining their ends in consonance with the needs and aspirations of the poorest groups of people, the proposed democratic delegation of power from the base level to the top level and the public accountability of the modes of exercise of that power by the State authority is likely to exist only on paper without being implemented in practice. In other words, it is only by effectively curbing the negative and conflicting features and functions of the well-entrenched and powerful intermediary groups that the State can really reflect the will of the most deserving and overwhelming majority of the people and thereby enable itself to be the widest possible area of convergence of the individual ends and the group ends. The negativism of the regimentationist may be accepted as a necessary and an intermediate step towards a positive end. The realistic drawback of idealism is not a negation of idealism itself. Nor does it involve any tacit commitment to moral positivism. For the sake of the ideal of human unity all types of diversity, good, bad and indifferent, cannot be equally tolerated on the basis of an untenable metaphysical assumption that whatever is actual is expressive of an undisclosed ideal. We all have to be very careful about one thing. And that is that the positive task of the regimentationist should receive ideological and institutional priority over that of the negative one so that the latter cannot distort or destroy the former. I know this is not an easy proposition.

Whether a society should resort to the method of integration or that of regimentation should not be decided *a priori* and only on the basis of some generalities. It should depend mainly, among other things, on the stage and character of its economic growth, geo-political factors and ideological considerations.

The needs and aspirations of the people in the developed and developing countries are not identical. This becomes evident from an analysis of the different policies and priorities of the planners of the developing countries. Even within the developing countries different models of economic growth are being followed. But one thing is becoming increasingly clear and that is the growing realisation of the people's power and the necessity of shaping State policies in accordance with their basic needs and aspirations. For achieving a faster rate of economic growth with social justice more and more developing countries, through struggle and turmoil, are veering round to an unorthodox model of economic growth and political organisation combining the principles of socialism with the sound characteristics of nationalism. Primary importance is being attached to the task of socialist transformation and the reconstruction of the nation-State on the basis of discipline and austerity, harnessing internal resources and indigenous technology. Though not formally rejected, the ideals of this or that communist internationalism are not being seriously entertained except by a handful of countries. The concept of military treaty organisations are fast outliving their original utility and are increasingly becoming suspect in the eyes of most of the developing countries. A real or imaginary fear of war is leading to increasing preparedness for war and expenditure on weaponry and also dependence on one or the other of the superpowers. But neither preparations nor dependence can provide the necessary strength and confidence to the countries of the third world, promoting their economic growth and the convergence of different group ends. On the contrary, it is being systematically observed that dependence on foreign countries for ostensible security reasons widens the gulf between authority and the people, making authority more vulnerable in the face of invasion from neighbouring countries synchronised with internal insurgency.

While the smaller and less powerful countries are mainly engaged in the task of national reconstruction and improving the quality of the life of their people, the superpowers are interested primarily in promoting their own national interests, maintaining their spheres of influence and trying to replace gradually the balance of fear by a balance of power and, of course, occasionally reiterating their respective ideologies and giving new interpretations to them, depending on the exigencies of the situation. The superpowers and their authorised nominee-States have virtually usurped the UNO's power of stopping war without of course seriously taking over its peace-keeping tasks and thereby reducing the organisation to a mere impressive forum of academic discussion of doubtful importance between international diplomats and dignitaries. The destiny of the world is being shaped not so much by the needs and aspirations of the people as by the wrong priorities of the ruling authorities of different States and their powerful patrons. Avoidable wars are being waged mainly for two reasons—either to secure the minimum needs of the people against the ruling power's policy of exploitation and suppression or because of some superpower's desire to retain an ugly stable for a wrong horse in defence of democracy. Frequently these two reasons overlap. The second type of reason is certainly not going to promote democracy, peace or the ideal of human unity. But the first type, either through the method of integration or that of regimentation, may pave the way for the realisation of these ends.

The fundamental question which consistently disturbs one in this context is, as we have not yet succeeded in removing the conflict and divergence of different group dynamics even in the case of one single State, whether it would be of any real importance to think of the ideal of human unity in its widest sense. It is true that even a theoretical discussion of the different ends and means of human unity has its own importance. Among other things it perhaps makes the people more conscious of the problems of human unity and also of the necessity of sorting them out in their own larger interest. The correct diagnosis of a disease enables one to treat it well. Even if this argument is conceded, and I think it should be, another equally fundamental question remains unanswered, and that is, how best can we promote the ideal of human unity?—whether (*a*) by tackling the pressing problems of in-group and inter-group conflicts and the paradox of the power structure within the State, or (*b*) by trying to abolish war, establish permanent peace and world government? Although there is no inconsistency in principle between these two alternatives and one could simultaneously pursue both, the issue of objectively deciding the priority has to be settled. The ideas of world-union and the world-state have often been regarded or even dismissed as purely utopian. I for one am not of this view. I think that these ideas or 'dreams' reveal a very real dimension and deep-rooted desire of human nature, and simply because these cannot be immediately realised their significance and value must not be underrated. Having recognised the reality of the human craving for the ideal, one should perhaps closely look into the issues involved in realising these ideals. One's commitment to an ideal and the difficulties involved in realising it should not lead one to pin one's faith in some metaphysical principle, 'ensuring' the practical success of the ideal within an undefined time-frame. For this metaphysical faith, although the expression of a noble sentiment, is hardly of any practical consequence.

To establish a world government, what is needed first is a real (*not* notional) world society. Unless there is a large community of interests and a wide area of convergence of State ends it is not clear how the concept of a global society could be given real content. Without a really existent global society the idea of the world-state or the world union with a government of its own, coordinating and super-ordinating the ends and means of other individual States, is bound to remain notional. The notion, basically idealistic in character, is influenced more by desires and hopes and less by a perception of the reality of the situation and trends marked by divergent and conflicting ends.[8]

Even to exist formally and to fulfil its basic responsibilities the world government needs sufficient authority and power. Otherwise it cannot abolish war, enforce law and order, maintain peace and promote the welfare of all citizens irrespective of their immediate group (in this case State) affiliation. We have already observed how within the limited scope of an individual State the governmental authority persistently fails to bring about a convergence of the ends of all individuals and group within its administrative control and also how it fails to reflect the wills of the poorest groups of people in its policies and priorities. Given these serious limitations of national society and its government, one perhaps does not know what is the real basis of one's optimism about the global society and government.

Lack of justice seems to be the main basis of in-group and inter-group conflict. Of all forms of justice perhaps the most important one is economic justice. I take justice as consisting of giving every man his due. It is not easy to define 'every man's due', for it depends on so many variables, individual and social, and the criteria of assessing their values and deciding their priority. Powerful groups have always their say both in framing and in the application of these criteria; and, therefore, although we speak of *every man's due* and *fundamental human rights*, when the time comes for according practical importance to them, groups and States differ and quarrel over their real content. Inter-group conflicts have their exact and inexact parallels in the inter-State sphere. International economic cooperation, for instance, is more an idea than a reality. In spite of several UNCTAD resolutions even one per cent of the GNP of the developed nations is not being made available to the developing nations for their development. The same is substantially true of the modes and areas of use of petrodollars.

The new world order needs, besides economic justice, a new moral and constitutional foundation, a new set of commitments from which individual States will not retreat even in the face of serious internal criticism and opposition. This new foundation and commitment cannot ensure the continued and purposeful existence of global unity, whatever name we give it. Adequate realisation of the significance of this unity within each State must be present and, further, this realisation must be genuine in the sense of being representative of the constituent groups. To be operationally significant at the base human level this ideal demands of different groups and individuals an altogether new approach—the gradual transformation of the allegiance to the national government into a commitment to world unity. International alliance should take precedence over national allegiance. Little analysis is required to understand the difficulties involved in the process of achieving this unity. The inter-group conflict which bedevils the function of the State as a whole will in all probability be reflected in the functioning of the envisaged world-state as well. If we analyse the views of the judges of the International Court on all major issues in the last four decades or so it will be evident that political considerations weighed rather heavily on the minds of the learned judges. I do not propose to say that the influence of politics on the legal process is necessarily pernicious. What I mean here is this: if the views of the Court on the major issues before it could be safely predicted on the basis of some political premises and the national identity of the members of the Bench, then they are bound to be taken more as political than legal. A more serious problem is encountered in evolving an international moral commitment to any cause of world unity. It seems that most of our moral rules result from the social environment as understood and transformed by reason. Unless the international environment takes a concrete perceptible shape and becomes something more than the projection of our own hopes and desires, it is difficult to believe that the moral rules of the world order yet to be born would be equally binding on all the citizens of the world, influencing their political and economic dispositions, decisions, and actions.

Evidently there is a gap between the ideal and the actual. World unity depends to a great extent on the conformity of the foreign policies of different States to moral and constitutional guidelines to be set forth in the binding instruments of international law. Patriotism and idealism require all governments, without any exceptions, to abide by the legal prohibitions on the recourse to force in the world society. Nobody can deny the extreme complexity of international problems relating to war and peace and the important extra-legal setting of these problems. But that is one more reason why we must have clear rules: otherwise, each State might try to act according to its wishes and interests and take refuge behind a self-serving selection of facts and arguments.

Whether we like it or not it is a fact that it is national egoism which puts even second-order self-interest over the first-order interests of other nations. The world society does not know as yet any uniform set of criteria in terms of which all nations can arrange their interests and objectives in a universally agreed value-scale. Therefore, as I have said before, it is not possible under the present-day circumstances to suggest a set of rules and norms on the basis of which the world-union can take a functional form. Obviously, these difficulties involved in realising the ideal of global unity must not be construed as an argument against accepting and trying to realise the ideal itself. But unless we are adequately aware of these difficulties our ideas and actions in this connection are likely to prove utopian and purely academic.

An interesting thing to note in this connection is that with the development of the idea of nationalism the people have become not only increasingly conscious of their own national interests but also of the interests of other nations. Certainly, in principle nationalism is not inconsistent with internationalism. But we learn from historical anthropology that during the early age and the medieval age when national consciousness among the people in general was nil or negligible and the international community of interests a mere concept, there took place a great deal of inter-continental and 'international' (or, should we say, inter-territorial) migration of population and racial intermixtures, whereas in the modern age, thanks to the arts, science and technology, when internationalism has become a living reality, though not a very organised one, large-scale migrations and racial mixtures have relatively gone down. The rules and norms of modern society are in many cases less permissive and liberal than what they had been in the past. Passports, visas, immigration control, emigration regulation, and various other subtle and not so subtle instruments are being used allegedly for the purpose of protecting economic interests, racial purity, cultural homogeneity and other considerations of uneven quality. My purpose in mentioning this well-known fact is not to question the competence of any sovereign society in the matter of framing its immigration or emigration policies. What I want to point out is the inconsistency between a profession of internationalism and the practice of nationalistic chauvinism.

Notwithstanding all these difficulties the modern world is gradually becoming one world, at any rate in some respects. Increasing meetings of human minds and the services provided by machines are all giving content to the concept of world unity. The modern communication system, mass media, fast transport system, well-institutionalised information and the various ramifications of all these are providing more and more points of contact between human minds separated by space and time. Trade and commerce, including the commerce of culture, are also bringing the concerned states closer to each other. The growing needs and aspirations of human beings have been creating objective conditions for the formation of appropriate international institutions which are influencing human minds in a manner which generates larger needs and higher aspirations in them. To sustain these objective conditions and to keep functional the still inadequate structural framework of unity the main desiderata are larger sympathies, deeper understanding of human problems and harmonious conduct of public affairs on the part of all concerned States. The objective and the subjective requirements of the ideal human unity have to be consciously organised into a comprehensive *ideology* and should not be left to the forces of history, spontaneity, or providence. In other words, mankind cannot afford to be a perpetual and passive learner in the school of experience marked by an irrational and avoidable divergence of ends. Whenever an individual or a society seriously intends in a determinate historical situation to exceed itself, it has to set before itself an articulate (as articulate as possible) system of ends and means. This is true also of the worldwide human unity which is in the making. Because of their inherent advantage, ideas can and do influence the course and composition of events not only contemporaneously but also in prospect. Some forms of culture, like religion, literature, music and painting, because of their popularity and immediate appeal to a very wide cross-section of the people, constitute a very important and forward-looking part of ideology. Whatever might be the inherent power and appeal of ideology, in practical affairs, as distinguished from theoretical ones, it cannot be left to work out its own method of propagation or effectuation. It has to be continuously supported by various functional infra-structures and an imaginatively organised *movement* which will take it, whenever possible, to the doorstep of the people rather than always waiting for their being drawn to it. Ideology is a self-exceeding form of experience, and conscious movement gives it the necessary direction and concrete shape.

It is very difficult to conceive of the complete success of mankind in evolving a global society in which the ends and means of individuals, groups and States will be absolutely consistent and the institutional means necessary for their realisation will also be equally coherent and convergent. The absence of ideal conditions should not, and in fact does not, deter us from dreaming the ideal of human unity and practically acting for it. This is a dream which has sustained and inspired mankind even in its darkest days of war and suffering and has been serving it continuously in a positive and optimistic manner. And this is a dream which does matter and makes a lot of difference in our practical attitude to the irrational and unjust gap between the ideal and the actual around us. Of course, dreaming is not enough and it has to be followed up by appropriate action; ideology has to be translated into movement. With courage and confidence we must dream, act and launch movements; but the future lies in the lap of the gods yet to be born.

# 12

# Possibility of Ideology: A Marxian De-construction

The nature and scope of ideology are not free from ambiguity. Etymologically speaking, it is the *logos* of *eidos*,—science of ideas or forms. Historically speaking, the term in its present sense has been first used in France in the eighteenth century. Because of its ambiguity, both etymological and conceptual, ideology lends itself to different,—quite different, if not possible, explications.[1]

Because of its association with the Greek root word *eidos* or form the practice-oriented empiricist is consistently critical of it. Further, the association of Plato's name with *eidos*/form has contributed to the empiricist's annoyance with and criticism of ideology. So, it is to be noted that the first explicatum of ideology assumes it as some proposition or proposal or belief which is essentially transcendental in character. As if it is not to be found in and around our life-world, the world of practice, and it is taken to be a product of transcendental speculation, disregarding the facts of life. Or, evaluatively speaking, it is construed as a product of visionary imagination, again disregarding and transcending social reality.

The first explicatum is obviously critical and pejorative. If ideologies are destined to be cognitively transcendental and evaluatively visionary, they are unlikely to be appreciated and commended. The question is whether by their very nature ideologies are condemned to be so. Or, one might ask, whether there is another type-appreciable and welcome-type of ideologies.

Fortunately, there is another explicatum of ideology which is received with approbation both by the social theorist and the political practitioner. Various forms of empiricism are not equally opposed to ideology.[2] The radical empiricist, who maintains that knowledge is reliable when it is close to experience, i.e. least transcendental in character, is understandably suspicious of the possibility of ideology. To him, ideology is an anathema; it means retreat from practical and living reality. But one can be an empiricist of the modest variety and for him modest extent of transcendentalism is necessary both in realm of knowledge and in that of ethics.

Undoubtedly Marx is an ardent critic of ideology.[3] But his view is to be understood against the backdrop of German idealism propounded by Kant and Fichte, and ingeniously defended by Hegel. The high tide of German idealism understandably led Marx to think that unless its excesses are *practically* corrected ideology could never be shown firm-foot on historical reality. If ideas and ideals are allowed to soar high in the realm of transcendentalism, the specifics of social reality and historical situation are bound to be downgraded. Besides, transcendentalism, excessively scared of social relativism and historical scepticism, tends to ignore the peculiarities of the life-world and is inclined to idealise the empirical, the social and the historical. Exaggerated idealisation inverts the shape of all concerned things. The familiarity of the practical life almost becomes unrecognisable through the eyes of transcendental idealisation. It is primarily for this reason that Marx accuses Hegelian idealism of its alleged programme to make thought to stand on and walk by head. In other words, the primacy of consciousness and indeterminacy of the material-practical world appear to Marx as the grounds for distortion of social reality and historical situation.

The transcendental methodology which the Cartesian and the Kantian philosophers initially thought for vindication of natural science, freeing it from scepticism and relativism, was extended by Hegel and his followers to social sciences. The former believed that science has a rightful claim to be regarded as *universal*. If the 'foundation' of science could be truly discovered, they hoped, this rightful claim would be really established. On the way of transcendental methodology leading to universal science the most formidable road-block was placed by David Hume, who was simultaneously a philosopher, a lawyer and professional historian. By questioning the very basic principle of Descartes, *cogito ergo sum*, I think, therefore, I am, and highlighting the non-availability of self and God within the bounds of human experience, he tried with considerable success to knock out the bottom of transcendental foundationalism and therewith to weaken the universality claim of natural sciences. His rejection of the Cartesian and Lockean arguments in defence of the then reigning paradigm of science, Newtonian mechanics, was basically *theoretical*. His main contention was that scientific inference—induction, eliminative and enumerative—could hardly be theoretically justified. Nonetheless, it has its justification and that justification, to his mind, is *practical*,—customary, conventional, traditional, etc. According to Hume, justification of all cognitive and evaluative statements are to be obtained from human praxis.

Hegel, otherwise committed to the transcendentalist programme for vindication of universal science, had to reckon seriously with the Humean critique of transcendentalism. Break down of the universality claim of science implies that its life and acceptability are confined to different historical epochs and human cultures. Unless Hegel could show the culture-neutral and history-invariant characters of science, its universality claim could not be sustained. Consequently, Hegel embarked upon the method of historism which is only seemingly historical but essentially metaphysical or philosophical. To Hegel *history* is identical with *philosophy* of history. It is only by philosophising history that its rationality could be shown. According to him, the micro event-structures of history do not reveal their underlying rationality. It is only for the metaphysical philosopher like Hegel, looking into the *essential* macro event-structures, to find out and exhibit the rationality of history.[4]

This programme of Hegel was thoroughly unacceptable to Marx. He thought that this Hegelian historiography is going to give rise to a pernicious, speculative and unpractical ideology. The basic reason of Marxian opposition to ideology consists in pointing out the unhistorical and transcendental characters of it. All human products, theoretical as well as practical, are historically situated. The material conditions of living shape these products. Of the material conditions Marx attaches highest importance to the economic ones. At different stages of social development man uses different sorts of technology. *Techne*, or artificial way of encountering nature and problems of living, influences and, in turn, is influenced by *episteme*, or valid mode of knowledge. Man is undoubtedly a tool-using animal. But different types of tools and their modes of use are determined by man's knowledge of his environment and awareness of his needs.

The main modes of economic production as evident from records of archaeology, anthropology and history are (*i*) hunting, fishing, cattle-breeding and agriculture; (*ii*) barter and trade, including maritime commerce ; (*iii*) extensive agricultural production, emergence of kingdom and conquest of foreign territory; (*iv*) large-scale industrial production, foreign trade and emergence of imperialism and capitalism; and, (*v*) decline of imperialism and capitalism, and emergence of socialism. Every mode of production has its own accompanied form of proprietory ownership and relationship. The first form is *tribal*. It is an undeveloped stage of production at which the basic labour unit is family or/and its extension. The second form is *communal*. In the community structure of ownership several tribes merge into an aggregate either by agreement or by conquest and form a *city*. At this stage the division of the labour becomes extra-familial and the antagonism between citizens and slaves becomes sharper. The third form of ownership is *feudal*. The scope of feudal property ownership is territorially extensive. If the second form is said to be *city*-based, it may be characterised as *country*-wide. At the feudal stage the hierarchical structure of land ownership becomes increasingly stratified and rigid, resulting in decrease in social mobility. The antagonism between cities and countrysides becomes wider and sharper. This period is also marked by the rise of the city-based corporative property,—the feudal organisations of trades or guilds. The feudal mode of property ownership chains labourers to their sources of living, reducing them to abject slavery and poverty. Simultaneously, the labour-market is created for trade and rising industry-based workers. On the one hand, feudalism promotes structural rigidity, and, on the other, market mobility. Fortune-seeking soldiers and migratory workers add new dimension to the labour phenomena.

The individuals entering into different modes of property-ownership becomes consciously or unconsciously subject to the forces generated by it. Productive *forces* weave the individuals into definite *relationships*. From productive forces are formed productive relationships. And from productive relationships arise appropriate ideas. The Marxian schemata may be put in this way : Productive Forces → Productive Relationships → Ideology. In brief: F → R → I. Or: (F + R) → 1.[5]

Though Marx is often criticised as a collectivist, it has to be borne in mind that it is he who affirmed, time and again, that the first premise of all human history is the existence and labour of human individuals. Marx's conceptual association with collectivism becomes clearly understandable in the context of his emphasis on the class-based interpretation of history. When he says, for example, that all history is history of class struggle, undoubtedly he takes an aggregates view of history. In many of his later writings he explicitly states that for abstract theoretical purposes it becomes often very necessary to treat individual human beings as embodiment(s) of different economic categories—capital, labour, land, etc. Rightly viewed, there is no incompatibility between (*a*) viewing individuals as authors of history, and (*b*) reviewing individuals *qua* members of different economic categories or classes.[6] History may be presented as individualistic and narrative as well as collectivistic or aggregative. In the narrativist form of history the emphasis is laid on individuals, their dispositions and actions; and the historian's attention is not focused on the concerned societal (or aggregative) pre-suppositions. In the collectivistic mode of presentation of history, though the individuals and their actions are not ignored, the historian's primary attention for theoretical consideration is focused on the societal pre-suppositions, or class affiliation, or collective behaviour of the individuals.

It is to be recalled that this blend of individualism and collectivism is found also in Hegel's historiography or philosophy of history. He also speaks in terms of different classes—bureaucracy, corporate sector and peasantry, and how they relate, differently mediate between, the people and the State (or the sovereign). It is not without justification that Popper presents both Hegel and Marx as defenders of what he calls methodological holism. The methodological holist primarily relies on some such aggregative concepts as class, historical epochs, group spirit for the purpose of constructing social and historical explanations.[7] It is to be noted that the aggregative concepts are theoretical constructs. At least Marx himself seems to be very clear on the point. But so far as thinkers like Hegel and Sri Aurobindo are concerned, the case is somewhat different. They believe in the existence and workings of what they call nation spirit, world spirit, etc. If Marx is a methodological holist, one might point out, extensively quoting both Hegel and Sri Aurobindo, that they are holist both methodologically and substantively.

There is of course a limited point of analogy in the historism of Hegel, Sri Aurobindo and Marx. At this place I am not concerned with the important distinction drawn by Popper between *historicism*, i.e., the law-governed and therefore predictable nature of history and historism, i.e., the changing character of all things due to human agency and action. It is in search of rationality of history and in a bid to avoid contextual—cultural and epochal—scepticism that both Marx and Hegel resort to aggregative exploration and explanation of history. The same point may be said also in respect of Sri Aurobindo's historiography. They all commonly believed that the "noisy" micro-events of history are mainly suppressive, not expressive, of the rationality of history. The fact that historians like H. L. A. Fisher and Peter Geyl are convinced of the possible emergence of endless contingencies, i.e., causally or rationally predictable factors, in history is often attributed to their own inability to go underneath the "noisy" micro event-structures or surface currents, of history. This view of history is intimately connected with the narrativist view of historiography defended by Croce and Collingwood and their modern interpreters like Arthur Danto and William Dray. But interweaving *particular* events in terms of individuals, their actions and situations, the narrativist tries to exhibit a sort of rationality of the concerned events which is no less respectable than the macro rationality of the large-sized events in which Hegel, Marx and Sri Aurobindo are evidently more interested. Additionally, they claim that the narrativist approach clearly unmasks the human face of history. What they leave unsaid is this: the Hegelian, the Marxian and the Aurobindite approaches to history, primarily addressed to solve the problem of rationality of macro events, are obliged to erase or, at any rate, undercut the role of individuals in history. However, Marx reserves his right to add a caveat here by pointing out that he does not highlight the roles of kings, heroes or *avataras* and the significance of political or dynastic history. On the contrary, he claims to have shown the importance of economic factors and the role of common man, especially of labourer, in shaping the course of history and in formation of different economic modes-linked social structures.

The point of disanalogy between Marx, on the one hand, and Hegel and Sri Aurobindo, on the other, is perhaps more central to our understanding of the former's critique or deconstruction of the latter's position. It should be clearly mentioned here that there are many important points of difference between the philosophical position of Hegel and that of Sri Aurobindo. But with reference to the question of ideology their views *vis-à-vis* Marx's have some very important points in common. Understandably, they too, like Marx, have to face the basic questions regarding the place of individuals and social forms in history, how history is made possible, and what are the roots of ideology.

The first premise of history, for both Hegel and Sri Aurobindo, is the *absolute* character of consciousness. By consciousness, to start with, they mean something pure in itself and unrelated to and unmanifested through history. This conceptually primitive, not historically primary, state of consciousness is essentially metaphysical. Hegel calls it Absolute Idea and thinks that it by its very nature is abstract. But as self-positing Subject it has in it the awareness of its abstractness and also the sublative dilectical power to get beyond or rise above this abstract state. Uninfluenced by Hegel, Sri Aurobindo also speaks of God in matter. He is not an absolutist in the strict Hegelian sense. The highest reality, Absolute, for him is intrinsically characterised and accompanied by what he calls executrix-force of consciousness. Consciousness in matter, though sleeping, is working all the time for developing its super-material potentialities,—vital, mental and supramental ones, for example. The movement of the Asbolute, according to Sri Aurobindo, is marked by two rhythms: descent and ascent,—descent of the Divine in matter and the ascent of matter to the Divine. It is for this reason that the base point or the original position of the ascent has often been described as Divine Materialism.

Hegel's position, as mentioned earlier, is substantially similar to Sri Aurobindo's, especially with reference to the gradual unfolding dynamics of evolution. Both are of the view that the basic propulsive force making evolution and its later phase, history, possible is the force of consciousness. This executrix-force is said to be inherent in consciousness itself. In this respect their difference from Marx is very important. The latter claims that the basic locus of consciousness is man and that he as a social being provides the basic dynamics or the propulsive force of evolution and history.

There is one important distinction between Hegel and Sri Aurobindo in respect of their base point or the original position wherefrom evolution starts. Corresponding to Sri Aurobindo's concept of the descent of the Divine in matter, Hegel has no concept in his system; but from the concept of *self-positing* Spirit one gets the impression that he assumes it without explicating it. It seems to me that this concept lends some added plausibility to Sri Aurobindo's account of the ascent of the material to the Divine through life, mind, over-mind and super-mind. The levels of materiality, vitality and consciousness enumerated by Sri Aurobindo are, on his own admission, are merely illustrative or typological, not exhaustive.

Even without the concept of the descent, Hegel takes care of different levels of formations of reality in terms of his dialectical ascent. Pressed by the critics, Hegel finds it difficult to explain why the Absolute Idea through different forms of Objective Spirit and Subjective Spirit will culminate or eventuate its journey in the Absolute Spirit. Besides, whether this journey is only of Thought or also of the experienceable Reality as found in history and science is not clear. Hegel speaks more of the 'dialectical movement' of Thought which, to him, is identical with Reality, and not only occasionally makes use of the concept of evolution. By contrast, Sri Aurobindo consistently speaks in terms of evolution. Only what is involved can and does evolve. Even when the evolution reaches its human level, when, one might say, history begins, Sri Aurobindo keeps on using such terms as cycle, development and unfoldment. Both Hegel and Sri Aurobindo in their historical accounts of human society take note of all social aggregates, small and large, mentioned by Marx—family, commune, tribe and nation. But world-order finds no place in Hegel's scheme of thought.

But Marx's basic objection against the idealist's and the spiritualist's explanation of social aggregates and their corresponding ideologies lies in the latter's *idealisation* of concrete historical situations, giving rise to different forms of theoretical and practical systems, religions, laws, ethics, etc. Ideology comprises both theoretical and practical modes of consciousness unless, of course, the practical ones are found to be firmly rooted in the *material* conditions of living.

Freedom from falsification of ideological consciousness is unobtainable except outside the hitherto known forms of society, i.e., the same are overthrown by the Communist form of revolution and the abolition of private property. Ideologies, whether these are of German or other origin, are by their very nature more or less distant from and alien to the material conditions of existence. Though Marx had German and some other ideologies of his time in the back of his mind while he was developing his critique of ideology, his own view on the subject has an obvious trans-European implication in it. Strictly speaking, in all non-communist forms of society, where private property-based relationships dominate, ideologies cannot assume a transcendental character without being subject to the process of *almost* inevitable falsification. In the case of Marx, his criticism or deconstruction of the feudal and bourgeois ideologies, the contingency of falsification of the true states of affairs is claimed to have been avoided by virtue of his own proximity to and the resulting true consciousness of the emerging revolutionary prospects of the then Europe. The special claim which has been made on behalf of Marx and in support of the Marxian ideology is exceptional to the general rule of falsifying ideology consciousness. This Marxist claim, though exceptional, proves at least one thing: that at least in the communist society, after the abolition of private property, *true* ideology is possible.

False ideologies, the ideologies to be deconstructed, are alien to the material activity and the material intercourse of men, the language of real life. If conception, thought, the mental communication of men and between men are not based on the language of real life, their meanings get inverted. When the human origin and authorship of ideas and ideals are forgotten, their links with the relevant productive forces and relations are not taken into account, these theoretical products turn out to be false,—false within the real life-situations. It is idle to claim that consciousness can be pure and independent of existence of man, from whose life-process and activity it emerges. Marx claims that in the Hegelian ideology things appear as upside-down as in a *camera obscura*. It is analogous to the reception of the physical-life process in a consistently inverted form in human retina. If the ideological forms are not *more or less* directly reflective of the historical life-process, the images they give rise to are both obscure and distorted.[8]

In the name of idealisation of history and in order to save it from scepticism what Hegel does turns out in effect falsification of history. In order to do it successfully, Marx argues, that Hegel first soars high about the concerned material conditions of life, form ideas and then tries to depict them as really transcendental. Their empirical co-relates are portrayed as expressions of the invisible Spirit. The German philosophy of Hegel and Kant, Marx complains, descend from heaven to earth. In their world-views the empirical is a shadowy appearance of the transcendental reality. In different ways both dismiss scientific view of nature and man as merely 'empirically real and transcendentally ideal'. Their refusal to accord the highest possible reality to the scientific world-view is rooted in their preference for some transcendental (and, in some cases, absolute) consciousness. To Kant this consciousness is *formal* and to Hegel it is *substantive*. Under these high sounding jargons the idealist philosopher tries to run away from the material life-process, sublimate it and immunise it against all possible verifications by referring the same to the material conditions of life. The phantoms formed in the head as the result of his historical and interactive life-process are unwittingly claimed by him as something really transcendental. He fails to see that these are not derived from the heaven but objectively rooted in the material existence of life. The philosopher as an ideologue first thinks and deludes himself, and then argues to make us believe that morality, religion, metaphysics, all the rest of ideology and their corresponding forms of consciousness are free, i.e., rootless, or transcendental in their origin. The idealist Kant, for example, defend goodness of Good Will by showing its 'autonomy', i.e., freedom not only from the material conditions of life but also from the physiological affections and the psychological inclinations. Hegel is accused of vindicating freedom of history by dehistorising itself, i.e. cutting it from its material roots and economic conditions.

Marx maintains that the ideologue's rootlessness may be shown in very many ways. To refute scepticism and relativism he hastily resorts to transcendental idealisation. The resulting philosophical system or the world-view which he develops knows no genuine history and knows no real development in it. All history, on scrutiny, turns out to be shadowy history, shadows cast by some imaginary transcendental reality into the cave of the empirical world of science and witnessed by some captive and unconscious cavemen like ourselves, ordinary mortals, the authors of history, Marx's own conclusion is that the real life-situation is not determined by consciousness, but consciousness by the former. Existence is not determined by consciousness, but consciousness by existence. Disembodied consciousness is the product of the empty and abstract speculation of the metaphysian. Unless speculation is put to a stop by real life-experiences, Marx affirms, positive science cannot begin. Positive science is the antithesis of speculative metaphysics. It is concerned with the repeatable practical activity, with the creative aspects of the practical process of the development of man, making positive science possible. Human praxis needs to be given primacy over the theoretical talk about consciousness.[9]

It is clear that Marx's deconstruction of ideology is highly polemical, and at times, it even suffers from over-simplification of the opponent's arguments and sketchiness of his own presentation. But these deficiencies, even if taken in their face value, are substantially removable provided we consult his major works of the later life, particularly, *The Capital.* Marx's arguments may be faulty or weak, but there is no denying of the fact that in support of his views he never fails to give us numerous examples from history. However, one might say, that his examples are very selective, purported only to *justify* his own theses, not to *test*, his favourite theses. Whether this criticism of Marx is just or not is a larger question which cannot be immediately taken up. For, this is precisely Marx's own criticism against Kant's anti-historism and, particularly, against Hegel's proto-historism. These two well known German idealists are criticised by Marx on the ground that their philosophical idealisation of history either negates history altogether, as it is the case with Kant, or reduces it to shadow-dance, as it is the case with Hegel. Whether Marx's arguments against the said ideologues are purely polemical and contrived or really substantial in character will be clearer after we first present schematically the idealist's philosophy or ideology.

I would like to add here that what Marx says against Hegel may be substantially extended against Sri Aurobindo. But since we will take up his view later on I am not going into his position here in details.

The idealist's basic premise is metaphysical and not historical. It affirms the absolute or divine nature of consciousness. Secondly, man is represented as an excerpt or a part of that reality which is essentially consciousness. Thirdly, society is said to be human beings institutionally inter-related. Though in the course of evolution man is posited first, he is not stated to be man without society. Society is a network, relatively durable network, of inter-human relationships. That is, individual men enter into, and disappear from societal relationships but the latter remain in existence. In this sense society may be described as real than individuals. But by *reductio* arguments it is often shown that without individual human beings the expression inter-human societal relationship makes no sense. Finally, ideology is the product of societally related human beings. It purports to give a systematic, not disjointed, image or theoretical picture of reality. Ideology has in it both a cognitive or theoretical component and a normative or practical component. In order to ensure their stability and internal relatability, i.e., freedom from scepticism and relativism, the philosopher tries to portray the philosophical, and not primarily the historical, picture of whole reality. Now, the above elements of the idealist's ideology may be schematically put in this form: Consciousness→Man→Society→Ideology. It may be rewritten thus: taking only the initial letters of the said terms C→M→S→I. Or: C→(M+S)→I. Because of the intimate relation between Man and Society one may like to rewrite the schema in a still simpler form: (C→SM)→I. '(M+S)' stands for Man and Society. 'SM' stands for Social Man. It is to be noted that in the idealist's schema sociality (of man) is rooted in consciousness without (substantive or effective) mediation of materiality. It is a fall-out of the thesis of autonomy. Secondly, the humanity of man is posited without making any explicit reference to the concept of labour, a concept which is consistently highlighted by Marx in transformation of sub-human anthropoids into full-fledged (social) men. Another characteristic of the idealist's ideology is its proclaimed "secular" character. To secularise the concept of Good Will, Kant insulates it both from social existence and human existence. Fear of what he calls anthropologism leads him to dehistorise and dehumanise anthropology. Arguments are offered by him to show that morality and justice based on Good Will are products of absolutely free rationality of man. Kant's treatment of Good Will may be, in effect has been, taken by Marx himself as a paradigm example of how to dehumanise and secularise a central ideological concept. True, neither Kant nor Hegel has any such specific thing to say which entails denial of the existence of social reality or empirical self. But in order to give *universal* status to their ideologies they are, at least they think that they are, required to ignore the association of Good Will with concrete human existence and specific social affiliation. However, it is to be admitted here that Hegel is more circumspective than Kant in formulating his version of Good Will which is destined to be universally acceptable. To Hegel, 'Good Will' is 'God's Will' and to be found only in the German philosophy propounded by himself. One might question: 'Why the *universal* World-Spirit would choose *a particular* philosophy of Germany for its best possible self-expression? From the thesis of chosen philosophy to the thesis of chosen race is not ideologically far off.'

While the "free rational man" of Kant is 'proved' to be the maker of the moral law categorically binding upon the whole of mankind, in 'the rational philosophy' of Hegel the world-spirit finds its consummation. Universal morality and universal rationality are the hall-marks of German ideology. From its transcendental or superstructural standpoint nothing *particular*, even if visible as a passing shadow, is recognised as truly real. Since with the fall of the dusk the owl of Minerva takes its flight and the particulars of history get too close to the philosopher to be seen by him, philosophisation or idealisation of the said contemporary events comes to a stop. History comes to a stop not only in Kant's Kingdom of Ends but also in Hegel's history of philosophy. In highly speculative metaphysical terms an arrogant thesis is politely whispered by Hegel: beyond him philosophy knows no history because in him it has realised its highest and leaving nothing else to be realised further. Self-realisation of philosophy marks the realisation of the highest end of the mankind itself. It is Hegel's Kingdom of God on the Earth, a theoretical surrogate of the World-State. Ideologies, like utopias, Nozick pertinently observes, tend to get frozen, exhausting their motive-force and momentum.[10]

In their ambitious bid to have too many things, one feels and Marx confirms, the German ideologists could achieve only too few ones. However, in fairness to Hegel one should point out that Marx has borrowed a lot from him on the issue of ideology. Even if his criticism of Hegel to the effectt hat the latter inverted the true relation between existence and ideology is accepted as correct, it exposes Marx to the opposite error as pointed out rather dramatically by Merleau-Ponty. If ideology depends on existence, this existential dependence does not itself make existence intelligible. Merleau-Ponty, himself a Marxist of a sort, puts the point thus: if Hegel has committed the error of trying to make dialectic *walk on head*, Marx may be accused of trying to make dialectic *think by feet*. Metaphors apart, the substance of the argument deserves careful attention. Existentially speaking, I am inclined to agree with Marx that ideologies are rooted, directly or indirectly, strongly or weakly, into existence. But that is the only one half,—the ascending half, of the total truth. The other half, the descending half, is equally important. Existence itself is not self-explanatory—certainly not the materialist's own conception of primary, i.e., material, existence. Everything and every being, living or dead, observable entities and theoretical ones, physical objects, numbers and classes, etc. have their existence, thick or thin. It goes without saying that all these things or beings, existentially speaking, are not of the same sort. Some existentialists like Heidegger and Sartre designate human consciousness as the paradigm of Being. Both are deeply 'concerned' with material things but that does not prevent them from affirming the primacy of consciousness as existential reality. There are other mathematical or logical minded materialists like Quine who will readily agree to recognise the being of man and that of a mathematical set, for instance, at par. To *be* is to be a value of a variable (of a proposition): that is how Quine is fond of putting across his case, levelling all sorts of existence nominalistically (or realistically?) at par.

The point I am trying to make is this. Existence, the primary category of Marx, is in need of explanation and that explanation has to come from some sort of ideology, whether it is philosophy or science. It is to be remembered that the terms 'philosophy' and 'science' themselves have been differently conceived by different thinkers down the centuries, from Kant and Hegel to Husserl and Quine. Both Kant and Hegel believed that they were engaged in the difficult task of justifying science showing their affiliation to philosophy. In different ways Comte and Marx tried to make philosophy scientific, preserving its human face. Husserl takes philosophy as 'rigorous science', tracing its origin into, and making it answerable to, the life-world. Quine told us earlier that philosophy is science, neither more nor less. But now he tells us: it is science self-reflective.

Without some sort of reflection on existence the latter cannot be made intelligible. This reflection may be scientific or ideological. Marx himself states that where speculation ends, positive sciences begin. It is true that natural sciences, concerned as they are with physical and chemical phenomena, stand very close to material existence and are verifiable in terms of it. Because of their very nature life-sciences are a little away from the material conditions of life and living. Still more distant from the latter are the social or human sciences like economics, anthropology and demography. Marx was not quite clear where to place economics in the pyramid of knowledge—near the bottom and close to natural sciences or at par with other human sciences. Strictly speaking, 'bourgeois economics' should be placed at par with other human sciences and above the level of life-sciences. But the sort of economics which Marx himself has written could be justifiably placed somewhere near the natural sciences. For, according to him, the due place of different branches of knowledge in the pyramid of knowledge is to be determined by their proximity to, or distance from, the material conditions of life or existence. The falsity-content of a branch of knowledge is due to the extent of its distance from the base of the pyramid, material existence. Judged by that criterion, philosophy, jurisprudence, theology, aesthetics, etc. are to be placed at the superstructure, forming the apex of the pyramid. I have said that material existence itself is in need of explanation in terms of sciences—physical, biological, social, and even of ideology. Marx himself concedes that the causal relation between the super-structure and the sub-structure, *via* the mid-structure of the pyramid, is creatively circular or dialectical, not unilateral. Certainly, according to him, material existence is causally more influential than ideology at the superstructure; but it cannot be said that the latter does not exert any influence at all on the sub-structure. Science *via* technology and propaganda has its own impact on the sub-structure. Even if one accepts Marx's view that ideology consists of the ruling ideas of the ruling class, it does not rule out the possibility of the battle of ideas and ideologies within the State-structure which itself is an expression of the irreconcilability of different class-interests. The more important point is that when the ruling class turns out to be proletarian, according to Marx, its ideology cannot be false. Because of the freedom of its consciousness from the falsity of the ideologies of the feudal and the bourgeois classes, the proletariat can produce a super-structure, which, in spite of its super-structural character, can truly reflect the conditions of material existence. In other words, ideology as such, because of its reflective character, is not condemned to be distortive.

To Marx undoubtedly goes the credit not only of de-constructing the false ideologies authored by others before him but also of leaving the cues for re-constructing the true ones. In the process of de-construction he attacks Kant and Hegel, particularly the latter, but it has not stopped there. Historically speaking, his attack on the young Hegelians like Feuerbach, the Bauer Brothers (Bruno and Edgar) and Stirner is also of deep conceptual significance. To him it appears that their criticism of Hegel is primarily based on the Hegelian premises and therefore could not be sufficiently radical. Commonly with Hegel they thought that the main task of ideology is to liberate man from illusory ideas. His complaint against them is that they are rephrasing the Hegelian view from the opposite end and that 'they are in no way combating the really existing world.' It is not enough to start from human consciousness to understand what God or the Absolute Spirit is like. It is not enough to invert the relation between theology and anthropology and to say that God is a product of man's imagination. The main obstacle to the correct understanding of the situation is not merely the inverted or erroneous relation between man and his ideologies but the real social contradictions which are at the root of this inversion. The young Hegelians could not clearly understand the property-based contradictions between the different ruling classes and their distorted ideologies.

In the second phase of his life, when Marx writes *Grundrisse* (1858), *A Contribution to the Critique of Political Economy* (1859) and *The Capital* (1867), his view on ideology undergoes a significant change. His economic analysis of the capitalist market forces convinces him that the relationship between 'inverted consciousness' (reflected in ideology) and 'inverted reality' is not immediate but mediate—mediated by the operation and competition of the market. The market forces (F) conceal the real economic relations (R) obtained between different classes. Ideology, thus, not only inverts the relation between existence and consciousness, between the sub-structure and the super-structure, but also conceals the contradictory character of the invisible pattern of the relation between the two by highlighting the superficial economic relations. The whole range of values, like freedom, equality, property, are distorted by the market and, what is worse, the distortion itself is sought to be concealed. For example, freedom is defined as freedom to compete; equality is taken to be equal opportunity to compete under the market forces; and property in included under the right of citizenship, which in turn is itself restricted by several interesting stipulations. In brief, all basic values in the bourgeois society are defined, explicitly or implicitly, in terms of free market forces and as exchange values. The second phase of Marx's critique of ideology speaks of double inversion of the relationship between the material conditions of life and the ideas which are said to be thrown up by the same. In his first phase he draws our attention only to the single level of inversion pointed out earlier.[11]

The talk of double inversion of ideology widens its scope and perhaps also makes it rather vague. So one finds that in the later years of his life all sorts of theoretical and practical defects, errors, distortions, and illusions are sought to be shown under the umbrella term 'ideology'. Engels and Kautsky in different ways apparently commit the same error of not discerning the different forms or elements of ideology. That all these are not equally vulnerable or negative is not explicitly understandable to them. For their errors of judgment Marx himself is to be made partly responsible and partly it is due to the fact that the text of *German Ideology* was not available, until the 1920s, to the Marxist thinkers. Plekhanov, Labriola, Lenin, Gramsci and Lukacs are understandably found to be deeply, almost exclusively, impressed by the polemical and negative aspects of ideology. Kautsky, Mehring and Plekhanov may be criticised for presenting Marxism as an eclectical whole of ideology without being very faithful to Marx's own texts. An element of revisionism already emerged in the writings of the first generation of the Marxists.[12]

It is not until 1898 that the positive aspect of the Marxist view of ideology was highlighted by any first-grade Marxist scholar. It stands to Bernstein's credit to point out emphatically that *Marxism as interpreted and practised by the proletariat* is to be taken as an ideology. In this respect his view, often dubbed as revisionist, is an extension of what Mehring and Kautsky had already been saying on the subject. Even in Bernstein's assessment Marxism as an ideology, in spite of its material-existential roots, is *reflective* in character and, therefore, lends itself to different interpretations. By implication he admits the *alien* character of ideology. But that does not prevent one from interpreting it as something positive and which can be used by the working class, under different circumstances, differently and to their advantage.

The more positive aspect of Marxism as an ideology has been brought out by the second and third generations of the Marxists like Lenin, Gramsci, Rosa Luxemberg, Lukacs and Mao Tse-tung who had to apply its basic tenets to different historical situations.

Since I am concerned here mainly with the *conceptual* elements of ideology I do not propose to enter into the details of the historical contexts in and through which it has undergone change. The main points to be noted here are: ideology (*a*) as a polemical critique of idealism making 'inverted' use of the Hegelian dialectic (1840-1844); (*b*) as explication of the basic elements of historical materialism and defining the relation between ideology and its neglected material base (1845-1856), and (*c*) as clarification of the role of the capitalist market forces in the redefinition of doubly inverted relationship between the material base and ideology. (*d*) After Marx's death the concept of ideology underwent two basic changes, viz., (*i*) construed as the totality of forms of social consciousness or ideology as the whole of super-structure and (*ii*) Marxism itself as an ideology. The defenders of *d*(*i*), viz., Plekhanov, Labriola, Gramsci, etc., for understandable reasons indicated earlier, could not spell out the intervening market variables between the material base and the ideological superstructure. The market is responsible not only for distorting the true relation between the super-structure and the sub-structure but also for fostering an increasingly clear awareness of it, the developing contradictions of capitalism, in the minds of the working class because of its direct involvement in the process of the capitalistic mode of production. The positive aspect of Marxism as an ideology became clear to the working class and its leaders because of their proximity to the real life-situations. Revisionists like Bernstein, though accused of distorting Marx's view on the subject, have brought out certain elements not expounded by Marx himself. On the contrary, it is to be recalled that Marx's own view was not uniform and entirely free from ambiguities. And this point has been conceded by Engels himself after Marx's death. The later transformation of the Marxist concept of ideology as a positive theoretical weapon for fighting the cause of the proletariat in different historical situations has, as we know, assumed various shapes and shades. These interpretations have been subjected to different, often confusingly contradictory, types of criticisms, both internal and external. The charge of revisionism and dogmatism have been freely traded by one against another. This shows, among other things, that Marxism, like Hegelianism, its predecessor, had in it many elements and strands which lent themselves not only to alternative but often to contrary interpretations. Creative application also accounts for the diversity of the Marxist concept of ideology.[13]

In spite of the strident Marxist critique of Hegel many significant elements of the latter are found in the Marxist ideology, especially in its positive aspect. The communist society visualised by Marx and Engels, negatively speaking, is not only free from class-antagonism but also, positively speaking, promotive of humanism and internationalism. The communist society knows no nationalism, State and Nation-State. At that stage nationalism gets merged in and attains its fulfilment by sublation or abolition of itself. The antagonism between naturalism and humanism and the antagonistic contradiction between man and nature disappears.

It is true that Marx and Engels were critical of Stirner, Proudhon and Bakunin because of their sympathy for anarchism. At one stage the attempt to link anarchism to Marxism was viewed as a petty bourgeois aberration. Bakunin was accused of adventurism and revolutionary rhetoric characteristic of de-classed intellectuals and the lumpen proletariat. It may be, perhaps it is, true that Bakunin did not get Marx's concept of the State and ideology right. But it is to be remembered that Bakunin was developing a line of thought on his own. A strong streak of anarchism is evident in his philosophy. In his anxiety to get rid of the State as the manifestation of the conflicting class-interests, Bakunin was primarily concerned with the abolition of the State. But Engels took pains to explain that the abolition of the State as such makes no sense to the communist. The disappearance of the State is to be conceived as the consequence of the abolition of private property, capital and the resulting contradictions. But it seems that both Marx and Engels over-simplified the complex contingency of the abolition of the State. It was not to come about automatically. At times both of them give the impression that the State will disappear automatically; but elsewhere, they are careful to point out that the abolition of the State has to be brought about by revolutionary means. In the second half of the twentieth century many leading spokesmen of Marxism have come round to the view that the transition to communism may be peaceful, i.e., without necessitating violent conflict or war. Some of them even go to the extent of suggesting that a new species-consciousness, man's consciousness of mankind, is steadily emerging. It has already been affirmed by the Communist Party of Soviet Union that USSR is no longer a class-State and that it is a State of the *whole* people. To what extent this description is in accord with Marx's own thought on the subject is debatable. But one point is clear: the Marxist is inclined to see that the State becomes free from class-conflict but continues to remain and function as State. But this idea, a part of a comprehensive Marxist ideology, cannot stop half-way-house. Short of the abolition of the State there cannot be a communist society in the true sense. But the modality of its bringing about has to be economic or material and not (class-interest-free) consciousness. To preserve the touch of orthodoxy the scientific Marxist highlights the nature and the end of the communist society and not the classlessness or Statelessness as such.

The pro-Hegelian critic of the Marx might intervene at this stage and remind us that Marx's concept of contradiction-free species-consciousness, man's consciousness of mankind as a whole, is a revived Hegelian concept of Universal Consciousness.[14] Though inverted, its Hegelian inspiration as well as content are unmistakable.

# 13

# Possibility of Utopia: Aurobindite Reconstruction

Aurobindo speaks of 'Two Negations' in the context of ideology in the positive sense. He rejects transcendental ascetism as well as materialist hedonism. The spirit of his 'Two Negations' may be extended to metaphysics, the science of reality. According to him, reality is one and indivisible. Its different parts and levels—matter, life, mind, super-mind-are integrally related. His Integral Monism (*Purnadvaitavad*) is claimed to be the only full-fledged system of philosophy that has been developed in India in the last five hundred years or so.[1] Its comprehensiveness is undeniable and impressive. There is at least one significant aspect of this philosophy which is not there in the Hegelian system and because of it in expounding his view on ideology and utopia, it seems to me, Sri Aurobindo is at an advantage *vis-à-vis* Hegel.

Hegel conceives Reality, to start with, as self-positing Absolute Idea. It is said to be identity of identity and non-identity. The reflection of man as subject makes it increasingly clear. Absolute Idea through historical development, which is hardly distinguishable from logical development of thought, becomes Absolute Spirit or Concrete Reality. This upward journey of Idea to Spirit is understandable. What is left unexplained is whether Spirit has any travel route towards Idea. The Hegelian account from the abstract to the concrete is borne out by history. But the philosopher's question remains: whether this journey has an undisclosed backdrop indicating the journey route of the concrete to the abstract. This philosophical question has an evident bearing on the relation between reality and ideology. Sri Aurobindo's concept of two movements, downward and upward, i.e., descent of the concrete into the abstract and the ascent of the abstract to the concrete, give us a complete, but not circular, account of the relation between reality as consciousness and what it throws up and how it throws up.

In the course of explicating the relation between the material base of the human life and the social and ideological transformations of it the terms often used—descent, ascent, upward journey, downward journey, pyramid etc.,—may rightly appear too much metaphorical. Metaphorical indeed they are. But these metaphors make sense only because of their underlying literal meanings. In science we always come across the concepts of matter, life, mind etc. But when the scientist is called upon to explain them clearly, he is obliged to use many theoretical, as distinguished from observational, terms. To explain the hard stuff of the sense-life we cannot avoid using certain concepts which are not exhaustively definable in terms of the sense-given. This is a scientific requirement which cannot be bypassed either by the materialists like Marx or the idealists like Sri Aurobindo. Because, persuasive presentation of any scientific or even metaphysical view has to follow certain logical laws and methodological rules. It is to be remembered here that neither Marx is a crass empiricist nor Sri Aurobindo oblivious of the obdurate reality of matter, despite his suspicion about empiricism as a theory of knowledge.

At whichever level of reality, material or spiritual, man may decide or is obliged to live, he has in him a suspicion, sleeping or roused, to go beyond it, to rise above it. Self-transcendence is native to human nature. The philosopher of biology may go further and affirm that self-transcendence is the defining characteristic of all living creatures, in general, and of man, in particular. Evolution is not necessarily species-specific. Transmutation of species is not an impossibility. Both internal needs and external causes work together, not necessarily in a complementary way, for transforming a species. Consequently, certain species in the process of transformation or transmutation become weakened, some get strengthened, and some remain stationary for a pretty long span of time. Intergeneration genetic drift is a well-established fact of life. The case of human evolution, with which we are especially concerned, has its own distinct characteristics. All the internal needs which man feels for his transformation are not blind in nature. He is aware not only of the needs but also of their causes and the possible means for fulfilment of the same. Equally he is aware of the constraints, natural and social, amidst which he has to follow up the needs for their fulfilment. By fulfilling his needs man creates for himself other needs. The pursuit of needs may be construed both positively as well as negatively. It may be said that the endless pursuit of needs, marked by multiplier effects, is symptomatic of materialism and consumerism of the modern age and that it is a craze. What is implied is that man as the citizen of a possible sane society will not pursue his needs in the way he is doing today. Positively speaking, the pursuit of needs may be interpreted as an indication of man's evolving and enlarging nature. To use Sri Aurobindo's language: man is a growing god.

The basic question to be dealt with by the student of utopian thought is whether there is a particular point of fulfilment of human needs which we may mark as the end-point of his experience and pursuit of new needs. It is interesting to note that in the tradition of both the eastern and the western thought and religion there is a persistently recurrent theme of utopianism. Had it been an intellectual freak of one individual visionary or another, of one romantic generation or another, the recurrence of the theme could somehow be explained in a dismissive fashion. But because of the continuity of the theme and the distinguished names associated with it, utopianism needs to be taken much more seriously.

If we have to believe thinkers like Marx, Sri Aurobindo and Mannheim, ideologies and utopias differ in degree and not in kind. In the Indian tradition we are told of different forms of utopias, viz., the choice of the eternal *Vrindavan*, the high beautitude of *Brahmaloka* and the ineffable *Nirvana* or the abode of immortal souls, the *Svargya*. In the western tradition we are told of Heaven, the Kingdom of God on the Earth, the Kingdom of Ends, *El Dorado*, etc. The point to be noted here is that when the writers of speculative-philosophical bent of mind speak of utopias, they highlight the *conceivable* forms of transcendent and ideal realms. But there are many thinkers who try to relate utopian modes of thinking with the perceptible-historical world around us. They maintain that these states of affairs amidst which we are placed need not be taken as given for ever and that by our knowledge and action, individual or collective or both, we may transform and transcend the same A moderate degree of transcendence beyond the existing states of affairs will take us to what may be called the ideological realm. But when the transcendence will be fundamental and very comprehensive in nature, we will reach a realm, which, from our present standpoint, will appear utopian. As the distinctions between the past, the present and the future are relative to a definite frame of reference, the differences between the actual, the ideological and the utopian also presuppose a specific point of view. It is not uncommon to speak and hear of the view that even in the squalor and poverty of our contemporary society certain people, the rich and the saints, for example, are living in a dreamland. Even if we discount the metaphoric aspect of this view, there is an element of truth in it, namely, that even in the framework of same time and same society people do believe that certain forms of life are cursed, or exploited or devilish and some others, by contrast, blessed, happy and affluent, or blissful. The utopian modes of thought, for the proper understanding, need not be construed always in theological or metaphysical terms. I think a clearer understanding of them may be found in terms of our available sociological and philosophical concepts.

Sri Aurobindo begins the chapter on 'Matter' in *The Life Divine* with the affirmation that life is 'neither an inexplicable dream nor an impossible evil that has yet become a dolorous fact, but a mighty pulsation of the divine'. In this connection he recalls verse II, chapter III, of *Taittiriya Upanisad,* where it is said that matter is *Brahma.* Though matter is recognised as a foundational principle, its potentiality is declared to be 'the out-flowering divine'. The matter is like a seed wherein the mind, life and body of man are held in a state of creative, organised and seminal form meant for gradual development.

The point which needs to be clarified here is the mechanism or method of development of the higher forms of life out of their material base. Marx, as we have noted, ascribes this evolutionary and creative power to *labour.* It is because of man's labour power that he, initially fastened to the material forces of nature, succeeds in disengaging or freeing himself from the said constraints. Further, labour fosters a power in his brain which is judgemental, inferential and argumentative. Gradually through labour he thus develops in himself the twin powers of reflective action and thought, manual labour and intellectual labour. Manual labour in the case of man, Marx concedes, is not purely physiological, reflexive or instinctive. Man's manual labour is imbued with an intellectual spirit. Similarly, Marx points out, man's intellectual power and its exercise are very much dependent on his biological competency and conditions. Thought is also a sort of activity, requiring organised and convergent exercise of the bodily conditions. The intimate connection between manual labour and intellectual labour may be made clearer by highlighting the fact that there cannot be any disembodied act. The acts or activities which lift man from his individual animal level to collective social one is basically body-based. Body is not exclusive in its nature. It has both a substantive and a mediumistic value and function. Nourished by the forces and resources of nature, it contributes, in turn, to the same, reinforcing it. In and through man nature affirms, expresses, and exceeds itself. Philosophically speaking, in tool-using and sign-using man, nature acquires new capacities and becomes social and self-reflective. Through labour nature becomes human. This very important role assigned to labour in shaping human destiny is not peculiar to Marx.

Sri Aurobindo takes sustained pains to explain the very significant role of body as the physical instrument capable of receiving and reinforcing the forces necessary for self-transcendence. This self-transcendence comprises different aspects of life—physical, mental and the beyond. The body is there not merely to hold the human life back in the case of material forces but prompts it in quest of a higher, richer and better life. Had the body been recalcitrantly self-affirmative, making the human life impervious to the nourishing forces of nature, its development into higher social and spiritual dimensions would have been an impossibility.[2]

Even then, Sri Aurobindo points out, the body has been often construed negatively as a 'continual stumbling-block and rock of offence'. Many spiritual seekers have spoken against the body making it responsible for the bonds which tie them down to the earth. The ascetic curses the body for keeping him earth-bound. The obscure burden of the body and its 'obstinate material grossness' appear unbearable to him. Somatic obsession accounts for his neurotic urge for deliverance from the desires of flesh to the 'purity' of the ascetic life. Collateral to this urge is his sufferings rooted in his body's place in the material world and efforts to deny the existence of that world. Sri Aurobindo fails to understand why many religious teachers curse matter and advise man to 'accept' the presence and the pressure of the physical life as a *negative* test of religious truth. This grudging acceptance, which is nothing but a veiled rejection, of the material conditions of existence, is spiritual failure to see through the positive forces stored in, and unleashed by, nature for man's benefit. The serious perusal of the myths and epics of the East and the West shows that this deeper truth was known to the ancient people who acknowledged Earth the Mother and Heaven the Father as their benevolent parents. Our formula-bound modern intellect, unable to decipher the meaning of the symbolic language of the ancient fails to cut the Gordian knot of the problem of material existence. The Marxist wants to cut it by labour, and the ascetic spiritualist refuses to recognise its reality and angrily withdraws from it. Sri Aurobindo demands of us patience and counsels us to look into the problems of matter seriously and constructively.

The development of contemporary physics appears to Sri Aurobindo as a definite cut in 'the knot of the great denial'. The age-old belief that there is an antagonism between the higher reaches of mind and life and the characteristics of the material bodies of nature seems increasingly unfounded and misunderstood. Inertia of the material bodies and death of the life-forms are not to be taken as a proof of the victory of matter over life. In fact there is no war at all between the two. This imaginary war appears with added complexity at the level of mind. At this level, because of its own limitations, and its subjection to the grossness and inertia of the material conditions, it seems that mind is unable to overcome the passions and sufferings of the bodily existence. Death is taken to be a defeat of mind in war against material inertia and somatic sufferings and the resulting decay. Even while mind gives the impression that it is winning the war, the win is marked by mind's distortion and deformity because of its constant supression of the natural cravings.

It is from Freud and his followers that Sri Aurobindo seems to have received this message. Their basic materialist ontology perhaps prevents them from seeing that the increasing "complexification" of human consciousness is not a set back for the process of human evolution. Viewed from a higher point of view, the principle of apparent discord which appears to govern the relation between mind, body and life may be 'condemned as the trinity of the world, the flesh and the devil'. This view is unacceptable to Sri Aurobindo. The ascetic wants to withdraw from this hopeless war, conceding, by implication, victory to the forces of the trinity. The Freudian finds that the repressions of the socially disapproved impulses, though inevitable, are not only ultimately unsuccessful but also self-corrosive, if not self-destructive. The attempts of man to solve his problems within himself prove tempting but unsuccessful. In his attempts to solve the same by subordinating his ego to the super-ego of society he finds no solace either. At one stage he feels very impotent, insecure and helpless and at another he finds himself supressed, subjected and humiliated. Freud does not find in the Marxist ideology of the communist society any satisfactory solution to the problems of man's natural, aggressive and exploitive tendencies. In search of security, for the time being, individuals may come together and even agree to give up their private rights to property. But that will provide no permanent solution to the problem of his instinctive aggressiveness and self-aggrandizement. What individuals might agree to abide by in search of the much needed security may not satisfy their natural instincts. The civilised man may exchange some part of his chances of happiness for a measure of security. But Freud is persuaded to hold that propertyless group-formation will not bring about the elusive and constantly sought-after happiness.

That the conditions of material existence and the complexity of human nature have to be taken seriously into account before any satisfactory solution of the said problems could be found is openly acknowledged by Sri Aurobindo. In this context his appreciation of the Marxist and the Freudian trends of thought are very noteworthy. The problems of human existence may be viewed from two different ends—the subjective and the objective. Marx, while criticises Hegelian idealism, openly disfavours the phenomenological or the subjective method of understanding the problems of human existence. He is sceptical of the efficacy of this method. While Freud grapples with the discontents of civilisation and looks into the causes and the future of an illusion called religion, he undoubtedly follows the method of psychology and makes use of the concepts of psychology. But that does not mean that he is either an idealist or his approach is subjective in the sense Sri Aurobindo commends. Sri Aurobindo's affirmation that human history has to undergo a Marxist phase but without achieving its elusive goal of an egalitarain utopia is instructive. Freud has promised us no land of eternal *eros*. But one must take due note of his rather realistic diagnosis that mankind's willing subordination of itself to the cultural ethics of the super-ego will not fundamentally change the nature of our problems. Our envisaged transition from the group of the family to the group of humanity as a whole, observes Freud, will not basically alter the inner discontents of our civilisation. For he thinks that 'the innate conflict of ambivalence, from the eternal struggle between the love and death trends' will remain 'inextricably bound up...until perhaps the sense of guilt may swell to a magnitude that individuals can hardly support'. By quoting Goethe he suggests that the course of life, marked by error and guilt, leaves us almost cursed on earth and far distant from God. The debt of materiality is almost sure to banish us from the realm of divinity. This perception may be represented in different idioms—psychological, poetic, theological and sociological. Sociologically speaking, if the individual in his quest of peace voluntarily agrees to identify his lot with that of all others, foregoing everything to be called his own or private, even then he is not going to reach his ideal goal, whether we call it utopia or not.

When Sri Aurobindo was engaged in writing, more or less simultaneously, his major works, *The Life Divine*, *The Ideal of Human Unity*, *The Human Cycle*, *The Foundations of Indian Culture*, etc., in the second decade of the century, Freud had already published his major works, namely, *The Interpretation of Dreams*. (1900), *The Origin and Development of Psychological Analysis* (1910), *Thoughts for the Times on War and Death* (1915), etc. The works of the second and third generations of the Marxists, Bernstein (1850-1932), Kautsky (1854-1938), Plekhanov (1856-1918), Lenin (1870-1924), Rosa Luxemburg (1871-1919), etc. were also published by that time. There is no documentary evidence to assert that Sri Aurobindo was textually familiar with the works of Freud and other Marxists, but it seems he was aware of the contents of their thoughts. The most strong point of Sri Aurobindo is certainly not his scholarship but his broad sweep of mind, deep penetration, power of discernment and, above all, the ability to come out with his own original perceptions of truth.

Sri Aurobindo's reconstruction of ideology and utopia may be claimed to be based on his theories of science and history. Essentially a mystic philosopher, he has tried to be as fair as possible to the facts of science and of history. He does not claim to have any first-hand familiarity with science. But his mastery of history, both of India and of Europe, is undoubtedly impressive. Like Hegel's, his historiography, is basically philosophical. Like the former, he is concerned primarily with the macro-structures and rhythms of history, and not with its micro-events or 'noisy factors'. For the understanding of history he follows the subjectivist method. This is subjectivity without subjectivism. In this respect he acknowledges his special debt to Nietzsche and Lamprecht. The former's philosophy of subjectivity and the latter's periodisation of the German history impressed Sri Aurobindo deeply. Like many European philosophers of the eighteenth and nineteenth centuries, Sri Aurobindo finds at least three rhythms in the history of all known cultures—symbolic (marked by symbolic flexible mentality), typal-conventional (defined by a relative rigidity of the mental cast), and subjective (to be understood in terms of increasing inwardisation of consciousness).[3] It is to be noted that Marx also believes in tri-rhythmic historiography primarily defined in terms of mode of production,—pastoral, feudal and capitalist. During Marx's own life-time communist society was more in the nature of a manifesto to be followed. In order to prepare the people, especially the working class, Marx was theoretically clarifying the historical situation of the time. His double inversion thesis (1857-1867) of the relation between the material existence and ideology was intended to lay the scientific foundation of ideology, freeing it from Hegelian idealism. But, as I have tried to show, if we take seriously the dialectical relation obtained between the material sub-structure and the ideological super-structure, the realm of consciousness as a whole, it becomes difficult to deny the influence of the latter on the former.

It is interesting to note that at about the same time when Marx was working to develop a philosophy against Hegelian idealism, highlighting the primacy of material existence but without denying the importance and influence of ideological consciousness, two European philosophers, starting from different standpoints, were engaged in developing another critique of Hegel, highlighting the primacy of subjectivity and consistently denying the role of straight-jacketed Hegelian rationalism. Kierkegaard (1813-1855) in Denmark and Nietzsche (1844-1900) in Germany were doing philosophy, serious philosophy,but in a rather non-professional style. Kierkegaard was both a philosopher and a religious thinker, who is now regarded as the first important existentialist. Nietzsche combined in himself both philosophical insight and poetic excellence. In 1840s, when Marx was busy in demolishing the influence of Kant and Hegel by writing such monographs as *Critique of Hegel's 'Philosophy of Right'* (1843), *Economic and Philosophical Manuscripts* (1844), *German Ideology* (1845) and the *Communist Manifesto* (1848), Kierkegaard was writing his epoch-making books, *Either/Or: A Fragment of Life* (1843), *The Concept of Dread* (1844), *Concluding Unscientific Postscripts* (1846), etc. His criticism of Hegelianism, apparently unlike Marx's, consists in pointing out the irrationality, insecurity and a sense of void that pervade the human life. Principally, it is opposed to the spirit of Enlightenment, boundless optimism. In ethico-religious terms Kierkegaard brings out the uncertainty of the human life and the necessity of inwardisation of man's consciousness in search of an authentic existence. From another standpoint Marx also highlights the contradiction, confusion and uncertainty of the capitalist society marked by 'free' competition of the market forces. Market pulverises authentic human relationships, alienates one from another, one from what one does and what one produces and even one from one's own self. Following the economic route, Marx shows the tragic and insecured situation of the human life in the capitalist society.

Nietzsche (1844-1900), though appears on the scene a little later, contributes substantially to the same basic theme, the nature of *human* existence, but from a still different point of view. His *The Birth of Tragedy* (1872), published five years after the publication of the *Capital*, Vol. I, also highlights the themes of pessimism and non-conformism. His understanding of the Hellenic history presents two contrasting tendencies—'Apollonian' and the 'Dionysian'. The first tendency is symbolic of the restraint, harmony and measure. All these features are manifest in Greek sculpture and architecture. The Dionysian tendency is marked by an urge for violating all established norms and forms in the drunken frenzy of the Dionysian festivals and the music associated with them. Nietzsche finds no opposition between Dionysus and Apollo, between normlessness and formlessness, on the one hand, and norm and form, on the other. What he means is this. Forms, unless transformed, lose their liveliness. Values, unless transvaluated, lose their value-character. Values, if conventionalised and typified, become dead. Human life and existence in their authentic forms are transparent, leaving nothing beyond, behind or beneath.

It is here one has to look for the reason of Sri Aurobindo's sympathy for Nietzsche. He thinks that the mid-nineteenth century witnessed a subjective turn of human civilisation not only in the history of Europe but also in that of India. In two of his important monographs, *The Renaissance in India* and *The Foundations of Indian Culture*, Sri Aurobindo tries, among other things, to show that the lingering and long typal-conventional summer of the Indian history comes to an end and the reawakening begins. If to Marx, Kierkegaard and Nietzsche go the credit of critical review and revaluation of the European history in the middle of the nineteenth century, the comparable credit, in the Indian context, should be extended to Raja Rammohun Roy, Ramakrishna, Dadabhai Naoroji and Dayanand. I would like to add here very clearly that this sort of historical comparison is bound to be more or less inaccurate. But the point to which I would like to draw people's attention is that both in India and Europe, the spirit of reawakening is mixed—partly religious and partly secular. For recapturing the cultural past of India the leaders of the Indian Renaissance heavily leaned on its interpretations provided by the western scholars. Indigenous ends were sought after and rediscovered by alien, but not necessarily objectionable, means. The difference of the Indian Renaissance from the European one is clear and does not merit our attention and detailed analysis at this place. Sri Aurobindo is perceptive enough to point out that our Renaissance should not be mechanically related to the European Renaissance of the Italian origin. He rightly likens it to the Celtic Renaissance of the nineteenth century, which was partly cultural and partly political. It is therefore no surprise that the pioneers of the Indian Renaissance were not necessarily philosophers and thinkers like Marx and Nietzsche.

The main point made out by Sri Aurobindo referring to Nietzsche is the importance of what he calls the beginning of the subjective age. The spirit of this age did not remain confined long in the land of its origin. It soon reached the shores of India. One might even claim that a halting beginning had started already in India. The European ideas, when reached India, accelarated the pace of it. The Indian reaction to the European cultural stimulus is marked by two trends: one was favourably, if not extra-favourably, disposed towards it and uncritically receptive of it[4] and the other wanted to shy away from it and lean heavily, if not exclusively, on the cultural past of India. Though Sri Aurobindo, because of the close association of his name with yoga and mysticism, is often unjustifiably shown as an exponent of the second trend. I think, it is largely a misrepresentation of his thought, which is yet to be seriously and professionally studied by the critical scholars.

Sri Aurobindo's thought-route to utopia is not apparently very different from that of Hegel and Marx. Having first studied the relation between the material world and human consciousness Sri Aurobindo, like his European counterparts, looks into the structure of such small human aggregates as family, clan, and community. He also analyses the formation-process and the structures of the larger human aggregates like nation, empire and federation of nation-States. His analysis of the concepts of the world-State and world-union are very interesting for two reasons: first, he anticipates the emergence of super-national or international political organisations and secondly, he is perceptive enough also to speak of the inadequacy of the emerging world-State. One who has carefully gone through Sri Aurobindo's critique of the cult of the State will clearly see why he has opposed the concept of the world-State. The mechanical character of the State which suffocates the freedom and the creative aptitudes of its citizens cannot hold them together in a peaceful state of society for long. The key to the understanding of Sri Aurobindo's reconstruction of the ideal of human unity is to be found in his concept of spiritual subjectivity.

Sri Aurobindo draws an important line of distinction between true subjectivism and false subjectivism. The subjectivist, having realised the superficial and the hopeless inadequacy of the objective view of life, the understanding of life from without, starts exploring the powers and potentialities which he has within himself. In a way it is a return of the self from the outer space to the inner space. In the earlier periods of history—the symbolic, the typal-conventional, man's touch with reality was external, other-mediated. The paradigm of other-mediated knowledge of the world finds expression in science. It gives the impression that in this so-called ideal form of knowledge the human nature has been totally excluded and, therefore, it could reach a sort of objectivity which ensures its reliability. Scientific knowledge is wrongly interpreted as antipodal to self-knowledge. When in the subjective age man realises the falsity of this view, he cannot get immediately to the true form of self-knowledge. It is not easy to get out of the veil of self-ignorance. Man's realisation that the deepest truth of his life, thought and action is to be found within himself, though correct, his way of translating it in practice is attended by many limitations. The most important limitation of man's self-knowledge is imposed by the most intimate and influential presence of the material world in him, i.e., his *body*. While Sri Aurobindo recognises the necessity of the material existence for making man realise that he must return to himself in order to get to his deepest truth, he, at the same time, imposes an *alienative* influence on his self-returning or home-coming tendency. The last road-block to man's home-coming is his own body. In his rejection of the ascetic denial Sri Aurobindo recognises the importance of the body; but simultaneously he reminds us that this body should not be confused with the self, the innermost nature of man. In other words, the body-based subjectivity is false. The true subjectivity is spiritual, which takes due note of the body but does not get lost in it. While Sri Aurobindo is not seeking the Kantian ideals of the transcendental self and autonomous will, he is clear about the advisability of withdrawing from man's material environment, without, however, rejecting it totally. The true law of social development requires of man and nation to act and think universalistically, not egoistically, shedding off the body-based egoism, individual as well collective.[5]

Man must make optimal use of his 'God-given impulses' to recognise other human beings, other cultures and countries as integral parts of his true subjective nature. He must not live by himself and for himself. It is in solidarity with all of his kind that the best in him is likely to flower out. Neither the society has any right to crush the individual in the name of socialism for its own betterment nor the individual has the right to disregard the similar rights of others in their individuality as well as collectivity. True subjectivism is a confluence of transcendental self-affirmation and identification of self with all others in the world. He recalls, in this connection, 'the old Indian discovery that our real "I" is the Supreme Being which is our true self and which it is our business to discover and consciously become and, secondly, that, that Being is one in all, expressed in the individual and in the collectivity and only by admitting and realising our unity with others can we entirely fulfil our true self-being'.[6]

The false subjectivist identifies himself with his life and ego. If one's own self-awareness is identified with one's own separate life and separate ego, one is led to believe that one's growth and survival requires exploitation and subjugation of others. False subjectivism may appear both in the life of an individual and that of a collectivity. In its later form, it gives rise to the cult of State and also hegemonism, expansionism and imperialism. The cult of State glorifies the State-machinery and undervalues the significance of the individual self, its potentiality and growth. The weakened individual cannot support long a strong and mindlessly growing State apparatus. Besides, when the individual starts living by his separative self-image, he cannot draw the sustenance he needs to draw from others to support the State apparatus. The upshot of false subjectivism, both individual and collective, makes the individual weak and the State seemingly strong. This unfortunate development cannot go on for any sufficient length of time. For it is against the very nature of man, human institutions and the law of human development.

Sri Aurobindo refers to the German history of the late nineteenth century and the early twentieth century to illustrate his concept of false subjectivism. Its Statism, hegemonism and persistent belligerency are taken to be the unmistakable symptoms of false subjectivism in which this otherwise very gifted nation slided into. It is instructive to recall that Shri Aurobindo's reference to the German ethos of racial superiority and war was made well before the rise of Nazism and the catastrophy of the Second World War. 'The whole root of the German error' seems to lie in its "mistaking life and the body for the self". This "bastered creed" is rejected by Sri Aurobindo on the ground of its 'objective subjectivism which is miles apart from the true goal of a subjective age'. To get out of this false subjectivism the individual and the collectivity have to recognise the distinction between superficial egoism and true self-identity. The former is associated with the physical, economic and cultural adjuncts of an individuals or an aggregative life. It is reinforced by the *analytic* reason which takes an external and mechanical view of the human situation. Beyond the 'bastered creed' of 'subjective materialism' Sri Aurobindo perceives that a new beginning is being made, a 'subjective idealism' is emerging which seeks to see that the inmost aesthetic, ethical, religious, emotional and intellectual aspirations and needs are harmoniously fulfilled without the intervention and distortion of the forces of life which are basically 'pragmatic and outwardgoing'. True subjectivism requires man to get back to his powers within himself as a consistent whole touched by the depth of his inner being and without the colouration of the external adjuncts of life.

The ideal law of social development fosters a spirit of unity in all members of mankind, despite their geographical distance and racial difference. Strictly speaking, the human race, though differently individuated, is gradually approaching 'in the cycles of progression and retrogression' and 'through the countless millenniums of its history' to a convergent goal. The Indian thinkers speak that the true object of all human action is *lokasamgraha*, 'the holding together of the race in its cyclic evolution'. Aggregation and dis-aggregation, totalisation and de-totalisation are not the features only of human history. Their constant feature is to preserve a basic identity amidst all changes. Man simultaneously belongs to his race-type, class-type and also to his kind. The many-sidedness of man's nature is the proof of his integral, not fragmentary or one-dimensional, nature. Man *qua* man does not immediately belong to humanity; the community stands and works as a mid-term between the two. The true law of his own development is not always consciously known to man. Often he follows it half-consciously which accounts for his not infrequent stumblings, hesitations and deviations. But since man cannot be totally alienated from his true nature, even through discord and regimentation he keeps on seeking the goal of liberty and harmony.

Man's ability to remain steadfast in his pursuit of the higher goal is often affected because the reason he relies on for the purpose is somewhat imperfect. The highest power of reason, according to Sri Aurobindo, is the *dis-interested* seeking of true knowledge. But, unfortunately, man's subjection to the external conditions of life makes it very difficult for him to be really *dis-interested* in his pursuit of knowledge. The power to pursue knowledge for its own sake proves often elusive to the common man. However, being influenced as he is by other things and beings, man, by making good use of the reason as governor of life conceives truths and principles of his nature and of others' nature and tries to generalise and formulate them. Since all of us are more or less affiliated to our intermediate modes of living, i.e., different communities, our conceptions turn out to be 'interested' and therefore not always very consistent. The light of reason by itself fails to lead us to the perception of the oneness of all human beings. In order to reach that 'distant' goal we need something else, some other power, other than that of reason. And Sri Aurobindo calls it spiritual power, the power which enables us to overcome the separative forces working against us and strengthens the *sense* of unity which brings us together, closer to our *inmost* unity.

Our dependence on what Sri Aurobindo calls *analytic* reason makes it difficult for us to grasp the inmost truth in us. This type of reason is parasitic in its nature and function. In Sri Aurobindo's language, when our thought-mind is obliged to work upon the materials provided by the sense-mind, the outcome is an abstract copy of reality. Analytic reason does not enable the human mind to get in direct 'touch' with reality; that is the work which can be performed only by intuition. While the latter succeeds in giving us concrete touch of reality, face-to-face encounter with reality, analytic reason, by piecing together the fragments of the sense-mind, can give us only something abstract, sketchy but clear. At times Sri Aurobindo's language gives one the impression that he is following the Kantian theory of knowledge. But that is not entirely correct. Nor does he defend the *dialectical* form and functioning of reason as suggested by Hegel. His view of *ideal* reason is neither dialectical in the Kantian, i.e., illusory, sense, nor in the Hegelian, i.e., progressively constructive, sense. He defends, instead, *integral* reason,—the reason which aims at integrating the sense-conveyed message of the senses with the intuitively or subjectively realised or available truths.[7] His pre-supposition is that the object-ward analytic reason and the reason that works primarily within our subjective mind are not at all unrelated. Our mistaken epistemological perception that they belong to two entirely different hemispheres is due to the analytical, i.e., dis-integrative, functioning of reason and its failure to see the underlying unity of the said two hemispheres. For 'pragmatic and outwardgoing' construction analytic reason has an important role to perform and the results of this performance are ordinarily known as scientific. This form of reason, though inadequate, presents us a picture of reality which is clear and formulable in precise language. Scientific reason informs us clearly of the material forces and conditions within which we are obliged to live. Scientific information is bound to be abstract and its clarity is mainly due to its mathematical treatment and formulation. For the purpose of *understanding* this information-based knowledge is extremely useful. But the highest good and the deepest truth of our life are not made available by it. For the purpose of *living*, for grasping the manysided, rich and complex truth of the life-world, analytic reason is found to be inadequate. Sri Aurobindo speaks of supra-rational good and the spiritual aim of life. In a sense this good is already available with us. In a sense this spiritual aim is also within us, and under it fall other—material, vital and mental—aims of life. The spiritual aim is both supra-rational and integrative of the diverse aims of life.

The term 'spiritual' is ambiguous and, in some quarters, much maligned. Aware of this difficulty with his main premise, Sri Aurobindo takes the trouble of explaining this key concept figuring in it. *Poesis* (Greek) or *poesia* (Latin) means *making* or *composing* which is said to be the life-breath of poetry. *Muse* and *mousike* (Greek) provide the symbolic underpinning of music. 'Spirit' is an idealised form of what is sensible, embodied, or material. Literally it means breath. As without breath life is not life and ceases to be what it is, similarly spirit is symbolic of life dwelling in the world of physical things available to senses and studied by science. The spiritual aim of life is not something alien to our own life. It is not something other-worldly. Every man has in him spirit in the form of self. To the highest, largest and the most perfect self, Sri Aurobindo says, 'we give the name of God'. To realise this highest spiritual presence in us, ordinarily, we follow the path of religion. However, Sri Aurobindo is skeptical about the rightness of this path. Because of its institutional and credal rigidity and conservatism religion, instead of promoting spiritualism, in effect suffocates it. He points out that it is clear from the history of religion that it has often 'stood violently in the way of philosophy and science, burned a Giordano Bruno, imprisoned a Galileo' and in self-defence harmed the very cause of religion itself. It is mainly because of religion's alienation from spiritualism and pinning its dogmatic faith in 'certain fixed intellectual conceptions about God and the world which could not stand scrutiny' of science and philosophy. Consequently, in the name of religion the scrutineers were sought to be suppressed by 'fire and sword'.[8] It is to be noted here that Sri Aurobindo's conception of spiritualism has something exceptional in it. It is neither a fixed concept nor appended to religion as ordinarily understood. This aspect of his thought merits the attention of those who summarily characterise him as a revivalist, if not an obscurantist.

Further, it is to be noted that while Sri Aurobindo recognises the role of scientific reason in shaping the ideal human society, he is also careful to indicate its inadequacy. The socialist solution of human conflict and fragmentation, though ideal in principle, is difficult to bring about in practice. The difficulty is mainly grounded in the inadequacy of the means conceived and the measures proposed by the rationalist mind of man. Taking science-making as its model achievement human reason draws the blue-print of collective being and living which, in practice, fails to take due note of man's intermediate or secondary group-identity. Individual beings are members of mankind only through their secondary group-reference, that is, through their race-group, ethnic type, linguistic type, national type, etc. If this intermediate diversity of mankind is ignored and, in haste, suppressed by reason, the resulting unity does not prove durable and can hardly fulfil the aspirations of the concerned people.

Not only of scientific socialism but also of spiritual anarchism Sri Aurobindo is skeptical. Impatient with the inadequacy of the rationalist blue-print of socialism and the measures adopted to satisfy the material and vital needs of man, the spiritual anarchist, in his eagerness to realise fast his ideal society, highlights the primacy of spiritual approach and the transformation of society. Sri Aurobindo feels that this well-meaning approach unwittingly negates the importance of the vital life 'and promotes an ascetism which instead of purifying and transforming' the *life* of man, 'seeks to suppress and even kill it'. In the name of spiritualism the spiritual anarchist, instead of facilitating the process of blossoming of human life, tends to stiffle it. And as a result of that 'life itself is impoverished or dried up by these severe austerities in its very spring'.[9] His means defeat the end.

In his quest for an ideal unity of mankind Sri Aurobindo spaeks of 'a deeper brotherhood'. This brotherhood will be gladly tolerant of man's intermediate group affiliation and yet will uphold the primacy of the inner unity of all men. It will abjure the path of suppression and regimentation and abandon the use of fire and sword. The true spiritual aim of the universal human society is comprised of the fullness of human life, both individual and collective. The puritanic denial of art and beauty will find no place in it. The aesthetic joy of life will be fully recognised. Science and philosophy will be accorded due importance and not merely tolerated as intellectual pabula. The ideal social order must be characterised by three requirements. Man must seek not only his own freedom but the freedom of all, not only his own perfection but that of all. Secondly, he must realise that his individuality remains imperfect unless it is viewed in the context of the largest universality. He must feel that his own life will not be full unless it becomes an integral part of the universal life. Thirdly, he must not live either for himself or for the secondary group and the State, i.e. for the individual ego or the collective ego. If he wants to get in touch with the highest ideal within his individual ego, he will end up either in the Olympian egoism of a Goethe or the Titanic egoism of a Nietzsche. When man's nature is prepared to answer the said three requirements, he will find the largest and the highest self called God within himself. And that is the take-off point of the 'Kingdom of God on the Earth'. He will then realise the divinity as the Light, Strength, Beauty, Good, Delight, and Immortality, not only indwelling within himself but also manifest in his outer life. It is in every way of his being, *sarvabhavena*, that man will start living in the best possible mode of social order.[10] This social order may be characterised both as human and as divine.

This ideal, however attractive it might appear in its intellectual formulation, is not totally satisfactory to Sri Aurobindo. For he feels, by projecting this ideal we may only create a psychological environment. For creating a new and an ideal social order something much more is needed. A general spiritual awakening and aspiration must be there in mankind for giving concrete shape to this ideal. The necessary motive force of realising this ideal has to be provided more or less by all human beings. Every man must aspire to become perfect in consciousness and action. He must live both inwardly and outwardly motivated by the force and poise of spiritual consciousness. This motive-force can hardly be strengthened by this or that religious movement. Sri Aurobindo fears that the imperfect man of religious movement cannot ordinarily serve this purpose. For, the sustained and free spiritual force which is needed to bring about this social transformation cannot be supplied by the creeds and institutions of any religious movement. Sri Aurobindo's scepticism about the role of institutional support for the realisation of any high-level spiritual aim is evident in his criticism of religious movements as the vehicle of social transformations. In this connection one must recall his criticism of the typal-convention period of history and the institutions ossified by the 'deadening mentality underlying it.' The necessity of the subjective age is to be understood against this 'hard' and discouraging background. Besides, Sri Aurobindo lays emphasis first on the subjectivity of the individual and only through it to that of the group. Otherwise we will commit the error of 'objective subjectivism', "a bastard creed", in Sri Aurobindo's language.

When the secret spirit in man finds its best expression in freedom, equality and brotherhood, the ideal of human unity stands on its firm foot. This firmness cannot be achieved through the 'external machinery' of society. These attributes are eternally there in the human spirit, but their efficacy depends upon their being practically recognised and followed by us in our thought and action. Time and again Sri Aurobindo expresses his doubt about the institutionalised form of religion in the matter of promoting and awakening the basic attributes of the human nature. We have been hearing for ages of this *spiritual religion of humanity*. In a sense it is 'the hope of the future'. In an equally respectable sense it is already there in us as a firm promise of our own nature or, one might say, super-nature. But this universal religion must not be construed in terms of creed, intellectual belief, dogma and ritualism. The failure of different religious orders in awakening the spirit of brotherhood in man is attributed by Sri Aurobindo to their dependence on institutional forms and intellectual formulation. Rightly understood, spiritual humanism is the realisation of the truth that humanity, in spite of its diverse expressions and different cultures, is basically one. This oneness makes our internal co-operation and cultural communication not only possible but also silently imperative. Every man must realise that he cannot reach his highest ideal if his fellowmen cannot also reach the same. The humanity as a race must also realise that unless the individual can enjoy freest and fullest life, its own perfection will not be attainable. Spiritual humanism must have its own discipline so that the richness and strength of spirit do not go waste, and are fully realised for the freest possible expression and development of each man. Sri Aurobindo is quite aware that such a radical development cannot ever take place suddenly and swiftly. The process of unification, the realisation of the highest of the human unity, has to be worked from 'the inner truth to the outer forms'. While the few enlightened human beings will remain engaged in this extremely difficult, important and rewarding work, the rest of the mankind will be obliged to follow 'the institutional and mechanical means'; and at times these means will be boosted and strengthened by the spiritually more gifted human beings. Sri Aurobindo recognises simultaneously the inadequacy of the institutional means for the purpose of the realisation of the ideal of human unity which may understandably be regarded as utopian because of its apparent moral distance from what we are and what we have around us.

Since the main dynamics of the transformation of the human race is in the very nature of man himself, Sri Aurobindo goes into the details of how it works. He speaks not only of the inadequacy of the institutional approach but also that of the mental approach. The powers of mind are analytic, abstract and disintegrative. Consequently what it can achieve is not enough to lift man from his narrow mental groove and enable him to realise his unity with the super-nature of him but above him and the co-operative Nature silently working around him. It is, in this connection, he speaks of the necessity of a supramental change of the whole substance of our being. The supermind is not to be taken as something quite beyond us. It is a 'veiled' part of our 'psychic entity' of which we are not always aware. It is veiled but not screened or enclosed for ever. It can be released and liberated. It evolves slowly and does not disclose its luminous powers all at once. But this slowness of the process can be changed and a faster pace imparted to it, provided we increasingly inwardise our consciousness, get in touch with our deeper powers and try to bring them to the fore of our mind.

Mind finds its expression only in and through a particular level of our 'personality'. Personality, etymologically speaking, is mask-like. In us are the different levels of our personality. The mental personality of today is not to be there for all time to come. It manifests itself in psychic impressions, intellectual ordering and intuitional intelligence. Our thought of Truth, Good and Beauty, the highest three symbols of the divine in us, kindles our spiritual awareness of our supramental power. While the spiritualised consciousness tends always to move above, to climb the higher reaches of consciousness, and to comprehend the distant regions of existence, our mentalised consciousness exhibits a conservative tendency, to stick fast to its own known grounds. By releasing more and more of our dormant powers of consciousness, we can try to lift the lid of our mental chamber. We can outgrow our mental existence also by facilitating freer inflow of all kinds of spiritual experiences. In different planes of our being—mental, vital and even physical—we can receive these higher spiritual experiences. There is something in our life which keeps us prepared to receive the higher powers of consciousness. Our mind can ascend above because there is also an inviting descent from above.

Our mental equipments are not enough for the realisation of the ideal utopia. It is being called utopia not because it is impossible to achieve. It appears utopian only to our limited mental powers. This given character of the limitation need not cramp us and make us believe that we cannot get beyond the same. Sri Aurobindo thinks that our mind is destined to reach the higher levels of Overmind and Super-mind. To put it from the other end, Supermind through Overmind is already at work in our human mind. Supramental nature is said to be a part, upper part, of our own nature. The Supermind does not work always uniformly. It can withhold or keep in reserve its power of knowledge and action. The work of Supermind is facilitated provided mind opens itself up more and more to its powers. Our imperfections and ignorance make it often difficult to open ourselves fully to the Supermind. But according to Sri Aurobindo, we have in us the very effective principle of our inmost being, and he calls it the gnosis. The gnosis is a highest dynamics of the spiritual existence. The gnostic being is fully self-determined and self-driven. Yet, it belongs to a particular group and period. A 'supramental or gnostic race of beings' would not be a race made according to a single type, moulded in a single fixed pattern; for the law of the Supermind is unity fulfilled in diversity and therefore there would be an infinite diversity in the manifestation of the gnostic consciousness although that consciousness would still be one in its basis, in its constitution, in its 'all-revealing and all-uniting order'.[11]

At this stage Sri Aurobindo addresses himself to a problem which is very interesting. Does the transition of the human race to the supramental level imply the end of the evolution from the materially inconscient level? If the spiritual superconscience succeeds in decisively overcoming inertia of the material inconscience, is there any reason still left for the continuation of the process of evolution? This question is likely to remind one of the critic's questions put to Marx whether dialectics would come to an end after the establishment of the ideal communist society? Marx answers these questions by pointing out that even after the abolition of property and property-based socio-economic division man's encounter with nature cannot come to an end. Man's interrogation and utilisation of nature are bound to go on. The resulting benefit might not be uniformly or mechanically accepted by all humans alike. Even when nature is humanised in a friendly way, humanised nature is not likely to be taken with an equal friendliness by all. Therefore, man's emergence out of nature can never reach the level of equal an acceptance or an equal indifference. To deepen man's knowledge of nature the exercises of cognitive exploration have to be carried forward. The results of cognitive exploration of nature being multiform in their feed-back effect on mankind, there will be some non-antagonistic contradictions within the mankind, necessitating internal review and resolution of the same. In other words, man's knowledge of nature will continue to be an on-going process; its resulting effect will generate some productive or creative difference in inter-human relationship; and as a consequence of the said two phenomena the dialectics will remain operative both in the sphere of man-nature and man-man relationship.

Somewhat in a vein analogous to Marx's, Sri Aurobindo affirms that the passage into a gnostic evolution of the supramental level does not bring to an end the movements between the superconscience and the inconscience. The materiality of the inconscience and the spirituality of the superconscience are not an interim law of the natural evolution. The material universe is so durable and pervasive in its character that it is very unlikely to be totally transformed, exhausted, and eliminated, rendering the movement between the said two poles of existence unnecessary. The ascent-descent dialectics operative between matter and spirit are subjected to the law of harmony, the law of unity in diversity and of diversity working out unity. Talking about the human evolution at the gnostic level and beyond Sri Aurobindo maintains that 'it would be no longer an evolution through strife; it would become a harmonious development from stage to stage, from lesser to greater light, from type to higher type of the Power and Beauty of a self-unfolding existence'. Referring to the contingency of the re-appearance of the night of strife because of man's fall from his super-nature to the lower sphere of nature, he observes that it is very unlikely to happen. Once the causes of human struggle and suffering are removed by the power and light of the supermind working in the mankind, it is not understandable why this contingency of relapse or fall should arise. Positively speaking, the change which will be set in motion after the 'firm appearance' of the gnostic personality of the human race is going to be irreversible. Spiritualised human nature is in no need of outer instrumentation. 'The kingdom of utopia within us', to use Sri Aurobindo's term, is potent in its self-existence and self-effectuation and does not depend on an external borrowing. This kingdom, though established by us, is also nature's aim in us. In spiritual self-awareness man becomes fully conscious not only of his existence but also of his being and the full delight of being. In this consciousness man is truly universal in the fullness and freedom of his universality. With the dawning of this consciousness the darkness of our divisive ego disappears.

Sri Aurobindo is quite aware that the picture of utopia drawn by him is likely to be taken with great scepticism by the modern mind because it does not conform to our present scientific conception of nature and seems inconsistent with our 'ignorant preconceptions founded on a limited experience'. He is also aware of the possibility that his view of the human life is likely to be rejected on the alleged ground that it is 'supernatural, miraculous and occult'. Sri Aurobindo is firm in the repudiation of this 'pseudo-scientific' criticism of his utopia. He argues that from the animal point of view human achievements would appear as meaningless and bizzare. That does not make our own achievements really meaningless. In the evolution of the life divine or the utopian super-society Sri Aurobindo finds nothing extraordinary or irrational.

> (T)here would be nothing super-natural or miraculous in such an evolution, except in so far as it would be super-nature or superior nature to ours just as human nature is a super-nature or superior nature to that of animal or plant or material objects. Our mind and its powers, our use of reason, our mental intuition and insight, speech, possibilities of philosophical, scientific, aesthetic discovery of the truths and potencies of being and a control of its forces are an evolution that has taken place; yet it would seem impossible if we took our stand on the limited animal consciousness and its aspects; for, there is nothing there to warrant so prodigious a progression.[12]

Sri Aurobindo is not content only with defending his own view, he also takes the criticism to a higher level or, one might say, to the critic's camp itself. He points out that the most rational and scientific ideal, till the date, [Sri Aurobindo was writing the concluding part of *The Life Divine* either in December, 1918 or January, 1919] that man could think of is marked by vitalistic and materialistic tendencies, 'a search for a perfected economy, and the democratic cults of the average men'. This is undoubtedly an institutional effort to bring in harmony the competitive egos and the conflicting interests of different classes. Sri Aurobindo anticipates, perhaps rightly, that in the name of socialism even if we substitute the communal ego for the individual ego, it would only increase the powers of the State and the forces of regimentation and that the emergence of this super-ego might turn out to be a fatal error. In the name of idealism mankind would remain badly divided. He is persuaded that the main two agencies of 'the socialised life' envisaged by the scientific mind, viz., the 'better mental knowledge' and the 'new social machinery', are not competent enough to tackle the crisis of the age. For neither can reach, touch or transform the human nature, the seed of social discord and global crisis. Imposed uniformity of life and borrowed light of knowledge cannot meet the deepest questions tormenting men.

Another objection which Sri Aurobindo seeks to meet is this. The utopia of his thought might be taken only as a distant dream. For, one apprehends, this radical transformation of the normal human nature is not easy to come about. But somehow even this objection does not appear very convincing to him. He characterises the human phenomenon itself as an abnormalcy in the normalcy of nature. The very evolution of man marks a major break-through, cutting off the gordian knot of matter. However, he is realistic enough to admit that the beginnings of 'this complete transformation of the earth-life', though in the offing, would not be achieved very quickly and decisively. To start with, this transformation will be achieved only in the supernature of some of us and, given time, through arduous efforts, it will reach and kindle others. If the transition of the animality to the humanity is taken as an achievement of our predecessors, it is difficult to disbelieve that with more powers and knowledge to our credit, we will not be able to establish a better society, even a super-society, answering the needs of our own nature. If in the face of the stiff opposition from nature and with relatively 'crude' tools at their disposal, the *homo sapiens* could establish a 'wonderful' social order mainly by their *labour*, it is difficult to believe that the mankind of today would not be able to build an enlarged and enlightened society characterised by unity, diversity, freedom and fraternity. True, human knowledge, especially its scientific form and technology, have created some unprecedented problems for ourselves, which were not there before. Even then human resources, pooled together and judiciously used, can certainly show us the way out. By human resources we must not understand only the institutionalised ones but also, perhaps more so, the internal or the spiritual ones.

The dialectic of development, whether we start from the Marxist premise or the Aurobindite one, will not possibly come to a stop. The exchange of powers between man and nature is going to be an endlessly creative process, disturbed occasionally by regressive or destructive curves.

# 14

# Ideology and Utopia: A Critique

If ideology is not respected, utopia is bound to be suspected. The respect (or lack thereof) for ideology is in most cases found to be utilitarian in its motivation. Even the word 'utilitarian' is somewhat misleading here. For, *utility* of one may be, in fact often is, the *disutility* of another. One's *value* may turn out to be another's *disvalue*. This asymmetry of utility/disutility, value/disvalue presupposes a social order (or arrested disorder) and is marked by heterogeneity, if not conflict, of interests, individual and/or group. There cannot be a universally acceptable value-schedule or preference-order for all persons in a highly stratified society.[1]

The considerations which underlie the lack of respect for ideology, if reinforced, can only explain popular suspicion towards utopia. But the interesting point is that the attitude of most of the people towards utopia is consistently ambivalent. On the one hand, we want to be in a state of individual life or social life which, given our values and beliefs, will be most ideal for us, and, on the other hand, we do not like to be placed in a state of life which might appear insecure and unsafe. The ideal society is expected to provide us such primary goods as justice, equality, freedom from hunger, want and other constraints, etc. in which we are interested.[2] True, if we get used to certain cherished rights and privileges, we almost absorb them in our system, send them down to our unconscious and ordinarily forget about them. Only when we are faced with a "threat" of being deprived of those valued objects, we wake up and get back the value-sense of those otherwise forgotten objects of our normal, at times highly roused, consciousness. The threat of *negation* heightens our sense of *position* as well as that of possession. The whole idea of forgetting or losing or getting back values makes sense only under the assumption that our consciousness is not stable, or that the influences to which our consciousness is exposed are not steady or both.

This issue of heterogeneity or the conflict-riddenness which draws our attention in the context of ideology and the issue of instability or unsteadiness which we encounter in the context of utopia are not totally unrelated. Their relation, though not apparent, may be approached from different points of view. Firstly, it may be contended that so long our individual life or social life, preferably both, is somehow freed from heterogeneity, hierarchy, unevenness, etc., i.e., unless a deep-rooted unity is firmly established in our life, in all its aspects, we would never feel that we have reached an ideal state. This demand of our nature, be it primarily emotional or rational in its origin, tends to be forgetful of the unwelcome consequences of levelling down the unequals or treating them equally. Secondly, the demand for stability is closely related to denial of historism, i.e., the flux view of life, and goads us to an ideal *status* of life which will not be visited and disturbed by the *dynamics* of historical thought and action. Somewhere Nozick remarks that utopian mode of thought is characterised essentially by changelessness. If the said two strands of the ideological and the utopian modes of thought, viz., (*a*) rejection of multiformity and hierarchy, entailing a sort of egalitarianism and (*b*) freezing history to fend off the threats to the human ideal, are interwoven, a new image of utopia seems to emerge. And, that is, the ideal state of life must be uniform and changeless.

I am aware that the above mode of presentation of the basic tenets of ideology and utopia may appear unfair both to the ideologists and the utopians. But, let me say clearly, I have no intention to play down or to undercut their contributions to our understanding of the human yearning for idealism, an almost inevitable outcome of the self-transcending nature of man. It is to be remembered that both Marx and Sri Aurobindo anticipate, though not in identical terms, the possible criticism of anti-historism or anti-dialectical character of their ideals of human unity. Neither the communist society of the former nor the life divine of the latter is a state of frozen history. There seems to be no good reason to regard the 'blueprint' of communism as ideological and the 'picture' of the life divine as utopian except that the idioms in which the former is presented appear familiar to us. But, let us recall Sri Aurobindo's insistence that the divine life is no more distant from the human life than the latter is from the animal life. On the contrary, rightly understood, it is much less. When the resistance of the material conditions of existence is overcome and the life-phenomena become possible, their evolution, evolution of the higher forms, prove to be relatively easy. This may be illustrated by the research findings of palaeontology and zoology. The point has been very persuasively made out, among others, by Pierre Teilhard de Chardin. A practising Christian priest and palaeontologist by professional training, Chardin, on the basis of studies and reflections, concludes that man as a phenomenon has a potentiality in him which is super-human or divine.[3] Many scientists like Julian Huxley finds his conclusion very plausible.

The same point is defended by the historical materialist in the context of sociology. Development of thought-phenomena is found to be less 'obstructed' than that of life-phenomena. When this point is presented in terms of science and technology, it is readily accepted by most of us. When a metaphysician like Sri Aurobindo argues the very same point in his own idioms we complain of obscurity and avoidable transcendentalism. Perhaps it is not surprising that our thought-habits, like our life-habits, exhibit a persistent tendency to move in the realm of familiarity and easy experiential confirmation and feel out of sort, if not baffled, in the face of things 'unknown', 'unfamiliar' and framed in a somewhat 'strange' language.

Certain anomalies of our thought are to be noted at this point. Firstly, at the instance of the scientific materialist many of us believe that our cognitive exploits, natural sciences, for example, because of their proximity to, and testable determinability by, the material conditions of living are more dependable and respectable than those forms of knowledge which do not readily satisfy the said conditions. By their very nature the theories of natural sciences, concerned as they are with the natural phenomena, are required to be experimentally or, at least, observationally testable. The fact that the outcome of tests does not always prove favourable makes one thing clear : in spite of their so-called proximity to the natural phenomena with which they are concerned and also the material conditions of the life of the people who frame these theories, theories do not turn out to be as dependable as ordinarily believed. Besides, the proximity argument appears even more suspect when we recall that all sciences, including the natural ones, are always theory-loaded and do have their metaphysical pre-suppositions.[4] It is methodologically well known that no worthwhile scientific theory can be formulated exclusively in an observational language. In other words, theoretical terms and metaphysical elements of scientific theories show that proximity argument is not as strong as uncritical commonsense prompts us to believe.

Even if it is assumed for the sake of argument that proximity of a theory or a discourse to the set of conditions of its causal origin makes it more respectable, and acceptable, we face another problem and which cannot be so easily solved. If we always try to remain close to our experience, conditions of life, customs, habits, etc., we are accused of conformism and conservatism. Hume, Mill and their modern followers in social sciences like Hayek and Oakeshott have been widely criticised by the socialist and other pro-changers on the ground that in the name of 'solid experience' the ultra-empiricist oppose, in effect, progress both in science and society. On the one hand, the socialist and the materialist are of the view that natural sciences because of their proximity to the material conditions of life, all things being equal, are likely to be more truthful than the social sciences and humanities which are relatively distant from their proclaimed base conditions; on the other hand, they favour progress and revolution in the field both of science and society. Progress requires disturbing the *status quo*, giving rise to puzzles, anomalies and problems. When our social habits and thought-habits are disturbed by new, unfamiliar and 'strange' modes of thought and action, we feel puzzled and we cannot immediately decide how to respond in terms of the available thought and action to the newly emerging situation. When the change in our social structure or thought-structure proves very 'radically' new, we call it revolutionary. Revolution is often described in terms of paradigm-shift or structure-shift. One need not be a Kuhnian to put the matter in this way. Even if it is assumed that many elements and substructures of revolutionary paradigms are different, that does not commit one to the incommensurability thesis. To give any rational verdict on the commensurability or otherwise of different paradigms one has to take a meta-paradigmatic or transcendental point of view. This is a pro-realistic and anti-relavistic requirement.[5]

Whether one stands for reform or revolution in science or society or both, one must be prepared to distance oneself from the already obtained state of affairs around and within oneself. If in order to undo the conservative miseffects of social and scientific positivism we favour distance from what we are and what the things are around us, it is not easy to justify the view that truly creative consciousness, theoretical as well as practical, is required to be proximate to the material conditions of living. Unless we succeed in disengaging ourselves from our old habits of living and the used modes of thinking, how can we be rationally expected to do something really innovative or creative ? If, on the other hand, in our bid to be creative and innovative we get far away from our moorings or roots, will not our creations exhibit an alien or outlandish character? This is the main dilemma which every protagonist of ideology or that of utopia has to face and answer.

A possible way out of the said dilemma may be explored along this line. We must first realise that method of constructing and deconstructing a sociological theory and that of forming and reforming an ideological view are not essentially the same. Our commitment to methodological monism needs to be critically reviewed. The logic of thought and the logic of action are not same all along the line. Admittedly, thought is an essential input for rational action. That input is necessary but not sufficient for ensuring the goal-achievement of the concerned action. In the course of performing an action, the actor is required to face and tackle many imponderables not previously thought out. In brief, the field of action proves much more complex than that of thought. One might say that the difference between the logic of thought and the logic of action is a matter of degree. If one is a methodological monist, be he a materialist like Marx or spiritualist like Hegel or Sri Aurobindo, every difference to him, *essentially* speaking, is a matter of degree and not of kind. But on this metaphysical ground one must not under-rate the important difference that is there between the ways of thinking and the ways of acting. Through action or praxis—the latter seems to be the more appropriate term in this context—thought is not only corrected but also gets more meaningfully articulated. One might almost say that thought needs praxis for its full or best possible self-articulation. If this requirement of the primacy of praxis is clearly borne in mind and actually followed, the possible blemishes of abstract or higher-level thoughts, due to their distance from the sub-structural material conditions of life, may be substantially removed. In that case, after encouraging 'daring thought', 'bold conjectures', and 'creative enterprises' we need not criticise and abandon them half-way-house on the alleged ground of their alienation or rootlessness, i.e. distance from the base conditions.[6]

A word of caution here. The term 'praxis' must not be narrowly conceived. One of the reasons, why we preferred 'praxis' to 'action' is that the connotation of the latter is rather limited. It is not clear to me why thought, at least some of its modes, should not be deemed very close to praxis. It is well understood that certain modes of thought, construction of axiomatic system or formulation of the proof of a theorem, for example, cannot be taken to be practical in any ordinary sense of the term. But there are certainly many other modes of thought which are intended to be tested or terminated in some or other practice and the logic of these modes of thoughts can certainly be brought close to the logic of praxis itself. Even with reference to the axiomatic and proof-formulating modes of thought it may be shown that they too have some or other practical terminal. For example, without its rules of interpretation being given, an axiomatic system by itself is not of much interest or use to us. Proof is language-bound; the language presupposed by rigorous proof is always constructed, i.e. not natural; and it is found, on scrutiny, that the adequacy or otherwise of a constructed language cannot be decided without reference to the concerned natural language, i.e., language in use.

That man is a self-exceeding creature is not disputed either by the critic of ideology and utopia or, certainly not, by their defender. The point is substantiated both by the recorded history of mankind and by the theories of evolution, genotypic and phenotypic. That we are progressing, discovering new secrets of the physical world and the life-world, and abandoning certain old views, beliefs and values is a commonplace conviction. Even those who are accused of traditionalism, conventionalism and anti-ideological disposition are not likely to controvert this widely shared belief. The dispute arises on the question whether all types of progress are welcome or good. When anthropologists like Levi-Strauss maintain that such value-loaded concepts as 'welcome' and 'good' are always to be understood intra-culturally, what they mean is that value-judgements are never universally valid. In his well-known controversy over the subject with Jean-Paul Sartre, Strauss says, defending his position, that he is neither anti-historical nor opposed to the ideal of progress. He seeks to rebut the Sartrean form of historism by affirming that historical explanation is not essentially different from, and certainly not superior to, structural explanation and that structural explanation is doubly historical, regressively as well as progressively. It is interesting to recall that both Sartre and Strauss, two very influential thinkers of our time, are professed Marxists. Upholding the primacy of *dialectical* reason, a surrogate of historical reason, Sartre tries to show that by conscious labour man is engaged in creating and recreating his social institutions, doing away with this 'practico-inert' character, and in trying to take the same forward. To him, *analytic* reason, essentially an anti-historical form of structuralism, is meant only for *understanding* and not for creating and recreating what is historical. Following Marx, he claims that our task is not so much to understand history as to change it. Strauss response to Sartre's criticism is that as an anthropologist though his main preoccupation is with the understanding of the primitive or the so-called frozen, i.e. static, societies, that does not mean either denial of historism or the ideal of change. On the contrary, the very fact that widely different human cultures, both modern and primitive, exhibit some structural universals shows their essential human or historical character. Structuralism is second-order historism and marks no departure at all from the humanism highlighted by Marx and Sartre. Additionally, he claims that structuralism by showing how cultural universals are at work in every society is promoting the cause of *universal* humanism, the main plank of Marxism. While the humanism underlying Strauss structuralism cannot be lightly dismissed, the point remains that his primary interest is structuralism as a method for the understanding of different human cultures, widely separated by geography and history.[7]

Structuralism is not antithetical to the idea of change. Undoubtedly, the ideas of historical change and progress have received special attention from Sartre. But the point for which I am referring to the Sartre-Strauss debate is that neither the structuralist nor the historist is opposed to the basic philosophy of ideology—ideological change. There is nothing wrong even for a frozen society in having an ideology for itself. That the primitives have their own do's and don'ts, legal and moral codes governing human conduct may be easily found from anthropological literature. What we, the 'modern' people, often forget in our progressive zeal is that we too are culture-bound and our moral and legal codes are not as universal as we often imagine them to be. *Enforceable* international laws, private or even public, are still a far-off dream. The United Nations's declaration of Human Rights is often described as a dead charter. The League of Nations is long dead and the United Nations Organisation has been languishing before our own eyes. All these are forgotten measures of our fall from our own ideologically proclaimed universal humanism. From the other end, one might point out that these are the unmistakable indicators of our surviving cultural provincialism or primitivity. This way of looking at the things makes us at least aware that the structuralist and the historist, in spite of their notable methodological difference, are in effect trying to understand similar human problems and their possible solutions, of course from different points of view. None of them, however, is refusing to recognise the place of ideology in a society, be it modern or frozen. Opposed to the 'practico-inert' or static form of our institutions, Sartre openly favours practical measures—action, movement, struggle—to change the same towards the chosen *ideal* direction. Though indirectly, Levi-Strauss can also rightly claim to have performed an ideological job by reminding the modern man (*a*) that his primitive counterpart, culturally speaking, is not *essentially* different from him and (*b*) that, given structurally understood *meanings* of life, the modern society and the primitive society are not very different. Straussian structuralism is a quite critique of modernism, especially of its epochal, i.e., historical, egoism, and polite reminder of human universalism.

In a way Levi-Strauss is a continuer of the French tradition of Montaigne, Montesquisu and, particularly, Rousseau. It is to be recalled that while progress is claimed by many to be the hall-mark of ideology, there are many thinkers like Rousseau who yearn to get back to a 'natural' state of society and criticise why the so-called modern ideology is more corrupting than elevating in its influence on the human life. It is equally instructive to recall that Rousseau's critique of the then modernism, together with its arts, science and education, roused the people's consciousness of their 'lost' equality and of the need to get it back, socially and morally in the civil State. In the process he turned to be the ideologist of the French Revolution.

The state of nature, according to Rousseau, was free and idyllic. By agreeing to have the civil State through the social compact or contract men agreed, rather strangely, to leave behind their utopia. In order to explain this 'strange' and free contract to live under the sovereign, Rousseau states that it is only under the pressure of the state of nature that men, under the felt need of self-preservation, agreed to barter their freedom for rights. The contractarian unity, which gives rise to the civil State, compromises only the *natural* freedom of man and gives him 'an unlimited right to everything he tries to get and succeeds in getting'. Without this liberty man cannot be the master of himself. Man cannot be the master of his own self disregarding the nature of his relation to other selves. To leave behind the natural freedom is not enough for man to be free in the highest sense. His true identity does not consist in his isolated will-to-be. His will is an indivisible part of the general will. When several men in the assembly regard themselves as a single body, their will is one and it is only in and through it that common interest and general well-being can be preserved and promoted. In the name of individual liberty if the general will is flouted and the social bond allowed to weaken, the interests of the individuals or those of the groups undercut and supervene over the common interest. When the general will ceases to be the will of all, contradictory views, debates and disputes arise. The ruin of the State is imminent when the general will, its true basis, turns out to be vain, illusory and formal.

Rousseau's Ideal State presupposes the indestructibility of the general will. This presupposition seems rather metaphysical. Rousseau can well conceive all individual men detaching their own interests from the common interest. But he points out that this process of disengagement cannot be taken to its farthest end. Individual interests cannot be entirely separated from the common interest. One's self-interest, whatever that might be, can hardly be fulfilled except in and through its relation to the common interest based on the general will. The promotion and preservation of the general good are necessary for the fulfilment of man's own interest. Taking his stand on this premise, Rousseau argues that when government is run by *all*, on the basis of the consent of all, its form is best and people's interest is served the best. This form is called democracy. To him it is the ideal form of government. The government by *few* (aristrocracy) is inferior to but better than the government by *one* (monarchy). The intention underlying Rousseau's argument is undoubtedly welcome. But it is clear that he did not anticipate that if in principle none is allowed to 'detach' his interest from the common interest, his will from the general will, individual liberty, as ordinarily understood, is in grave jeopardy. In different ways Rousseau's mistake has been repeated by Kant and Hegel.[8]

It is to be recalled that in the bloody feud which followed the French Revolution both the factions referred to and invoked the authority of Rousseau. Robespierre, defending the Jacobins, claimed that he and his followers represented the general will of the French people: 'our will is the general will'. Justifying their factional despotism they invoked 'the great cause' of the Revolution, i.e., vindication of liberty. 'The government of the Revolution is the despotism of liberty against tyranny'. Interestingly enough, the enemies of Robespierre, who later on succeeded in liquidating him, also tried to justify their action in the name of the Revolution and for the sake of liberty. The danger of Rousseau's affirmation that the general will is indivisible has been practically illustrated by the post-revolutionary anarchy and the rise of the

Napoleanic dictatorship. How badly divisible in effect it was became clear in the last decade of the eighteenth century.

Its theoretical fall-out found its way into the writings of Kant and Hegel, for example. When Kant argues that goodwill in its purest, i.e. most autonomous, form is universal, it appears unexceptionable. But when one goes into its implication, it shows its grave problem. The Moral Law which issues forth from the goodwill is universal in its scope, knows no exception whatsoever. It is in the form of Categorical Imperative, i.e., unconditionally binding on all rational human beings alike. In order to ensure the universality of the Moral Law Kant is obliged to formulate it in a context-insensitive form. If the Moral Law, however laudable might be its objective, fails to recognise the importance of different circumstances, the logic of the varying situations, it becomes trivially true. A man endowed with the Kantian Goodwill is unable to will which is good for some and bad for others, or just for some and not so for others. This historical and contextual blindness of the Moral Law has another grave, more dangerous, implication. Kant claims, consistently with his view on the Moral Law, that the constitutional law of a country is 'holy and irresistible'. As the absolute command of the practical reason it is said to be binding on every people. What is rather unexpected from a libertarian like Kant is his pronouncement that 'even if the organisation of the State is defective by itself, still no subordinate authority in that State can bring any active resistance against the legislative chief of that State'.[9] Apparently disturbed by the bloody aftermath of the French Revolution, Kant was not prepared to recognise the moral authority of individuals or groups under the State to defy or rise against the sovereign. Scared of the possible anarchy, Kant maintains that even if the State authority is found to be defective it is for the sovereign, the legislative chief, to remove the deficiencies by reforms, *not* revolution. Otherwise, he argues, if the supreme law of the realm is allowed to be contradicted or contested by the will of the subordinate authority, individual or collective, the foundation of the political constitution is bound to collapse. For once the unquestionable supremacy of the sovereign authority is allowed to be questioned, 'irrational' questions will be raised from many quarters and veritable anarchy would be let loose on the regime. Whether Kant's fear of anarchy is unduly exaggerated or not, it is clear that in his ideal realm, Kingdom of Ends, individual dissent or group dissent would not be tolerated. The 'perpetual peace' of the supra-rational States would never be visited by conflict and war.[10] The old question again reappears here: is not Kant's Ideal realm too good to be believed in the face of the history of endless wars? Has the Goodwill, the basis of the ideal realm (of ends), been deliberately dehistorised, portrayed as autonomous, to forestall the inevitable criticism?

Hegel, who criticises Kant's notion of goodwill as formal and empty, himself speaks of the State as the supreme and the most concrete expression of freedom. He, too, thinks that individuals and groups can have no freedom or right except under the sovereignty of the State. The freedom of the individual and that of the group consist in their subordination to and identification with the supreme sovereign. What Kant said of freedom in his "formal" idioms Hegel repeats, with a slight variation, in his 'material' idioms.

The common point which one notices in them is their anti-naturalism. Natural laws provide no guarantee for the highest possible human freedom. Nature is either inimical to or at least not cooperative enough with man in his venture, personal and institutional, to be free. Freedom is to be found within some or other human 'arrangement', whether we call it contract (following Hobbes and Locke) or convention (following Hume) or compact (following Rousseau). For the enlargement of this freedom we cannot depend on nature and its initiative, if any. Expressions like 'nature's initiative' are either metaphorical or grounded in some metaphysical principle like God.

Hume's conception of 'the natural' is full of ambiguity. When it is said that he is a naturalist, it is mainly because of his pro-scientific and anti-metaphysical views. But unlike the divine teleologist, he tries to explain every phenomenon in terms of cause-effect relationship. Even in the realm of causes and effects he endeavours to show by his penetrating analysis that the higher-level truths of nature, laws and theories, for example, are not to be taken as valid exclusively on logical or methodological ground. The secrets of nature are not open or manifest. Therefore, their truth-claims have to be rigorously tested by reason. Here again it is to be shown that Hume's conception of reason is 'natural' only in a special sense, not in the sense it is used by a Leibniz or a Kant. Here he comes down from abstract reason to concrete reason or what is crystalised experience. The consideration for which Hume attaches special importance to customs and conventions, human habits and practices, is to avoid the misleading formalism and unnecessary abstractionism. In Hume's writings 'natural' sometimes means what is anti-speculative or experiential. Sometimes the term stands for what is traditional and customary. But his anti-speculative pro-naturalism does not lead him to any sort of narrow utilitarianism. He refuses to believe that man is invariably subject to the passing impulses of pleasure-seeking and pain-avoiding. As a cultural being and enriched by convention and custom, man can, and in fact does, rise above the forces of instincts and blind habits. Influenced by tradition, man can interrogate and change tradition.

Kant takes note of the ambiguity in Hume's treatment of the concept of the natural. Further, he appreciates Rousseau's view of the 'natural reason of heart'. Besides, the effect of the historism defended by Rousseau and Hume posed a challenge to the abstract and justificationist philosophy of Newtonian science proposed by Kant. On the one hand, Kant is not prepared to debunk science on the Rousseauite ground that it alienates man from nature and debases the goodness of his heart. On the other hand, given historism and traditionalism of Hume, he is not clear how to justify the Newtonian paradigm as the culmination of theoretical reason. Kant's own deep moral impulses and religious sentiments compounded the nature of his problem. In this respect he feels a 'theoretically unjustifiable' sympathy with the views of Hume and Rousseau, two of his most influential and elderly contemporaries. Kant's response to the said cluster of issues has been formulated in the trifurcation of human reason—Pure or Theoretical, Practical or Moral, and Aesthetic or Artistic. The first form of reason, primarily cognitive in its structure and function, is intended to justify, not falsify, scientific knowledge. This may be called Reason of Head. The second form of reason primarily pertains to human will and conduct and is purported to justify, not to test, Moral Law in terms of transcendental freedom available to every rational being and which is claimed to be totally independent of the causal forces of nature. This may be called Reason of Heart. Even after delineating the structures and functions of these two 'types' of reason Kant feels that to explain the universal possibility and 'validity' of aesthetic creativity and judgment he is obliged to further enquire into such human powers as *taste* and *genius*. To him these terms carry very special connotations. In every sphere of reason Kant tries to show by elaborate arguments, basically transcendental and anti-historical, how synthetic judgments *a priori* are possible and become *necessarily* valid. Kant's transcendental argument-strategy, purported to save him from the Humean scepticism, lands him in the static two structural frameworks of 'facts' and 'values', requiring him to explore their relation in terms of the third.

Whether Kant's tripartite or trifurcated reason succeeds in removing the ambiguity of Hume's and Rousseau's notions of the natural and the rational still remains a debatable question. But it is clear that his analysis raises two problems for himself. Firstly, if the different types of reason are so different from one another, how their products or performances could be shown to be consistent with one another? If the man, who as a scientist or a philosopher of science, is engaged in knowing the inviolable laws of nature, how it is so that he, the same person, as author of Moral Law, which is equally binding on all human beings, does not find a great divide within himself? Further, the proclaimed *affinity* of the natural and the moral, of pure reason and practical reason, raises the additional question regarding the place of aesthetic or judgmental reason vis-a-vis the other two forms of reason. Is the aesthetic genius in man inclined towards 'value-making' or allied to 'fact-finding' or stands equi-distant from or equally close to the two? Are not all sorts of "finding" in Kant turn out to be basically exercises in 'making'? Are they really three separate types of reason—separated from each other both structurally and functionally? Or, are they merely three different forms of articulation of one and the same transcendental reason having their empirical correlates? The affinity between (*a*) the reason that knows and what it knows and (*b*) the reason that wills and what it wills can hardly be explained without a compresence, simultaneous and consilient presence, of the both before human reason itself, whether we call it transcendental or not. Kant's preference for teleological argument to other forms of theological arguments indicates his inclination to show at least a *formal affinity* between the different spheres of reason's activities. His aim is sobre. He wants to show only the affinity, not the unity, of the universe as a whole.

Kant's attempted synthesis of pure reason, practical reason and aesthetic reason, though weak or sobre in its formulation and execution, is ambitious from another point of view. Firstly, it tries to establish that the apparent diversity of the modes of human experience is no road-block to their eventual convergence or synthesis. The man as a part of nature is not debarred from either artistically creating and enjoying the sublime beauty of nature or being a citizen of the Kingdom of God on the Earth. Man's empirical nature is in no way an obstacle to his transcendental activities—scientific, artistic and ethical. In other words, Kant's world-view tries to carve out a secure, perhaps a little too secure, place for man in nature. Kant's dream of the Kingdom of Ends on the Earth and the perpetual peace which is likely to characterise it is bound to appear as little too utopian to every student of history. His conception of history is somewhat structurally static, marked by approximation to the ideal of the Categorical Imperative, or the presence of God on the Earth, and not by that of growth or development.

Kant's exaggerated demand for autonomous Good Will is criticised by Hegel and sought to be corrected by Marx. True, by applying his supreme moral principle to the realm of nature, Kant has tried to rebut in the third *Critique* the charge of dualism raised against him. That nature is not necessarily hostile to human aspiration is proved by him by pointing out that man can have *disinterested pleasure* from his experience of the beautiful and the sublime natural phenomena. But this sort of defence of the 'harmony' between the natural and the human is not enough to satisfy Hegel. The experience of aesthetic harmony, Hegel thinks, is sustained by a deeper unity of thought, feeling and willing in Spirit. It is not enough to say that nature is merely helpful in producing disinterested aesthetic pleasure in the human mind. What remains to be further shown is that the forms of nature are there as necessary conditions for the production of aesthetic experience in the human mind. This is collateral to the point that nature is not hostile to human moral aspiration but necessary for its development and satisfaction. Anti-naturalism of Kant is thus criticised and corrected by Hegel. Unification of nature, human thought and action is felt additionally necessary for rejecting the static conception of history. The realisation of the World-Spirit in history becomes impossible unless human beings are recognised as its dynamic agents. But dualistic tension of the Kantian thought is fully exploited by Hegel to his own advantage. Even after emphasising the autonomy of the Goodwill while Kant draws a distinction between Goodwill and Holy (God's) Will, it is pointed out that the 'limitation' of the former explains why man *needs to be* moral, although this question (the question of being moral) does not arise in the case of the Holy Will. The implication is : the Holy Will is so fully perfect that the question of its being further morally perfect does not arise at all. And, by contrast, the Will of man, though autonomous by virtue of his rationality, has an element of natural limitation or imperfection in it and without acknowledging which the idea of man's moral aspiration and endeavour makes little sense. Pressing this point of Kant further, Hegel argues that nature cannot be separated from man's moral existence and adventure. On the contrary, nature's challenge kindles and strengthens his moral consciousness. The very body of man is a part of nature. This is a point which Kant himself recognises. But its fuller implication, not exploited by himself, is taken up and pressed forward by Hegel. Hegel serves his twin purposes by this strategic move. Firstly, he ascribes to nature a positive contribution to man's moral consciousness and action, rejecting thereby the anti-naturalism of Kant. Secondly, by the same token, he injects a mild dose of *historical realism* into the Kantian utopia of Kingdom of Ends entailing perpetual peace and the supra-national World-State.

It may be contended that Hegel's opposition to Kantian idealism and naturalism and his attempt to introduce historical realism are somewhat inconsistent with his own professed aim. It is not clear why he thinks that Spirit for its fullest possible realisation does not need a world-State and that Objective Spirit finds its highest expression in the nation-State or the aggregate of such States. The point has been persuasively argued by some writers.[11] Rational Will of Spirit is unlikely to find its highest expression in any State or aggregate of States (empire ?). Hegel concedes that the universal will, as expressed in the nation-States, is not realised in its best possible form because of the presence of the elements of conflict in the relation between individuals and associations. If nation-States are themselves not free from internal conflict, it seems, Hegel feels that a World State consisting of them, even if established, would not prove ideal or durable. This realistic perception of Hegel, though understandable, is somewhat incongruous with Hegel's historical background consisting of Kant's theory of a peaceful World-State and his own conception of Spirit having all-rational will in it. Besides, given his conception of Spirit, it is difficult to see how in the nation-State the best possible form of freedom would be realised. For, he himself recognises that none of the classes mediating between the State and the people are not free from self-interest and successful in unifying the two. It is one thing to say that the internal structure of the State is yet to reach that character, given which, it would be entirely conflict-free or free in the perfect sense and another thing to affirm that in the nation-State itself Objective Spirit will find its highest form of freedom. The question remains: 'What would be the freest possible form of history in the scheme of Spirit itself?' I think it has been rightly observed by Plamenatz that 'it seems to follow from Hegel's conception of Mind or Spirit that the fully rational and free community must be a World-State'.

If Kant's anti-naturalism has been pointedly criticised by Hegel, the task of adequately correcting it was left to Marx. Marx pits materialism against the anti-naturalism of Kant and the spiritualism of Hegel. Opposed to Kant's constructivism, a variant of idealism, and influenced by Hegel's dialectic, Marx improves upon the materialism of the eighteenth century and styles it as scientific materialism. Its basic characteristic is the recognition of not only the influence of existence on consciousness but also of the consciousness on existence. The initial primacy of the influence of matter on mind does not mean that it remains so for ever. The development of human civilisation is marked by the increasing powers of mental consciousness and its freedom. Though it is based on the knowledge of the secrets and the powers of the material world, that does not impede its dialectical growth. By his manual and intellectual labour man succeeds in gradually freeing himself from the one-sided forces of nature and in utilising the same for his own benefit without defacing nature.

Following the foot-steps of Hegel and the classical economists, Marx takes serious note of the existence of conflict in society and analyses its property-based economic causes. From the commonsense point of view it is bound to appear that the propertied and the afluent class is more free than other classes. However, Marx shows that though by exploiting the working class the bourgeoisie become rich but, paradoxically enough, their money and property do not buy real freedom for them. The capitalist system which yields undue profit to the rich people also binds them to the fetters inherent in the system. In the process of exploiting the poor, interestingly enough, the bourgeoisie not only make the proletariat poorer but also make their consciousness more authentic and better equipped to fight for their own freedom. By depriving them of their property and relatively freeing them from property-based relationship, the bourgeoisie unintentionally prepare the proletariat for launching a determined struggle against themselves. In other words, in the capitalist mode of production the bourgeoisie and the proletariat are caught in a vicious circle in which the former gain more and more materially, i.e., in terms of money and property, while the latter get materially impoverished but organisationally and spiritually more and more strengthened. In effect, poverty of the proletariat proves to be its disguised boon.

In the context of ideology Marx's concept of authentic consciousness assumes deep significance. Authenticity is not rooted in good will. It consists in freedom from exploitive and proprietory web of relations. In the capitalist system this freedom can never reach its best possible form. The conditions which sustain this exploitive system and keep it going cannot allow the emergence of authentic consciousness. Admittedly the poor are blessed in the sense that they are not burdened with and tied down to profit-making activities and machinations. But this is only one part of the story. Their poverty or propertylessness by itself cannot give them the creative joy of authentic consciousness. Though impoverished, they remain bonded within the exploitive conditions and constraints of the systems. The joylessness or drudgery of the work is always with them unless they die or succeed in throwing over the system itself.

As I have pointed out earlier, Marx is primarily committed to the illusory notion of ideology. When he says that ideology consists of the ideas and ideals of the ruling class, the ruling power of ideology is directly grounded in the economic power of the ruling economic class. But there are at least two important concepts in Marx's own writings which, if critically developed, might provide the clues for reconstructing the positive aspect of his concept of ideology. Firstly, he recognises, at least in principle, that all members of the bourgeois class are not identically committed and fastened to their class interests. One's affiliation to one's class, determined by birth or the mode of earning the livelihood, is not *mechanically* binding on one's life. A member may get *de-classed* from his original class; he may withdraw, both mentally and in action, from the web of his class relationship. Numerous historical examples are available showing that the members of ruling class are promoting the interest of the ruled.

Secondly, the proletariat as a class, though ordinarily more homogenous than the bourgeoisie, are not always and necessarily so. Some members of the proletariat get corrupted, deviate from their path, and become *lumpen*. At times we find that, lured by the bourgeois values, the proletariat betray their own class interests. The very fact that members of a class can get out of their own class-orbits shows that they are free enough to do so. Unless many men are deemed to be organic analogues of machines, it is difficult to deny them the freedom of changing class-affiliation.

The efficacy of this freedom may be indicated in another way. At one stage it was thought that the gradual pauperisation of the proletariat would make it more and more unified or homogenous. But it has been found later that increasing division of labour within the working class makes their composition gradually heterogeneous, if not conflict-ridden. The history of the working class movement not only in the capitalist countries but also in the socialist ones shows that the proletariat are prepared to work both politically and economically, in cooperation with the capitalist even before the cherished proletarian victory against the ruling bourgeoisie has been achieved. In the last fifty years or so two forms of coalition between the proletariat and the capitalist have emerged in different parts of the world. While in some parts of the world the peasants' and workers' parties have become the major partners in the coalition government allowing other parties to work with them, in some other parts of the world they have agreed to form government as junior or minor partner with the bourgeois and social democratic parties. Even if one remembers the relevance of the Dimitrov-thesis that to the communists the coalition form of government is only an interim and strategic step forward towards the goal of capturing the State power, some major theoretical questions of deep practical significance remain unanswered. For example, in many bourgeois States the local communist parties have been taking part for a long period without succeeding in capturing the State power or even without attempting to do so. The other question which seems to be more important is this. Even in the socialist countries where the dictatorship of the proletariat has been established, there is no appreciable sign of withering away of the State,—the State which is said to be the expression of the irreconcilability of conflicting class interest. To say, as it has been said, for example, that some of the socialist States are now States of the *whole people* and not of any particular class, is not enough to get into the crux of the problem. The question is : 'why the State authority is still so dependent on the armed forces?' To answer it by pointing out the external threat and the on-going war-preparation, though very pertinent, does not go to the theoretical depth of Marxism. For, again the question may be raised: 'since the instant globalisation of communism was never envisaged by Marx and his followers like Lenin and Mao, was it not easily conceivable at the time of formulating the thesis of the withering away of the State that the danger of external threat will remain in force for a long time to come?' In the light of development of the last ten years or so especially the 'open door policy' of some socialist countries, the substance, if not the whole of the original thesis, has become suspect and is now in need of serious review.[12]

It is evident from the history of last fifty years or so that theoreticians and/or activists of a particular class may be critical of the ideology of their own class without being inimical or hostile to it. Internal criticism is not only being allowed but at times even encouraged. Besides, external criticism is not being regarded necessarily as destructive or slanderous. This positive development indirectly indicates that authentic consciousness is not antithetical to critical consciousness. One might go a step forward and affirm that authentic consciousness, to preserve its authenticity amidst changing historical situations, is obliged to be critical. If the critical dialectic internal to authentic consciousness is not allowed to operate freely, its authenticity is bound to be compromised, embourgeoisment of the proletarian values become inevitable, and dogmatism would set in.

Ideology by its very nature is not condemned to be an expression of false consciousness—illusory consciousness. To predicate falsity of consciousness in general makes little or no sense. The issue has to be meaningfully formulated only with reference to this or that particular mode of consciousness. The main reason for which the scientific mode of consciousness is said to be truest is because of its clear formulability and easy testability. The clarity of scientific theories is due to the well-defined nature of the concepts used in it. Its testability is the pre-requisite of its being accepted as scientific. But neither its clarity nor its testability can save any open-ended science from its being false. At times, to highlight this point instead of testability we hear of falsifiability as the hall-mark of what is scientific as distinguished from what is non-scientific. History of science is replete with scientific theories which were taken to be true once upon a time and rejected, partly or wholly, thereafter, in course of time. If science is taken to be the paradigmatic mode of human consciousness and if that science is historically bound to undergo falsification, it is of no use to examine separately the other modes of consciousness, scientific or humanistic, unless, of course, we are prepared to question the superiority of the scientific mode itself.

From the ancient to the modern time we have come across many thinkers who are not prepared to take scientific knowledge, as we understand it today, as the highest form of knowledge. From Kant and Hegel to Husserl, for example, many philosophers are of the view that science is authentic only in a limited sense. Its findings are not relevant, certainly not central, to various other modes of consciousness and the established pursuits of values. At one point or another the findings of science face the testing tribunal of experience not within the narrow confines of experimental laboratories but in the wider spheres of human praxis. Man does not live by the scientific mode of knowledge alone. The needs of living and solving the problems of the various spheres of life, theoretical and practical, oblige man to take science into the large account of relation with the other branches of knowledge and practice. The question of authenticity or truthfulness cannot be decided in isolation. One's view of the world and every class-view of the world are exposed to other's and other classes' view of the same before the concerned views' truth-claim or authenticity can be established or dis-established. The quest for truth is not a self-bound or class-bound exercise. Solipsism, individual or collective, is untenable. Solipsism, factual and valuational, is unsustainable. The reason is very simple. Every man is obliged to be fair not only to his own experience of the world but also to others' experiences of the same. Similarly, every class-experience of the world is required to be fair, at least factually, to other class-experiences. True, for gathering knowledge of the world we must have a definite standpoint. But that standpoint need not be fixed for ever. For, in view of the changing character of needs, interests and problems of our life we have to change our standpoints from time to time. There is no one single standpoint, empirical or transcendental, individual or collective, which can be defended and stuck to in the face of all sorts of problems. It is for this sort of considerations that we often hear of different sorts of reasons, of head and of heart, theoretical and practical. Without seriously disregarding different qualitative features of the diverse modes of our life-experiences we cannot huddle them together into a unified whole claiming it to be the supreme or superior to all the possible forms of life, including their 'facts' and 'values'. Short of being dogmatic and self-righteous one cannot uphold the class-bound view of ideological authenticity. How can only one class enjoy the privileged access right to the non-illusory ideology, while it shares the 'same' socio-economic space with other classes? Unless the State withers away or finds another basis for its existence, the criticism of all forms of ideology except one seems untenable.

To brand ideological consciousness as false is to disregard its necessity, insistent necessity, not only for, say, aesthetic enjoyment but also for changing our social forms of living for development, betterment and enlargement.[13]

Man's social life is not merely an external adjunct of his life. In a very important way society is he in an enlarged form of the human life. In fact, the social dimension of human existence is nothing incidental or passing in nature. It is by mastery of tools and symbols that man has been able to enlarge himself in family, in community and in larger social aggregates. Both thought and action underlie his capacity to use tools and symbols. Conversely speaking, tools and symbols have facilitated and improved his modes of thought and action and made their scope more and more comprehensive. Only in terms of property-relationship man's growing world cannot be accounted for. Property has both enlarging and alienative influences on the human life. The whole of man's being cannot be fully expressed in one or other form of its expression. Undoubtedly, action or labour has contributed to man's growth, but, unless this category is elevated to the metaphysical level of, say, 'consciousness-force', to use a term of Sri Aurobindo, it is difficult to explain other facets of the growth of human personality.

The self-exceeding nature of man is not confined only to his increasing action-capacity. It is there in knowing as well. But even knowing does not exhibit the fullness of man's potentiality. It is not surprising that, besides action, the will-power is also accorded special recognition in shaping the human personality. The richness and resources of human consciousness are not exhaustively manifest in the traditional tripartite classification of human phenomena—cognition, volition, and conation. For example, when we speak of human *hope* or inspiration, it does not fall neatly under any one of the said three forms of human consciousness. Hope has a peculiarity of its own. To spell out the ontology of human hopes and aspirations, is not a very easy job.

Consciousness is not a freak of nature. It is the result of the orderly and convergent function of the laws of nature. Mental consciousness and its different forms—knowing, willing, feeling, doing, hoping, etc., have a systematic ambivalence in their workings. Such concepts as Absolute Knowledge, the World as Will, the World as *Rasaghana* (as Delight) and Reality as Perfect Being, are 'proofs' of the fall-out of man's own supernature. The supermind is nothing but what lies above the body-bound mind but the glimpses of which are available, though not continuously and steadily, to the ordinary human mind. In and through the glimpses of his supernature, man feels assured of the existence and truth of the ultimate unity of different visions, formulations, arrangements, expressions, actions and movements of reality. Law-governed harmony of reality appears as luminous truth to the mental being (*Manomaya Purusa*). The ambivalence of the analytic or divisive consciousness of mind is due to its being pulled and pushed, though not arbitrarily, by the forces of the supernature and those of the lower nature. The multiple forces of nature, perpetual in influx, often tend to bewilder the human mind, making it rather difficult for it to grasp the laws which relate them to the physical nature. Though basically triune, the human mind ordinarily conceives itself as biune, i.e., the meeting seat of many-in-one and one-in-many. When the ambivalence of our mind is steadied and we start exploring, reflectively and actively, our existence, we realise that the different levels of our consciousness are graded and complementary, and not really divisive or antagonistic. But this realisation does not readily dawn upon our mind. First we have it in the form of *hope*.

Once it becomes clear to us that our mental phenomena are not *exclusively* mental, naturally the question which haunts us is this. To what our hopes and aspirations, for example, are due. I deliberately raise the question of hope and not that of perception or even feeling, because the *objective reference* of perception is easily traceable, and the *representative character* of feeling is also, though not easily, determinable. That neither perception nor feeling is rootless is likely to be conceded. But the same concession is not ordinarily made to hope. True, in some cases 'rootless' feeling of fear, for example, is regarded as neurotic and therefore dismissed lightly as if there is not much behind it to think about. But the psychoanalyst, by his patient investigation, often succeeds in finding out that what is ordinarily dismissed as rootless is not really so. The roots of certain mental phenomena are not easily visible or manifest. Their objectward reference is oblique, devious and not quickly traceable. Most of our mental *representations* of worldly objects are not picturesque. Our own mental interpretations have always an important say in determining the meaning of the mental representations. Though sometimes it is claimed that all mental phenomena have their *intentional* or object-ward character, it is difficult to deny that, on scrutiny, while some objects (mainly cognitive) turn out to be *'factual'*, some others (mainly artistic and ethical) '*fictional*'. But further scrutiny reveals the difficulty involved in drawing a sharp line of distinction between the two. For what is regarded 'factual' to-day in cognitive or scientific discourse may, as a result of test, turn out to be corrigible, if not clearly false. If the corrigibility of facts or cognised objects is once admitted, their difference from what is fictitious becomes very indefinite. When the 'internal realist' speaks of his difficulty in drawing a sharp line of demarcation between 'finding of fact' and 'fabrication of fiction', he has precisely this point in mind.

Let us now return to the concept of hope. There are certain forms of hope which are like 'rootless' orchid, suspended on air and deriving its nourishment from light, air and other elements of atmospheric nature. Nothing living, be it botanic or biological, is really rootless. The ways of drawing their sustenance by different living beings are not evidently identical. All human hopes are also not same in nature. Some are primarily socio-political with such economic underpinnings as propertylessness and egalitarianism. Some are primarily religious by such highly unearthly characteristics as immortality and all-round perfection. Interestingly enough, all utopias, despite their difference, are intended to satisfy some very practical and spiritual needs of human beings. When the utopias are *primarily* meant for the human beings like ourselves—finite, fallible and mortal—these are generally called ideologies. In spite of their added transcendental character, utopias, like ideologies, are historically informed and rooted. Even in their highest flight of imagination the utopian thinkers do not get entirely beyond their own cultural gravitational fields. This fact may be more constructively interpreted by pointing out the rootedness even of our 'wildest' hopes into the life-world. The human character of all our hopes is grounded in our life-experience and the perception of absent or negated values in it. We hope and long for those 'things' and 'values' which either we do not have at all or do not have in sufficient measure and believe that *somehow or other* we may possibly have the same. Our sense of *lack* or *not having* (something), is secretly historical, i.e., peculiar to different societies and different ages. There is no universal ontology of hope. It is to be gathered from its diverse sociological conditions. If some utopian thinkers utterly fail to indicate the *modus operandi* to get to their cherished utopias where the missing or negated values would be available, their views are rightly criticised as purely romantic or figment of imagination. This implicitly suggests that even utopias must satisfy the requirement of the historical rootedness. In other words, the respectability accorded to ideologies may be extended to utopias only on the satisfaction of the condition that the latter, like the former, could somehow be shown to relatable to some or other historical situation.

The historical rootedness or situatedness of ideologies and utopias can well be presented in a different way. By highlighting the self-exceeding character of man it has often been argued that yearning for better, larger and nobler forms of life is an integral part of the human nature itself. The establishment of Kingdom of God on the Earth or the realisation of *The Divine Life* or the supramentalisation of man is claimed to be the fulfilment of a promise which we have in our inmost being. This is substantially a line of argument of the thinkers like Sri Aurobindo, Samuel Alexander and Chardin. The history of ideological and utopian thought clearly shows the hidden histority of numerous ideologies. Sometimes the views are couched in such mystic or metaphorical language that it is not easy to decipher it. Some utopias and ideologies are theological but there are few others which are 'secular'. Sri Aurobindo justifiably claims that *The Life Divine* has nothing to do with institutional religion. He is prepared to call it spiritual but not religious. William James, himself not a believer in any ordinary sense, recognises the existence of a 'religious propensity' in almost all human beings. The hidden histority of utopianism has been expressed in different ways. Plato's *Republic*, for example, is undoubtedly an idealised picture of some Hellenic city-state of his time. Some commentators on chapter II of *Genesis* ask us to believe that the Garden of Eden, the canonical version of Paradise, is a reconstruction of an ideal state of human order visualised by some priests of Israel around the ninth century before Christ. Thomas More's *Utopia* (1516) bears the stamp of his time and place. He makes no secret of his indebtedness, though often critically, to Plato. He proposes to build a 'philosophical city' under King Utopus but without the aid of 'abstract philosophy', a veiled critical reference to Plato. More affirms that his utopia is not a second paradise and that it is an earthly society. The commentator has added that it is not only an earthly society but also 'an urban society conceived by the son of a London lawyer and the grandson of a London baker'.[14]

By analysing the contents of different utopias, as it has been said earlier, it is not at all difficult to show how human and historical they are in their basic inspiration. The sense in which men are 'growing gods' in a closely comparable sense *their* societies, in spite of (or because of?) all attending problems, are bound to be ideology-inspired, if not utopia-seeking. Justification of ideologies and utopias are, therefore, basically socio-historical or empirical and not transcendental. The changing character of human hopes and fears and their causes do *not* lend themselves to any uniform and eternal justification. Ideas and ideals do not have any independent identity of their own,-independent of their socio-historically situated human loci. Questioning regarding the acceptability or otherwise of ideologies and utopias of one epoch or culture by another is very natural. There is nothing surprising even in intra-cultural ideological scepticism because every culture has in it many individuals who are unequal but more or less free. To resort to transcendental argument for forestalling ideological diversity, utopian pluralism and the resulting scepticism amounts to denial of the reality of history and human freedom.

Ideology and utopia need demythologization, socio-historical interpretation and demystification—not hasty rejection.

# References

## Chapter One


1. Harry Elmer Barnes, *An Intellectual and Cultural History of the Western World*, Vols. 2 and 3, Dover Publications, New York, 1965.
2. P. F. Strawson, *The Bounds of Sense: An Essay on Kant's Critique of Pure Reason*, pp. 38–42, 188–99, Methuen and Co., London, 1966.
3. Sri Aurobindo, *The Human Cycle* (HC), Sri Aurobindo Ashram, Pondicherry, 1949. All page references of HC in this book are from this edition. Together with two other significant works of Sri Aurobindo on the related areas of thought, *The Ideal of Human Unity* and *War and Self-Determination*, HC may be found in the Vol. 15 of Sri Aurobindo's Collected Works, Birth Centenary Library, Pondicherry, 1971.
4. See Shlomo Avineri, *The Social and Political Thought of Karl Marx*, Cambridge University Press, 1968.
5. G. D. H. Cole, *A History of Socialist Thought*, Vols. 1 and 2, Macmillan, London, 1953.
6. Sri Aurobindo, *The Life Divine*, Vols. 18 and 19 especially Bk. 2, Part I, Chs. I, II, III and Part II, Chs. XV–XVIII, Birth Centenary Library.
7. Sri Aurobindo, *The Ideal of Human Unity* (IHU), p. 2, Pondicherry, 1950. All page references of IHU in this book are from this edition.
8. G. H. von Wright, *Explanation and Understanding*, Cornell University Press, Ithaca, New York, 1971; Theodore Abel, ' The Operation called "Verstehen" ' in *Readings in the Philosophy of Science*, H. Feigl and M. Brodbeck (eds.), Appleton-Century-Crofts, New York, 1953.
9. K. R. Popper, *The Logic of Scientific Discovery*, Hutchinson, London, 1959; C. G. Hempel, *Aspects of Scientific Explanation*, Free Press Paperback, 1970; R. B. Braithwaite, *Scientific Explanation*, Cambridge University Press, 1953.
10. E. B. Tylor, *Primitive Culture*, 2 Vols., Gloucester, Mass, 1958. First published in 1871. E. Westermarck, *Ethical Relativity*, Littlefield Paperback, 1960; S. Andreski (ed.), *Herbert Spencer*, Thomas Nelson, London, 1970.
11. Isiah Berlin, *Four Essays on Liberty*, Oxford University Press, London, 1969; K. R. Popper, *The Open Society and Its Enemies*, 2 Vols., Routledge and Kegan Paul, London, 1962.
12. A. N. Whitehead, *Science and the Modern World*, Macmillan, New York, 1960.
13. Abraham Edel, *Ethical Judgement*, Free Press Paperback, 1955; Gerald Dworkin (ed.), *Determinism, Free Will and Moral Responsibility*, Prentice-Hall, 1970.
14. IHU, p. 174.
15. W. Dilthey, *Meaning in History*, H. P. Richman (ed.), Allen and Unwin, London, 1961; Alfred Schutz, *Collected Papers*, 3 Vols., Nijhoff, The Hague, 1962–65.
16. A. R. Radcliffe-Brown, *Structure and Function in Primitive Society*, Cohen and West, London, 1961; Claude Lévi-Strauss, *Structural Anthropology*, Allen Lane, Penguin Press, London, 1969; E. Nagel, *Structure of Science*, Routledge and Kegan Paul, London, 1960.
17. HC, pp. 28–29.
18. IHU, p. 176.
19. K. R. Popper, ' Prediction and Prophecy in Social Science ' in *Theories of History*, Patrick Gardiner (ed.), Free Press, Glencoe, 1959.

## Chapter Two

1. HC, p. 332.
2. IHU, p. 388.
3. *The Life Divine* (LD), p. 47, 1 Vol. edn., New York, 1949. All page references of LD in this book are from this edition.
4. LD, p. 627.
5. IHU, p. 14.
6. LD, p. 217.
7. HC, pp. 74–75.
8. LD, p. 261.
9. LD, p. 316.
10. T. B. Bottomore and M. Rubel (eds.), *Karl Marx*, pp. 243–44.
11. LD, p. 90.
12. IHU, pp. 226–28.
13. LD, p. 903.
14. HC, p. 99.

## Chapter Three

1. LD, pp. 659–60. See also, Pierre Teilhard de Chardin, *The Phenomenon of Man*, Fontana Books, 1971.
2. F. A. Hayek, *The Counter-Revolution of Science*, 1964, pp. 17–24.
3. HC, p. 292.
4. LD, p. 737.
5. LD, p. 743.
6. *Anti-Dühring*, p. 115, Moscow, 1954. See also, Jacques Barzun, *Darwin, Marx and Wagner: Critique of a Heritage*, 2nd ed., New York, 1958.
7. LD, p. 662. See, also Jack Lindsay, *Marxism and Contemporary Science*, London, 1949.
8. LD, pp. 744–45.
9. LD, p. 738. See also, Julian Huxley, *Soviet Genetics*, London, 1949.
10. LD, p. 739.
11. LD, p. 740.
12. IHU, p. 176.
13. LD, p. 749.
14. HC, p. 98.
15. J.B.S. Haldane, *The Marxist Philosophy and the Sciences*, p. 104, London, 1939.
16. *Dialectical Materialism: A Historical and Systematic Survey of Philosophy in the Soviet Union*, Gustav A. Wetter, translated by Peter Health, pp. 455–69, London, 1958. See also, C. H. Waddington, *Introduction to Modern Genetics*, London, 1950.

## Chapter Four

1. HC, p. 2.
2. IFC, New York, 1953.
3. IFC, p. 16.
4. L. Lévy-Bruhl, *Primitive Mentality*, New York, 1923. Also see his *How Natives Think*, London, 1926. J. B. S. Haldane tells us that Engels in his unpublished manuscript notes for *Anti-Dürhing* expressed a curious view that 'uncivilised man would probably be incapable of getting a mathematical achievement and other forms of intellectual activity, because their ancestors had not practised them' (*The Marxist Philosophy and the Sciences*, p. 117). Lévy-Bruhl tells us of the difficulties the modern logical-minded people experience to understand

the pre-logical mentality of the primitive man. See Sri Aurobindo, *The Secret of the Veda*, Birth Centenary Library, Vol. 10, Pondicherry, 1972.

5. HC, p. 7.
6. Cf., ' We must dissipate the illusions of the repetitiveness of history and of the rigid persistence of its products, generated by the misunderstanding of classificatory concepts, we must on the contrary be fully aware that in history everything lasts only in so far as everything changes.' Benedetto Croce, *History as the Story of Liberty*, pp. 270–71.
7. HC, p. 12.
8. HC, p. 88. See also ' Modern Attempts to Periodize World History ' and ' The Periodization of World History According to Marxism-Leninism ' in *Marxism, Communism and Western Society, A Comparative Encyclopedia*, C. D. Kering (ed.), pp. 281–91, Vol. 6.
9. HC, p. 8. The point may be supported also by tracing the growth of the human mind from its early stage to the mature one. See, for instance, Jean Piaget, *Judgement and Reasoning in the Child*, pp. 130–34, Routledge and Kegan Paul, London, 1969.
10. LD, pp. 771–72.
11. Frazer thinks that magic appears first, and that religion grows out of it when its insufficiency is realised by deeper minds. Durkheim tells us that totemism is the basis of religion. It is to taboos resulting from instinctual renunciation that Freud traces the origin of morality and religion. See also, Claude Lévi Strauss, *Structural Anthropology*, translated by Jacobson and Schoeph, Chs. IX-XI, Allen Lane, Penguin Press, London, 1969; E. E. Evans-Pritchard, *Theories of Primitive Religion*, Oxford, Clarendon Press, 1965.
12. FIC, pp. 124–25.
13. HC, p. 2.
14. FIC, pp. 124–25, 177–78 and 363.
15. FIC, p. 390.
16. Max Weber, *Methodology of the Social Sciences*, translated by Shils and Finch, Free Press, Glencoe, 1949.
17. R.C. Majumdar et al., (eds.), *The Age of Imperial Unity*, Chs. XVI–XXIII, Bharatiya Vidya Bhavan, Bombay, 1968. See also, *The Classical Age*, Chs. XV–XXII, Bharatiya Vidya Bhavan, Bombay, 1970.
18. Abbé J. A. Dubois, *Hindu Manners, Customs and Ceremonies*, Part I, Clarendon Press, Oxford, 1972.
19. HC, p. 10.
20. Cf., ' . . . as reform reveals itself engaged on subduing pressure and protest, so does the emphasis shift towards repression, coercion, police power, law and order, struggle against subversion, etc.' Ralph Miliband, *The State in Capitalist Society*, London, 1969, p. 271.
21. HC., p. 11.
22. ' Understanding a Primitive Society ' in *Ethics and Action* by Peter Winch, Routledge and Kegan Paul, London, 1972.
23. FIC, pp. 167–68.
24. HC, pp. 11–12; see also, FIC, pp. 382–83.
25. Max Weber, *The Protestant Ethic and the Spirit of Capitalism*, Unwin University Books, London, 1970.
26. J. R. Hale, *Renaissance Europe, 1480-1520*, Ch. III, Fontana Library, 1972. See also, G. R. Elton, *Reformation Europe, 1517-1559*, Ch. X, Fontana Library, 1972.
27. Perhaps it is Kant more than anybody else has most effectively argued the point. Later on, the neo-Kantians of the last century elaborated it further.
28. HC, p. 22.
29. Sri Aurobindo, *The Synthesis of Yoga*, Vols. 20 and 21, Pondicherry, 1972.
30. Oswald Spengler, *The Decline of the West*, p. 361, Vol. I.
31. See, for example, *Readings in Indian History, Politics and Philosophy*, K. Satchidananda Murty (ed.) Allied Publishers and George Allen and Unwin, London, 1967.
32. HC, Chs. XXI–XXIV.

## Chapter Five

1. Karl Popper, *The Open Society and Its Enemies*, p. 270, Vol. II, London, 1962.
2. Isiah Berlin, ' The Concept of Scientific History ' in *History and Theory*, Vol. 1, No. 1.
3. *The Open Society* ..., p. 278.
4. Marx and Engels, *Selected Works*, p. 98, Vol. 2, Moscow, 1969.
5. Engels, *Feuerbach and the End of Classical German Philosophy*, sec. IV.
6. *The Monist View of History*, Moscow, p. 249.
7. Ibid., pp. 205–6.
8. See K. R. Popper, *Poverty of Historicism*, London, 1961.
9. LD, p. 890.
10. Sidney Hook (ed.), *Philosophy and History*, New York University Press, 1970.
11. *A History of Europe*, p. v, London, 1946.
12. E. H. Carr, *Wha' is History?* Penguin Books.
13. Johan Huizinga, *Men and Ideas*, translated by Holmes and Marle, pp. 51–52, London, 1960.
14. See Vilfred Pareto, *Mind and Society*, Vol. 4, London, 1935.
15. *A System of Logic*, p. 2, VI, VII.
16. K. R. Popper, *The Open Society and Its Enemies*, Ch. 14, Vol. 2.
17. *Pattern and Meaning in History*, H. P. Rickman (ed.), p. 72, Harper Torch Books, 1962.
18. H. A. Hodges, *The Philosophy of Wilhelm Dilthey*, London, 1952.
19. Gustav A. Wetter, *Soviet Ideology Today*, London, 1966, Part Two.
20. LD, p. 332.
21. *The Two Sources of Morality and Religion*, London, 1935.
22. Sidney Hook, *The Hero in History*, New York, 1943.
23. HC, p. 13.
24. See Charles Oman, *On the Writing of History*, New York, 1939.
25. IHU, p. 213.
26. Stalin, *Collected Works*, Vol. 13.
27. *Political Theories*, p. 165, Vol. III.
28. William Dray, *Laws and Explanation in History*, London, 1957.
29. *The Rise of Rationalism in Europe*, p. 36, Vol. II.
30. *The Meaning of Human History*, p. 67.
31. *The Methodology of the Social Sciences*, p. 79, New York, 1964.
32. HC, p. 54.
33. LD, p. 578.
34. LD, p. 579.

## Chapter Six

1. HC, pp. 82–83.
2. Ibid., p. 16.
3. Ibid., p. 17.
4. Ibid., p. 9.
5. HC, p. 39.
6. R. H. Lowie, *The Primitive Society*, p. 60, London.
7. Ogburn and Nimkoff, *A Handbook of Sociology*, p. 459.
8. G. P. Murdock, *Social Structure*, p. 1, Free Press Edn.
9. Ralph Linton, *A Study of Man*, p. 153, London, 1965.
10. G. P. Murdock, op. cit., p. 45.
11. Ralph Linton, op. cit., p. 201.
12. G. P. Murdock, op. cit., p. 85.
13. Ralph Linton, op. cit., pp. 229–30.
14. R. H. Lowie, op. cit., pp. 378–81.
15. IHU, pp. 102–5.
16. F. Engels, *The Origin of the Family, Private Property and the State.*

17. L. H. Morgan, *Ancient Society*, p. 394.
18. R. H. Lowie, op. cit., p. 184.

## Chapter Seven

1. A. C. Das, *Sri Aurobindo and Some Modern Problems*, pp. 162–63.
2. IHU, p. 109.
3. Karl Popper, *The Poverty of Historicism*, London, 1961.
4. IHU, pp. 115–17.
5. D. P. Chattopadhyaya, *Individuals and Societies: A Methodological Inquiry*, 2nd edn., Ch. 3, Scientific Book Agency, Calcutta, 1975.
6. See, for example, the controversy between Sartre and Lévi-Strauss. E. Nelson Hayes and Tanya Hayes (eds.), *Claude Lévi-Strauss: The Anthropologist as Hero*, MIT Press, Camb., Mass. and London, 1972. See also, Ernest Gellner, *Cause and Meaning in Social Sciences*, Routledge and Kegan Paul, London, 1973.
7. Albert Hourani, *Arabic Thought in the Liberal Age, 1798–1939*, Oxford Paperbacks, 1970.
8. IHU, p. 118.
9. HC, p. 40; italics mine.
10. Cf. Telford Taylor, *Sword and Swastika: Generals and Nazis in the Third Reich*, Simon and Schuster, New York, 1952.
11. HC, p. 53.
12. HC, pp. 56–58. See also, K. R. Popper, *Open Society and Its Enemies*, Vol. 2, London, 1962.
13. HC, pp. 61–62. See also, Ralph Miliband, *The State in Capitalist Society*, Quartel Books, London, 1973.
14. *Nationalities and National Minorities*, pp. 77–79, New York, 1945.
15. See Tom Kemp, *Theories of Imperialism*, London, 1967.
16. *The Ideal of Human Unity*, p. 275.
17. *On Nationalism*, First Series, Pondicherry, 1965, p. 13.
18. *A Study of History*, pp. 536–39, Vol. VIII, London, 1954.
19. *The Politics and Culture of New Democracy*, 15 January 1941, Section XV. Quoted from Snyder's, *The Dynamics of Nationalism*, p. 332.
20. *The Historical Evolution of Modern Nationalism*, New York, 1931.
21. Hans Kohn, *The Idea of Nationalism*, New York, 1967.
22. Seton-Watson, *Nationalism, Old and New*, London, 1965.
23. Anthony Smith, *Theories of Nationalism*, London, 1971.
24. IHU, p. 350.
25. IHU, pp. 323–24.
26. HC, pp. 53–63.
27. HC, pp. 48–49.
28. *Nationalism*, p. 106.
29. IHU, p. 37.
30. Marx and Engels on Colonialism, pp. 77–78.
31. IHU, p. 39.

## Chapter Eight

1. *Philosophical Theory of the State*, p. 292, London, 1951.
2. This has to be decided by the logic of the situation. In a general way only this much can be suggested that the State power should be exercised in order to help the deserving individuals to take over more and more power of the State to perfect themselves and the society.
3. This is the underlying principle of negative utilitarianism. Beyond a point it turns out to be a plea for non-interference.

4. IHU, pp. 14–17.
5. Gilbert Ryle, *The Concept of Mind*, London, 1949.
6. J. H. Woodger, *Biological Principles*, London, 1929. See also, Ernest Nagel, *The Structure of Science*, London, 1961.
7. HC, p. 81.
8. HC, pp. 82–83.
9. IHU, p. 9
10. Fritz Stern (ed.), *The Varieties of History*, Macmillan, 1956.
11. IHU, p. 5.
12. *Principles of Social Reconstruction*, p. 94
13. See, for example, R. C. Majumdar (ed.), *The Age of Imperial Unity*, Chs. XVI, XIX, XX, Bharatiya Vidya Bhavan, 1968; J. S. Bromley (ed.), *The New Cambridge Modern History*, Ch. III, Vol. VI, 1970.
14. Jacques Droz, *Europe Between Revolutions, 1815–1848*, Chs. V and VI, Fontana, London, 1967.
15. Hannah Arendt, *The Origins of Totalitarianism*, Harcourt, New York, 1951.
16. Shlomo Avineri, *Hegel's Theory of the Modern State*, Cambrdige University Press, 1972.
17. IHU, p. 26.
18. IHU, p. 21.
19. Max Weber, *The Methodology of the Social Sciences*, Free Press, 1949.
20. H. B. Acton, *The Illusion of the Epoch*, pp. 236–50, London, 1973.
21. IHU, p. 22.
22. IHU, p. 27.
23. IHU, p. 27.
24. Bertrand Russell, *Principles of Social Reconstruction*, p. 34. See also, Bertrand Russell, *Power*, pp. 197–98.
25. IHU, p. 332.
26. L. T. Hobhouse, *The Metaphysical Theory of the State*, pp. 143–44.
27. HC, pp. 239–40.
28. H. A. L. Fisher, *History of Europe*.
29. Lord Acton, *Lectures on Modern History*, p. 79, Fontana, 1970.
30. B. Russell, *A History of Western Philosophy*, London, 1946.
31. HC, p. 243.
32. John Plamenatz, *Democracy and Illusion*, Longman, London, 1973.
33. HC, p. 248.
34. *The State and the Revolution*.
35. Nicos Poulantzas, *Political Power and Social Classes*, London, 1973.
36. HC, pp. 249–50.
37. HC, p. 255.
38. Isaiah Berlin, *Four Essays on Liberty*, London, 1969.
39. John Rees, *Equality*, Macmillan, London, 1971.
40. HC, p. 253.
41. HC, p. 254, my emphasis.
42. R. H. Tawney, *Equality*, Ch. III, London, 1971.
43. Louis Althuser, *For Marx*, Penguin Books, 1969. See also, B. Olman, *Alienation*, Cambridge University Press, 1971.
44. HC, p. 266.
45. HC, pp. 263–64.
46. HC, p. 268.
47. Mikhail A. Bakunin, *The Political Philosophy of Bakunin: Scientific Anarchism*, G. P. Maximoff (ed.), Glencoe Illinois, 1953; and George Sorel, *Reflections on Violence*, Glencoe, Illinois, 1950.
48. *Political Justice, What is Property and Mutual Aid.*
49. *Human Society in Ethics and Politics*, pp. 15–16.
50. HC, p. 273.

51. *Economics and Political Manuscripts*, quoted from the *Essential Marx*, Ernst Fischer and Franz Marek (eds.), p. 23, New York, 1971.

## Chapter Nine

1. HC, p. 90.
2. *The Protestant Ethic and the Spirit of Capitalism*, p. 72, Unwin University Books, London, 1970.
3. Ibid., pp. 170–71.
4. HC, p. 118.
5. E. Zeller, *Outlines of the History of Greek Philosophy*, p. 92.
6. *A History of Political Theory*, p. 43, Vol. I.
7. *A Study of History*, abridged by Somervell, p. 183.
8. HC, p. 120.
9. *Negations*, Ch. III, Penguin, 1968.
10. *LD*, Birth Centenary Library, p. 23, Vol. 18, 1970.
11. Ibid., p. 24.
12. *The Renaissance in India*, Birth Centenary Library, pp. 401–4, Vol. 14.
13. HC, pp. 183–84.
14. HC, p. 168.
15. A. N. Whitehead, *Adventures of Ideas*, Free Press, New York, 1967, p. 252.
16. Collingwood, *Principles of Art*, Oxford University Press, 1970, pp. 286–87.
17. *The Future Poetry*, Birth Centenary Library, p. 243, Vol. 9.
18. HC, pp. 171–72.
19. Cristopher Caudwell, *Further Studies in a Dying Culture*, p. 106.
20. Gustav A. Wetter, *Soviet Ideology Today*, London, 1966.
21. Lucien Goldmann, *The Hidden God*, Ch. V, Routledge and Kegan Paul, London, 1964.
22. Alvin W. Gouldner, 'Anti-Minotaur: The Myth of a Value-free Sociology', in *The Relevance of Sociology*, Jack D. Douglas (ed.), pp. 64–84, New York, 1970.
23. K. Gilbert and H. Kuhn, *A History of Aesthetics*, pp. 392--93.
24. HC, p. 95.
25. P. Sorokin, *Social and Cultural Dynamics*, p. 535, Vol. III.
26. *The Open Society and Its Enemies*, p. 199, Vol. II.
27. *The Modern State*, Oxford University Press, 1966, p. 325.
28. M. Marleau-Ponty, *Phenomenology of Perception*, p. XIX, Routledge and Kegan Paul, London, 1970. See also, his *Adventures of the Dialectic*, Heinemann, London, 1974.

## Chapter Ten

1. The Cuban Crisis, the Arab-Israeli War and the Vietnam War and some other similar issues illustrate the point very clearly.
2. IHU, p. 144.
3. The structure, function and programme of action of political and economic organisations like EEC, EFTA, COMECON, OAS and ESCAP are interesting in this connection.
4. M. M. Drackovitch (ed.), *The Revolutionary Internationals, 1864–1943*, Stanford, California, 1966.
5. IHU, p. 166.
6. Edgar A. J. Johnson (ed.), *The Dimensions of Diplomacy*, John Hopkins Press, Baltimore, 1964.
7. Unlike Plato Sri Aurobindo is a spiritual anarchist. The spirit as the governor of life perceives the inner unity of all human beings and, therefore, cannot favour any aristocratic form of government or class rule.
8. According to him, reality is a spiritual whole and the object of perception exists in some

conceptual form even before its being perceived, one is reminded more of Hegel than of Plato in this connection.

9. Harold G. Nicolson, *Kings, Courts and Monarchy*, Simon and Schuster, New York, 1962.
10. John Plamenatz, *Democracy and Illusion*, Longman, 1973.
11. He favours parliamentarianism not because he thinks it is perfect, which it is not, but perhaps because it hinders least the evolution of the ideal form of government.
12. Alfred Vagts, *A History of Militarism*, Meridian, New York, 1959. See also, John U. Nef, *War and Human Progress*, Harvard University Press, Cambridge, 1950.
13. Raymond Aron, *Peace and War: A Theory of International Relations*, Doubleday and Co., N. Y., 1966.
14. IHU, pp. 386–88.
15. Jackson H. Ralston, *International Arbitration: From Athens to Locarno*, Oxford University Press, 1929. See also, Elmore Jackson, *Meeting of Minds: A Way to Peace Through Mediation*, McGraw-Hill, New York, 1952.
16. Fred M. Gottheil, *Marx's Economic Predictions*, Evanston, 1966. See also, J. A. Schumpeter, *Capitalism, Socialism and Democracy*, New York, 1962.
17. Stalin, *The Problems of Leninism*, p. 147, Moscow, 1954.
18. Mario Pei, *The Story of Language*, George Allen and Unwin, London, 1908.
19. Ottovon Gierke, *Natural Law and the Theory of Society*: *1500* to *1800*, translated with an introduction by E. Barker, 2 Vols., Cambridge University Press, 1934. See also, Hans Kelsen's *A General Theory of Law and State*, New York, 1961.
20. IHU, p. 330.
21. Irving Louis Horowitz, *War and Peace in Contemporary Social and Philosophical Theory*, Condor Book, London, 1973.
22. *Basic Writings of Nietzsche*, translated and edited by Walter Kaufmann, New York, 1966. See also, Nietzsche's *The Will to Power*, translated and edited by Walter Kaufmann, New York, 1966.
23. B. Nelson (ed.), *Freud and the Twentieth Century*, New York, 1957. See also, J. A. C. Brown, *Freud and the Post-Freudians*, London, 1961.
24. J. P. Sartre, *Existentialism and Humanism*, p. 55.
25. G. D. H. Cole, *A History of Socialist Thought*, 5 Vols., Macmillan, London, 1969–70.
26. C. D. Broad, *The Mind and Its Place in Nature*, London 1925. See also, H. Feigl's 'The Mind-Body Problem in the Development of Logical Empiricism' in Feigl and Brodbeck (eds.), *Readings in the Philosophy of Science*, New York, 1953.
27. Barrington Moore, Jr., *Social Origins of Dictatorship and Democracy*, Peregrine Book, London, 1966. See also, C. J. Friedrich and Z. K. Brzezinski, *Totalitarian Dictatorship and Autocracy*, Harvard University Press, Cambridge, Mass., 1956.
28. Martin Buber, *Paths in Utopia*, Macmillan, New York, 1950. See also, J. C. Davies (ed.), *When Men Revolt and Why: A Reader in Political Violence and Revolution*, Free Press, New York, 1971.
29. HC, p. 268.
30. *The Positive Philosophy of Auguste Comte*, translated and edited by Harriet Martineau, 3 Vols., London, 1896. See also, F. A. Von Hayek, *The Counter-Revolution of Science*, Free Press, 1952.
31. *Economic and Philosophical Manuscripts*, 1944.
32. See A. S. Pringle-Patison, *The Idea of God*, Oxford, 1917.
33. P. Worsley, *The Third World*, Weidenfeld and Nicolson, London, 1964. See also, H. Bernstein, *Under-development and Development: The Third World Today*, Penguin Books, 1973.

## Chapter Eleven

1. Gustav A. Wetter, *Dialectical Materialism*, translated by Peter Heath, London, 1958.
2. John O'Neil (ed.), *Modes of Individualism and Collectivism*, London, 1973. See also,

D. P. Chattopadhyaya, *Individuals and Societies: A Methodological Inquiry*, 2nd. ed., Calcutta, 1975.
3. Karl R. Popper, *The Poverty of Historicism*, London, 1961. See also, Isaiah Berlin, *Four Essays on Liberty*, OUP, 1969.
4. D. P. Chattopadhyaya, *Societies and Cultures*, Bombay, 1973.
5. Hans Gerth and C. Wright Mills, *Character and Social Structure*, London, 1969.
6. B. Russell, *The Problems of Philosophy*, OUP, 1973.
7. Sri Aurobindo, *The Human Cycle*, Pondicherry, 1949.
8. Morton A. Kaplan, *Great Issues of International Politics*, Chicago, 1970.

## Chapter Twelve

1. Ideology has two well-known connotations: (a) negative or pejorative, and (b) positive or programmatic. Ideologies are often taken as normative social outlooks. At times, the term stands for systems and movements of thought. Its proximity to politics is understandable. Daniel Bell, *The Cultural Contradictions of Capitalism*, Basic Books, New York, 1978. See also, Talcott Parsons, *Sociological Theory and Modern Society*, Free Press, New York, 1967. pp. 128-9, 153-4, 159-64, 484-5.
2. Both Karl Popper and Michael Oakeshott are empiricist, though of different shades. Their difference on the concepts of tradition and ideology are interesting. Michael Oakeshott, *Experience and its Modes*, Cambridge University Press, Cambridge, 1985, Ch. 5, and Karl R. Popper. *Conjectures and Refutations*, Routledge & Kegan Paul, London, 1969, pp. 120-35.
3. In most of his books Karl Marx critically expresses his view against the concept of ideology. Understandably he has chosen the ideology of Germany as the background of his own 'ideology'. But the work in which he (with Engels) has gone deep into the issue is *The German Ideology*, Progressive Publishers, 1976, Moscow.
4. See, for example, C.J. Friedrich's Introduction to *Hegel's Philosophy of History* (Dover Edition) Friedrich rightly observes: 'Hegel not only did not pretend that his work was "history" or "sociology" but very explicitly rejected this notion, declaring very definitely that he was putting forward a philosophical framework for history, that he was not writing history, but philosophy'. Hegel himself puts the point in this way: 'Philosophy concerns itself only with the glory of the Idea mirroring itself in the History of the World'. As a philosopher he wants to 'escape from the weary types of passion that agitated the surface of society into the calm region of contemplation'.
5. See, for example, Michio Morishima, *Marx's Economics*, Cambridge University Press, Cambridge, 1974, and Meghnad Desai, *Marxian Economic Theory*, Gray-Mills Publishing Limited, London, 1974.
6. It is true that *all* theorems of macro-economics cannot be derived from the theorems of micro-economics. But the point remains that *most* of the theorems can be formulated in alternative ways. I have argued the point elsewhere. See below.
7. D.P. Chattopadhyaya, *Individuals and Societies: A Methodological Inquiry*, Scientific Book Agency, Calcutta 1973, pp. 153-62, see also pp. 188-92.
8. Marx and Engels, *The German Ideology*, 1976, pp. 188-90, 279-81, 323-34, 436-37, 504-05.
9. Marx is never tired of emphasising the primacy of the practical modes of consciousness. Related to this thesis is his emphasis on the concept of labour. His main complaint against theorisation is that it is abstract, often anti-historical and, therefore, leads to anomalies and puzzles, if not falsity.
10. Robert Nozick, *State, Anarchy and Utopia* Basil Blackwell, Oxford, 1974.
11. Karl Marx, *Capital*, Vol. III, Progress Publishers, Moscow, 1966. pp. 852-886.
12. Leszek Kolakowski, 1978, *Main Currents of Marxism: The Golden Age*, Clarendon Press, Oxford, 1978.
13. Leszek Kolakowski, *Main Currents of Marxism: The Breakdown*, Clarendon Press, Oxford, 1978. I am referring to the work of Kolakowski because it is very comprehensive

and contains very useful references. Every author in this area has his own view on the subject. The same may be said of the famous multi-volume work of G.D.H. Cole.

14. In all his works of 1840s Marx highlights the mutuality of naturalism and humanism. In this respect he is definitely anti-Kantian and pro-Hegelian.

## Chapter Thirteen

1. After Sri Caitanya nobody has developed such a comprehensive system, comprising different aspects of philosophy like metaphysics, epistemology, ethics, social philosophy and aesthetics. To the discerning scholar his philosophy of language is bound to appear very interesting. In this connection, his work, *The Secret of the Veda*, is highly insightful.
2. Sri Aurobindo's philosophy pays serious attention to contemporary concepts of the philosophy of body and mind. Ordinarily, metaphysicians of his type are not found to take such interest in these areas. In fact, one finds a concept of subjectivity of body in his philosophy.
3. His main work on the philosophy of history is entitled *The Human Cycle*. Originally when it was published in the *Arya* (from August 15, 1916 to July 15, 1918), its title was *The Psychology of Social Development*.
4. For example, the Derozians of Bengal in the middle of the nineteenth century were steeped in the then newly imported British ideas and ideals. Utilitarianism, naturalism and scientific temper marked their anglophilism.
5. See, ch. 5, 'Truth and False Subjectivism'. *The Human Cycle, Social and Political Thought*, Birth Centenary Library, Vol. 15.
6. *ibid.*, pp. 40-1.
7. See, ch. 10, Book Two, Part I, 'Knowledge by Identity and Subjective Knowledge'. *The Life Divine*, Birth Centenary Library, Vol. 18, Pondicherry, 1970.
8. *The Human Cycle*, Birth Centenary Library, Vol. 15, p. 165.
9. *ibid.*, p. 206.
10. *ibid.*, pp. 217; see also pp. 244-45.
11. *The Life Divine*, Birth Centenary Library, Vol. 19, Pondicherry, 1971, p. 971.
12. *ibid.*, p. 1042.

## Chapter Fourteen

1. It is not easy to devise universally acceptable way of aggregating the value-schedules of different individuals and groups. Kant's principle of Categorical Imperative may be interpreted as a principle of utility distribution. John Rawls has also addressed himself to this problem in terms of his Difference Principle. In this connection, see, for example, Kenneth J. Arrow, *Social Choice and Individual Values*, Tata McGraw-Hill, New Delhi, 1963.
2. Little reflection is necessary to show that such primary goods as justice, freedom and equality demand of us a lot of self-restraint, consideration for others and foregoing or surrendering certain otherwise available pleasures and comforts. It is no surprise that we often hear of 'fear of freedom', 'equality as mechanical levelling down', etc.
3. See my papers, 'Pierre Teilhard de Chardin: A Revolutionary View of Man' and 'Sri Aurobindo and Pierre Teilhard de Chardin: On Human Evolution' in D.P. Chattopadhyaya, *Environment, Evolution and Values*, South Asian Publishers, New Delhi, 1983.
4. In this connection, I have particularly in mind the works of Husserl (*The Crisis of European Science*), Cassierer, Popper and Gerd Buchdal. I also find Collingwood's treatment of the subject (in his *Metaphysics*) very interesting.
5. Thomas Kuhn's incommensurability thesis is widely misunderstood. Its realistic undertone has gone largely unrecognised. This appears particularly unfortunate in view of his later publications like *The Essential Tension*.

6. It is interesting to note that the contrast between Marx and Popper on the relation between theories and their social determinants. While the former favours social revolution and discourages adventure in thought, the latter takes a pro-normative and pro-revolutionary stand in the context of theory-formation but strongly opposes the ideas of social revolution.
7. See my paper, 'Remarks on Historiography of Science: Historism and Structuralism' in the *Journal of Indian Council of Philosophical Research* (*JICPR*), Vol. I, No. 2, 1984.
8. Rousseau's views on the General Will and its relation to the State are not found to be uniform. For example, in *The Social Contract* (1762), he glorifies the General Will, relatively downgrading the importance of individual freedom; but in some other works like (*Discourses on the Sciences and Arts* and *Discourse on the Origin and Foundation of Inequality* (1750-55) he emphasises the notion of *natural* freedom.
9. Immanuel Kant, *The Metaphysical Elements of Justice*; trans. by John Ladd, Bobbs- Merrill, Indianapolis, 1965, p. 140; see also, pp. 77-78 and 84-86.
10. Kant's familiarity with jurisprudence is evident in his work on *Perpetual Peace*. He thought of the problem not only from a purely ethical point of view, but also from the point of international relations. He was one of the few thinkers of the eighteenth century who anticipated the world organisations like League of Nations and United Nations Organisations.
11. John Plamenatz, *Man and Society*, Vol. II, Longman, London, 1974, pp. 266-7.
12. Both China and USSR are increasingly following 'open door policy' both in internal matter and in external relations. Many of the things, which were initially prohibited or proscribed for their 'revisionist' or 'deviationist' features, are now being officially allowed and even encouraged. This is a new development which is bound to have far-reaching consequences.
13. The relation between sociology, on the one hand, and ideology and utopia, on the other, has been carefully studied, among others, by Weber, Mannheim, Parsons and Merton. In this connection I find the work of Wright Mills and Dahrendorf also very interesting.
14. Frank E. Manuel and Fritzie P. Manuel, *Utopian Thought in the Western World*, Basil Blackwell, Oxford, 1979.

# Index